SIMPLICIUS
On Aristotle Categories 9-15

SIMPLICIUS
On Aristotle
Categories 9-15

Translated by
Richard Gaskin

BLOOMSBURY
LONDON · NEW DELHI · NEW YORK · SYDNEY

Bloomsbury Academic

An imprint of Bloomsbury Publishing Plc

50 Bedford Square	1385 Broadway
London	New York
WC1B 3DP	NY 10018
UK	USA

www.bloomsbury.com

Bloomsbury is a registered trade mark of Bloomsbury Publishing Plc

First published in 2000 by Gerald Duckworth & Co. Ltd.
Paperback edition first published 2014

British Library Cataloguing-in-Publication Data
A catalogue record for this book is available from the British Library.

ISBN HB:	978-0-7156-2900-0
PB:	978-1-4725-5851-0
ePDF:	978-1-4725-0193-6

Library of Congress Cataloging-in-Publication Data
A catalog record for this book is available from the Library of Congress.

The present translations have been made possible by generous
and imaginative funding from the following sources: the National
Endowment for the Humanities, Division of Research Programs,
an independent federal agency of the USA; the Leverhulme Trust;
the British Academy; the Jowett Copyright Trustees; the Royal
Society (UK); Centro Internazionale A. Beltrame di Storia dello
Spazio e del Tempo (Padua); Mario Mignucci; Liverpool University;
the Leventis Foundation; the Humanities Research Board of the
British Academy; the Esmée Fairbairn Charitable Trust; the Henry
Brown Trust; Mr and Mrs N. Egon; The Netherlands Foundation
for Scientific Research (NWO/GW). The editor wishes to thank
Michael Chase, Manuel Correia, John Dillon, John Ellis, Frans
de Haas, Pamela Huby, Donald Russell and C.W.A. Whitaker for
their comments and Sylvia Berryman for preparing the volume
for press.

Typeset by Ray Davies

Contents

Introduction

The last third of Simplicius' commentary on Aristotle's *Categories*, here translated, falls into two distinct parts: (1) an examination of the six categories dealt with by Aristotle in chapter 9 of the extant *Categories* text, namely *acting* (*poiein*), *undergoing* (*paskhein*), *being-in-a-position* (*keisthai*), *when* (*pote*), *where* (*pou*) and *having* (*ekhein*); and (2) an examination of chapters 10-15 of Aristotle's text (the so-called *Postpraedicamenta*), which comprise a discussion of four kinds of opposition, namely the relatives (*ta pros ti*), the contraries (*ta enantia*), possession and privation (*hexis, sterêsis*), and affirmation and negation (*kataphasis, apophasis*), as well as of priority (*proteron*), simultaneity (*hama*), movement (*kinêsis*), and having (*ekhein*).

In his commentary on Chapter 9 Simplicius was, like the interpreters on whom he relies and like all commentators since, hampered by the imperfect state of the extant text. For the text of this chapter, as it has come down to us, is almost certainly incomplete. The discussion of the categories of acting and undergoing (11b1-8) is begun, but no more than that, and there is no consideration at all of the remaining four categories. We are indeed told in the continuation of our text after the presumed lacuna, i.e. at 11b10-16, that enough has been said about the category of being-in-a-position in the discussion of the relatives to make further consideration of it superfluous, and that a separate examination of the remaining three categories, namely when, where and having, is unnecessary in view of their obviousness: but 11b10-16 are probably a later interpolation, inserted to close the evident gap between the abortive discussion of acting and undergoing and the ensuing discussion of the four kinds of opposition. In his commentary Simplicius shows no awareness of the probable fragmentary state of chapter 9, treating its abruptness as sufficiently explained by an Aristotelian disdain for detail (297,23), and he plainly regards 11b10-16 as genuine. On this latter point he follows his predecessors, for although he indeed reports Andronicus' view that the materials of the *Postpraedicamenta* are not authentic (379,8-10), he reports no similar misgivings in the tradition concerning the authenticity of 11b10-16, which he would surely have done if these lines had to his knowledge been subject to challenge.

Despite the paucity of the Aristotelian material relating to the last six categories, Simplicius is able to fill over 80 pages in the Berlin edition with commentary. His discussion is greatly indebted to his predecessors in the commentary tradition, and especially to Porphyry's and Iamblichus' com-

mentaries on the *Categories*. Porphyry in fact wrote two commentaries on
this text: of these one, dedicated to Gedalius, is entirely lost, and the other,
written in dialogue form, is only partially extant and unfortunately deals
in its extant portion only very cursorily with the six categories which are
the topic of our part of Simplicius' commentary, breaking off abruptly
before any consideration at all either of the category of having or of the
Postpraedicamenta, and in a way which leaves unclear to what extent
Porphyry intends to discuss the last six categories.[1] Simplicius credits
Porphyry with the responsibility for 'all the good things' in his own
commentary (*in Cat.* 2,5-6), and it is likely that, if only we knew how to do
it, we could in principle recover large parts of the Gedalian commentary
from Simplicius' text. It is at the very least reasonable, on the basis of what
we are told by Simplicius at *in Cat.* 2,5-9, to trace many of the objections
(*enstaseis*) to Aristotle's account and difficulties (*aporiai*) for it mentioned
by Simplicius (whether anonymously or together with an attribution to a
critic such as the Platonist Nicostratus), as well as the solutions (*luseis*)
conveyed, to Porphyry. It is also reasonable, on the basis of the same text,
to credit Porphyry with the citations from Stoic sources richly scattered
throughout Simplicius' commentary.[2]

In Iamblichus' case we are able to gauge the extent of Simplicius' debt
more precisely, for Simplicius regularly quotes large excerpts from Iamblichus' no longer extant commentary on the *Categories*.[3] Iamblichus, we
are told (2,9ff.), followed Porphyry closely, while compressing the latter's
long-windedness, but introduced two significant novel features to the
tradition of *Categories* commentaries. Firstly 'throughout his work he
appended to more or less every chapter an intellectual theory (*noera
theôria*)' (2,13-14), and secondly he inserted into his commentary relevant
extracts from a treatise on the categories by a philosopher whom he calls
'Archytas the Pythagorean' (2,15).

In our part of the *Categories* commentary, Simplicius cites Iamblichan
'intellectual theory' on the categories of acting and undergoing (327,6ff.; cf.
also 305,5ff.), being-in-a-position (339,34ff.), when/time (350,10ff.),
where/place (361,7ff.) and having (374,7ff.). The inclusion of such an
'intellectual theory' – which is intended to demonstrate that Aristotelian
categories have an application beyond the sensible world, to the mind or
intellect, and even to the One itself (see e.g. 364,3 with my note ad loc.) –
is important for the project of justifying the prime place accorded to
Aristotle's *Categories* within the Neoplatonic curriculum. The special importance of the *Categories* among Aristotle's writings was fixed early in the
Peripatetic tradition, and it became established for the Neoplatonists too
in the wake of Porphyry's decision not to maintain the hostile stance
towards the *Categories* adopted by his teacher Plotinus. The aggressive-
ness of Plotinus' attack on Aristotelian category theory in *Enneads* 6.1-3
certainly meant that there was some work for Porphyry and Iamblichus to
do in justifying the Neoplatonic credentials of a text which seems at first

blush to offer rather unpromising material to friends of the *kosmos noêtos*. But it is important to note that Simplicius, though by and large subscribing to the justificatory project, and to the Porphyrian thesis of the harmony of Plato's and Aristotle's doctrines, is not an uncritical supporter of the tendency to Platonise the *Categories*. We can illustrate this well from our part of the commentary.

In the case of the categories of acting and undergoing Simplicius appears to cite Iamblichus' 'intellectual theory' with approval: according to this theory, the pure and primary cases of acting are the most perfect operations (*energeiai*), which are free of potentiality and *a fortiori* free of movement (328,16ff.). Simplicius is even prepared to follow Iamblichus in his Neoplatonising interpretation of the definition of time given by 'Archytas the Pythagorean'. According to that definition, time is 'the number of a certain movement, or, more generally, the extension of the nature of the universe too' (350,11-12). This definition is interpreted by Simplicius, evidently following Iamblichus, as positing the *soul* as the proximate cause of time, an interpretation for which it is rather hard to find a basis in what Archytas actually said. (This is a nice case of Iamblichus' technique of 'unravelling the things which were intellectually wrapped up' by Archytas, as Simplicius puts it at 2,21.)

On the other side of the account, however, Simplicius not infrequently expresses reservations about Iamblichus' interpretations of Aristotle. After citing Iamblichus' 'intellectual theory' about the category of where, according to which that category applies primarily to the intelligible rather than to the sensible world, Simplicius rebukes him (364,7ff.) with the remark that if one investigates 'in a more balanced way the use and nature of place strictly and not metaphorically so called', one will say that the denizens of the intelligible world do not need either place or time, but exist as indivisible unities in eternity, whereas the material and perishable denizens of the sensible world need both time and place to house their divisible being. Similarly, after quoting Iamblichus' intellectual theory concerning the category of being-in-a-position, according to which reasonings (*logoi*) are positioned in the soul, forms in the mind, and everything in god (339,34ff.), Simplicius remarks laconically that being-in-a-position is, in the strict sense, ascribed to bodies (340,12-13). Again, at the close of a long citation of Iamblichus' 'intellectual theory' about the category of having, Simplicius objects in strong terms (376,13ff.) to Iamblichus' wanton extension of the scope of this category well beyond the strict limits laid down (as Simplicius takes it) by Aristotle, according to which it applies just to the placing of a corporeal item of clothing, ornament or protection about the human body. Simplicius especially objects to what he sees as an inconsistency in Iamblichus' approach, since he claims (376,18-19) that Iamblichus too recognises that things had in the sense of the category are bodies placed around bodies.

The charge of inconsistency provides a nice illustration of a distich which occurs several times in one of the manuscripts of Simplicius' commentary, the Codex Ambrosianus 306 (E99 sup.):[4]

> This is the work of Simplicius: O Iamblichus, giver of all goods, be gracious unto me, though you have been conquered. You have been conquered by your own words.

Accordingly, while Simplicius on the whole concurs with Iamblichus' aim, in respect of the *Categories*, to (as John Dillon puts it)[5] 'salvage Aristotle, reconciling him both with his perceived doctrine elsewhere (as, for example, in the *Metaphysics* and the *Physics*), and with that of Plato and the Pythagoreans', there are limits on the extent to which he thinks the *Categories* can really be Platonised.

As far as reconciling Aristotle with the Pythagoreans is concerned, both Iamblichus and Simplicius identify the Archytas presumed to have written the treatise on the categories from which Simplicius (following Iamblichus) extracts extensive passages for citation with the Pythagorean philosopher of that name, a contemporary of Plato's. In fact, however, the treatise in question is relatively late, probably written in the first or second century AD, and is heavily dependent on Aristotle's *Categories*, not *vice versa*.[6] The aim of the treatise is to systematise the *Categories* by 'setting out clearly by means of examples their [i.e. the categories'] distinguishing marks and explaining the order they have towards one another, the specific differentiae of each one, and the things that belong to them in common and individually' (2,17-20). Since the treatise is actually dependent on the *Categories*, Simplicius does not in general have a difficulty rendering its presumed Pythagoreanism consistent with Aristotelianism, but since, again, the treatise is *more* systematic than Aristotle's *Categories*, Simplicius now and then encounters the exegetical problem why Aristotle, though apparently basing his own work on the prior treatise by 'Archytas the Pythagorean', nevertheless failed to avail himself of the insights of that treatise at every point. Thus Simplicius feels obliged to defend Aristotle against the charge that, compared with Archytas' lengthier examination of the last six categories, Aristotle's treatment of these categories in the *Categories* is defective (300,9ff.); there is a *prima facie* problem (which Simplicius thinks he can solve, however: 342,21ff.) why Aristotle assigns time and place to the category of quantity and not, like Archytas, to the categories of when and where respectively; it is unclear why Aristotle regards time, the number of movement, as 'an externally supervening measure of what is continuous', when Archytas had – according to Iamblichus – clearly and correctly established it to be an inherent and substantial part of what it measures (350,29ff.).

In spite of these difficulties, and what seems to the modern eye to be the very evident dependence of the Pseudo-Archytan treatise on Aristotle rather than *vice versa*, Simplicius does not question Iamblichus' identification of the treatise's author with the Pythagorean Archytas;[7] nor in his commentary on the *Postpraedicamenta* does he question the assumed dependence of the Peripatetic tract *de Oppositis* (not certainly by Aristotle himself, though Simplicius assumes that it is) on the pseudepigraphical treatise of the same name, whose author Simplicius again identifies with the Pythagorean Archytas.[8]

Apart from his citations from Pseudo-Archytas' treatise on the categories, and his reports of Iamblichus' intellectual theories, Simplicius' discussion of the last six categories in his commentary on chapter 9 of the *Categories* largely consists of an examination of *aporiai* and possible solutions to them. Many of these difficulties are raised by Plotinus in his treatise *On the Genera of Being* (*peri tôn Genôn tou Ontos*), which takes up the first three parts of *Enneads* 6. Plotinus regards Aristotle's first four categories (substance, quantity, relation and quality) as genuinely applicable to the sensible world, and he also admits a category of movement (*kinêsis*), concocted out of Aristotle's two categories of acting and undergoing, but he regards the remaining four categories – i.e., when, where, being-in-a-position, and having – as spurious. Much of Simplicius' commentary on chapter 9 is given over to a sustained polemic against Plotinus, both for his conflation of acting and undergoing into a single category of movement, and for his rejection of the remaining four categories.

The first and most obvious objection to Plotinus' conflation of acting and undergoing into a single category of movement is that it fails to accommodate cases of acting which involve no undergoing, such as Aristotle's unmoved mover (302,5ff., 306,13ff., 311,13ff.), or objects of thought or sight (312,22ff.). More generally, Simplicius criticises the conflation on the basis that, even in cases where an agent does undergo, or a patient acts, the *principles* of acting and undergoing are distinct. As he puts it at one point: 'the agent does not undergo *qua* agent, nor the patient act *qua* patient' (312,10-11; cf. 313,8ff. and *passim*). Of course it is true that in the case of composite things these principles are generally observed working together: tin which purifies silver acts by purifying the silver and undergoes by being consumed in the process, while the silver undergoes by being purified, and acts by using up the tin (316,31ff.). But we should not be misled by the practical difficulty of distinguishing active from affective processes in composite things into supposing that nothing in principle distinguishes action from affection.

Plotinus claims that the categories of when and where are superfluous: for expressions like 'yesterday', 'tomorrow' and 'last year' specify a time, which according to Aristotle belongs to the category of quantity, and expressions like 'in the Lyceum' and 'above' specify a place, which likewise belongs in Aristotle's view to the category of quantity. Pseudo-Archytas, too, assimilates the concept of when to that of time and the concept of where to that of place, but unlike Aristotle, and unlike Plotinus (who reduces time and place to the relatives: 342,29ff.), he does not seek to reduce time and place to other categories; hence his tally of categories remains at ten. Simplicius, though taking the opportunity offered by a consideration of the concepts of when and where to incorporate extended Neoplatonic, intellectualising discussions of time and place, resists the assimilation of Aristotle's categories of when and where to other categories, insisting that there is a distinction between time and place on the one hand, and what is *in* time or *in* place on the other. But Plotinus and his followers have a counter to this line of defence (347,18ff.): if the categories of when and where signify a relation of a particular thing, such as Socrates, to time or place, are they not decomposable into the categories of substance on the one hand and quantity (housing time and place) on the other? Simplicius insists that there is something special about the *relation* of a thing to the time or place which accommodates it. But Plotinus presses the objection (348,35ff.): what is so special about *these* relations, meriting their elevation to separate categorial status? Simplicius replies (349,19ff.) that these relations are unique in involving both (1) a relation of containment and (2) the separation of the natures of container and contained, so that neither is part of, or constitutes, the other.

In his discussion of the category of where Simplicius is prompted by suggestions put forward by the Stoic Cornutus to enunciate again a fundamental principle governing the interpretation of the *Categories*. Cornutus thought that the categories are purely linguistic, and consequently more than ten in number. Simplicius rebuts this view (359,1ff.) on the basis of his adherence to the Porphyrian characterisation of the categories as simple meaningful words, insofar as they are meaningful (i.e. signify concepts and things), and not insofar as they are mere expressions (10,20-3; 13,11-15). That is, in arriving at a fundamental division of categories, one must take account of the meanings of words, and not of their forms. On Cornutus' approach, one would assign very different things, such as horse and time, to the same category, on the basis that the corresponding Greek words have the same linguistic character (in this case *hippos* and *khronos* are both masculine nouns of the second declension); and one would make spurious categorial distinctions, such as assigning masculine and feminine demonstrative adjectives (*houtos* and *hautê*) to distinct categories, even where their referents are both substances. It cannot be the point of a category theory merely to mimic grammar and morphology: rather, it must have ontological import.

Plotinus' attack on the inclusion among the categories of being-in-a-position and having centres on two charges: that these two concepts apply to only a few cases, and that they are both reducible to other categories, in particular to those of substance and relation. Simplicius is easily able to rebut the first charge, for the number of sublunary and celestial bodies (all of which enjoy a position) is not few (338,21ff.); and, as for the category of having, the phoenix is a species, even though it only has one member (371,10ff.). But what is so special about the relations of substances which these concepts undeniably introduce? Of course Simplicius is able to specify what is distinctive about these concepts: being-in-a-position signifies the spatial configuration of an object (although he cites a view which rejected even this much specification, regarding configuration and place as not basic to the category, but supervenient: 338,21ff.); and having signifies the control or possession of an acquired inanimate object which is placed around the body of an animate owner and which does not, as an accident does, qualify the owner's substance. In the latter case Simplicius is even able, further to the general project of demonstrating the harmony of Plato and Aristotle, to quote a long passage from Plato's *Theaetetus* in which having in the sense of the Aristotelian genus is allegedly distinguished from mere legal ownership. But in spite of Simplicius' efforts it remains obscure what the point of singling out these concepts for inclusion in the list of categories is.

In the case of the category of having, the problem is exacerbated by the last chapter of the *Categories*, in which Aristotle (or whoever the author of the *Postpraedicamenta* was) enumerates eight senses of having, with no indication how the enumeration is to be reconciled with the official category theory. This point was pounced on by Nicostratus, who charged Aristotle with a failure to integrate the final chapter with the rest of the work (368,12ff.). In his discussion of the category of having in chapter 9, Simplicius accepts a response to this *aporia* derived from Iamblichus, according to which two of the senses listed in the last chapter on the homonymy of having are indeed of having in the sense of the genus, and that Aristotle omitted to point this out, partly (as usual) out of a desire for concision, and partly to test the wit of his readers (369,37ff.). One answer which seems to us at least worth considering – that whoever wrote the chapter on having which appears at the very end of our text of the *Categories* did not have in mind the category theory developed in the first part of that work – is excluded *a priori* from the list of possible explanations which a commentator of Iamblichus' or Simplicius' cast of mind is prepared to entertain. On the other hand, in the final part of his commentary, Simplicius mentions another speculation of Iamblichus', according to which *all* the eight senses of having listed at the end of the *Categories* fall under the category of having, and hence that having, like the category of quality (8b26), though said 'in many ways', is not said homonymously (438,18ff.). Although the suggestion seems quite plausible – perhaps the final chapter of our *Categories* text belongs with the main part of the work (chapters 4-9) and not with the other material in the *Postpraedicamenta* – Simplicius dismisses it on the basis (in effect) that the only examples Aristotle gives us of having in chapters 4 and 9 of the *Categories* (being shod and being armed) envisage a restriction of the category to just these and closely similar cases.

Simplicius' discussion of the *Postpraedicamenta* contains much interesting material, and is especially rich in discussion of Stoic doctrines.

There are also useful excerpts from the Pseudo-Archytan treatise *de Oppositis* and from the Peripatetic treatise of the same name. (As noted, Simplicius takes the former of these texts to be by Archytas the Pythagorean – hence reversing the correct order of dependence – and the latter to be genuine Aristotle.) Simplicius assumes that this part of the *Categories* is authentic (379,3ff.), though he mentions Andronicus' opinion that it is not genuine, and that it was added by someone who saw the work as a propaedeutic to the *Topics*. He thinks, however, that this reservation is sufficiently answered by observing that the *Postpraedicamenta* contain materials which relate closely to the subject-matter of the *Categories* as well as to that of the *Topics*, since they treat of important auxiliary concepts which Aristotle requires in the main body of the former text. He suggests that Aristotle dealt with those auxiliary concepts which were unfamiliar to readers (e.g. homonymy and synonymy) right at the start, postponing his treatment of those auxiliary concepts which were relatively familiar until the very end. And Simplicius is able (379,20ff.) to find a rationale behind the order of presentation of the themes of the *Postpraedicamenta*, corresponding to the order of presentation of the categories in the earlier chapters. But whether these coincidences really warrant more than saying that the *Postpraedicamenta* – whatever their provenance and whatever their connection to the main part of the text – consist of apparently Aristotelian treatments of a miscellany of genuinely Aristotelian themes, is doubtful.

Acknowledgements

I am grateful to the University of Sussex for granting me periods of leave, and to the Alexander von Humbolt-Stiftung for awarding me a Fellowship at the University of Bonn, in order to work on this translation. Richard Sorabji, Han Baltussen and Sylvia Berryman have been of considerable assistance to me throughout the period of its execution; I have profited greatly from the comments of the series readers on an earlier draft, and have also had the benefit of advice on individual passages from David Langslow and Oliver Primavesi: to all these I offer my warmest thanks. My greatest debt of gratitude is to my wife Cathrin for her unfailing forbearance and support.

Note

My translations of the Aristotelian lemmas follow L. Minio-Paluello's text of the *Categories, Aristotelis Categoriae et Liber De Interpretatione* (Oxford: Clarendon, 1949); I have also made some use of J.L. Ackrill's translation of it in his *Aristotle's Categories* and *de Interpretatione* (Oxford: Clarendon, 1963).

Notes

1. On this text see C. Evangeliou, *Aristotle's Categories and Porphyry*, Leiden 1988.

2. See here J. Dillon, 'Iamblichus' *Noera Theôria* of Aristotle's *Categories*', *Syllecta Classica* 8, 1997, 65-77 at p. 66.

3. These have been collected and supplied with a commentary by Bent Dalsgaard Larsen, *Jamblique de Chalcis: Exégète et philosophe* 2 vols., Aarhus 1972.

4. K. Kalbfleisch, *Simplicii In Aristotelis Categorias Commentarium*, Berlin 1907 = *CAG* 8, p. xii; I. Hadot, 'The Life and Work of Simplicius in Greek and Arabic Sources', in R. Sorabji ed., *Aristotle Transformed*, London 1990, 275-303, pp. 296-7.

5. 'Iamblichus' *Noera Theôria* of Aristotle's *Categories*', p. 77.

6. See further n. 10 to the translation.

7. But he does at one point in our part of the text show a fleeting awareness that the chronological question is not closed: at 350,13-14 he briefly refers to unnamed critics of Archytas who accused him (correctly, in fact) of conflating the opinions of Aristotle and the Stoics: these critics must therefore have got the chronology right. The source of this objection may be Themistius: see my note ad loc.

8. See 382,7-10 with my note ad loc.

Textual Emendations

316,32	Delete *auto.*
316,34	Delete *<eis>.*
317,12	Read *kai <tin'> oukh hupotattei.*
317,15	Read *hoion <geometren>.*
318,15	Read *houtôs <hê>.*
319,2	Read *ta sômata* instead of *to sôma tas.*
319,7	Read *theôrountai <kai>.*
321,2	Delete *ê engus.*
322,28	Read *hôs hup' allou <huph'> heautou diaphtheiromenos.*
323,31	Read *aph' heautou* instead of *aph' heautês.*
324,11	Read *<ê> ei.*
325,4	Read *ou deêi* instead of *oude êi.*
327,7	I translate Kalbfleisch's suggested supplement *Iamblikhos <paradidôsi> peri tou poiein.*
328,10	Read *pros alla* instead of *pros allêla.*
328,21	Read *energein <kai> poiein.*
328,31-2	Read *kata tina diadokhon* instead of *kata tên adiadokhon.*
329,10	Read *to poiein te* instead of *tôi poiounti.*
329,17	Delete *hê.*
330,10	Delete the first occurrence of *ta.*
330,25-6	Read *kai hosa <. hosai te gar>.*
331,7	Read *hê* instead of *kai.*
331,17	Read *deuterôi* instead of *prôtôi.*
332,18	Read *holên* instead of *allên.*
332,20	Read *ekhei <ti>.*
333,20	Read *ethesan <to peras> tou poiêin.*
333,26	Read *<en> tôi pros ti.*
333,33	Read *de <kai>.*
335,9	Read *tina* instead of *tên.*
336,6	Read *hotan <tis> huptiôteros.*
336,32	Read *eskhen* instead of *eskhon.*
337,32	Read *<ananka> toigaroun.*
338,15	Delete the third *kai.*
338,29	I translate Kalbfleisch's suggested supplement *hautai <phônai>.*
339,11	Read *eite sômatôn <eite asômatôn>.*
339,15	Read *anapim<p>latai.*
340,6	Read *mia kai <hê> autê.*
342,26	Read *epeita <hoti>.*
342,33	Read *<ou> bouletai.*
343,1	Read *ê gar psukhê ê to nun* instead of *ê gar psukhên ê ton noun.*
343,1	Read *kata men* instead of *ei men kata.*
343,6	Read *en de tôi tritôi tôn* instead of *en de tôi tritôi tôi.*
343,10	Read *autês* instead of *autois.*

343,13	Read *ôn* instead of *on*.
344,13	Read *autês* instead of *autou*.
344,18	Read *hen* instead of *hena*.
344,21	Read *hôsper* <*gar*>.
344,23	Read *autêi ekhei kai autê* instead of *autôi ekhei kai auto*.
344,29	Read *kai* instead of *ê*.
344,29-30	Read *hê ousia autou* instead of *autos*.
345,24	Read <*hê*> *kinêsis*.
347,11	Read *proêgoumenois* instead of *proêgoumenôs*.
349,8	Read *meresi* instead of *merei*.
350,26	Read *autou* instead of *auton*.
351,1	Delete *ou*.
352,6-8	Read *hò … touto* instead of *hôs … houtôs*.
352,25	Read *to gar nun ameres on hama nooumenon kai legomenon*.
353,8	Read *hopoka khronos* <*ouk ên*>.
354,31	Read <*ton*> *auton*.
355,19	Read *tên* <*ousian*>.
355,31	Read *apophainoito* instead of *apophainointo*.
355,32	Read *diameneî* instead of *diaménei*.
356,4-5	Read <*pros to ekeinou*> *hama kai aei* <*ta onta*>.
357,32	Read *hôs* <*gar*> *to* instead of *hôs ta*.
359,7	Read *lektikas* instead of *dialektikas*.
359,21	Read *parakeimenon* <*kai hupokeimenon*>.
360,2	Read *ta pragmata* <*ta*> *en*.
360,19	Delete *tôn*.
360,23	Delete *kai*.
360,31	Read <*ê hêde*>.
361,25	Read *epeidê* <*de*>.
362,29	Read *to eskhaton tou periekhomenou topou* instead of *to periekhomenon eskhaton tou topou*.
362,30	Read *kat' autên* instead of *kata tautên*.
362,34	Read *noêt*<*ik*>*ê*.
363,25	Read *houtôs* <*ekhen*>.
365,6	Read *tôn* instead of *tinôn*.
365,24	Read *gen*<*nêt*>*ikên*.
365,27	Read *gar* instead of *te* and <*kai*> *oute*.
365,28	Read *m*<*el*>*anotas*.
368,5	Read *holôs* instead of *hoti*.
369,16	Read *hên en* instead of *en men*.
369,28	Delete *apo ktêmatôn: ou gar perikeimetha ekeina: kai apo*.
371,20	Read <*tês*> *tou ekhein*.
371,30	Read *kai gar* <*to agon*>.
372,8	Read *boun* instead of *noun*.
372,15	Read *pheromenên* <*ousian*>.
374,15	Read *pheromenên* <*ousian*>.

374,25   Read *houtô* instead of *autôi*.
375,9   Read *heautêi* instead of *autêi*.
375,12   Read *periekhousês* instead of *periekhousêi*.
375,22   Read *<hê> thalassa*.
375,24-5 Read *apaidei … merikês … merika* instead of *apodei … meristês … merista*.
375,28   Read *<ta> tettara*.
376,5   Read *autais* instead of *autois*.
376,20-1 Read *to ekhein kat' aitian kai to ekhein* instead of *to kat' aitian kai to ekhon*.
376,31   Read *ta mikrotera* instead of *mikrotera ta*.
377,3   Read *hêi … hêi* instead of *ei … hê*.
378,5   Read *tô logô* instead of *tôn logôn*.
378,8   Read *poson <êmen> kai*.
378,11-12 Read *pot' heteron ti pôs* instead of *pote gerontikôs*.
379,1   Read *hôs oikeian tais arkhais kai têi epistêmêi hôrismenais
          ousais dia touto en arithmô* etc.
380,21   Read *asunuparxia* instead of *anuparxia*.
380,31   Read *asunuparxias* instead of *anuparxias*.
381,7   Read *to auto* instead of *ta auta*.
381,8   Read *asunuparkta* instead of *anuparkta*.
382,12   Read *ta men <hôs> enantia*.
384,17   Read *ou legetai tou kakou <agathon>*.
384,30   Read *<to> epistêton*.
384,32   Read *esti* instead of *legetai*.
386,5   I translate Kalbfleisch's suggested supplement *to gar leukon
          ou legetai <tou melanos leukon, all' enantion> tôi melani*.
387,19-20 Delete the comma after *exergasiai*, and insert a comma after
          enantiôn.
387,30   Read *ei tauton <to> ta pleiston apekhonta*.
388,4-5   I translate Kalbfleisch's suggested supplement *hoti mê monon
          en tôi autôi genei <ta enantia huphestêken, alla kai en enan­
          tiois: en men gar tôi autôi genei> tôi khrômati*.
388,28   Read *kai <ou> touton toutôi, alla mesôs ton phronimon*.
388,30   Read *epi ta amesa <blepontes>*.
389,9   Read *kinêsis <kai> stasis*.
389,12   Read *<hôs> hou*.
389,13   Read *parônumon* instead of *parônuma*.
389,21   Read *<enantia> estin ta kata ta hapla monon ê <kai ta>*.
389,27   Read *phêsin* instead of *phasin*.
390,5-6   Read *kai … enantioi esontai* instead of *kan … enantia estai*.
390,34-5 Read *ta hôs kataphasis kai apophasis* instead of *tên hôs
          kataphasin kai apophasin*.
391,8-9   Read *to katholô ôn, hôn men enantiotatôn anagkaion* instead
          of *to katholô men anagkaiotaton*.

391,21   Read *oudeteron <oud>eterôi*.

392,4   Read *<kai> enti eidea*.

392,6   I translate Kalbfleisch's suggested supplement *epidekhetai <monon tan eis genê> toman.* (Omit *men.*)

392,7-8   I translate Kalbfleisch's suggested supplement *ta d' eskhata eidea kai poti tan aisthasin <oikeiotata tan eis atoma monon, ta de mesa> ouk an genê.*

392,9   I translate Kalbfleisch's suggested supplement *skalênos genos, <tô de epipedô eidos, kai ha areta tas men phronasios kai andreias kai sôphrosunas kai dikaiosunas genos,> tô de agathô eidos.*

392,13   Read *<tên> tôn*.

393,4   Read *topon* instead of *tropon*.

394,4   Read *ekhein <hetera onta, kai tên hexin kai to hexin ekhein,>*.

396,32   Read *kai <allo> to sterêsin*.

396,33   I translate Kalbfleisch's suggested supplement *sterêseôs, <tauto palin eipôn kai peri tês kataphaseôs kai apophaseôs,> pistoutai.*

397,5   Read *hôsautôs <hôs>*.

397,9   Read *onomatos <kai rhêmatos>*.

397,17   Read *tôi <gar>*.

397,33   Read *kai <tou>*.

398,3   Read *tês <tôn>*.

398,11   Delete the second *tôn*.

399,33   Read *apo prôtês ge<neseôs>*.

400,22   Delete *pantôs*.

401,27   Delete *phêsin*.

402,8   Read *estin <hê>*.

402,35   Read *<tôn> en*.

403,12   Delete *hôs*.

403,24   Read *kataphaseôs <kai apophaseôs>*.

403,33   Read *pros <tous> allous tropous*.

405,19   Read *<ek>pesein*.

406,11-12   Read *<hoion> 'hôs kalos ge ho Peiraieus', <'ou kalos ge ho Peiraieus'>, kai tois psektikois, hoion '<hôs> phaulos estin', 'ou phaulos estin'.*

407,7   Read *autês* instead of *autôn*.

407,31   Delete *genesios*.

407,31   Read *toutôn* instead of *toutôi*.

408,10   Read *<logou> eidea mallon enti*.

408,25   Read *kataphasios <kai apophasios>*.

409,2   Read *sunuparkhen* (= *sunuparkhein*) instead of *sunuparkhon*.

409,4   Read *sunuparkhen* (= *sunuparkhein*) instead of *sunuparkhon*.

409,12   Delete *hupo*.

411,31   Delete *tade*.

412,2 Read *auto* instead of *auta*.
412,5 Punctuate *elleipsei. kai* etc.
414,13 Delete the first *to*.
415,33 Read *proskeisthai* instead of *prokeisthai*.
415,34 Delete closing quotation mark after *mallon*.
416,2 Insert closing quotation mark after *paralipô*.
416,29 Read *bouletai <einai>*.
417,1 Read *apotukhiai* instead of *apotukhia*.
417,7 Read *<hê> antithesis*.
417,22 Read *to ptilôssein* instead of *to ptilôsson*.
419,6 Read *poieisthai* instead of *hêgeisthai*.
419,11 Read *<ê> hê*.
420,3 Read *akolouthêsin* instead of *akolouthian*.
421,8-9 Read *hôs ek gês kai hudatos pêlos* instead of *hôs ek gês kai pêlou*.
421,16 Read *ei de <e>ti*.
423,6 Read *hupo <to> têi*.
423,27 Read *hupo de <to en> tois*.
423,31 Read *<to> auto*.
424,20 Read *<tôi> hôs aitiôi*.
425,23 Read *tou tôi haplôi* instead of *toutou kai haplou*.
426,35 Read *hosa* instead of *hosas*.
428,4 Read *autas* instead of *autos*.
428,7 Delete *tauto*.
428,17 Read *dokein* instead of *dokei*.
429,8 Read *kai mên kai sunkrinomena men auxanetai*.
429,19 Read *poiotêtos* instead of *posotêtos*.
430,19 Read *<ta men bk kg> tetragôna esti*.
431,29 Read *kat' autas* instead of *kat' auta*.
432,20 Read *kai <hai> kata*.
433,12 I translate Kalbfleisch's suggested supplement: *kai tên en tôi leukôi êremian: hê gar en tôi melani êremia antikeitai têi leukansei*.
433,17 Read *tôi pro tou einai* instead of *tôi prôteuein*.
433,21 Read *dio* instead of *dioti*.
433,22 Read *hêkei* instead of *hê ekei*. Delete *esti*.
433,29-30 Read *megethos <megethos> oude tên kat' ousian <ousian>*.
433,31-2 Read *kata tauta* instead of *kat' autas*.
434,6 Read *topon* instead of *touto*.
434,22 Delete *kathaper*.
436,24-5 Read *mêpote de tou hebdomou touto esti sêmainomenou tou hôs ktêma*.
437,20 Delete *hothen oukh*.
438,30 Read *all' oute ho huios oute ho agros oute to tôi apsukhôi perikeimenon krateitai*.

Simplicius
On Aristotle
Categories 9-15

Translation

The Commentary of Simplicius on
Aristotle *Categories 9-15*

CHAPTER 9

On Acting and Undergoing[1]   295,1

11b1-16 Both acting and undergoing admit of contrariety [and
of more and less: for heating is contrary to cooling and being
heated to being cooled and being pleased to being grieved, so
that they admit of contrariety. And of more and less too: for it
is possible to heat more and less, and to be heated more and less,
and to be grieved more and less. Hence acting and undergoing
admit of more and less. <...> That suffices for an account
concerning these; and concerning being-in-a-position, too, it has
been said, in the discussion of the relatives, that they are said
derivately from the positions. But concerning the remaining
ones – when and where and having – owing to their obviousness
nothing more is said about them than was said at the beginning,
namely that being shod and being armed signify having, that
being in the Lyceum, for example, signifies where – and all the
other things that were said about them.] Concerning the [pro-
posed] genera, then, what has been said is sufficient.

Since the four of the ten genera which he has already gone through
are more general and admit of a more ample theory, they were
deemed by Aristotle worthy of an extended account; and he will [now]   5
speak of the remaining ones, even if in a more concise manner. It
would have been possible to say many fine words about these [genera]
as well, but he is satisfied, as befits an introduction, with exhibiting
their [sc. general] content, so that students, by referring simple things
to their proper genera, may be able properly to establish the categories for themselves, which [Aristotle] did at the beginning by means
of his examples. He produced precise accounts of each of these in   10
separate works, however: of the [category of] acting (*poiein*) and [that
of] undergoing (*paskhein*) in the [treatise] *On Generation and Destruction* (323b1ff.); of the [category of] when (*pote*) and the [category
of] where (*pou*)[2] in the *Physics* (208a27ff.), where he gave complete
instruction on time and place; and he established thoroughly complete accounts of all [these categories] in the *Metaphysics*.[3] For the

principles are made clear, so far as their significant expression is
15   concerned, in the logical treatise;[4] as regards the objects signified,
they are appropriately expounded in the *Metaphysics*.

Among these [remaining genera] he mentioned the [category of]
acting and [that of] undergoing first because, they say, acting and
undergoing exist in respect of the quality (*poiotês*) [of something]: so
it is reasonable that they were put forward immediately after the
[category of] quality.[5] And yet acting also exists in respect of substance (*ousia*), as for example begetting and housebuilding, and in
20   respect of quantity (*posotês*), as for example counting, and it is
inherently related to the relatives (*pros ti*), since acting and undergoing are relatives.[6] Hence it is better to say that the [category of] acting
and [that of] undergoing, being inherently related to the [first] four
categories, as operation (*energeia*)[7] and affection (*pathos*) to an underlying reality (*huparxis*), reasonably received their account after
the four [initial categories], and [this was] also because these [first
four categories] belong to incorporeals as well [as to corporeals], all
296,1 the subsequent genera being observed solely in bodies. [Aristotle]
mentioned them[8] at the same time because they coexist at the same
time – that is, where there is the one, there is also the other – so that
some people do not think one should even define separate categories
for them, but rather arrange them under the relatives.[9] But Archytas[10] arranged both the [category of] having (*ekhein*) and the
[category of] where before the [category of] acting and [that of]
5   undergoing, giving his reason thus:[11] 'Since everything moved is
moved in a particular place, and [since] acting and undergoing are
particular movements in operation, it is clear that place, in which
acting and undergoing exist, must subsist first of all.'

The [category of] acting signifies an operation, and that of undergoing an affection (*pathos*), not in respect of the *character* of the
10   affection (*peisis*) – for this is a quality – but in respect of the *movement*
in the affection.[12] This is the obvious conception of them, which is why
[Aristotle] has omitted to allude to it, as being [anyway] clear, but he
does mention the *attributes* of these [categories] as well [as of the
other categories], and the first of these is that acting and undergoing
'admit of contrariety' (11b1-2). For heating and cooling are contrary,
each being in the [category of] acting, and being heated [is contrary]
15   to being cooled,[13] each of these being in the [category of] undergoing,
just as are being pleased and being grieved. For if such contrarieties
[are constituted] in accordance with [sc. contrary] qualities ([and they
are], for the [sc. quality] hot is contrary to the [sc. quality] cold), and
[if] contraries are productive of contraries,[14] then (1) contrariety will
obtain in the [category of] acting as well, whenever it is construed as
the operation of those genera which admit of contrariety; and (2) if
[contrariety obtains] in the [category of] acting, then [it does so] in

the [category of] undergoing too: for what the agent brings about is   20
what the undergoer undergoes.

Next, some contraries have something in between, and some do
not. And of all those qualities which have something in between it is
also the case that their contrariety in respect of acting and undergoing
has something in between, such as making lukewarm and making
red, since lukewarm is between hot and cold, and red or grey [be-
tween] white and black. Of all those things whose qualities have
nothing in between, on the other hand, neither the operations nor the   25
affections [have anything in between] – as for instance making
healthy and making sick.

The account [of action] is twofold: of actions some are opposed to
something else, namely the undergoer, as for example the [action] of
heating (for the heating thing heats the heated thing), whereas others
are absolute, as for example the [action] of speaking.

Contraries are not the distinguishing mark of acting and undergoing: this [feature] does not belong to them alone, nor to all cases of   30
them, for [it does] not [belong] to speaking or writing or constructing,
because none of these is observed in a state of contrariety; rather, [it
belongs] only to those things which, in respect of their operation or
affection, are among those things possessing contrariety.

Acting and undergoing also admit of more and less. For it is   297,1
possible to heat and be heated and to do and undergo the other things
we have mentioned both to a greater and to a lesser extent, for[15]
because there is, in the qualities themselves, more and less, the
things acting and undergoing in respect of these [qualities] will also
possess more and less.[16] However, one should not look for more and   5
less in all cases of acting and undergoing, but [only] in those cases
which possess acting and undergoing in respect of the genera which
admit of more and less, since it is not possible to beget, or count, more
or less (for neither the [category of] substance nor the [category of]
quantity admits of more and less). There will be a division of acting
and undergoing both in respect of operations, [which are] divided in   10
many ways, and in respect of affective qualities.[17]

Concerning the [category of] being-in-a-position (*keisthai*) [Aris-
totle] directs the reader to the foregoing. It has been said that *position*
(*thesis*), since it is *of* something, namely the thing positioned, is
among the relatives, but that the *being-in-a-position* [of that thing],
called derivatively (*parônumôs*) from its position, is of another category.[18] Examples are reclining, standing and sitting: these are not   15
positions, but their names are derived (*parônomastai*) from the [cor-
responding] position.[19] And we also have conveyed by him the division
of the [category of] being-in-a-position.[20] But concerning 'the remaining' three [categories] – 'the [category of] where, that of when and that
of having – owing to their obviousness,' he says, 'nothing more is

said'[21] about them 'than what was said at the beginning' (11b11-13).
And all he did there was set down examples of them, saying: 'where
20   – for example, in the Lyceum; when – for example, yesterday, last
year; having – for example, he is shod, he is armed' (2a1-3). Further
on he will also convey a division of the [category of] having as
something which is said in many ways.[22]

    But as these matters have been disdained by Aristotle,[23] it may be
as well to learn the [doctrines] concerning them developed by Porphyry[24] and Iamblichus.[25] They say that the [category of] where and
25   [that of] when, like the relatives too, are not among the *primary*
things observed in the case of objects, but are among the things
supervening on other things.[26] For when quantity is present as underlying subject, along with the things which follow upon it, namely
place and time, then the [category of] where and that of when are
constituted together with them: place is not the [category of] where,
nor is time the [category of] when, but rather place and time have
prior existence, and subsequently, when something else is in this
30   [place or time], what is in place is said to be some*where* and what is
in time some*when* – such as *Socrates in the Lyceum*, or <*the festival
of Dionysus> yesterday*.[27] The [category of] where does <not>[28] appear
to have just one species or to fail to admit of differentiae.[29] For some
things are said to be in a place in an indefinite sense, for example *in
the city*, and others in a definite sense, for example *in the Painted
Portico*, or *in this particular part of the Portico*. And [the category of
298,1   where] admits of all the differentiae of place: for *above* and *below* [are
said][30] in accordance with the neighbouring place, the common
[place], the [place] *per se* (*kath' hauto*), and the [place] which is
accidentally so (*kata sumbebêkos*). It is possible for [the category of]
where to obtain in each of these cases. Similarly, too, the [category
of] when is not time, but rather time has prior existence, and what is
5   in[31] time is said to be some*when*, such as *the festival of Dionysus last
year* or *this year* or *next year*. Time itself, however, in which that which
is said to be some*when* is said to be, is not in the category of when,
but in that of quantity. The [category of] when also admits of the
differentiae of time.[32] For *last year* is said in respect of past [time], *this
year* in respect of present [time], and *next year* in respect of future [time].
10   The [category of] having signifies whenever some acquired thing,
which belongs to something and is separated from the substance of
the body [which has it], coexists with it; so the [category of] having is
the possession (*skhesis*) of certain acquired things.[33] For being clothed
is having a garment and being shod is having shoes, and these things
are different from the haver and separated from his substance,
belonging to him neither in respect of substance nor as accidents, as
15   do blackness and brightness of the eye. The [category of] having does
not *per se* have species-forming differentiae, but can admit of division

in virtue of the differences of the things had, since some will be animate, such as a household slave or an ox, and others inanimate, such as a cloak or weapons. And [the category of having] can also admit of division in virtue of the difference among the things in respect of which [someone] has, as when, for example, they[34] say that one has one's acquired [sc. mental] states (*hexeis*) *in the soul*, or acquired [properties] with regard to the body *in the body* – but no 20 differentiation will come about in virtue of the sheer *having* or the *being had*. But while both Porphyry and Iamblichus admitted the [category of] having in the case of the soul in respect of its acquired states, one might raise the question whether those [states] are not rather *qualities* and the things [affected] by them *qualified*, like the bodies too which participate in acquired blackness. For the states are not *placed on* the soul like shoes [on the feet], but, since they alter it 25 to a greater or lesser degree, they are particular *conditions* (*diatheseis*) with regard to it.

What has been said provides the solution to such puzzles as how, assuming that there are no species of them, the [last] six categories[35] can be genera (for genera are said in relation to species and are genera of species). That the categories *are* genera Aristotle has himself made clear by saying: 'Concerning the proposed genera, then, what has 30 been said is sufficient' (11b15-16). Given, therefore, that there *are* species of these [last six] genera too, as we have shown, the puzzle then no longer has any place. For if these genera are indeed of this sort, then they are *said of* the mentioned species. But perhaps[36] someone will say that these genera are not said in the same way as are things predicated of several specifically different things in the [category] of what a thing is,[37] but that [these six categories] above all signify *natures* [which are] different and separate from one an- 35 other, just as we say in the case of the branches of knowledge too that each of them is defined around a particular *genus*, [thereby] saying as much as[38] that [each is defined] around a certain nature which is separate from the others. And that is why [Aristotle] calls them[39] categories.[40]

Again, some contradict [Aristotle's view] and want acting and 299,1 undergoing to be said in relation to each other and to be relatives rather than, as Aristotle says, separate categories. But they are wrong; for [acting and undergoing] do not have their being in their relation to each other.[41] For they do not, like right and left, consist merely in a relation, but there is additionally something which is 5 brought into being by them, in accordance with which the one [component] is the agent, and the other the patient. And even if it be granted that the [category of] *acting* and [that of] *undergoing* are said in relation to each other, nevertheless the *particulars*[42] are not: for walking and running are not relatives, although they are acting. Nor indeed was grammar in relation to anything either,[43] for all that its genus [consists] in knowledge, which is one of the relatives.[44] In

10 general acting is said in respect of every operating thing, but not every operation [is] in relation to a patient: for the absolute actions, such as speaking, running, reading and such, are not [in relation to a patient], so that not all acting will be among the relatives. For even if the ground does undergo some [effect] from the walking man, still it is not in virtue of this fact that walking is called acting, but in virtue of the sort of movement involved; and likewise being in pain or

15 becoming black or white [are cases of undergoing] in virtue of the way they are.[45] For just as the contrary taken generally [is] a relative,[46] but each of them [i.e. each of the contrary things] [falls] under its appropriate genus, so too even though the [category of] acting and that of undergoing are said in relation to each other, it does not follow that the things [falling] under them will be relatives too. So since [acting and undergoing] are not under the relatives, nor under any of the other categories, they will be separate categories. But perhaps

20 someone will say that acting and undergoing [as such] should have been ranged under the relatives, just like the contraries, but the particular actings and undergoings each under their appropriate genera – founding a city, as it might be, and begetting under substance, counting and speaking under quantity (because speech and number are quantities),[47] and whitening and blackening under qual-

25 ity. Perhaps therefore acting and undergoing are related to the other categories as operation and affection are to substance. For it is possible to operate – for example, to love – both in accordance with the relatives, and in accordance with the rest of the ten[48] categories.[49]

Now someone might say that [Aristotle] has specified the general features of acting and undergoing, but has not demonstrated the particular features. In response to this Iamblichus says: 'In the

30 features which are held to be general their particular features are also displayed. For [Aristotle] does not adduce contraries and more and less *simpliciter*, but [adduces] some of these in the case of operation, others in the case of affection.' It is quite easy to reply to this that in the case of the other categories too not any random contraries and [cases of] more and less were adduced, but [only] the appropriate ones for each [category], and none the less [Aristotle] still thought he ought to set out the particular features [of each category]

35 in addition to the general ones. Hence what [was said] at the beginning is nearer the truth, namely that [Aristotle] was satisfied in these cases [i.e. acting and undergoing] with more general [characterisations].

But why, if acting and undergoing are both genera, and given that *having* is a genus, is *being had* not also a genus? For having is

300,1 contradistinguished from being had just as undergoing is from acting.

Well, [the reason is] that within the [category of] having being had is also included: for whatever haver is taken, it necessarily *has* the had thing connected with it. But undergoing is *not* included in acting *simpliciter*: for shouting, walking, running and writing are acting, and none of these has a patient connected with it. And indeed it is not 5 even the case that having is in relation to something – to being had, as it might seem: for the [species] it is predicated of, such as being shod and being armed, are not said in relation to anything. The haver might be spoken of in relation to the thing had, but having – which is not the same as the haver – is not [spoken of] in relation to another thing.[50]

Some criticise Aristotle on the ground that he has said little about the [last] six categories and has neither described (*hupographein*) 10 what their nature is,[51] nor divided them into their differentiae, even though it would be possible, as we have said (298,1.7), to divide the [category of] where into the differentiae of place and the [category of] when into the [differentiae] of time. That Aristotle has spoken defectively is also evident anyway from Archytas' lengthier teaching concerning them [i.e. these six categories], since he conveys the particular features of each of these [categories] as well as of the preceding ones. But people defend Aristotle by saying that he gave 15 full instruction on the things which are not fully assumed in common-sense conceptions [of these categories]; those matters which are assumed and were obvious he omitted on account of their obviousness. He makes this clear himself by saying: 'Owing to their obviousness nothing more is said about them than was said at the beginning' (11b14-15). And even if each of these [categories] is connected with a physical theory – as, for instance, the [category of] acting [with a theory] of movement, and the [category of] where and [that of] when 20 [with a theory] of place and time – in a logical treatise there is no need to take excessive pains beyond [expressing] the conception which manifests itself immediately in accordance with the meaning [of these categories], given also that it would have been difficult to give a precise theory concerning place and time. And they add this, that since these six genera have an adventitious nature it was appropriate that they receive a more passing treatment. For some [categories], such as quality and relative, come along with the perceivable and 25 physical substance,[52] whereas others, such as acting and undergoing, supervene on it when it is already being moved in relation to what it was possible [for it to be moved in relation to]; and the [category of] in time and [that of] in place,[53] the [category of] being-in-a-position and the [category of] having accompany these [categories].[54] For someone acting acts in time, and is moved in respect of place, and someone undergoing necessarily[55] undergoes in time, and what comes to be [sc. a substance] is positioned or has something. 30

Some wonder too why Aristotle did not join the account concerning the [category of] having to the simple categories, but talked first[56] about opposition, prior and posterior, the simultaneous, movement and some other things, and only then[57] produced the division of the [category of] having. But others[58] solve [this problem] nicely, [saying]
35 that he arranged [i.e. listed] the [category of] having together with that of where and [that of] when,[59] and remarked [there] that there was no need – in view of their obviousness – to say anything else about
301,1 them, but then wishing after the [treatment of the] categories to give a more technical analysis of the matters which he had dealt with according to the popular conceptions of them – I mean with regard to opposites and the prior and posterior and the rest – [and] since having is homonymous, lest anyone think that he was establishing a single
5 genus of homonymous things, he reasonably defined the homonymy of having at the end.[60]

But surely, they say, the six last categories can be reduced to the ones already mentioned, the [category] of when to time, and this to quantity, the [category] of where to place, and this too to quantity, and the [category] of acting and [that] of undergoing and [that] of being-in-a-position and [that] of having to the [category of] relative.
10 The response to this view too is clear from what has been said. For there is a distinction between what is in something and what the thing which is in something is in. If that is right, what is in place will differ from place and what is in time [will differ] from time. The genera of where and when will then be distinct from place and time. And acting and undergoing too have been previously shown to have their own particular natures going beyond the relatives, as do being-
15 in-a-position and having also: for *they*[61] have different sorts of relation (*skheseis*) – for being-in-a-position is of something in relation to something different, whereas having is of something different in relation to something – but the relative itself has a common relation towards each [of the relata].[62] So these genera are distinguished according to their particular differentiae and are not [to be] reduced to the relatives. But so much for these general and disparate problems and solutions.
20 Next we should make distinct investigations into the appropriate questions concerning each one.[63] And first, that it is consistent that acting and undergoing are genera is clear from the ensuing considerations. For just as quantity came after substance,[64] and on account of this quantity was posited as one genus, and again, just as quality [came] after substance, [and] concerns substance, and [so] quality
25 became another genus, so too operation and acting [come] after substance, and [so] in accordance with these [precedents] operation too should be posited as a genus after substance (*huparxis*), and also its[65] kin, affection or undergoing. But would it have been possible to

posit as the genus [either] the *acting* (*to poiein*) or the *agent* (*to poioun*) or the *action* (*hê poiêsis*), just as quality was a genus and so was the qualified thing [derived] from it?[66] Perhaps we should say: in this case too action, acting and agent obtain conjointly, but the agent encompasses the subject as well, and imports a composite meaning deriving from both the operating [thing] and the operation, whereas the action and the acting are simpler and do not possess composition, so that these latter are more suitable than the agent for the definition of the genus.[67] Again, of these [i.e. action and acting] [Aristotle] has given precedence to acting over the action as well [sc. as over the agent], because action (*poiêsis*) is said in two ways: for both the *operation* is said to be a *poiêsis* (an action) and the finished *product* of the operation, as when we talk of Homer's 'creation' (*poiêsis*).[68] But what we want is not the finished product, but the operation, which *operate* signifies uniformly. Hence *acting* is posited as the genus: for acting signifies an operation which is still coming about, just as action [signifies] rather what has come to a stop, and the agent's finished product.[69]

But if acting exhibits operating, why do we not posit *operation* as the genus rather than acting? And if operation is more appropriate than action for the reason that it manifests the [process] in movement, and not the [result] of the movement, as does action, then [Aristotle] should have posited *movement* as one genus among the categories. For just as the other [categories] concern substance, so too does movement, in which there is both acting and undergoing: for both [of these are involved] in movement. But those who say this, such as Plotinus,[70] do not avail themselves of Aristotle's hypotheses. For the latter says that the prime mover and agent is unmoved.[71] Because of this, too, acting was separated in his treatment from undergoing, and they were not both arranged under one genus, so that we should not reduce both of these to one [genus] either, but define them as two [separate genera], just as Aristotle too separated them. That is indeed how both Boethus[72] and Iamblichus objected to the puzzle which claims that movement should be established as a single genus prior to acting and undergoing.[73]

But Porphyry says: 'In some cases movement seems to be single and continuous in respect of acting and undergoing, as for example in the case of movements by impact (*plêgê*) like throwing and pushing.[74] For the movement of the thrown piece of wood is just like that of the man throwing it, and that of the pushed thing is just like the pushing of the man who pushes it. Hence also each [movement is] single and continuous. But [movement] does not have the same sort of being in relation to the striker and the thing struck, but rather [the movement] of the struck thing becomes an affection, that of the

30

35
302,1

5

10

15

20

striker an action. Thus acting and undergoing are not simply of a
25   single genus – namely movement – but maintain a difference.'
        Iamblichus censures this solution of the difficulty as far-fetched
and as not based on entirely familiar [principles] nor on Aristotle's
doctrines: 'It does not follow that if some *particular* action is thus and
so, *every* action is thereby also [the same way], and one ought not to
have begun from the lowest actions (I mean those of impact and
30   pushing), nor to have agreed with the Stoics [in a matter] concerning
which we continue to differ from them, namely [their view] that the
agent acts by means of some sort of approach and contact. It is better
to say that not all things act by approach and contact, but that action
comes about according to the suitability of the agent towards the
patient, and that many things act without contact – as we all know –
and that even in the case of agents which we see needing juxtaposition
35   [in order to act], contact [only] comes about accidentally because the
things partaking of the capacity to undergo or act are in a place: for
that is what bodies and those things which partake of active or
affective capacities are like. But in cases where the separation be-
303,1 tween the bodies does not in any way prevent the one from acting and
the other from undergoing and receiving the operation of the agent,
in these cases the operation comes about dimensionlessly (*adiastatos*)[75] and unhindered,[76] as the strings of a lyre sound together[77]
although separated from each other, and naphtha receives the form
of fire from a distance.[78] And, on the other hand, many things which
are connected do not act [on one another], such as a plaster or some
5   other medicinal preparation applied to a stone. If, therefore, touching
things often do not act [on each other], and things which are not
touching do, action in the strictest sense is not impact and pushing,
not even in the cases where we see some things striking [others], nor
in these cases is the *touching* the cause, but rather it is the kinship
of capacity[79] which, in these cases too, supplies the efficacy (*to kuros*)
of acting.
10   'Now if someone were to say that the essence of the agent and of
the patient is the same, then the mover will also itself be moved, the
moved thing will move, and [such a thing] will as a whole and
throughout its whole [extent] both move and be moved, and the
axioms concerning movement will be demolished in their entirety –
namely that movement proceeds *from* something and *concerns* something [sc. else], and that the origin of movement is a different
particular thing from the movement itself, this being *produced* from
the origin; and in the cases where the causes of the movement lie
15   separated,[80] [these axioms] will be all the more demolished. So we
should not allow true opinions, if they are to distinguish the origins
of the genera and divide them in the natural places, to be mistaken
about these [axioms]. For even if we ought also, on the basis of the

operation of the agent and the change undergone by the patient, to conjecture some sort of mixed movement, this generation [sc. of a mixed movement] does not obtain in the case of the simple and unmixed [movements]. Being mixed together out of the agent and the 20 patient, it will reasonably enough be extruded from the primary genera, as being secondary, just as [are] all the other composite things too. So we should not concede that movement includes actions and affections and joins them together in a single continuity, nor that it partakes of an essence shared with both [action and affection], nor that it is partitioned into these and that one part of it displays [the] action of the things it contains, while the other part [displays their] 25 affection. For according to all these ways [of treating movement], movement becomes something common to acting and undergoing, and the movement is distinguished from the agent and patient as being an intermediate between both, proceeding from the agent, and producing the affection in the patient. Hence,[81] just as the mover and the moved exist as two things, so too the agent and the patient are distinguished from each other.' Let that then suffice as a response to 30 Porphyry, or rather to the opinions transmitted by him.

The great Plotinus says[82] that Aristotle refuses to place movement in a genus on the ground that movement is said to be an imperfect operation: 'But if this is the case,' [Plotinus] says, 'nothing prevented him from placing operation foremost, and treating movement as posterior, as one species of operation, since it is an imperfect opera- 35 tion.' Iamblichus rebuts this, saying: 'Let us see, in the first place, whether movement is called imperfect operation in the sense that it is inferior (*hupheimenos*)[83] within the same nature, or rather as departing into a [sc. different] nature which is in all respects weaker. For if it is called imperfect in the sense of being inferior within the *same* nature, nothing prevents us from placing operation foremost, 304,1 as a genus, and treating movement as posterior, as its species. But if it departs into a *different* genus, operation cannot be its genus. If, therefore, movement strives *towards* its goal because it comes into being for the sake of that, and does not yet possess it within itself, and [if], on the other hand, operation stands fast *at* the goal, being 5 full of itself and its own perfection, then what is entirely perfect will not have any community of nature with what strives towards perfection. And if operation contains within itself the perfect form, whereas movement journeys towards the form, possessing it only potentially, and in accordance with a material and formless *suitability* [sc. for perfection], then what has been claimed will be obvious in this way too.[84] Again, if movement is considered in terms of its passage and 10 continuity, as being infinitely divisible into [stretches which are themselves] always continuous, whereas operation stands fast at one limit, deriving its being from itself, and simultaneously comprehend-

ing the single universe *per se*, then, on these assumptions too, operation will not be the genus of movement. And if movement is divisible
into parts and is infinite and indefinite, while operation is indivisible,
15   is a limit, and rejoices in its stable identity, how could the one be the
genus of the other? And if, further, movement has a compounded
subsistence (*hupostasis*) in relation to what is contrary – that is to
say, it always changes from one thing to its contrary, as for example
when black comes to be from white (for movement from one thing to
another is [itself identical with] neither of the extremes, but is
20   compounded from both) – whereas operation is completely unmixed
and stands fast in one of the contraries, being in no way infected by
the nature of the other contrary, then how can operation be the genus
of movement? And if one were to say that movement is coextensive
with time,[85] since it has dimension, whereas operation [is coextensive]
with eternity, since it exists dimensionlessly and is present all together as a whole in the instant, there would still not in that way
25   either be some homogeneous nature covering eternal things and
things in time; all the more so if operation, [being] unmoved, has prior
existence, containing the origin and the goal of movement together in
a single state of rest, while movement is differentiated [from opera-
tion] in virtue of a passage proceeding in accordance with number.

'But,' continues [Iamblichus], 'Plotinus seems not to agree with the
purer opinions concerning operation, but instead to be misled into
that conception of it according to which some people define operating
30   in terms of being-moved, and suppose that movement – in the sense
of being-moved – and operation are the same thing; which is far from
the truth. Further, we should be persuaded by Theophrastus:[86] he
thinks that movement is separate from operation, but that movement
is also operation, since it is included in it, whereas operation is not
thereby also movement.[87] For [he thinks that] the essence and the
35   peculiar form of each thing is the operation of each thing, although
305,1 this is not movement. And indeed nothing prevents the perfection [sc.
of operation] from existing also among intelligibles and things by
nature unmoved. But there are many such [perfections] among the
perceivables too, as for instance that[88] in the shape of a statue: for the
shape stands fast in accordance with the same perfection.[89] But if
operation surpasses movement to such an extent, [Plotinus] should
5   not have conjoined them or made the one the genus of the other.[90]

'Now[91] if someone says that operation produces being-moved in
virtue of being placed in the same class as that, whereas the *operational* (*to energeiâi*), which stands fast in the case of the shape of the
statue and [in general] the actuality (*entelekheia*) of each thing, is
spoken of in contrast to the [merely] *potential* (*to dunamei*), as
transcending that – but it is not [on this view] that the operation
[transcends] *movement* – well, this person fails to recognise that *the*

operational, on the one hand, is opposed to the potential, is the   10
perfection of what is imperfect, and adopts a relation towards its
contrary, whereas *operation itself*, on the other hand, is *per se* absolute, is not said in relation to any contrary, and endows the [merely]
operational with its perfection. So it is far from correct [to say] that
the shape [sc. of the statue] exists [merely] operationally, and that
operation [as such] does not belong [to it]. In general, those who say
this are not aware of the pure genus of operation, nor of its separate-
ness from movement, nor of its priority over the [merely] operational;   15
nor do they recall the way in which we say that thoughts are
operations, namely by adducing the partlessness of the knowledge
belonging to these [thoughts], [the fact that this knowledge is] simultaneous, instantaneous, all at once in the instant, and similar such
things. For what the instant is in the case of time, this [we say] is
what operation is thought of as being in the case of movement, and
[we say] that pure operation exists outside of movement, and that   20
other operations, which are not observed without movement, proceed
from it [i.e. pure operation], as for example we say that imagination
and perception are movements in respect of affection, but an operation in respect of form, and thus that some [operations] are not
separate from movements, whereas others are separate: not separate
are all those which are perfective of movements, preceding them[92]
and leading them forward into operation; separate are all those which   25
are uniform and entirely unmoved.

‘To this extent, certainly, one might tolerate those who drag down
operations in this way,[93] since [after all] it is also the case that some
forms are enmattered, and the enmattered operations are seen to
coexist with these. But one cannot in any way tolerate those who go
further and drag them [i.e. operations] down to *movements*, nor those
who suppose that, of the so-called common operation, some [opera-   30
tions] are partless and all at once, whereas others [consist] in coming
to be and [are] *generations*,[94] which [they say] are also called movements. For there could not be just one genus of partless things and
things divisible into parts, nor of things in being and things in [a state
of] coming to be, nor could the very same operation both be partless
and extend to the things [which are] divisible into parts, and obtain
both all at once and in [a state of] coming to be. For all these obliterate
the nature of the things that are[95] and fail to preserve the essence of   306,1
operation. And it is clear too that to make movement a common genus
of actions and affections is contrary to the opinion of Aristotle, [as
expressed] both elsewhere and here in the arrangement of the division of the categories. For acting and undergoing will then no longer
be two genera, but there will be a single [genus], movement, prior to   5
them. But things in the [category of] undergoing and things in the
[category of] acting do both extend to being-moved, [when they are]

considered in respect of a movement, such as walking, or a relation, such as putting on one's clothes, [or] sitting down. For these are mixtures of affection and operation – not [operation] in the strict sense, but the [sort which is] mixed with affection. But, again, to

10   speak of operation with regard *only* to actions is to speak without proper investigation: for neither is every operation an action – in particular thought is not[96] – nor is every action an operation, for some actions are also affective.'[97]

It is to be inferred from these [remarks] that Plotinus and the others who transfer the claim that movement is the common [genus] of acting and undergoing from the Stoic usage to Aristotle's philo-

15   sophical system [wrongly] conflate together movement and operation, and do not keep action pure and freed from affection, since they consider it [i.e. action] along with movement, and moreover indeed do not keep the origin of movement unmoved, as in Aristotle's doctrine. Furthermore,[98] when the Stoics treat as different genera (1)

20   being moved *out of* (*ex*) oneself, as a knife possesses cutting out of its own constitution (for the action [of cutting] is accomplished by virtue of its shape and form); and[99] (2) the operating of a movement *by means of* (*dia*) oneself, as the natures [of things] and medicinal powers produce the [appropriate] action (for once the seed has been planted it unfolds its own principles, draws to itself the neighbouring matter and gives form to the principles in itself); and further (3) acting *from*

25   (*apo*) oneself, which is generally acting from one's own impetus, but is more particularly[100] [acting] from a rational impetus, and which is also called acting practically (*prattein*),[101] or even more specifically than this operating in accordance with virtue – well, when [the Stoics] make these divisions they commit the contrary mistake to that [examined] in the foregoing: for they wrongly separate all these [ways of acting], which ought to be arranged under one genus (since they are all in the [category of] acting), into many genera, on the ground

30   that there are many origins from which the [mentioned] actions come about. Moreover their definition of operation is confused: for they expound it [i.e. the definition] in terms of movement.[102] When they make acting and undergoing a genus, they certainly speak correctly; but when they arrange being-moved [so as] to include moving they contradict themselves, in both making being-moved the genus of

35   moving (on the ground that it includes it), and not [making it] its genus, because it is contradistinguished from that [i.e. moving], since

307,1   the one [i.e. moving] is acting, and the other [i.e. being-moved] is undergoing.

'And,'[103] says Iamblichus, 'the Stoics grasp movement in a mistaken way, when they say[104] that imperfection is ascribed to movement not on the ground that it is not operation – for they say that it necessarily is operation – but [because] it has an accretive nature

(*ekhei to palin kai palin*), not in order to reach operation (for it is that already), but in order that it produce somewhere something else 5
which then exists after it.' This is indeed what the Stoics say. 'But how,' asks Iamblichus, 'is it possible to say that operation, which is the most perfect of all things, is imperfect? In what way is it, once it stands fast in its operating, multiplied accretively, like those things which proceed in accordance with number?'[105] Movement in general is called imperfect by the ancients by way of *contrast* with operation:[106] for it was not operation but *actuality* (*entelekheia*) which was 10
called imperfect, because although one sort of actuality[107] is a con-
tainment of perfection in respect of the form, the other [sort of actuality][108] is a drawing on of the potentially moveable (*kinêtos*) into the form,[109] and this [sort of actuality], being movement, is called imperfect actuality by way of contrast with perfect actuality. For example, the chasing and casting of a statue [is] a movement and an imperfect actuality, whereas its form, and the statue itself, [consti- 15
tute] the perfect actuality. For this reason Aristotle defined move-
ment as the actuality of a moveable thing *qua* moveable,[110] which is to say an actuality always remaining in [a state of] imperfection, since it is separated from operation. Not that all movement is imperfect, but [only] that indeed which has a beginning and a limit. Hence the [movement] of the heavens is in no way imperfect (*atelês*), being always at its goal (*telos*).

'The confounding of the *operational* with *operation* [itself] throws 20
the present reasoning into confusion. For what is [in the process of] changing from the potential into what it is capable [of becoming] is said to be *operational*, whether it is a form, or an affection, or a state of rest: for a piece of bronze which progresses from the potential to the operational, and which becomes a statue, is perfected into *form*;[111] and when something which is capable of being heated is heated it progresses to [a state of] *affection*; and the operational [aspect] of movement becomes a state of *rest*, when it is completed into this [state 25
of rest]. But the *operational* differs from *operation*, insofar as the operational exists in relation to the potential, whereas operation exists *per se*.' To which I think one might add that even if the operational is spoken of in relation to the potential, the operational still does not manifest *movement*, but rather the perfection of what was previously imperfect.

But Plotinus does not concede[112] that movement is imperfect, nor, 30
he says, does *it* get perfected, but rather the object at which it aims: for example, walking is walking right from the beginning. 'If one had undertaken to walk a stade, but had not yet achieved this, the falling short lies not the walking or the movement, but in the walking such-and-such a distance. For there was already walking and movement no matter how short the distance [from the start].' But Iam-

308,1   blichus, responding to him, says: 'You are not construing the function
of movement *qua* [something] moveable, nor are you conjoining it [i.e.
the moveable] to its potentiality, since insofar as it is moveable, it is
not yet a whole. Nor, therefore, are you construing its actuality as
that of a moveable thing.' And I think [Iamblichus] is right about this,
for [Plotinus] seems to me to be falling victim to somewhat the same
sort of mistake as if someone were to say that even the imperfect
5   itself, when it is imperfect, is, considered in respect of its imperfection,
perfect.[113] Likewise too movement [really] is imperfect, because its
nature is mixed out of the potential and actual, being a thing which
comes about[114] out of the indefinite and the definite, of formlessness
and form, of what is not together with what is. It emerges clearly from
this that there is nothing common to movement and pure operation.
10   For the latter is purified of all infinite and indefinite commixture, and
excels such things.

        While the Peripatetics thought that one should reduce movement
to quantity, Plotinus wants to reduce it to operation, so that just as
operation is not quantity, so also movement may be demonstrated not
to be quantity. That movement is indeed quantity is clear, not from
the fact that it is in time (for this belongs to it accidentally), but in
15   virtue of its dimensionality (*diastasis*), and insofar as it is diversity,
as Plato says, and unlikeness.[115] For as long as they remain one and
the same, all things are at rest; whereas insofar as they assume a[116]
differentiation, they have been moved. So since the state of rest is
necessarily a single thing, and movement necessarily many things,
movement is a quantity. And that not all operation is movement is
20   anyway clear: for indeed the operation of the mind is not [movement],
since it is motionless. But there has been some dispute about *particular* [mental activities], to see if one ought to call them movements, as
for example perception and the soul's thought: these things seem to
some not [to occur] *without* movement, although they are not [them-
selves] movements, since indeed they are indivisible, as has been
shown [by Aristotle] in the *de Anima*,[117] whereas all movement is
divisible into parts. Further, if perception and thought are accom-
25   plished in the instant, they would not then be movements either, but
would more correctly be called operations. While Melissus says that
everything which comes to be has a beginning,[118] Aristotle denies that
there is in all cases of things which have come to be a beginning for
the object:[119] there is indeed a beginning of the *period*, but not
therefore of the *object* too. For it is possible for there to be change all
at once, as in the case of illuminated air.[120] [In this case] everything
is illuminated all at once, but not outside time as well: for it is
30   illuminated at the rising of the sun, but the sunrise is not outside
time, for it is not instantaneous, nor is the [process of] illumination

instantaneous, even though the air is illuminated all at once and not one part after another.

Now, while Aristotle says that the change is all at once, in this way, Plotinus says: 'If the change is all at once, there is a *movement* which is both all at once and outside time.' Well, Aristotle would say that there is change in the sense of *changing*, and change in the sense of *having changed*. The former – [change] in the sense of changing – is movement, but the latter – [change] in the sense of having changed – is a state of rest. And now if change in the sense of having changed necessarily comes into existence out of [change] in the sense of changing, and [if change] in the sense of changing has prior existence [at the time] when the sun is about to rise, and [if] only the [change] in the sense of having changed comes upon us imperceptibly, it follows that it[121] could not exist *without* movement, but it does *not* follow that the onset of the illumination *is* movement.[122] If, on the other hand, it is possible for [change] in the sense of having changed to come about without the [process of] changing, then that sort of change, namely the one [consisting] in the [state of] having changed, would [*a fortiori*] not be movement nor even [come about] with movement. Rather,[123] such changes are operations and not movements.

Many of the things said by Plotinus about movement do not fit with [the nature of] movements [themselves]. That movement is said to be outside time conflicts with the distance it traverses and its passage; that it [on his view] originates at some point in the timeless destroys the continuity of its nature; and to consider that the same movement is accomplished by *accretion*[124] (*palin kai palin*) is impossible for continuous [movement]: for only in the case of those things divided discretely in accordance with [sc. natural] number is it possible to think of [first] one unit and [then] additionally another unit, and in this way to arrange together the discretely divided plurality into the same [class]. But in the case of things where there is an infinite continuity,[125] it is not possible for these to be summed under one and the same head as a discretely divided plurality. Nor is it correct to say that just because an all-at-once and timeless change comes about, a movement of that sort also comes about. For if presences of forms come about motionlessly, in respect of form, there will indeed be timeless *changes*, but not [timeless] *movements*. And they[126] are wrong too in their supposition that there is one account[127] of movements and operations, and that if operation is timeless, movement is likewise timeless. For operation stands fast in accordance with the unmoved presence and perfection of its form as [one and] the same thing, whereas movement is always in progress, until it arrives at its actuality. And quantity should not, in the case of movement, be construed after the manner of a *denumerable plurality* (for this sort [of plurality] does not have continuity),[128] but rather in accordance

with *passage*, similarly to the dimension of body. If, therefore, movement is a quantity, it cannot be established in a separate genus. But
that is enough on this topic.

    Some say that Aristotle did not posit a genus of movement or
30 operation among the categories for the reason that these are ranged
under the relatives, because operation is *of* what is potentially operative, and movement is *of* what is potentially moved. Plotinus well
replies that:[129] 'What generated the relatives was *relation* (*skhesis*)
itself, not simply being *said in relation to* something else. For whenever there is some subsistent reality (*hupostasis*), even if it is *of*
something else, and even if [it is said] *in relation to* something else,
35 it has still received its nature before [receiving that of] the relative.
Therefore even if this operation, movement and state are [each] *of*
310,1 something else, they nevertheless do not forfeit being something prior
to the relative,[130] and being thought of *per se.*' And in general relatives
are considered just according to the relation itself, as for example
being on the right and likeness, whereas things which are *of* other
things in the manner of things which subsist by participation – as for
example movement is *in* the thing moved, and operation is *in* the
5 operating thing[131] – do not [as such] exhibit the relation *relative*, but
rather *participation* in movement. And participations do not create
the [category of] relative,[132] since on that basis everything would be
a relative by virtue of a single account.

    <But why, they ask, did Aristotle not posit acting and undergoing
as one genus?>[133] Especially since acting is conjoined by him with
undergoing because of its relation to that, in such a way that Aristotle
established the same account concerning both, and if the number of
10 ten genera did not demand that they be divided, some people might
have thought that he does [indeed] reduce the two into a single
category. Well, perhaps [they are divided] because acting, taken as a
genus and standing fast in accordance with pure action, is completely
separated from undergoing. For Aristotle did not construe heating
and cooling like the [predicates][134] called 'active' by the Stoics,[135]
which possess their movement as one which inclines towards some-
15 thing else, but rather [he construes them] according to the movement's primary cause itself, which has prior existence in the form of
heat and cold. Thus the action will be purely and utterly separated
from the undergoing. Nor are being-heated and being-cooled what
[the Stoics] call 'passive' [predicates], which are considered in their
relation to the heating [or cooling] thing. Now we would not reject the
20 view that some such [predicates, i.e. 'passive' ones] are *also* signified
by these words, but [we would insist that] *they* are not what Aristotle
places in the [category of] undergoing.[136] For just as there is another,
pure action, distinct from the sort which inclines towards the patient,
and altogether unmixed with that, so also there is pure affection,

embracing only the affection in the patient, and possessing neither reference nor relation nor connection to action, so that these [predicates] are neither 'active' nor 'passive', as the Stoics customarily call 25 [their predicates]. In those cases where the affection is not freed from a relation to an agent, both 'active' and 'passive' [predicates] are reasonably enough held [to be present], the former directing the operation towards the other thing [i.e. the patient], the latter harmonising the movement of something [i.e. the agent] with the patient, and referring it [i.e. the movement] to something else [i.e. the patient]. But even though such [predicates] really exist, they are nevertheless 30 not simple, unmixed and primary genera which subsist *per se* and do not have their being in one another.

It is also rightly said that the relative ought not to be counted in with the primary predicates (*katêgorêmata*), but with those which coexist[137] and are a certain way,[138] such as the burner and the striker: he is someone who strikes *another* and who burns *another*.[139] For since the striker is in some sort of [state of] composition, being thought of 311,1 together with an underlying subject (*hupokeimenon*),[140] his action too manifests some sort of mixed [state], and 'being a certain way in relation to something else' (*to ekhon pôs pros heteron*). Acting, however, because it is conjoined purely and solely with operation, for this reason it stands fast in its purity in accordance with that [i.e. operation] alone, and *it* [i.e. acting] is not infected either with relation 5 or with mixture in respect of a patient. And really the relative[141] is not even among the predicates; but if someone *does* so take it, at least notionally, then it is being thought of as a *secondary* [predicate]. For those-who-are-a-certain-way (*hoi pôs ekhontes*)[142] will themselves in the first instance be *relatives*, and only in another sense, and for a secondary reason, are *predicates* of that kind additionally thought of. It has been well said too that relation alone supports the relatives, 10 whereas acting and undergoing have their own separate natures, beyond which the relatives are additionally thought of, if at all, in a secondary way. That is why each [of acting and undergoing] does not depart from the separate category which it has *per se*.

But why, people ask, is there not one genus of being-moved, and two species of this, namely moving, which is the same as acting, and being-moved, which is spoken of homonymously with the genus,[143] in which undergoing [is placed], with the result that there would be one 15 category of being-moved and not two (acting and undergoing)? The solution to this has already been set out at length (302,16ff.); let us just say here that acting is not included in being-moved, if one is thinking of pure actions, but only undergoing has been embraced [therein]. Hence being-moved cannot be a genus of actions, since it is not predicated of them at all in their being.[144] For movement coexists 20 with a certain alteration and change, whereas pure action, which is indeed contradistinguished from undergoing as having nothing in common with it,[145] is without affection, unmoveable and unchangeable. Accordingly, it only acts; it does not itself receive any affection: it will therefore act motionlessly. It follows that acting in the primary sense does not reside in being-moved, taken as its genus, but rather

25   in not-being-moved. That is a full solution to the objection. But if someone were to extend the [category of] acting to movements as well, then one should say that according to the ancients being-moved subsists on the basis of movement, but that, given that it is that way, [being-moved] was not applied [by them] to all *operations*, but only to those which were the same as movements. The [category of] acting,[146] however, was inclusive not only of movement, but also of operations.

30   So [Aristotle] appropriately located it in a place of its own genus, because it is appropriate both for operations, which being-moved did not include, and for active movements which are completely separate from affections. Hence [Aristotle] consistently posited acting as a genus distinct from that of undergoing. And [he laid down] that being-moved is in no way [set] over these [i.e. acting and undergoing] as their genus, not because being-moved is not said of actions at all,

35   as the first solution aimed to argue, but because acting also included movements in respect of an *operation*, and it is these which are not included in being-moved.[147]

312,1   One might note the fact that acting and undergoing are also two genera because of the nature [of things] in the universe. For if one thing generates, and another receives the generation, and [if] one thing is active, and another affective, then necessarily too the genera must be two, in agreement with the [two] principles. And since the

5   unmixed everywhere precedes the mixed, necessarily both the purely acting and [the purely] undergoing have existence prior to the mixed genus of movement: for this[148] [movement] comes about from one thing and acts on another, and if it really were a genus,[149] the genera would consist in participatory and mixed things, which is absurd. Many things which act, however, also undergo, in virtue of the fact that the two principles – the affective and the active – often coincide

10   in a single nature, although if one is distinguishing the objects purely, the agent does not undergo *qua* agent, nor the patient act *qua* patient. Hence the first causes are *unmoved* [causes] of the movements of which they are causes, whereas some of the succeeding movers are also *moved*, by virtue of their possessing in themselves both [active and affective] principles, and of there being a part of them which moves, and another [part] which is moved; and thus the whole thing

15   appears to move and be moved. The view that actions come about because of pushings and leverings – rather than, as the ancients thought, by virtue of the active power [of the agent] and the [mutual] suitability of the agent and patient – misleads the generality of people

into positing movements in actions as well. For pushing and dragging things and the like are mixed out of acting and undergoing. So whether one differentiates the *cause* of acting from that of under- 20
going, or the *form* [of the one from the other], there will certainly not be a genus common to both.

Being-thought-of and being-seen are shown for the same reason to belong to the category of acting and not to that of undergoing. For the thing which is thought of does not undergo anything in order to generate a thought, but rather being-thought-of is the *creation* of a thought, and being-seen [the creation of] a seeing, the expression 25
having only the [grammatical] form of undergoing. So one ought not to have regard to the form of the expression, but to the objects [meant].[150] For certainly, some [words] have the [meaning of] acting by virtue both of the object [meant] and of the form of expression, as for example 'to doctor'. Others are active in respect of the object [meant], but affective[151] in respect of the form of expression, such as being-thought-of and being-seen (for this is [a matter of] impressing, 30
and impressing is acting); others again are the reverse, such as seeing and thinking (for these are [a matter of] being impressed, and being impressed is undergoing). But it is worth raising the question whether perhaps thinking and seeing are not merely undergoing and being impressed, but also possess some sort of operation awakened inside them, by which the apprehension comes about. I do not think it would be at all astonishing, if something commingled[152] obtained in their case. For it is consistent that some [things signify] acting 35
alone, others undergoing alone, and still others, such as thinking and seeing, [signify] acting and undergoing simultaneously.

Again, Plotinus says:[153] 'We should examine (1) whether they[154] will say that in the [category of] acting some [actions] are operations, and others are movements, <saying that the all-at-once [actions] are 313,1
operations, and the rest movements>, such as cutting <(for cutting is in time)>,[155] or that all actions are movements or are accompanied by movement;[156] and (2) whether [they will say that] all actions are [defined] in relation to undergoing, or [whether] there are also abso-lute ones, such as walking and speaking; and (3) whether [they will say that] all the [actions construed] in relation to undergoing are 5
movements, while the absolute ones are operations, or whether both sorts are of each sort;[157] for clearly everyone would say that walking, although it is[158] absolute, is a movement, whereas thinking, although it has a patient, namely the thing thought, should, I think, be called an operation.'[159]

(1) With regard to the first of these points it should be said that it is not to be conceded that every action is a movement or accompanied by movement, but on the contrary [we should say] that the agent insofar as it acts and possesses pure operation is not moved at all, so 10

that one should not say that in the [category of] acting some [actions]
are operations and some movements, since, in general, movements
are not in the [category of] acting, for the reasons mentioned.[160] But
nor are we simply to say that the all-at-once [actions], insofar as they
are all at once, are operations, since the [property of being] all at once
was a distinguishing mark of changes too, and operation is never
contradistinguished from movement in this way – namely that the
15   one is all at once, the other in time[161] – but rather in virtue of certain
other differences.

(2) With regard to the second point – whether all actions are
[defined] in relation to undergoing, or whether there are also some
absolute ones – it can be said that Aristotle did not posit as a genus
the [kind of] acting which is ranged over against undergoing, but
rather the more general [kind], which is identical with operating and
20   acting out-of-oneself, so that walking and sitting and all the absolute
[actions] fall under it, but the [kind of acting] which is ranged over
against undergoing also falls under it, [the division proceeding]
according as the former has the principle and cause of movement in
itself, while the latter [has them] in something else. We can also say
this, that it is not the [kind of] acting which is ranged over against
undergoing, and which is called 'active' by the Stoics, which has been
the present subject of discussion, but rather the general [kind of
25   acting], although the [kind] ranged over against [undergoing] was
chosen in the examples as being perhaps clearer.[162] Likewise the
undergoing [here in question] is not the so-called 'passive' [kind],
[defined] in relation to the agent, but the general [kind]. It is prefer-
able to posit the primary and most legitimate genus of acting [as] pure
and untrammelled by any combination with the patient; for thus
operation out-of-itself is considered pure. But if someone wanted to
consider in addition the opposition between acting and undergoing,
30   we should construe this too not in terms of a *relation*, but in terms of
the separate subsistent reality (*hupostasis*) of each one – [a reality]
which, being in each, takes on in a supplementary and secondary
manner the principle of contrariety.

(3) The third point is not readily decidable owing to the mixture of
314,1   the two principles[163] in many [actions]. Walking is really a mixture of
movement and operation, and perhaps too thinking [is a mixture] of
undergoing and operating. As a result it is not easy to give an opinion
on what sort of genus the proposed items are in. But generally one
should say that the pure and unmixed actions are the primary ones,
and distinguish the ones [deriving] from those [as] secondary, [put-
5   ting these latter] into the mixed genera. Of these [mixed genera] there
are several differentiae: some of them are combined with undergoing,
some with certain other things; some control by virtue of an operation
out-of-themselves, while some are controlled by others of the mixed

[kinds of action]; others are woven together in a variety of further ways.

Iamblichus ranges himself in opposition to Plotinus in the follow- 10 ing terms: 'It is more systematic,' he says, 'first to distinguish the special feature of these genera – of acting and undergoing – [taken together], and to demonstrate the differentia of each of them in relation to the other. For from this it will be clear both which things one should range under them, and what the mixed things between them are like.' But if we should set down Archytas' account of the distinguishing marks of acting and undergoing before that of Iam- 15 blichus (for after all Iamblichus expounds that [account]), well then, Archytas writes as follows:[164] 'The distinguishing mark of the agent is that it possesses in itself the cause of the movement, whereas that of the thing brought about and the patient [is] that [it has its cause] in something else.[165] For the statue-maker has in himself the cause of the bringing about of the statue, whereas the lump of bronze [has the cause] of the [statue's] being brought about both in itself and [in] 20 the statue-maker. And in the case of the affections of the soul the principle is the same: for anger (*thumos*) is naturally aroused [in one] because of something else, and provoked from outside by something else,[166] for example [it is provoked by] contemptuous treatment, dishonour or insolence, whereas the man who acts in this way[167] has in himself the cause of acting thus.' In expounding this point Iamblichus says that acting possesses in itself the cause of its operation, whereas undergoing [possesses] the [cause] of its movement in some- 25 thing else and in itself, as for example the lump of bronze [has it] in itself and [in] the statue-maker, because the patient[168] also has a certain stability of its own essence peculiar to it, and is not entirely dependent on the agent.

Next, [Iamblichus] mentions the objections to this account. For he says: 'Some people counter that there are also cases of acting which have their cause in something else, as for example thinking. Alterna- tively, if one places in the [category of] acting not thinking but 30 being-thought-of, on the ground that thinking [belongs] in the [cate- gory of] undergoing, even so being-thought-of does not bestow the whole cause of being-moved on the thinker. But the manner of association, in the case of the mind and the thing thought of, is not of the kind that these doubters suppose.' But then *that* [way] is 315,1 relevant to the theory of the mind, whereas I think the puzzle should be solved in conformity with the points already set out, by saying that Archytas gave an account of the *pure* actions and affections, and that even if thinking is a kind of undergoing, it still has a certain internally awakened operation, just like seeing and in general knowing, and 5 [Iamblichus] should not have adduced the objection to the account [given by Archytas] on the basis of these mixed [kinds].

Others adduce the same difficulty on the basis of desiring and having an impulse, on the ground that although these things do indeed have the cause of movement in themselves, they are not entirely free of the [sort of] cause which originates from another thing and externally. In solving this puzzle, Iamblichus says that 'things
10 which have an impulse and which desire are not simple, and since they are composite they possess the cause of their operating neither throughout all their parts, nor, strictly taken, from themselves,[169] but the impulse to perform their actions comes from a particular one of their parts, and from a capacity. Hence they also need co-operation – either originating or contributory – from external things,[170] and they partake of an affective movement, arising in connection with one
15 thing (namely the composite animal [itself]), but provided by another (namely the capacity responsible for the operations). Hence this [movement] is not pure action, nor mere affection, and one should not on its basis object to the account of acting which has been given – the one which says that the cause of [an agent's] operating from itself is present to it. One should only add [to that account] (says Iamblichus)
20 the [kind of acting] which is strictly and primarily so called, which supplies the cause from itself, and from the whole of itself, and which possesses this [cause] solely in itself, and distributes it at its own discretion among all [its parts].' It is clear that the account [of acting] is thus rendered more perspicuous through the addition, but that Archytas too did indicate all these things in his brief account: for the phrase 'in itself' was, strictly and primarily, taken as [meaning] *in the whole thing*. Again, he says that the distinguishing mark of
25 undergoing is the possession in something else of the cause of the movement. For either the affection is causeless, which would be absurd – that one of the things which come to be should come to be without any cause – or it has a cause, and if so, then either in the patient itself, in which case it is not merely a patient, but also an agent,[171] or externally and in something else: for as the agent acts [so the patient undergoes], and whatever that [agent] brings about is
30 what the patient undergoes.

Plotinus wonders[172] in relation to this (1) how there can be absolute [properties], not being [derived] from other things, in the [category of] undergoing too, such as rotting and rusting. (2) And many things which have the cause of their movement in something else do not undergo, as for example the swan, which, we may suppose, is made white on the basis of the principle [of constitution] in itself, and thus is led to attain its own actuality, but this sort of thing is not the
316,1 consequence of an *affection* [received] from something else.[173] And a thing which increases in size as a result of its internal principle is certainly not led into its increase as a matter of *affection*. But against this it must be said that it is neither the case that a swan has

the cause of its being white in something else – rather [it has it] in itself – nor is it the case that any of the other things which are led to attain their own particular naturally inhering form gain their par- 5
ticipation in their own particular form from outside. We do indeed call this way of participating affection, *not* because such an affection comes about from something else,[174] but because the participation in the form is a matter of receiving *substance*, in accordance with the operation <of its own internal principle [of constitution]. And rotting and rusting, though they are indeed in the [category of] undergoing, are not *absolute* affections, but rather have the cause of their move- ment from outside, since>[175] they come about from airs or waters or some other moist exhalation. But perhaps, owing to the composition of rotting or rusting things, there are also certain [components] in them 10
some of which are in the [category of] acting, and others in the [category of] undergoing, and those who are incapable of differentiating hypothe- sise the latter to be absolute affections of the sort mentioned.

But many things, they say, which possess in themselves the cause of their acting, behave passionately, inasmuch as we say that all bad men are, owing to their inner wickedness, in a state of passion. Now Plotinus himself thinks that the affections of the soul are not affec- tions but operations; that is, operations are in it [i.e. the soul], 15
whereas affections [are] in the body.[176] Accordingly, just as bad men have the cause of their wickedness in themselves, so too they have its operation in the [category of] acting, given that affection is not said in the case of the soul. But [even] if the undergoing comes about in connection with the body, it will still be the case that the affection is in one thing [i.e. the body] and [derives] from another thing [i.e. the soul], and so the definition of undergoing will be true [in this case]. And perhaps indeed there are in the soul several parts or several 20
distinct principles, and several sorts of imagination or capacities or opinions, differing from one another by virtue of their inconsistency, and so bad men get into a state of passion as some of these contrarie- ties act, and others undergo, and [thus] the account of undergoing remains sound, since they [i.e. the bad men] possess their undergoing in something other [than the acting part].

But how is it that the suitability of matter [to receive a form], being an affection of the matter, does not derive from the matter itself, but 25
from outside [it]?[177] Well, one could say that this suitability, being a reflection (*emphasis*) of the form, is also bestowed on matter by the form – but some say that matter *is* the very essence of affection. If, however, it is not [identical with] affection, but rather [merely] *is affected*, then we should ask about its suitability [to be so affected]. Now if [the matter] *undergoes* the suitability, then what brings it [i.e. the suitability] about is necessarily something;[178] if, on the other hand, [the matter] does not *undergo* [the suitability], but itself actu-

30   ally *is* the suitability, then this is matter's essence, but the account
      concerns the *affection*, whether [it comes] from inside or from out-
      side.[179]

      But [Plotinus] says that it does not seem appropriate either to
      characterise acting as the [principle of moving] from oneself[180] and
      not from anything else, or undergoing as the [principle of being
      moved] from another and not from oneself, since it is also the case
      that what acts on another thing is itself manifestly a patient, though
      [of course] it is not undergoing what it brings about, but bringing it
35   about.[181] For clearly, when tin acts on silver it is itself a patient [in
      the transaction], being used up and destroyed; but it purifies the
317,1 silver, by getting rid of what destroys that, so that it conserves the
      silver itself, in its quality, better. But since in the case of composite
      objects actings and undergoings have been taken as being mixed
      together, it is not the case that the tin merely acts: it also undergoes.
      It acts in that it purifies the silver, and undergoes in being used up
5   by that; the silver undergoes in being purified, and acts in using up
      [the tin]. [They each act and undergo] in different respects.

      Since we have defined in general what acting is and what under-
      going is, and what the specific features of each are, we should proceed
      next to distinguish the species of acting and undergoing. When we
      have defined these it will be quite clear which things are incorrectly
      referred to the principal genera, and which things correctly, which
10   are mixed, applying to both [genera], and which are simply referred
      to one or the other [genus]. As a result it will also become clear
      whether Plotinus was right to range some things under the [category
      of] acting, and not to range other things.[182] We must also here set
      down Archytas' division of the [category of] acting. He writes thus:[183]
      'The highest kind of acting is operation, and there are three differen-
      tiae of operation: (1) part of it consists in theorising (*theôren*), such as
15   doing geometry[184] and astronomy; (2) part in bringing about (*poien*),
      such as healing or building; and (3) part in acting practically (*pras-
      sen*), such as being a general or a statesman. And operation also comes
      about without thought (*dianoia*), as in the case of the non-rational
      animals; but this [i.e. operation *with* thought] is the principal
      (*genikôtata*) kind.' Here the highest and common (*koinon*)[185] kind of
      acting is defined in accordance with operation *simpliciter*, which
      comprehends in itself all the various operations differentiated by
20   species, is free of all movement, and possesses the pure moving
      [principle] and cause from itself, and not from some other originating
      or co-operating thing.

      (1) Various species of actions derive severally from this [highest
      kind of acting], of which the first is the theoretical, which employs
      immaterial and unmoving operations, and is itself partitioned into
      several species, of which (1a) the first will be homonymous with its

proximate genus,[186] since it is itself theoretical, and this is [indeed]   25
what is strictly called theoretical. This is the [species of theorising]
which engages in reflection, with simple acts of thought, upon intelligible and indivisible substances: the *intellectual* (*to noeron*) [species]
is of this kind. Archytas omitted this, even though he is [a member]
of the Pythagorean school, because of the possible inappropriateness
of this sort of theory to an introduction. (1b) The [species of theorising]
which concerns motionless mathematical substances produces dis-   30
cursive thought (*dianoêsis*) – doing geometry is like this – and the
intuitions (*epibolai*) it employs are defined and no longer basic, but
are already composite ones, and in accordance with passage [of
thought]. The operations of *pure discursive thought* (*dianoia*) are of   318,1
the same kind as these [notions]. (1c) Third among these [species of
theorising] is the one which produces the theory relating to the
eternal and ever-moving perceivable substances, which makes use of
perception along with reasoning – doing astronomy is like this – and
which renders accounts in harmony with the phenomena. Thus the
whole operation of theory descends from the pure thoughts at the top   5
down to the discursive reasonings with perception.

(2) After this Archytas sets down the productive (*poiêtikos*) species
[of the genus, acting], which is homonymous with the genus,[187] and
which principally consists in the bringing into existence of things
which do not yet partake of being. (2a) Much of this is [the province
of] the divine – whatever is included in the creative activity of the
gods; (2b) much too [lies] in the nature of the universe, and especially
what descends from heaven and embraces everything that comes to   10
be; (2c) much again lies in the skills which imitate nature and make
good what is has left undone. For just as nature places the form of
health in bodies, so too the doctor, by healing, preserves nature's
perfection in bodies; and just as nature has provided animals with
the protection of caves and naturally grown garments, so building[188]   15
and carpentry and weaving and the other skills make good the things
in which men fall short, constituting what is needful for the self-
sufficiency of our life.

(3) As the third [sub]genus of acting is reckoned that [which
consists] in acting practically, which organises the actions of reason
regarding perceivable and composite things, and produces choice,   20
wish, opinion, inquiry and such actions. Part of this is general –
managing the practical affairs of cities, commanding in war, and
governing cities in peace; and part is more particular – setting one's
own household in order, which is called housekeeping. The whole of
this genus relates to the soul's opinion-forming reasonings operating
with regard to perceivables, and admitting of virtue and vice, because   25
it is accomplished in the domain of choice and vital impulse. That is
how Archytas distinguishes acting practically (*prattein*) from acting

[in general] (*poiein*). Some people say, however, that the *productive* [actions] are those of which the finished products remain *after* the action [is over], as for example carpentry and housekeeping, whereas the *practical* [actions] are those of which the products have their being *in* their coming to be, as for example flute-playing and dancing and the like.[189]

30   After these is another kind of operation, which Archytas dubs generally 'without thought', namely the [kind found] in the case of the non-rational animals, and it is clear that there are, within the [category of] acting, as many and as various different species in respect of this kind of operation as ever there are numbers and kinds of species of the non-rational animals; we usually give a reckoning of these [species of action] in the natural histories.

35   Iamblichus says:[190] 'There is a final kind of operation which needs to be considered, one which does not indicate action of a soul, of
319,1 nature, of reason and of life, but which renders perspicuous the corporeal operation of bodies *qua* inanimate bodies, in accordance firstly with all the manifest special features of bodies,[191] and in accordance secondly with all their capacities, not only those in virtue of which they are solid and impenetrable, but also those in virtue of which they have many active capacities in themselves. For the naturally inhering operations of the elements, and the movements of
5   inclination whether downwards or upwards, and the striking [movements] and those which come about through pushing – these exist at the lowest level, and are observed in the case of composite things, and[192] are commingled with other natures. They are not any more [to be regarded as] operations and do not possess the active principle in the same way [as the soul], but are mixed with affection, since while they exist *per se* they also receive a sort of intercourse from other
10   things towards themselves.' It has certainly been made evident through these [words] just how many things are subsumed under the [category of] acting. It is worth considering why Archytas completely omits this last species, the one observed in the case of inanimate things. My view is that he set himself the task of distinguishing actions strictly so called, which have in themselves, strictly taken, the principle of movement, and rejected these bodily [actions] on the
15   ground that they are mixed with affection, and come to be along with movement and alteration.[193]

These distinctions having been made, it is a suitable point to examine next what Plotinus has said.[194] So then, to say that movements which incline towards undergoing are actions is to confound the two genera [acting and undergoing] with one another. For the movements which are combined with undergoing are not in the [category of] acting *simpliciter*. But if someone says that movements
20   are *also* included in the [category of] acting, it is clear that he will

have in mind the causes of being-moved *in respect of their moving*, and these include – as [being] in the account of cause – all the principles of the [caused] movements. But nor should we characterise operations in an absolute way. For being absolute belongs to [sc. some] movements as well, such as walking, and it does not belong to [sc. all] operations, as in the case of thinking of [something], since being-thought-of is either acting or undergoing.[195] But to say that perhaps thinking and walking are not even [cases] of acting, *given* 25 that they are absolute, rightly [viewed] achieves rather the opposite [of what was intended]: for [thinking and walking] will then all the more *belong* in the [category of] acting, just because the primary actions in it *were* absolute. 'But,' [Plotinus] says,[196] 'thinking is rather one of the relatives.' Now, first of all, it is not the case that thought in general is in relation to something *simpliciter*. For [even] if one were to posit it as being a relative as well, it still has prior existence *per se*, and then assumes the relation in addition. And indeed Plotinus 30 himself says[197] about perception: 'Perception also is an operation or an affection in advance of [being] a relation.' And likewise thought [is so] too. And [even] if one regards *thought* as being one of the relatives as well, nevertheless *thinking* will be in the [category] of acting, since it is, among other things, the origin of the relatives, and *originating* belongs to the [category of] acting.

Since, in hypothesising that movement and operation are the 320,1 same, Plotinus represented it as a single genus, namely movement, let us see how he divides up this genus. He says[198] that some movements are bodily, others of the soul, and that among those of the soul some are rational and others non-rational. It is clear that compared with the things which partake [of these movements], in which they arise, such a differentiation follows in an accidental manner, and does 5 not come about in accordance with the proper differentiation of the genus. Both those [movements] which employ the body as an instrument, as in the case of striking, and those which are the body's own [natural movements], such as being weighed down, are bodily movements in the [category of] acting. In the case of the soul, doing geometry is movement by *means* of the soul in the [category of] acting, whereas life is the soul's *own* operation. One can also[199] posit [such actions] in the soul and in the body, after the manner of those who 10 posit affections arising in the soul as well [sc. as the body].

Again, [Plotinus] says that some movements [proceed] from things themselves towards other things, whereas other [movements proceed] from other things towards them. And it is clear that these points do indeed distinguish the *active and the affective movement* from each other, insofar as the former kind [of movement] possesses its operating from things themselves towards other things (this is action[200]), whereas the latter [possesses it] from other things or out of other 15

things towards itself (this is the affective [movement]). But the
unsullied and pure specific feature of *acting* lies in its [acting] from
itself, that of *undergoing*, on the other hand, in its possessing its cause
in something else. [Plotinus], however, does not uphold their purity,
since, on the one hand,[201] to the [operating] from itself he adds the
operating towards other things – for with the commixture and the
inclination towards something else he fails to preserve the pure

20   operation – and, on the other hand,[202] to the [operating] from another
thing he adds the [operating] towards [the things] them[selves],
[thereby in each case] producing a kind of composition [of the two].
For there is a big difference between having the cause of the affection
in another separate thing, and being joined to the cause of the
affection: for[203] in a certain sense the two origins in the case of these
[categories][204] are confounded into one and the same thing. The
reason for this has been the preferential honouring of movement
as a common genus [of acting and undergoing], as a result of which
it is not then possible to distinguish acting and undergoing in pure
terms.

25   Hence in the case of a cut (*tmêsis*)[205] also this [Plotinian] account
confounds these [categories], since it posits that movements *towards*
other things are the same as movements *from* other things. For then
it will be the case that 'the cut (*tmêsis*) is a single thing, whereas the
cutting (*temnein*) and the being-cut (*temnesthai*) are different [from
each other]':[206] but this is by no means to be conceded. For as the cut
is, so too are the cutting and the being-cut.[207] Hence, just as the

30   operation from the side of the cutter is separate from the affection in
the thing being cut, so also the cut (*tomê*) [which comes about] by
virtue of the *cutting* differs from the [cut which comes about] by virtue
of the *being-cut*.[208] For the cause which originates out of the operation
and from the active movement is one thing; quite another thing, and
subsequent to this, is the affective change which comes about in the
thing cut, since in the case of hair, as well, there is a difference
between the separation of the hands which are spreading out the hair,

35   and the unfolding of the hair.[209] So too in the case of the cut (*tomê*),
therefore, there will be a difference between the cut (*tmêsis*) in respect

321,1 of the *operation* and the *cutting* on the one hand, and the [cut] in
respect of the *being-cut* on the other. But because the one lies close to
the other,[210] the fact that there are two of them escapes notice, and
sometimes occasions the opinion in some people that both, taken
together, reside in the *operating*, at other times that they are in the
undergoing. But the truth is quite otherwise, and there are in fact

5   two motions, naturally differing from one another, but confused
together in the case of composite things. This escapes notice owing to
their commixture [in composites], and because people reduce acting
and undergoing to one genus.

Plotinus also investigates[211] successively, for the so-called species of movement, whether acting is everywhere connected to undergoing. Now the species of movement were [taken to be] generation and destruction, increase and diminution, alteration, and finally change   10
in respect of place. But Iamblichus says: 'We object straight away to the beginning of the procedure, since we do not think it right that actions are being characterised on the basis of movement, for the genus of things which move [sc. other things] and the genus of things which are moved are distinct. And we further reject [his approach], since in our view agents and patients should not be characterised on the basis of the same thing, as for example on the basis of being-   15
moved.' But perhaps one should say in reply to Iamblichus, that [at any rate] the same species *of movement* apply to both the things which move [sc. other things] and to the things which are moved. For what comes to be comes to be as a result of an agent, and what is destroyed is destroyed by something which destroys, and the same reasoning applies to alteration, as well as to change in respect of place. Those who came after Plotinus have put forward solutions of this kind to   20
his difficulties.

Since Plotinus accepted another definition of acting and undergoing instead of the one expounded by the Pythagoreans,[212] let us try to consider this [alternative] one too, including a brief summary of what Iamblichus and the others have said in response to it. Plotinus says,[213] then, that some have thought that one should not characterise acting and undergoing on the basis of [whether the movement proceeds]   25
from the thing itself, or from something else, but on the basis of [whether the movement is] in accordance with nature or against nature. For things which achieve their appropriate end (*telos*) are said to be in the [category of] acting, and the contraries of these in the [category of] undergoing. For clearly one says that the man who dies for the sake of his country does not undergo but acts, since he preserves what accords with his principle [of humanity] and what accords with his own perfection, whereas one says that the man who commits injustice undergoes rather than acts, even if he obliterates the whole of mankind, since he destroys what accords with his   30
principle [of humanity] and his natural impulses. Hence it can happen that the same movement is a case of acting and a case of undergoing.[214] For the same thing acts in accordance with nature *qua* artificial thing, and against nature *qua* natural thing: for example, in the case of animals the fire which is moved downwards and the earth [which is moved] upwards[215] [sc. in their creation] are, [when viewed] according to the skill of the creator, moved in accordance with nature, so that such movement is not affective but active, though   35
[considered] in relation to its original essence it is affective.

Those who argue against these claims say that the active cause   322,1

and the purposive [cause] are distinct, and that even if, among causes, the purposive [cause] has superior worth, nevertheless in the case of acting the active [cause] is more important and in this case needs no other [cause] in addition. So whenever some agent *fails* to achieve its
5   end, it would [still], in respect of the active cause in itself, rightly be said to *act*, while in respect of the failure to achieve the end [it would be said] to undergo, if it is [then] disposed against its nature. And perhaps in the case where it does attain its end, whenever it is disposed in accordance with nature, it could even so be said to undergo: for not every affection is indicative of what is against nature, but there is a kind which is in accordance with nature too.[216] But if what is called acting does contain in itself the end and the good, as
10   they[217] claim, then on this score too the account we have specified concerning acting will be fitting – namely that what contains in itself the cause [of the action] is acting.

    Perhaps, however, in the case of simple things the active [cause] and the end are not distinguished, but converge together. If, on the other hand, they are distinguished, there is nothing strange if something acts in respect of the active [cause], and undergoes in respect of its end. But when it acts to bring about its end, it is also said to act
15   in respect of that [end]. For clearly the man who dies for his country puts into operation that action in respect of his end by means of which he preserves what is natural and [what] accords with his principle [of humanity], and he has within himself the cause of this sort of operation, namely one which procures his proper end; the participation in the end is indeed a passivity, but [one put into operation] by the man himself. Of course, he is no longer in possession of the operation which preserves and safeguards *himself*,[218] at the moment
20   when he dies: someone else is the cause of his dying.[219] Accordingly, insofar as he does not have within himself the cause [of his death], but [has it] in someone else, to that extent he undergoes rather than acts. It seems that unless he voluntarily surrenders himself [to the enemy], on behalf of his country, then he is the agent in one sense and the patient in another. Hence insofar as anything acts, it has the cause of the acting in itself; insofar as any patient undergoes, [it has the cause of its undergoing] in something else. Hence also when one
25   says that the unjust man undergoes – even if he obliterates the whole of mankind – because what accords in him with his principle [of humanity] is destroyed, one is considering more than one feature in this man. For he himself *acts* to bring about the destruction in himself of what accords with his principle [of humanity], since he destroys himself,[220] and he *undergoes*, since he is destroyed by himself as though by another,[221] and of course he also *acts* to bring about the obliteration of the other men. But if he becomes unjust through [the agency of] another, then that [other] acts towards him, and he

undergoes at the hands of that man who acts against him, but he *acts*   30
against those who are obliterated [by him]. Iamblichus says: 'If the
fire which is [used] in [the creation of] animals is moved downwards,
and the earth upwards, then in relation to the skill of the creator, this
being itself an origin of action too, it acts, but in relation to the
principle (*aitia*) of its nature it undergoes, since it is moved against
nature.'

I would be surprised if we are not also saying here just what
Plotinus wants [to say] – that what is in accord with nature is in the   35
[category of] acting, and what is against nature is in the [category of]
undergoing. Then perhaps it is clearer to say that the movement of
fire downwards and that of earth upwards are affections arising in   323,1
them from the creative action, but are perfective, and form the
species, of the composite thing. If someone is investigating the affective action of the elements themselves,[222] namely the [action] in
respect of the form and the cause operating in them,[223] he should
define just this [affective action], on account of which although [the
elements] are strengthened and increased in respect of their *opera-*   5
tions, in respect of their *affections*, even though these are things
arising [in them] from creative principles, while [the elements] contribute to the constitution of the form of composites (and it is towards
this [constitution] that the creator gazes[224]), they themselves are
confined, diminished and enfeebled. In the case of animals, they say,
since the [elements'] impulses sort ill with the [animals'] form, and
since the [elements'] movements retreat from their [i.e. the animals']
active principle, [these impulses and movements] are disposed   10
against nature, and rebel towards the contrary of the cause of acting,[225] which is why they must be ascribed to the [category of]
undergoing, among other reasons because the principle of the acting
constrains them into [constituting] the being [sc. of the animal], while
those [elements themselves] decline[226] into destruction.

But if this is so, the origins of these [elemental impulses and
movements] also will not be in them, but from outside, given that they
are in the [category of] undergoing. If, however, the origins are inside
them, then they too should be called actions, even if they retreat from   15
what accords with nature. For there are destructive actions too, just
as there are also perfective affections, and not every kind of acting
leads to being, but [there is] also [a kind which leads] to not-being,
whether the thing operates towards itself or towards something else.
And indeed what is disposed against nature does perform certain
operations on the basis of this very condition of being against nature,
even if [these operations are] not pure, because they are commingled   20
with affection (since they are produced from an affective condition).[227]

And in the case of external movers when these move [something]
towards [its own] nature,[228] as farmers and teachers do, since the

active origin belonging to the nature [of the thing] and that belonging to the skill [of the external mover] coalesce and the two operations proceed together, the [operations] of the skill *qua* skill, having their origin outside [what they operate on], become affections in the thing [they operate on], which has [the origin of those operations] in accordance with nature, while the [operations] which preserve the nature [of the thing], having their origin inside, remain in the form of operation. Thus when the teacher's voice enters the learner, the operation from the voice holds the affection [arising] through the [learner's] hearing conjointly [with itself], and thus here the acting is conjoined with the undergoing, the operation in respect of the voice being one thing, and the affection in respect of the hearing being another.[229] But when the thing affected by the voice does not stay any longer in the [mere state of] affection, but projects another operation from itself[230] – namely the apprehension – then another origin comes about, [this time] of an operation from the side of [the affected subject] itself, which is the [hearer's] knowledge of what is said. But if he who receives the former operation by virtue of an affection [then] produces another operation out of the affection, that does not mean that one should join the latter [operation] to the operation which preceded the affection, omitting the affection in the middle. Nor should one locate the origin of the second operation in the teacher, in order that the cause of the action may appear to lie in something else, but rather [the origin of the second operation] is as it were conjoint: the cause of the affection in the learner [brought about] by means of the [teacher's] voice in his hearing resides in someone else (namely the teacher), but we should [also] hypothesise an origin of apprehension in the soul of the learner, peculiar to him, and awakened by the rational principles (*logoi*) in his soul, so that he may truly understand what is said and receive it properly, and not remain subject to the mere impact and hearing[231] [of the sounds]. Thus the origin of the [latter] operation will be in some [affected] thing itself and not in another thing.

Plotinus adds the following points based on the same conception:[232] 'Is it the case that where there is no operation, but only affection, these things will be in the [category of] undergoing? – What then if the patient should become finer, and the operation have the worse outcome?[233] Or[234] if someone should operate evilly and rule intemperately over someone else? – Are we to put these cases just in the [category of] undergoing?'[235] These remarks are delivered from a conception of acting and undergoing which says that acting is preservative, whereas undergoing is destructive, and that the former is more noble and the latter worse. But [this conception] conflicts with the usage which says that operations and actions can be both bad and against nature, and which contrariwise reckons with perfective and natural affections. For action [taken] *simpliciter* is not some single [i.e. monolithic] genus of operations, but all the possible differentiae of actions divided discretely by species are included under the unified [category of] acting. Likewise too there are perfecting affections under the [category of] undergoing, as well as the imperfect ones; and some 20 are noble, others base; and [there are] in each [category] some things which are according to nature, others which are against nature. If one only takes into consideration one side of all the oppositions applying to them, one contracts these genera too far, just as if one called the whole of the [category of] quality a state only in accordance with nature, or only against nature.

'But,' [Plotinus] says,[236] 'not all acting [derives] from the thing itself, but it can also [derive] from something else. The absolute kind, 25 such as walking, and the "active" (*orthon*)[237] kind, such as striking, [derive] from the thing itself, but desiring, for example, [derives] from something else. For when the object of desire (he says) overpowers one's longing, how does this differ from being struck or being pushed down to the ground?' In these cases [Plotinus] claims that the desires, although operations, derive their impulse not from the [desiring] things themselves, but from the object of desire. Yet they *do* get their impulse from the things themselves, and the object of desire precedes 30 them in quite another manner, not heaving or pushing the desire, but appealing to it on the basis of the suitability [of the object to the desire]. For it would be strange if the [state of] desire in the self-moving or unmoved soul, in the way Aristotle conceives it,[238] were such [as Plotinus describes]. Of course if desire is an undergoing, as [Plotinus] says,[239] then there is nothing strange if it has its moving [principle] outside. Yet it is strange to introduce a desire which lacks choice, and which does not have its origin from itself, and still more 35 strange to range this sort [of desire] under the [category of] acting. 323,1 So much, then, in response to Plotinus on the subject of acting.

We must now turn to speak about undergoing, since Plotinus himself also examines this in a separate treatment.[240] He says:[241] 'Perhaps one ought not[242] to characterise undergoing in terms of [derivation] from something else. For it is also possible for some [undergoing to derive] from the thing itself, and not every [undergo- 5 ing derives] from something else: rotting [derives] from the thing itself, while being struck [derives] from something else. But then [undergoing] is no different from acting, since that too is from the thing itself and from something else.' But it has already been said (315,31ff.) that we should not either in the case of the [category of] acting adjoin the [possibility of the action's deriving] from something else, or in the case of the [category of] undergoing [adjoin] the [possibility of the affection's deriving] from the thing itself, and, as regards rotting, it has already been explained how that comes about 10 from outside. 'But,' he says,[243] 'when the thing, without making any

contribution of its own, is subject to an alteration which does not lead it to substance, but which displaces it towards what is worse, or [at least] not towards what is better, then such an alteration is affection.' This does not tell us what the cause of the affection is, and leads to the opposite of what he wants.[244] For if the thing itself contributes
15　nothing to the undergoing, either the affection will be causeless, or [it will derive] from some other thing external to it. Even if some of its components act, and others undergo, the affection will still be *as from* something else. And Iamblichus says: 'Why is it that affections ought not lead to substance, given that some affections – those which are generative – do indeed lead to substance?' But perhaps the following point is appropriate to affection: if the substance has to have
20　prior existence if it is to receive the affection, then the affection is not substance-creating; just as alteration is not a distinguishing mark [of affection] either (but [Plotinus] said that the undergoing thing is subject to an alteration which does not lead it to substance).[245]

　　But how are we to concede that affections contribute towards the worse state, or [at least] not towards the better, when some of them produce what is more noble in us? Well, given that Plotinus himself also expressed puzzlement about this, let us see what he opposes to
25　himself:[246] 'But if the bronze is a more beautiful thing from being heated, nothing stops us [saying] that it undergoes: for undergoing is of two sorts, the one [consisting] in becoming worse, the other in becoming better, or neither.' Now it is clear that he previously located undergoing in the [process of] becoming worse, whereas he here grants that there are also some affections which lead to what is better. Iamblichus says: 'Given that an inclination in both directions[247] is
30　located [by Plotinus] in the [category of] undergoing, it was not correct [of him] to add the phrase "or neither". For this remark is in conflict with his hypothesis about acting and undergoing, since the former was placed in what is in accordance with nature and in the better, whereas the latter [was placed] in what is against nature and in the worse.'[248] However, if the undergoing thing comes to be *similar* [to the way it was before], then it is clear that it will not become either worse or better, hence neither. And it is also possible for a [merely] *differ-*
326,1　*ent*[249] thing to come to be, one which does not bear comparison in respect of worse or better, as when a red thing comes to be from grey one.

　　But Plotinus also raises doubts in relation to [his statement that] affections do not lead to substance. He says:[250] 'If being heated is receiving heat, and the bronze's being heated contributes to the
5　substance of the statue, but not [to that] of the bronze, undergoing and not undergoing will be the same thing, if undergoing really is what does not contribute to substance.' Against this Iamblichus says that 'it was wrong to adopt the definition of undergoing according to

which it does not contribute to substance. For whether being heated contributes to substance or to alteration or to anything else, it belongs to the [category of] undergoing alone.' But perhaps [the proviso] that affection does *not* contribute to substance was indeed rightly laid down, for the reason I have already given:[251] and in this case the bronze is heated [*per se*] and, in being heated, undergoes, whereas the statue is heated *accidentally*, in virtue of the fact that it is made of bronze.[252]

Iamblichus does not accept the following point either,[253] that undergoing comes about in virtue of the thing's having in itself a movement, namely the alteration [of the thing] in the sense of any sort of altering at all. He says: 'It is not only the movement in respect of alteration which should be placed in the [category of] undergoing, but many other [movements] too. For a thing which increases in size will also be said to undergo, as well as something which is moved in respect of place, and (so Iamblichus says) something led into substance as well.'

'But,' says Plotinus,[254] 'it further looks as if both [acting and undergoing] are relatives, in those cases where acting relates to undergoing.[255] This thing moves [another thing] and that thing is moved, and each [transaction] is [in] two categories, both the [category of] relative and that of acting or undergoing.[256] And this thing gives movement to that, so that the other receives it, with the result that there is a giving and a receiving and a relation. Indeed, if the recipient *has*, as it is said to *have* colour, why should it not *have* movement? And perhaps not only are the relatives [to be] ranged under the category of having as well, but the absolute [actions] too.[257] For indeed the absolute movement of walking[258] *has* the walk.'[259] Against this it is easy to say that in this sense everything will belong to the [category of] having, since [everything] is considered under the aspect of participation. For the white man has whiteness, and the thing that is two cubits long has so much length, and similarly in the case of the other [categories]. But each thing should be referred to the genus in respect of which it is said. It has often been mentioned[260] that the relative, considered as it is *per se*, in respect of the relation alone, has its being in the other categories: for relation does not exist *per se*. Accordingly, just as in the [category of] substance the relative [exists] in respect of father and son, and in the [category of] quality in respect of like and unlike, and in the [category of] quantity in respect of equal and unequal, so also in the [category of] acting and undergoing [it exists] in respect of striking and being struck. There is nothing odd about the same thing's falling under two categories, [the one] in respect of its subsistent reality *per se*, [the other] in respect of the relation between relatives.[261]

After such puzzles and solutions Iamblichus turns to his more theoretical systematic treatment,[262] and <conveys [instruction]>[263] about acting and undergoing – what kind of subsistent reality they have *per se*, how they are conformed to one another, and to which and what kind of things each extends. He begins from Plato's conception of acting:[264] he [i.e. Plato] says that the agent differs [only] in name

10 from the cause. And it is anyway clear that the agent is the active cause. But why does he not say that the agent does not differ from some one *particular* cause [sc. among other causes], rather than from *the* cause *simpliciter*? Presumably because the agent is cause in the strict sense: matter and form are rather *co*-causes, but not causes. And the paradigm and the end are not proximate causes of the finished product, but since they are causes of the acting *for* the agent,

15 they should be called *relations* of the thing which comes to be in the strict sense [sc. with the agent]. Hence the agent will be the main cause, so that in an exact account the theory of acting is about cause.

Accordingly, the number and nature of causes, the different varieties of them that there are, which of them are first, which second and which third – all of these [questions] are properly to be transferred to the [category of] acting as well. And again, since some of the incorpo-

20 real causes are operations – either [operations] of those [causes] which are separate *per se*, or of those which are present in the world and inseparable from the universe, as for example those heavenly [causes acting] on all sublunary things which come into being – while other [incorporeal causes] belong to nature in accordance with its own principles, and yet others belong to divisible forms, [it follows that] the [category of] acting and the theory of it permeate all of these too. And in terms of another distinction, since some of the operations are

25 pure and unmixed with any of the other genera, whereas others are mixed with the other [genera] – and these latter also produce multifarious combinations – while yet others lying at the lowest level communicate with the [corresponding] undergoings, both the beginning and the middle and end points of the [category of] acting also will be [defined] in accordance with all such differences. And since some agents are generative, whereas others are species-forming, and

30 some are perfecting – and of these some are unifying, others separative – while yet others have some other action among existents, the [category of] acting, strictly so called, will also be ascribed to all of these. Further, some [actions] are physical, such as heating and cooling, others involve skill, such as healing and carpentry, and some are limited, like those [occurring] in skills, while others are without limit and incessant, as in the case of divine actions and those of the

35 heavenly [bodies], given that the world is eternal. And whatever [agents] there may be which produce [their effects] in virtue of their

328,1 being, as for example the sun illuminates in virtue of its being, or which act by thinking, such as the world's mind, or by reasoning, such as the soul of the universe, all of these too are in the [category of] acting. And those operations in them [i.e. in these agents] which [operate] *per se* and in relation to themselves, such as the [operations] of the immaterial and separate thoughts,[265] as well as those which are brought into operation by means of other things, such as those [brought about] by means of the soul or by bodies or by bodily 5 capacities – these [operations] do not fall outside the assignment to the [category of] acting either. Likewise too those operations which operate towards themselves and need nothing else, and those which operate towards something else, and those [which operate] towards themselves and simultaneously towards something else, and those [which operate] towards themselves primarily, but which in a secondary sense also have an operation towards other things[266] – these too 10 will be included in the [category of] acting. What is more, the [category of] acting also extends, in accordance with the present division, over all the forms of the categories: as regards substance [it consists] in bringing into existence that which comes to be; as regards quality, [it consists] in bringing into a quality that which is altered; as regards quantity, [it consists] in making bigger or smaller; and similarly in the case of the other genera the cause permeating them all is in the 15 [category of] acting.

If we are completely to comprehend the genus of acting under a single account, let us consider, in respect of all the things that are, however many and various they are, the most perfect operations – the ones which are most of all free of any potentiality – to be everywhere primary. Of these we will rightly call those [operations] which also come to be *uniform per se* the principal ones in the 20 [category of] acting. For these [operations] possess operating and acting[267] from themselves, produce it all [i.e. operating-and-acting] from a single cause, and present it indivisibly to those things arranged after them, and contain them [i.e. operating and acting] uniformly, and render them very powerful and very self-sufficient. The operations here below, when they are disposed adequately and completely, imitate them as well, receiving a kind of fulfilment from 25 them. So much, then, for the [category of] acting.

We should embrace the complete view of the [category of] undergoing in just the same way.[268] This does not have a *contrariety* towards the [category of] acting, even if it employs the most opposed forms of expression: we ought [rather] to consider it *together* [with acting] and as *conjoined* with the operations which devolve from agents. Accordingly, when operations, proceeding outwards together with a relation, 30 are able to assimilate to themselves those things which can partake of them – not in respect of the operation, but in respect of a kind of movement which is successive[269] to the operation – in such cases these movements characterise the general genus of undergoing. But in

respect of another sort of impulse *every* movement and generation in
the universe[270] possesses, on the one hand, the moving and generative
thing and, on the other hand, the thing moved and the thing gener-
35   ated, considered as it were in the order of the finished product, [each]
in respect of a different impulse. If therefore we embrace in our
reasoning the genus which permeates all of these things in the whole
of the world and in respect of all the kinds of movement, we will
329,1 discover the full magnitude of the [category of] undergoing, and the
extent of its power.

In general, everything that is acquired and which enters adventitiously from something else, which is in no way of the thing itself but
from another, which accompanies the operations of the primary thing
[i.e. the agent], and which is changed by those [operations], is properly
placed in the [category of] undergoing. Further, that which is opposed
5   to form, and that which as material subject both receives a share of
form and possesses the capacity to be perfected, and that which
receives everything in itself – this[271] too will be one particular common
mark of the [category of] undergoing. And if someone were also to
posit the constitution of the sublunary material elements as being
affective in relation to the active heavenly cause, in this way too he
10   would be able to demonstrate a particular common feature[272] in the
universe. And it is possible to contemplate both acting[273] and undergoing in a single thing. For nature, in acting *towards* herself, also
undergoes *from* herself: insofar as she establishes principles [of
constitution] for the things which come to be, we define her as *active*,
whereas insofar as she herself receives from herself the ordering of
these principles [of constitution], she is rightly said to *undergo*. And
even if it is not exactly like this in the case of the soul, nevertheless
15   in this case too there are many divisions of the affective [principle].
Again, on the strength of a different analogy, a certain[274] passive
receptivity of the more perfect thoughts is observed in the case of
reasoning and in the case of the soul's mind.

And in general, in the case of everything which has a more perfect
and a more imperfect [part], and in which the former [part] produces
perfection, while the latter receives it, a certain analogy with affection
20   is observed, in accordance with which the former [principle] imports
the perfect form, while the latter [principle] receives this into itself,
but it is always the case that such participation in affection is
bestowed from *something else*, and [even] if it sometimes seems that
something undergoes *from itself*, it is not right to suppose [that] any
such thing [is in fact occurring]: for it is not by virtue of the same
thing in it that it both undergoes and provides itself with the cause
of the undergoing, so that in this case too the affection comes about
25   from another thing. For the active operation is able both to be the
cause of itself and to begin from itself, while the affection, being in all

respects imperfect, is by nature unable to be induced to generate itself. For if what possesses from itself the cause of the operating is the active thing, then the patient, being bereft of any causality, will not even possess in itself the cause of the undergoing.[275] Hence no undergoing will be absolute, in the way for example that walking was an absolute operation. And that is what you would expect: for the 30 better things, being independent of a relation towards other things, exist self-sufficiently *per se* and in themselves, while the worse things need the better ones to support them, and, in depending on these [better things] and acquiring a kind of participation from them, they receive a share of being. So [undergoings] should not be arranged in the same way as those [principles obtaining] in the case of the [category of] acting, to the effect that among undergoings too some 35 are [held to be] absolute and others passive: for patients are *always* dependent on agents.

Since Archytas conveyed a distinction between the affection (*to* 330,1 *pathos*), the thing which passively undergoes (*to peponthos*), the production (*to poiêma*) and the undergoing (*to pathêma*), this should not be left unexamined either. He says the following:[276] 'Affection differs from the thing which passively undergoes: for affection comes about along with perception – for example rage, pleasure, and fear – whereas something can passively undergo even without perception, such as wax when it is softened or mud when it is dried. Likewise too 5 the production (*to poiêma*) [differs] from the thing which passively undergoes: for the thing which has been brought about (*to poiêthen*) has also in a way passively undergone, but the thing which has passively undergone has not automatically been brought about (*pe-poiêtai*). For something can also passively undergo by virtue of a deficiency and a privation.'

In these words Iamblichus understands as *affection* that which, together with perception and apprehension, remains throughout the [process of] being altered,[277] and which includes the affections of the soul and of animals, as well as any [affections] which are higher than 10 these and come about together with self-consciousness (*sunais-thêsis*)[278] or some other kind of conscious accompaniment (*parakol-outhêsis*),[279] and which he says is also opposed to the primary genus of acting. For just as the latter was placed in theorising, [this being] foremost [in the category of acting],[280] so he posits the former[281] in the [category of] undergoing, together with its proper kind of knowledge, which he calls self-consciousness. This [sc. primary affection] is divided in multifarious ways according to the species of self-con- 15 sciousness: for [to these species] we should assign the conscious accompaniments to the capacities of the life in the soul, and we should also assign the [self-consciousness] which belongs to the perceptions of men and the other animals, and we must also posit a certain lowest

kind of self-consciousness in the case of those things which have a
dim, physical apprehension of undergoing. And thus, [Iamblichus]
20   says, this whole genus of undergoing[282] has acquired for us an opposition to the primary genus of acting.

He says that the *passively undergoing thing* is whatever does not,
in the [process of] coming about, manifest the affection along with
[the undergoing], but whose change, after completion of the [process
of] coming to be, clearly appears, as for example that the wax has been
softened, or that the mud has been dried. Hence, even although this
thing too goes through a process of *affection*, he nevertheless characterises it as *passively undergoing*. This [sort of] thing is without
25   perception, and includes all the various and many undergoings that
there are in nature. For all[283] the alterations lacking a conscious
accompaniment (*aparakolouthêtoi*) that come about in the physical
elements and in composite and simple bodies – all of these are
characterised in terms of passively undergoing. There will be multifarious divisions of these [alterations] too, since we shall want to bear
30   in mind those things which, insofar as they are bodies, are divided or
increased or altered or which are in any other of many ways observed
to be in [a state of] passively undergoing. This genus[284] is in opposition
to the actions of inanimate things.

[Iamblichus] says that the *production* differs from the *affection* not
in the way people think, namely by virtue of the latter's arising from
another, operating, thing, whereas the former in no way does so (for
there is in general no such thing as an affection [derived] from
oneself),[285] but because productions contribute to substance,
35   [whereas] the undergoings which are contrasted with them result in
no finished product, and displace [the patient] from its being.

(Since[286] substance is of two kinds – that of the form, and that of
the material underlying subject – the destructions [of substance] are
also said to be twofold: the one sort [proceeding] on the basis of a
331,1   privation, which is an absence of the form and yields the displacement
[of a thing] from its being thus and so, the other [proceeding] on the
basis of a deficiency of the kind of fulfilment which flows into the
material [parts], and on the basis of a consumption of the matter in
them. But if privation is an affection, why is it said in the *Physics* to
be an active cause (*poiêtikê aitia*)?[287] Iamblichus says: 'Privation [sc.
5   of the form] too can indeed become an active cause, just like the
presence of the form. The privation itself becomes one thing, and the
deprived thing another, so that in this case too the[288] affection in the
deprived thing comes about from something else[289] – namely [from]
the preceding active cause of the privation.[290] The same account holds
[sc. in respect of matter] for deficiency and fulfilment. [In the latter
case] there is in one thing the fulfilling, and in another thing there is
10   the being-fulfilled;[291] and [in the former case there is] in one thing the

being-in-need, and in another thing [there is] the producing of the cause of the deficiency in [the first thing].'[292] Against this I think it is worth asking what other active cause of a privation there could be, apart from the [privation] in the deprived thing.[293] Is the contrary which destroys what is contrary to itself the cause? Or perhaps this is accidental, and just as the necessity of generation and destruction in the sublunary [world] demands preceding causes of the *presence* of forms, so also [it demands such causes] of their *absence*, and the   15 inventors of legends range these in opposition to the creative causes.)

This production (*poiêma*)[294] should be ranged over against the second[295] species of the [category of] acting, namely the one considered in respect of what is productive (*poiêtikos*), for this [production] is also defined in terms of [something's] being brought into existence. For just as house-building is properly called productive, so a house's being   20 built is called a production. As many and as various as are the forms we have assigned to the productive *operations* – whether [these forms are] divine or human, whether they are products of skill or objects of knowledge, or whether divided up in whatever other way – so many and so various [are the forms] we should apportion to the *productions* produced by actions. For it is clear that the things which are brought about are brought about together with an affection. Such, then, is the particular division of the [category of] undergoing, as of that of acting,   25 conveyed by Archytas.

In the *Metaphysics* Aristotle distinguishes the physical affections roughly thus:[296] 'Affection (*pathos*) is said (1) in one sense to be a quality by which it is possible [for something] to be altered, for example white and black, sweet and bitter, heavy and light, and all other such things. (2) In another [sense] the operations and altera-   30 tions of these [are said to be affections], and especially those that are harmful. Further, [great] magnitudes of (3) misfortunes and (4) griefs are called affections.'[297] In the case of the first of these I suggest he   332,1 calls the affective product itself an affection, in the second case [he calls] the affective movement [an affection], and in the third and fourth cases he has employed the meaning favoured by usage. But we have now up to this point sufficiently considered the two genera as a whole, and the number and nature of their component species, to enable us to comprehend each of them taken *per se*.   5

But we must also look at their commixture with each another. For Archytas conveyed this too along with [what he says about] the simple [categories], saying:[298] 'One thing is an agent, another a patient, and yet another is both an agent and a patient: for example in the case of physical things god is an agent, matter is a patient, and the elements are both agent and patient.' The claim is clear, and he has appended the principal examples, saying that god, whom the other active causes   10 too accompany, acts, and that matter, by means of which also [all] the

other things [which undergo] partake of undergoing, is a patient, and
that the elements, since they are things which partake indeed of both
matter and form, both act and undergo. Those who investigate their
relation to each other say that although [acting and undergoing] are
15   said *oppositely*, they are not *contraries*, as Andronicus[299] thought. For
how could a contrary come about as the product of its contrary?

Next, after the general[300] systematic treatment [of acting and
undergoing], it is worth considering here too, even though it has been
said before (296,12ff.), what the attributes are in the case of these
[categories] as well, just as we did in the case of the other genera.
Well then, there is contrariety in the case of acting and also in the
20   case of undergoing, and of the contraries in these cases some have
something[301] in between, whereas others do not. Accordingly, things
which are contraries in respect of contrary *qualities* – as for example
'heating [is contrary] to cooling, and being heated to being cooled'
(11b2-3)[302] – and of which the [corresponding] qualities have something in between, of these [contraries] those which belong to the
[categories of] acting and undergoing also have something in between,
such as making lukewarm and making red. But [in the case of those
contraries] whose [corresponding qualities] do not have [something
in between], it is not the case that these [corresponding actions and
affections have anything in between] either, such as for example
25   making healthy and making sick. (And yet doctors posit the 'neutral'
condition intermediate between health and sickness.[303])

Acting and undergoing 'admit of more and less' (11b1-2), but these
are not present in all cases. 'For,' Iamblichus says, 'these will not be
present in the case of the kind of thinking which pertains to the
perfect [kind of] thought, but [acting and undergoing] do admit [of
more and less] in the case of the imperfect [kind of thought].' And
30   perhaps indeed in the case of all things admitting of more and less,
the main things do *not* admit of them, whereas the imperfect things
are the ones which *do* admit them. But perhaps we should rather
make the distinction in the following way: the things which possess
acting and undergoing in those genera where there is more and less
admit of [more and less], such as for example whitening and being
whitened in the [category of] quality. But all those things [possessing
acting and undergoing] which are in genera not admitting of more
35   and less – such as counting and measuring in the case of quantity –
do not admit of [more and less], and nor do begetting and being
333,1   begotten, or anything at all of the things spoken of in [the category
of] substance. And that is reasonable: for acting is operating, and
operation is uniform with the underlying reality (*huparxis*) of which
it is the operation.

And acting and undergoing are observed in each of the categories.
5   For each [category], being as it were a kind of substance and under-

lying reality, possesses a certain proper operation of its own underlying reality. In respect of [the category of] substance, acting would
be, for example, procreating, house-building, ship-building, while
undergoing in respect of substance [would be for example] being
procreated, a house's being built. But here Iamblichus raises the
question whether perhaps these [latter] things should be said to be
led into substance, rather than to *undergo in respect of substance*,
because, as I said before (325,19-20), [something] must *first* exist and
[only] thus [can it] undergo. Acting and undergoing in respect of   10
quantity are for example lengthening and being lengthened, widen-
ing and being widened, deepening and being deepened, and counting,
taking time, moving, saying and the affective opposites of these. In
respect of quality [acting and undergoing would be for example]
whitening and being whitened, making healthy and being made
healthy; in respect of the [category of] relative, doubling and being
doubled; in respect of the [category of] being-in-a-position laying
down and being laid down; in respect of the [category of] having,   15
arming with a breastplate and being armed with a breastplate.

The limit of acting is a function (*ergon*) or form: function is what
has its being in the coming about [of something], as dancing [is the
function] of the dancer; form is the enduring product, as for example
the painter's shape.[304] There is a limit of undergoing, and it is the
same as that of acting. People ask when acting is circumscribed and
changes into having-acted, and some place the limit[305] of acting at the   20
last [instant of] time [of the action], others in the first [instant] after
the last [instant of acting]: for [they say] that the last [instant] is still
part of the acting. (This is a quite general inquiry concerning the man
who has run a race, or who has healed, or who has died.) But perhaps
the limit of acting is the [state of] having for the first time acted, not
over a long period of time, just as the limit of movement, which we
call a motion, is not [over a long period of time] either.

Beside the acting, accompanying it, there is action [and the] agent,   25
while beside the undergoing [there is] affection [and the] patient. And
in all cases[306] action and affection have already been reckoned in[307] to
the [category of] relative, as too in the case of being-in-a-position
position [is counted as a relative, sc. as well]. We must also look
closely to see when the operation or the affection is active and when
passive. For example causing grief seems to the majority of people to
be active, being grieved to be passive – not that it always happens
just in the way it does in the case of the striker and the thing struck: 30
for the thing which causes grief need not always coexist [sc. with the
griever], such as a dead son (if someone is grieved on his account),
and it is also possible [in such cases] not to be grieved, so long, that
is, as one's imagination, which is something active and itself a cause,
does not persist. It can sometimes happen too[308] that even if the agent

ceases [acting], the patient [still] undergoes, since its condition persists, as for example in the case of something heated by a fire and
35 which still undergoes being heated, even after its retreat from the fire. For there are two kinds of undergoing, one kind connected to acting, and the other considered in respect of its condition. But perhaps in the latter case too the agent – whether the imagination, or the [sc. effect of the] fire impressed on [the patient] from outside – is conjoined [with the patient] internally.[309] It is well, therefore, in the examination of these matters to be guided by the objects themselves
334,1 and not by [mere] expressions. There is extensive treatment of such matters among the Stoics, whose teaching and the majority of whose writings have been unavailable in our time. But since we have dealt sufficiently with acting and undergoing, it is a suitable moment to
5 move on now to deal with the remaining genera as well.

On Being-in-a-Position

After the [categories of] acting and undergoing Aristotle placed the [category of] being-in-a-position (*to keisthai*), whereas Archytas [placed] the [category of] having. For the former had regard to the fact that being-in-a-position is the goal of acting and undergoing: for something [acting or undergoing] either places or is placed,[310] so that in this way the [category of] being-in-a-position comes about. Placing
10 is acting, and being placed is undergoing. Or else, since each thing which is positioned in its own place, or in an alien [place], acts and undergoes by nature,[311] it was for this reason that [Aristotle] conjoined the [category of] being-in-a-position to [those of] acting and undergoing – although on this basis [being-in-a-position] ought really to have preceded them, and also for the reason that the primary relation of every body is towards the thing which receives its position (*thesis*), and [only when it is positioned] thus does it subsequently receive possession of its acquired [properties].[312] Archytas, on the
15 other hand, having regard to the relations [which a body has] both from itself towards something else and from other things towards itself, and in view of the fact that the [category of] *having* comes about in virtue of the former [relation], while that of *being-in-a-position* does so in virtue of the latter [relation], ranked the [category of] having before that of being-in-a-position, on the grounds (1) that the relation [running] from other things towards the things themselves is in a sense *less relational* (*askhetôtera*) than that [running] from the things themselves towards other things; (2) that having indicates [a body's] *operation* more than does being-in-a-position; and (3) that having is
20 more *general* than being-in-a-position.

Each [of Aristotle and Archytas] assigned to these genera[313] the order appropriate to his own particular hypotheses concerning them.

For since Archytas placed the *pure* genera of acting and undergoing
in the principal things – [the pure genus] of acting in the divine, that
of undergoing in matter – he reasonably enough arranged the [cate-
gory of] having together [with acting and undergoing], given that this
[i.e. having] accrues to matter from the divine. And when having
accrues to matter from the divine, at that point the composite form   25
comes into existence, and this is already body, but still lacks being-
in-a-position: hence the [category of] having, as well [sc. as acting and
undergoing], is primary [with respect to being-in-a-position]. And it
is also more general than being-in-a-position: for having belongs to
incorporeal things as well [as to corporeal ones], as for example the
sound belongs to the soul (and has no tendency to qualify that[314]),
whereas being-in-a-position [belongs] to bodies alone and to the limits
of sizes, i.e. to surface, line and point. But since Aristotle conveys [sc.   30
as his primary cases of actions] *physical* actions, namely those in
respect of heating and cooling, which obtain in connection with bodies
and in bodies, he consistently with himself arranged the [category of]
being-in-a-position together with that of acting and [that of] undergoing, while since he defines the [category of] having only in the case
of possessions which are divisible into parts, such as shoes and
weapons, he reasonably placed it later, and did not, in the *Categories*,   35
convey the total and primary genus of it. And that both the [category
of] being-in-a-position and that of having enjoy an equal right to claim   335,1
precedence over each other (*antipleonektei allêla*) Archytas himself
made clear by placing the [category of] being-in-a-position before that
of having, in [specifying] the ends [of each], where he says 'and
furthermore [the individual necessarily] *acts* and *undergoes* and *is
positioned* and *has* …', and again, 'nor indeed [is man as such
something] which *acts to bring about* something, or which *undergoes*
something, nor [is it something] which *is positioned*, nor which *has*
something'.[315] But Archytas also frequently neglects the [category of]
being-in-a-position. Let this suffice for an account of the order of the   5
[category of] being-in-a-position [in the enumeration of the catego-
ries].

[Aristotle's method of] describing[316] its content (*ennoia*) by means
of examples, such as 'he is seated' or 'he is reclining', or his mentioning
infinitives like 'to be seated', 'to be standing', does indeed provide a
certain[317] instruction, but it is not sufficient for full knowledge [of that
content]: it produces rather an enumeration of the things which are   10
included in the [category of] being-in-a-position. Hence it is better to
cleanse its content thoroughly, firstly by removing the adventitious
relation (*skhesis*) of the [category of] relative, and secondly by removing movement and rest, and also acting and undergoing, and [then]
by considering just the simple relation of position. For just as the
relation to place creates the [category of] where, and [the relation] to

time [creates] the [category of] when, so [the relation] to a position
15   creates the [category of] being-in-a-position. So one should think of
the [category of] being-in-a-position not by embracing in thought
either the body which is positioned or the place in which it is
positioned, but by counting just the position-which-is-a-certain-way
(*hê ekhousa pôs thesis*) as being in the genus of being-in-a-position –
[and that] in respect of all those existents which are naturally
sustained (*anekhesthai*) by or situated (*enidruesthai*) in other things.
For it is just this sort of combination of things which are situated and
20   things which provide a location (*hedra*) that is the strictest and most
primary description of the [category of] being-in-a-position. Supposing, now, one adds [to being-in-a-position] a relation or acting or
undergoing or quality or some other such thing, then if, on the one
hand, the genus of being-in-a-position predominates in these mixed
cases too, so that it is thought of in that way on one's first approach
(*prosbolê*) [to these mixed cases], then [these mixed cases] will be no
less in the [category of] being-in-a-position [sc. than in the other
categories]; while if, on the other hand, some other one of the [addi-
tional] genera renders the apparent specification (*eidopoiia*) [of a
mixed case] more obvious [than does being-in-a-position], then the
25   control of the species will be defined in terms of the victorious genera
[sc. rather than in terms of being-in-a-position].

But we should next go through the attributes of the [category of]
being-in-a-position, just as [we did] in the case of the other genera
too. Contrariety seems to be one of the things in the [category of]
being-in-a-position: for since something supine has a contrary position to something prone, it is contrarily positioned. This contrariety
30   [in the category of being-in-a-position] obtains both by virtue of the
position [of something] – for a prone position is contrary to a supine
one – and by virtue of the *place* [holding something] – for there is
contrariety in this case too, which is why something positioned above
is positioned contrarily to what is positioned below, having adopted
the contrariety in respect of place. And everything, I think, in the
[category of] being-in-a-position admits of this latter [contrariety],
since it is indeed the case that everything [in that category] is in some
place having an opposition towards another place, whereas the con-
35   trariety [arising] by virtue of position does not apply to everything
[sc. in the category of being-in-a-position]. For a cube and a sphere
and many other inanimate things, though they enjoy *difference* of
positions – as for instance on a corner or on a side – nevertheless do
not thereby [enjoy] *contrariety* [of position] as well, in the way that
prone and supine things do, as observed particularly in the case of
336,1 animals which have a physical front and back or above and below,
and right and left.

More and less are sometimes applied idiomatically to the case of

being-in-a-position, when the positioned things admit of breadth (*platos*), as in the case of reclining,[318] and sometimes [being-in-a-position] manifests more and less by a form of expression, but signi- 5
fies a hyperbole in respect of the putative comparison, as when a particular[319] bowl is said to be more supine [i.e. shallower] [than another]. More and less are not present in all cases of things in the [category of] being-in-a-position: for clearly surface and line and point, and any other incorporeal thing among those in the [category of] being-in-a-position, do not have [degrees of] more and less. And just as action and affection were [also] among the relatives, although 10
acting and undergoing [each] received its own category, so too *position* is one of the relatives, although *being-in-a-position* characterises its own particular genus, quite different from that of relative.

Next we must examine too the division of the [category of] being-in-a-position, both that in respect of the species-forming differentiae, and that in respect of other ways [of being positioned], even where 15
they are not species-forming but do distinguish the things arranged under it [i.e. being-in-a-position]. Well then, of the things observed in the [category of] being-in-a-position some are [in it] by *nature*, as for instance the four elements, situated in their appropriate places, and the heavens, in possession of the highest domain, whereas others [are in it] by [sc. artificial] *position*, as for instance statues and images and implements, and in general things placed by dint of some sort of skill or [to provide some] service. Further, some things have their position in a state of rest, such as the earth and those of the elements 20
which stand still, while others [have it] in a state of movement, such as the revolutions of the heavens, which are situated in one an-other,[320] and those of the elements which are moved. And of the things which are moved and the things which stand still, some have their being-in-a-position eternally, such as those bodies which are eternal, while others do so temporally, such as those subsisting in a part of time.

'It may seem,' says Iamblichus, 'that everything in the [category 25
of] being-in-a-position has its situation in some particular *place*, but that is not so: things which are situated in *capacities* also have the same generic nature [as other positioned things] – for they are positioned by virtue of having their location *in* these capacities and *in* life (for these things are sustained by life) – and being-in-a-position is also reasonably regarded as [obtaining] in the case of those things which are contained from all sides in the causes most strictly so called.' But perhaps being-in-a-position does not signify every kind of 30
situation, unless one were to take it metaphorically, but rather the 'falling' (*ptôsis*), as it were, of *bodies*, which they have[321] when they retreat from the independent nature of the indivisible forms and require [situations] to receive and properly arrange (*euthetizein*) their

'falling'.[322] And in fact *place* provides this service – that is, of receiving and properly arranging things which are not able to sustain them-
35 selves, but which have 'fallen away' (*peptôkota*) [sc. from the forms] and been scattered. For the things which retreat from an indivisible nature [each] have both of the following: an existence in something else rather than in itself, and a dispersal [into parts] (*diespasthai*) rather than remaining indivisible. That is why they also require a place which both receives them and provides an order (*taxis*) and proper arrangement (*euthetismos*) for their [sc. newly acquired] parts:
337,1 for things once dispersed stand in need of proper arrangement, so that [for example] the head may have its appropriate place, and the neck too, and it not be the case that 'many neckless heads spring forth', as Empedocles puts it.[323] And that being-in-a-position (*keisthai*) also signifies 'having fallen' (*to peptôkenai*) Homer made clear, when he
5 said: 'Patroclus lies fallen (*keitai*), and they fight around his dead body'.[324] Hence those things situated in capacities and in life and in the causes most strictly so called are said to be 'positioned' in an extended sense, not in the strict sense.

It is agreed by everyone that being-in-a-position is an accident of every body, which is why[325] every body is in a place and has a position in respect of place, except that the body of a fixed [sphere][326] and that
10 of the universe are not in the [category of] being-in-a-position: for [the body of the universe] is not in a place either, according to Aristotle's disposition regarding place,[327] because there is no body containing it,[328] but place was [held to be] the [sc. inner] limit of the containing thing, at which it contains the contained thing. Being-in-a-position also applies to incorporeals, for example to the limits of bodies (for it
15 belongs to place and, *simpliciter*, to surface, line and point, since all of these have a position). But being-in-a-position surely does not belong to things which are incorporeal *per se*, unless one were to say that in a metaphorical sense all things are positioned in mind and god, as being contained in their origin and cause: 'They lie positioned (*keintai*) in god, drawing in the blossoming flames', the oracle says.[329]

One should note that while body is positioned in place, and place
20 indeed is *positioned* – for it surrounds bodies and also possesses, itself, the [various] differences of position, namely above, below and the rest, as well as the definite and the indefinite – place is not [itself] positioned *in place*, as bodies are. For there is no such thing as the place of a place, lest the account proceed to infinity, seeking place prior to place. But it is worth puzzling over what – if place is positioned at all – it is positioned *in*. For what is positioned tends to
25 be positioned *in* something. Well, Aristotle would say, given his assertion that place is the limit of the containing body, that it [i.e. place] is positioned in that [i.e. containing body], just as the other surfaces are also positioned *in* the bodies of which they are the

limits.[330] Now if someone says that place is an extension (*diastêma*), or a measure and a proper arrangement of the juxtaposition of magnitudes, just as time is the measure of continuation (*paratasis*) in respect of movement, then it will not be necessary to look for anything else in which place might be positioned. For being itself the   30
location of other things it will have no further need of a location [for itself], just as too the limits of magnitudes, being self-limits (*auto-perata*), have no further need of [other] things to limit them. That is why Archytas too says:[331] 'It is therefore necessary[332] that while other things are in place, place [itself] is in nothing, but rather relates to existents as limits relate to the things which are limited.'

Some positioned things have a single being-in-a-position, others a   35
double one: for an empty jar is positioned in a stone [container], as it   338,1
might be, whereas wine in the jar is positioned both in the jar and in whatever the jar is positioned in. According to another notion, the jar itself is positioned somewhere and its parts [are positioned] in the whole [jar], while the wine is itself positioned in the jar, and its parts in the whole [wine]: so that the full jar will have being-in-a-position   5
in four ways. But it is worth considering whether it is strictly correct to say that the parts are *positioned* in the whole: for not everything *in* something [else] is also *positioned* in what it is in, but only things which are in a *place* are said [strictly] to be *positioned* (in that place). The differentiae of the [category of] being-in-a-position will be [speci-fied] both in terms of the shapes and in terms of the spatial dimen-sions [of things in a place].[333] Archytas, however, in speaking of the differentiae of being-in-a-position, says:[334] 'Part of it [consists] in   10
potentiality (*en dunamei*), part in a state of rest (*en stasei*), and of the [part consisting] in potentiality part again [consists] in operating, part in undergoing'. The [category of] being-in-a-position is certainly considered in connection with a state of rest, for this [i.e. being-in-a-position] remains in the same [condition], whether the thing posi-tioned in a state of rest be incorporeal or a body. And in connection with potentiality, [being-in-a-position] is considered in two ways, in respect of both contraries,[335] namely in the case of acting and under-going, and in the case of moving and being moved, since[336] potentiality   15
too can be brought into both contrary [conditions]. But if one considers not the imperfect kind of potentiality but the sort which is perfect and able to cause operations, and which sustains within itself positioned things, then on this basis it is also necessary that the more primary causes be more inclusive than the secondary ones, and we will reasonably say that the secondary things are positioned in the prior   20
things.

But we should next proceed to the puzzles raised by Plotinus concerning the [category of] being-in-a-position.[337] Well, he says that being-in-a-position is found in only a few cases and that because of

this it is wrong for it to be separated in a genus of its own. But if it belongs to all bodies, both eternal and sublunary ones, how is it wrong for this too [i.e. being-in-a-position] to get a genus of its own? And
25 Archytas too says that it extends to many things. 'But reclining and sitting,' [Plotinus] says, 'are not simple, but signify being positioned, that is to say being in a place, in some sort of *configuration*. Now the configuration is one thing and the place another, and we have accounted for both,[338] and [so] there was then no necessity to conjoin two categories into one.' In response to this one should say that these <words>[339] for configurations, such as that for sitting and [that for]
30 reclining, signify the differentiae not of configurations *simpliciter* but of configurations in respect of *position*: even though [these words] denote a quality, since configuration is a quality, they will not mention the quality *simpliciter*, but rather the [quality] of *being-in-a-position*. Even [Plotinus] himself thought it right to refer the qualities constitutive of something to that genus under which the constituted thing is also referred: for example, straightness concerns
35 a line, and line is [in the category] of quantity; therefore straightness will also be [in the category of] of quantity, and this whole thing[340] will be a quality of a quantity.[341] Hence just as carrying (*pherein*) does
339,1 not depart from its own particular category when we talk of carrying *upwards* (*anapherein*), in the same way neither does being set *up* (*anakeisthai*[342]) or lying *down* (*katakeisthai*).[343] Those who came after him [i.e. Plotinus] objected even more to his difficulty, contending that being-in-a-position is connected neither with configuration nor with place, but that these things are random concomitants [of being-in-a-position], just as several things are observed going together with [sc.
5 each of] the other categories too, and that the special category of being-in-a-position is thought of barely, in terms just of the *position* itself [of the positioned thing], without our in any way considering in addition to that what the thing is positioned *in* and *in what particular way* (*pôs ekhon*)[344] it is positioned.

Iamblichus says: 'But nor is being-in-a-position even necessarily in a place,[345] since place too is positioned somewhere, but it is not in a place. So it is not correct that place is embraced within the [category of] being-in-a-position. And if it is possible to think of some position
10 without configuration either, namely [the position] of things lacking configuration (*askhêmatistoi*) – whether bodies or incorporeals[346] like line and point – then there will be [such a thing as] being-in-a-position without configuration as well.'[347] 'But if being-in-a-position,' [Plotinus] says,[348] 'signifies an operation, it should be arranged among the operations; if [it signifies] an affection, then [it should be put] in the [category of] undergoing.' Well, here too it must be repeated that
15 being-in-a-position, thought of purely, is not infected[349] whatsoever by actions or affections, and since it lies outside of both it has its own

special category *per se*. So if someone says that acting and undergoing are also manifested along with being-in-a-position,[350] then [acting and undergoing] will coexist with it as distinct genera with a distinct [genus], in consequence of the mixed convergence of [categories in] perceivable things. But it is better to define the [category of] being-in-a-position with precision, as Boethus too thinks one should: for he says that just those things belong to the category [of being-in-a-position] in the case of which neither acting nor undergoing is additionally present [merely] in virtue of the position in which they are positioned   20
or in virtue of the order in which they are arranged, as for example standing or sitting said of a statue, or an image's being set up. In our case it is indeed true that such things[351] co-manifest an *operation*,[352] but in the case of inanimate things these [positions] do not indicate either acting or undergoing, but only the pure [category of] being-in-a-position. Now since, in the cases of being set up and lying down, the place *up* and [the place] *down* are additionally thought of along with them, and a relation to particular places is co-manifested, we ought   25
to take the view that being-in-a-position exists *per se*, prior [to any further determinations], and that the relation to *up* and *down* then supervenes on it, in just the way also that the [category of] relative was always a natural offshoot growing beside the other categories.[353] But being-in-a-position has acquired its nature prior to the relative, and exists *per se*, as does each of the other genera which precede the [genus of] relative, too. If we placed everything on which relatives   30
supervene among the relatives, we should inevitably, as Plotinus himself said,[354] place all the genera among the relatives. These things, then, are what I have to say in response to Plotinus' puzzles.

Iamblichus says that being-in-a-position is considered in one way in the case of bodies – in terms of their having dimension and being divisible into parts and having a place which [likewise] has dimension   35
– and in another way in the case of the soul: 'For indeed the latter is said to be the place of the reasonings (*logoi*) in it, since it provides a domain for them in order that they may be situated and operate in it. In another sense the mind is said to be a place for the forms, since   340,1
it has the same substance as the forms, and contains its thoughts together with the forms within itself. In the strictest sense everything is said to be positioned in god, since all that comes after him is comprehended in him. But perhaps (he goes on) it will seem to some that being-in-a-position, thus [said], is being said in many ways, in one way in the case of bodies, and in another way in the case of   5
incorporeals. But that is not so: if one reflects more precisely on the matter, one and the[355] same analogy is observed in the cases of containing and being contained, and in the cases of providing a location and being situated. For the same account of being-in-a-position runs through all of these cases, namely of *one thing being limited*

within another, in respect of cause, or potentiality, or operation, or substance, or dimension. A difference [among the cases] comes about
10   in view of the fact that the objects are different and establish their position in relation to different things, but that [difference] does not displace the single account of being-in-a-position out of itself.' Let this be our account of the [category of] being-in-a-position, in addition [to the others], bearing in mind that being-in-a-position is, in the strict sense, ascribed to bodies.

On When and Where

15   After the [category of] being-in-a-position the order of the remaining categories is doubtful. For even Aristotle refers to the order differently on different occasions, at the beginning (ch. 4) placing the [category of] where and that of when before that of being-in-a-position and that of having, and putting acting and undergoing last of all; but as he proceeds he puts acting and undergoing before [these others], and places being-in-a-position before when and where, although he previously placed it after them. The others too he arranges differently
20   on different occasions, sometimes indeed manifestly changing their order in the same place. For in saying 'concerning when, where and having' (11b11-12), he is clearly distinguishing [the order of these categories] in one way, but in his supplementary explanation (11b13-14) he distinguishes their order differently. And he manifestly does not keep to the same order in the case of the preceding categories either, for which he produces the bulk of his account, but rather
25   whereas at one point (1b29) he places the [category of] quality before that of relative, in his discursive treatment of them [he places] the [category of] relative [before] that of quality.

In general, Aristotle nowhere expressed any reason for the order of the genera. Archytas, on the other hand, specifies the order of the categories together with a reason for it, and preserves the same one on the whole, except that he too changes their order at some points.
30   For in his account of the order [of acting, undergoing and where], he says:[356] 'Since everything which is moved is moved in a particular place, and [since] acting and undergoing are particular movements in operation, it is clear that place, in which the agent and the patient exist, must subsist first of all.' But when he comes to convey their differences and distinguishing marks, he places both the [category of]
341,1   acting and that of undergoing before that of where. And perhaps the reason for this kind of indifference regarding the order of the genera is the equal right to precedence (*antipleonektêsis*), in many cases, of the genera. Nevertheless a practice dominates among Aristotle's interpreters, with the effect that they place the category of when before that of where, since [Aristotle] himself here (11b11-12), having

mentioned being-in-a-position, added 'Concerning the remaining 5
ones – when and where' as though he were specifying this order for
them.

Now some people indeed think it right to advocate this particular
order, and they say that although everything moved is moved in time
and in place, the [category of] when is nevertheless prior to that of
where, because among generated things none can exist or have
existed or be going to exist without time, but many can do so without 10
place, as for instance place itself.[357] Deeds too are not in a place but
are in time, even though the doer is in a place. Against this Iamblichus
– though he keeps to the [Aristotelian] practice and discourses on the
[category of] when before [that of where] – gives the following rebut-
tal, saying: 'One ought not to refer the reason for the order of the
genera to *movement*. Rather, given that the [non-substantial] genera
subsist in connection with substance – since that [alone] enjoys its 15
existence *per se*, whereas these [non-substantial genera] subsist in
connection with it and in relation to it, contributing to the formation
of a unified combination – let us derive the order of the genera from
their order in relation to substance. So then, if place coexists with the
substance of bodies, while time coexists with movement, and [if] the
existence of things which come to be is prior to their *being moved*, the
genus which coexists with the *subsistent reality* of things which come 20
to be will be prior, and that which accompanies their *movement*
posterior.' But perhaps time too measures not merely the movement
of things coming to be in the sense of their *operation*, but also their
substantial [movement] (for the whole [process of] generation is a
movement),[358] just as place too contains the dimension [of a body] not
merely in respect of its *substance*, but also in respect of its *operation*.

But it is plausible that place is considered rather in connection with 25
the state of rest [of a body], while time [is considered] in connection
with its movement,[359] because even though time does measure a state
of rest, nevertheless the state of rest [of a body], as well [as its
movement], is measured by time in respect of the continuation and
flux of its existence. And besides, all the parts of place exist simultaneously, while those of time do not do so, and place has a clear
subsistent reality, while time [has an] obscure one, since its existence
is grasped by reason alone. But perhaps the truth is that just as the 30
parts of time do not exist at the same time, so also [the parts] of place,
in consequence of their dimension, do not exist in the same place, even
though they do exist at the same time.

But if someone should contend that time belongs to more things
than place, since all generated things are in time, whereas not all of
them are in a place – for neither is place in a place, nor deeds, which
are many and various – let him first of all bear in mind that even 35
though time belongs to more things [than place], this does not suffice

342,1 for superiority in their order. 'For clearly,' says Iamblichus, 'no one could reasonably put the relatives – which extend through all things – before the [category of] substance or that of quality, on the ground that these latter do not permeate the whole of reality.' But perhaps it is not actually true that the relatives permeate more things than do substance and quality: for the very character of the relative is
5 defined in terms of quality, and in the absence of substance neither the relative nor any other of the genera can subsist.

And it is possible to prove the following point by itself, namely that place too permeates everything, to no lesser degree than does time: for everything that comes to be does so in place. And though place is not in a place, neither is time in another time, since neither of these
10 stands in need of the containment (*sunokhê*) which it provides for other things – for nor is any of the other primary causes *itself* in need of the bestowal of benefits [which flows] from itself to other things. Even deeds do not in fact come about without place. Thus the order of these categories adopted by Archytas[360] does indeed have much reason to it. Some categories are arranged together in conjunction because of their inclination towards each other, such as that of acting
15 and that of undergoing: for the movement of the patient is conjoined with the operation of the [agent] moving it. Thus too the [category of] where and [that of] when are in a certain sense siblings of each other, since they make a common and equal contribution towards the whole [process of] generation, and perform an equal service for things which are moved. But the [category of] when should be put before [that of] where for the [purposes of] investigation, given that such is the nature
20 of Aristotle's enumeration (*aparithmêsis*).

It should be understood that although Aristotle put time and place in the [category of] quantity, but established when and where as two separate categories, Archytas, and following Archytas Andronicus, arranged when together with time, and where with place, and posited two categories in this way, so that they too preserved the number of
25 ten genera.[361] Those who follow Aristotle need to show firstly that time and place belong to the [category of] quantity, and secondly that[362] the [concept] when and [the concept] where do not denote time and place, but a *relation* to time and place, and that they deserve to be received into the number of most generic things. But Plotinus, in arranging the [concept] when together with time,[363] and claiming that
30 there are five categories in all, namely substance, quantity, quality, relative, and movement,[364] ought to have shown that time belongs either to quantity or to some one other of these five categories, if time was not to be completely thrown out of the [class of] existents. But that he does not[365] want it to be a quantity he made clear in his account of quantity,[366] saying: 'Now if time is construed as that which *measures*, we need to understand what it is that measures: either the soul

or the present instant.[367] But if [it is construed] as that which *is*   343,1
measured, then in respect of being[368] a certain duration, such as a
year, let it be a quantity, but in respect of being time [let it be] some
other nature: for duration is duration while being something other
[than time]. Time is indeed not [identical with] quantity, for (1)
quantity does not partake of anything else, and so will itself be
quantity in the strict sense;[369] and (2) if one lays down that all things
participating in quantity are quantities, then substance too will be   5
the same as quantity'. In the third book of the ones[370] on the genera
of being, [Plotinus] says:[371] '[It has frequently been said] that place
and time should not be thought of under the [category of] quantity,
but that time, by virtue of being the measure of movement, should be
assigned to the [category of] relative, and that place contains body,
so that this too resides in relation and the [category of] relative,
further, movement too is continuous and so was not put in [the   10
category of] quantity.' For Plotinus defined a single separate category
for it,[372] namely that of movement. Now in his remarks on time he
represents it not as a measure but rather as what is measured;[373] but
whether he represents it as a measure or as what is measured, given
that it is[374] *distinct* from measuring and being measured it will
possess measuring and being measured *accidentally*. Hence, just as
what is measured by a cubit-rule is not [*eo ipso*] said to be what it
is,[375] and if someone specifies movement as what is measured by   15
something, he does not say what this movement itself is, so also
someone mentioning a measuring thing or a measured thing does not
[*eo ipso*] mention time, but if anything a particular *accident* of time.
If, on the other hand, [Plotinus], like Plato,[376] says that it [i.e. time]
is a moving image of eternity,[377] then he obliterates its being a
relative: for then even if measuring and being measured belong to it
by virtue of a relation, they belong to it not as something which *is* a
relation but as something else subsisting *before* that relation: so in   20
this way too [time will have been characterised] neither *per se* nor as
a relative.[378] So much against Plotinus.

It is, however, possible to say on his behalf that time is observed
in *substances*, here being neither a quantity nor a relative, and in this
way will be subsumed under one of the five categories which he
posited. For if [time] is a moving image of eternity, then, just as
eternity [contains] the things which *are*, so too [time], analogously,   25
contains the things here [below];[379] and so if *that* [i.e. eternity] is a
mind containing all thoughts and all forms, then *this* [i.e. time]
embraces in itself all principles of things coming to be; and if *that* is
defined in terms of its state of rest and persistence in a single
[condition], then *this* has its being in being-moved in accordance with
a certain substantial life and movement, as well as in changing from
one principle (*logos*) to another principle. And if time consists in the   30

principles of the soul and in the transitional operation of these [principles], then it will be in the same genus as the one in which the principle of the soul is. For indeed if Plotinus too, like some others, abandoned the idea that the movement of the principles [of the soul] is substantial, he would have to say that one should put time not under the [category of] substance, but under the [category of] movement, in accordance with the transitional movement of the soul. But if, in the view of these people too, the operations of the principles [of the soul] *are* substantial, then time too will fall under the [category of] substance – the sort of substance which is intermediate between intelligible things and perceivable things. And on this approach [Plotinus] would say that the [concept] when does not need to be added to the categories:[380] for it belongs to time, and time has been arranged under substance. And he clearly says this on the basis that if the [concept] when and time do not differ, or even if they do differ, the [concept] when does not deserve a position as a separate category. But these matters will be examined shortly.

Since Aristotle[381] was persuaded that time derives from operation itself,[382] and noting that its essence is unclear, he returned to it on many occasions, sometimes to it as the number of movement,[383] sometimes as a measure [of movement],[384] sometimes as a part of movement,[385] and sometimes as [a part] of rest too.[386] And since he construed that [essence] as a concept of [the] continuous which accrues to everything, he placed it in the same genus as the continuous and the quantum (*pêlikon*), and this was the [category of] quantity. Now, just as in the case of all the other quanta and quantities some are measured by the [units] yielded by one item[387] among themselves, as for example ten men [are measured] by the [units] yielded by a single [man],[388] whereas others [are measured only] when we place some measure against them, such as a foot or a gallon (*khous*) or a bushel (*medimnos*), so too in the same way time, being a particular one of the continuous quantities, is measured by its own parts. For[389] just as in the case of a large surface no [naturally] separated or circumscribed part is observed, but when we place some measure on it, such as a foot or one of the other measures, [the surface] itself thereby gains[390] a boundary in accordance with that measure, so also, once we have posited a perceptually very short time bounded by durationless instants, such as an hour or the time called [an hour] by the makers of sun-dials, time is measured by this. We also circumscribe some things naturally with larger bounds, such as in terms of a day, a night, the revolution of the sun consisting of both, a month, a year, and other such [bounds].[391] Hence quantum and[392] quantity are [at least] naturally united with it [i.e. time] – even though its essence is not quantity[393] – whereas it possesses measuring and being measured and relative in general [merely] adventitiously.

So in consequence of this [Aristotle] arranged time not in the [category of] relative but in the [category of] quantity, this being naturally united [with time], and he thought those things which have a *relation* to temporal measures deserving of another category. For *yesterday* and *tomorrow* have a certain relation to the period of twenty-four hours (*to nukhthêmeron*), the former to the one that has gone by, the latter to the one that is to come; *the current day* [has a relation] to the motion [of the sun] from sunrise to sunset; *the last year* [has a relation] to the past orbit of the sun, *the current year* to the present one; finally, *just now* and *presently* [relate] indefinitely to the present [moment], *formerly* to the past, and *not yet* to the future. So he set up another genus for all these [phenomena], of which there are many, namely the [category of] when.

'We have reached this solution,' says Iamblichus, 'on the basis of the contribution of others, but (he goes on) when we pursue the issue regarding these matters by ourselves, we affirm that the essence of time is not at all incomprehensible, but is quite evidently located in the [category of] quantity. For in addition to everything else, the following statement conflicts with itself, that the essence of time is not quantity, but that quantity is in a special way naturally united with it [i.e. time]: for everything naturally united [with something] inheres in it as a matter of its *essence*, and what coexists [with something] as a special feature of its *being* does not stand aloof from its essence. (However, the [concept] when is not at all the same as time, but if anything [it exists] by virtue of a *relation towards* time: for it is formally constituted strictly in virtue of its being *different* from time on the one hand and *observed in* time on the other.) That time *is* a quantity is to be proved as follows. Not only does it measure movement, but it is also measured by it, just as Aristotle says:[394] for we define greater and lesser time by having regard to all the in-between things, the amount and length of these, and the long and short movements, just as, again, we also measure magnitude and movement by one another. For we call a route long if the journey along it is long, and again [we call] a journey long when the route has a sufficient length. And it is reasonable that this should obtain: for the[395] movement is consequential upon the magnitude, and the time taken upon this [movement]: for these three things are continuous and divisible in exactly the same way. Hence time as well [as magnitude], it seems, is a quantity, since each of these is measured by what is kin to it: units will be measured by a unit, and whole movements by a movement.

'So what is this [movement], if not circular motion? For that is regular (*homalês*), and the measure must be regular and determinate. Hence, since time is measured by movement, circular motion will be the measure of time as of movements too. In agreement with this also

345,1

5

10

15

20

25

30

is the common saying that human affairs and all things that come to be [move] in a circle, and that time is a kind of circle and revolution, just as are the things in it as well: for [time] is a measure of such motion and is also itself measured by such [motion]. Hence Aristotle, being aware that in the common conceptions the following is clearly
35   defined, namely that time is continuous and a quantity, employed this as a commonly accepted axiom. That is also why [Aristotle] completely denies[396] that things which are not naturally either moved or at rest, but are by nature motionless (*akinêta*)[397] – such as are
346,1   thoughts – are in time.

    'Given that movement is in time, rest must also exist together with time: for time is also a measure for this [i.e. rest], since not every motionless thing is *at rest*, but [only] what can, by its nature, be moved, although it is at that instant deprived of movement. Hence, since a state of rest has both a temporal beginning and a [temporal]
5   end, it is clear that it too is measured by time. But primarily time is the measure of *movement* [sc. rather than rest]. And just as being numerical (*en arithmôi*) is the same as the object's being measured by number, so too being temporal (*en khronôi*) is the same as the object's being measured by time. Hence again time is the measure of continuous quantity and continuous movement, so that we reason-
10   ably define it in terms of the quantified and the continuous. And that is also why its definition has been appropriately expounded [by Aristotle][398] as the number of every kind of movement and the measure of before and after in respect of movement. And there seems to be the same conception of time among the ancient opinions: for they take time to be either movement or some part of movement, whether separable or inseparable. Strato,[399] for example, in saying that time
15   was the quantity of movement, hypothesised it as an inseparable part of movement, whereas Theophrastus, in saying that it is a particular accident [of movement], and Aristotle, [in saying] that it is the number [of movement], [both] regarded it as separable [from movement]; but whenever [Aristotle] says that it is a state or an affection of movement,[400] he too construes it as inseparable. He does not touch on these matters here [i.e. in the *Categories*], however, since owing to their intricacy they go beyond the scope of an introductory treatise,
20   but [simply] adopts, as a commonly accepted axiom, the claim that time is continuous and quantified.

    'And he said that it is not the number of [discrete] *units*; but instead of the word "measure" he has employed the word "number" – [inaccu-rately,] for measuring is not the same as numbering.[401] Measurement is of before and after in movement, regardless of what kind of movement it is, whether of generation or destruction, of increase or diminution, or of alteration or change of place. And that time is a
25   *continuous* quantity and not divided discretely is clear from the fact

that any given part of it is [further] divisible:[402] for as we divide [time]
we do not come to an end at something indivisible, as we do, in the
case of [discrete] number, at the unit, which is indivisible. And it is
clear that [time] is consequential upon magnitude and movement,
which are by common consent continuous. As a result Aristotle
neither thinks that time is incomprehensible, nor does he think that
its nature is something apart from quantity. And indeed it would in   30
any case have been absurd, as has been said (345,11ff.), not to regard
the essence of time as quantity, while construing quantity as being
naturally united with it: for nothing which is naturally united [with
something] is outside its essence. And nor would [Aristotle] ever have
made the received physical measurements of time, such as the revolution of the sun or moon, another kind of category:[403] rather, these   35
things complement time, and embrace it with measurements. But
whenever some object which is different from time and not construed   347,1
as a part of time has a *relation* to time and is therefore *in* time – as
for instance the sea battle at Salamis [occurred] *in* this particular
time – then another category comes into being, namely that of when,
which is different from the [category of] quantity.' And this is indeed
Aristotle's opinion.   5

Archytas and Andronicus posited as a particular separate nature
[i.e. category] that of time, and they arranged the [concept] when
together with it, since it [i.e. when] subsists in connection with time.
For he [i.e. Archytas] proposes to construe the primary [and] first
genera of reality, around which the other things subsist, as the
principal ones. Since therefore time has been treated as prior to when,
and place as prior to where, in respect of their very existence, he   10
reasonably regards them [i.e. time and place] as primary [genera],[404]
passing over the things included in them as being secondary to them.
Accordingly, it has been shown in what has been said how on the one
hand Aristotle, paying heed to the differences in their meanings, puts
the [concept] when in another category [from time]; and how on the
other hand Archytas, having regard to the kinship in respect of their
objects, arranged the [concept] when together with time; and how   15
finally Plotinus, in reducing the primary genera to the smallest
number, and in not granting much significance to the divergences
(*parallagai*) between the conceptions and meanings [of time and
when], did away with the category of when.[405]

But we must next turn to the puzzles which have been mooted in
connection with the [category of] when, and match their solutions to
them. So then, when the followers of Plotinus and Andronicus say
that *yesterday* and *tomorrow* and *last year* are parts of time, and on   20
account of this think that they should be arranged together with time,
we shall reply that these things are not *parts* of time, but contain a
relation of the objects which are *in* time *towards* time, and that each

of these things[406] is different from the other. 'But,' they say, 'if *yesterday* is past time, or a measure of time, it will be a kind of composite, given that the past is one thing and time another, and so
25   the [concept] *when* will be two categories, and not one simple one.' Well, by the same reasoning we shall say that if animal is one thing, rational another, and mortal another, then they will not be simple, but will be three categories. But if in this case we comprehend the three things together in one species [i.e. man], then time and the past, too, contribute to one object and do not make two categories.

    But perhaps *yesterday* is not past time *simpliciter*, and [perhaps]
30   in this case it is not that a plurality of concepts coalesce in the same thing: for *yesterday* is formally constituted just by the relation itself of the [relevant] object to time. 'But,' they say, 'if the [concept] *when* is said to be what is *in* time, and if you say that this thing which is in time is a particular object, such as Socrates – because Socrates existed last year [say] – well, he belongs to another category [i.e. substance]; if, on the other hand, [you say] that [what is in time is] time, this too belongs to another [category, i.e. quantity]; and if [you say] that [what
35   is in time is] the composite, then there will not be just one category [of *when*].' In fact, neither the objects in time, nor time itself, nor the composite of both of these formally constitute the category of *when*, but rather the bare *relation* of the [relevant] object towards time. That
348,1 is why we shall admit into the [category of] *when* neither *parts* of time nor the *objects* [in time], but rather this [category] too will be simple, just as the other genera are. And Boethus indeed hypothesises that time is a different thing from what partakes of time and is in time, and [says that] *a year* and *a month* are time, whereas *yearly* and
5   *monthly* partake of time, just as wisdom is of a different category from [what is done] in accordance with wisdom, such as is acting wisely: the former belongs to the [category of] quality, the latter to the [category of] acting. In this way too *time* and what is *in respect of time* differ.

    But since, on the basis of the unclarity of the thing, some people conflate these different things into the same [genus], something should be said to these people too by way of reassurance, namely that
10   the [concept] *when* has two aspects: *time*, and what is peculiarly *in time*. In just the same way *always* too [has two aspects to it]: what is in time, in accordance with which we say, 'There is always action', and time [itself], [the word 'always' (*aei*) being] a derivative (*parônumon*) of the word 'eternity' (*aiôn*). Likewise too *last year* has two aspects, but *next year* and *this year* do not: they just denote what is in time.[407] And people posit as differences of time *past, present* and *future*, but as differences of the [concept] *when* *last year, next year*
15   and *this year*. And *long ago*, when we say 'So-and-so, being long ago (*ho palai ôn*) ...', denotes time [*simpliciter*], but when [we say] 'He did

it long ago', [it denotes what is] in time. And in just the same way *just now*[408] and *now* and *already* denote both time [itself] and [what is] in time. But *taking time* [denotes] what is in time, not time [itself]: for taking time does not [itself] take time,[409] because time is not in time, and taking time in fact belongs to the [category of] when, even though it employs the [grammatical] *form* of acting (for both the man being cut and the man cutting take time), as for instance we speak of 20 hastening and dallying.[410] And time is infinite, whereas the [concept] when is limited, since a deed *in* it [i.e. in time] is also limited, which is why the [category of] when has been expelled from the divine. But let this suffice as an additional account covering the usage of the names.

Concerning the [category of] when and that of where I admire Aristotle's sagacity in the way he – despite following Archytas in other 25 respects – nevertheless saw the difference between what is *in time* and [what is] *in place* [sc. from time and place respectively], and that they could be placed in different genera [sc. from time and place]. But one can obviously raise the question why, given that there are many ways things are said to be *in* something (at least eleven),[411] [Aristotle] characterised for us only these two out of [all] the [ways of being] in something – being in time and in place – as separate categories. [Something] is said to be in something [else] (1) as the accident in the substance, and in general what is in the underlying subject, and (2) 30 as the parts in the whole, and (3) as the whole in the parts, and (4) as the form in the matter, and furthermore (5) as the genus in the species, and (6) as the species in the genus,[412] and in addition to these (7) as the things belonging to the ruled in the ruler, and (8) the ruler's things in the ruled, and (9) as what is in a vessel, and [as] the things now before us, (10) what is in place and (11) what is in time. 35

Given that being in something is said in so many ways, why do separate categories come into existence only in the case of these two relations? For if white is one thing and body another, and the being 349,1 of white *in* a body yet another thing, and [if] white is analogous to Socrates, body to time, and white's being in a body [analogous] to Socrates' being in time, why does a separate category not come into existence for this kind of *being in* too? Plotinus too raises this difficulty in his treatment of the [category of] where, saying the 5 following:[413] 'If what is in time is different from time and what is in place is different from place, why will not what is in a vessel create an additional category, and what is in matter another, and what is in an underlying subject another, and the part in a whole [another], and the whole in its parts[414] [another], and a genus in its species [another], and a species in its genus [yet another]? But on that basis our categories will be more [than Aristotle envisaged].'

In solving this puzzle Iamblichus says that what is [in something] 10 as in a vessel, or as in matter, or as in an underlying subject, manifests *spatial* relations, whereas the whole in relation to the parts and the parts in relation to the whole have the relation of the [category of] *relative*, and likewise too the genus in relation to the species and the species in relation to the genus; and that the relation of the [category of] relative has nothing in common with the relation to place

15 and the relation to time. But I rather think that someone will say that in these cases [i.e. place and time] the [category of] relative *is* observed in one way, and being in something [is observed] in another way: for what is in place, insofar as it is accommodated [in place] and the place accommodates it, will indeed belong to the relatives. And[415] how could *both* what [is in something] as in an underlying subject *and* what [is in something] as in a vessel be the same as what is in place?[416] So perhaps one should say that not everything which is in something deserves a specific category, but only those in which (1) one [compo-

20 nent] contains and the other is contained, and (2) each [component] preserves its own nature, neither becoming part of the other, nor constituting the other – for in these cases alone does it happen that the thing itself which is in something [else] is a certain determinate nature subsisting in accordance with the relation itself [sc. of being in something] – and when (3) the universal has necessarily also to obtain, as for example the body's being in place and time:[417] but the things which are in them [i.e. in place and time] subsist *in addition*

25 [to them], and are separated from the *particular* time and place [in which they subsist].

Of the other significations of [being] in something, however, some are constitutive, such as the parts and the whole and the genera and the species and the ruler and the ruled, and others cannot subsist separately [from what they are in], such the form in matter, and the accident in an underlying subject, and this [accident] also becomes the form of the subject, which explains why the subject is also called

30 after that [accident] – as for instance 'white' or 'increased' – and similarly for the other categories belonging to substance. How then could one thing be strictly *in* another thing when the things are not distinguished from each other *simpliciter*, in terms of their subsistent reality, but only notionally, in the way we distinguish the genera? But the things in time and in place are [genuinely] different from place

350,1 and time. Hence also things which are the same in number sometimes come to be in one [sc. place or time] and sometimes in another, whereas it is impossible for numerically the same thing to come to be sometimes in one underlying subject and sometimes in another.[418] And what is in a vessel is in place: for a vessel is a portable place. For this reason the legislators of names have established different names[419] for the [category of] when – 'yesterday', 'tomorrow', 'last

5 year', 'this year' and 'next year' – and for the [category of] where – 'in

the Lyceum', 'in the market-pace' – whereas in the other cases of *being in* it is not customary to say 'the white is in the body', but rather 'the body is white', and 'the head is an animal's', 'man is an animal', 'the composite is [composed] out of matter and form'. This seems to me to solve the matter for the time being, but if it is possible to do it in another way too, that would be good.

In conveying the nature of time more theoretically, Iamblichus   10
again chooses as his guide Archytas, who says that 'time is the number of a certain movement or, more generally, the extension (*diastêma*) of the nature of the universe too'.[420] In this he does not conflate together the opinions of Aristotle and the Stoics, as some think,[421] because Aristotle says that time is the number of *movement* [sc. without qualification],[422] whereas of the Stoics Zeno[423] said that   15
time is the extension of *all* movement *simpliciter*, while Chrysippus[424] [called it] the extension of the movement of the world. Now [Archytas] does not join [these] two definitions[425] together, but establishes a single definition, one which is special [to time] and goes beyond the assertions of the other [definitions]: for he did not say that time is the number of *all* movement, as Aristotle defined it, but rather [the number] of a *certain* movement – not [the movement] of one of the *particulars* (*ta en merei*), such as the [movement] of the heavens or that of the sun or of some other definite thing among the particulars,   20
since on that basis time would not be of the nature of a principle, nor would it extend commonly to everything, nor would it deserve to be defined among the primary genera. Instead, by means of this [definition], [Archytas] altogether expresses a movement which is of the nature of a principle and is the cause of being for the other movements. For people are accustomed in all cases to place foremost what has prior existence as a single form and is predicated homonymously   25
of what [exists] subsequently,[426] as for example the principle of man himself[427] [is predicated] of the many men. So too here [Archytas] places a single movement foremost, as cause of the many [individual] movements, and, being the origin of movement, this [movement] had according to Plato[428] necessarily to be self-moving, while according to Aristotle[429] [it had to be] unmoved.

In consequence it is plausible that [Archytas] is, by means of these [characterisations], expressing the substantial movement of the soul, and the projection (*probolê*) [into the world] of the principles belong-   30
ing to it by virtue of its substance, and the transition from some [principles] to others: for he says that this single and particular movement is appropriate to time.[430] And he says that its number is the one which is at this moment generative, proceeding to the creation of the things in the world, and which continuously produces passages or transitions by virtue of the projections of the things brought forth from it, and this clearly is time. This differs[431] considerably from the

351,1   number [of movement] referred to by Aristotle: for he considers it to
be an externally supervening measure of what is continuous, whereas
Archytas establishes it as a measure of movement itself, inherent [in
it] and not external [to it], as Aristotle [thinks]. 'And,' says Iamblichus, 'the Peripatetic opinion seems to have deviated from the
5   Pythagorean instruction. The reason for this is that the recent [think-
ers] have not held the same view of number and movement as the
ancients, but think that they are accidents, and consider them to be
externally adventitious, whereas [the ancients] regard them as substantial.'

But I admire the following feature of Aristotle's sagacity, namely
how he too[432] posited the soul as the proximate cause of time: for in
10   seeking what it is which *numbers* [time], he talked of the soul.[433] For
if the soul is the origin and cause of all movement – whether *qua*
self-moving, as Plato thought, or *qua* unmoved, as Aristotle thought
– it will also, in all probability, be the cause of *temporal* movement.
But given that Archytas says that the number [of time] is the
generative time, which proceeds from the soul-movement as from its
unit (*monas*), it is clear that he also regarded that movement as a unit
15   of time, and so it would seem that he posits as time the primary
movement in, and proceeding from, the soul, and within which all
other movement is contained, arranged and measured – for the
measurer ought to be articulated alongside the measured, and be
more of the nature of a principle than it.

The Stoics, in taking over [from Archytas] the definition [of time]
which calls it 'the general extension of the nature of the universe',
20   changed the account to 'the extension of movement', and [in so doing]
they go wrong, because, while the Pythagoreans define the extension
[of time] as one which is physical and [inherent] in physical principles,
and indeed, if one wanted so to call them, in the seminal principles
(*spermatikoi logoi*)[434] – just as indeed Cornutus later on surmised was
the case[435] – or, as one might say more accurately, they define the
extension [of time] in accordance with principles which are prior even
to the seminal principles, namely the [principles] of the entire nature
25   of the world, in which the soul too is embraced, the Stoics are not able
to distinguish clearly what sort of extension they are talking about,
but seem rather to construe it as the corporeal extension of corporeal
movements or to explain it as something linear (*grammoeides*) – a
view which is shown to be full of absurdity in their very own accounts
of time. But this is not the sort of account we get from the ancients.
30   For the phrase 'of the nature of the universe', combined with the word
'extension', makes clear what sort of thing they are explaining extension to be: for this sort [of extension] fits the principles of nature.[436]

The opinion of still more ancient [thinkers] also agrees in giving
the same [account].[437] Some of them define time, as indeed the name

[i.e. *khronos*] makes clear, in terms of a kind of dance (*khoreia*) of the soul around the mind (*nous*),[438] others in terms of the revolutions of the soul and its mind, still others in terms of the physical dance around the mind, and yet others in terms of the circular orbits [sc. of the heavenly bodies] – all of which the Pythagorean philosophical system embraced. For the general extension of the nature of the universe embraces all the universe's natures in general, and permeates them wholly and completely; and it determines time [as] originating from the first principles above and permeating as far as a particular point, and as determining its extension in general in terms of the transition and movement of the principles as a whole. For what,[439] in the case of things in generation, this present instant indicates as [being] a *change* in comparison with the previous instant, and [what] this [i.e. the current] movement [indicates as being a change] in comparison with the first[440] movement, just this is observed, though in a way which is very much prior and more primary, as having prior existence in the case of the essence of the physical principles as a whole, and strictly constitutes the extension of the time which is the eldest of all things.[441]

But now the account has expounded these as *two* definitions of time, and it is necessary to unite them both into one:[442] for in this way the whole nature of time will be being considered. For the generative time, being the number of self-moving movement taken as a temporal unit, is an extension of physical principles – not the [extension] in respect of size, nor that in respect of external movement *simpliciter*, but the extension in respect of the order which pre-exists movement, in which the prior and posterior are first arranged and provide both deeds and movements with their order. For the prior and the secondary among things cannot be calculated unless time – to which the order of our deeds too is referred – pre-exists *per se*. But that will suffice on the essence of time.

Archytas conveyed its distinguishing mark by appeal to a number of features, and there is nothing untoward, especially in view of the scarcity of Pythagorean writings, in transcribing the whole of his text concerning this topic:[443] 'The [concept] when and time have in general partlessness and insubstantiality as their distinguishing mark.[444] For the present instant, being[445] partless, is no sooner thought of and mentioned than it has become past and is not enduring. For since it is continuously coming to be, it is never preserved as numerically the same thing, though [it is preserved] formally.[446] The time which is now current, and the [time] which is going to be, are not the same as the previous [time]: for the latter has vanished and is no more, while the former, as soon as it is thought of and has become current, has gone. In this way the present instant always joins [things] together in a continuum, by coming to be one [point] after another, and being destroyed, though [remaining] the same in form. For every instant is partless and indivisible and a limit of what has previously been, but the beginning of what will be, just as, when a straight line is broken,

353,1   the point at which the fracture occurs becomes the beginning of one line, and the limit of another.[447] Time is continuous and not divided discretely like number, speech and harmony:[448] the parts of speech are the syllables – and these are divided discretely – of harmony [they are] the sounds, and of number [they are] the units. Line and area

5   and place are continuous: their parts, when divided up, create shared boundaries. For a line is cut at a point, a surface at a line, and a solid at a surface. Now time too is continuous: for there never was nature when there was no time,[449] nor movement when the instant was not there. But the instant always was and will be and will never fail, as

10   it comes to be one [point] after another – different in number, but the same in form. And indeed [time] differs from the other continuous [quantities], because the parts of a line and of an area and of a place subsist, whereas the [parts] of time which have come to be have been destroyed,[450] and those which will come to be will be destroyed. Hence either time does not exist at all, or it exists obscurely and only just. For how can something of which the past no longer exists, the future

15   does not yet exist, and the present instant is partless and indivisible, really exist?'

Now in [interpreting] this account some consider the partlessness of time in connection with the present instant – which is both a limit and a beginning of time – and [they also consider] the insubstantiality [of time in connection with the present instant], to the extent that the past has been destroyed, while the present instant is no sooner thought of and mentioned than it has become past.[451] Iamblichus,[452] however, in asking how partlessness and insubstantiality belong to

20   time, says that they are incompatible, and so denies that one can ascribe them both to the same thing; rather, he defines the *partlessness* [of time] in terms of the forms – in themselves stationary – of the principles [of time], and he posits its *insubstantiality* in terms of the movements proceeding from those [forms], since these [movements] do not preserve the indivisible and motionless essence [of time]. And

25   he further defines the *indivisibility* [of time] in terms of the operation and perfection residing in its essence, distinguishing its *insubstanti-*

354,1   *ality* in his account in terms of its inclination away from being, issuing forth in generation. Hence, so Iamblichus says, neither will its partlessness, which is time's distinguishing feature, be insubstantial, nor its substantial reality (*to hupostaton*) be insubstantial (*anupostaton*) – for that is a contradiction – but rather its partlessness and its insubstantiality are discretely divided in application to different natures, on the one hand [to] the more noble [natures], and on the

5   other hand [to] those lacking the elder nature and on that account

called insubstantial – not because they do not exist at all, but because they do not preserve the purity and immaculacy of the first essence. For of this kind are all things which have their existence in coming to be and are not strictly said either to be or not to be. Since, therefore, the past [portion] of time no longer exists and the future [portion] does not yet exist, but only the current one appears to exist, as something which is partless (since it is taken as the present instant) and which retires, simultaneously with its being, into not-being, [Iamblichus] accordingly says that it is for this reason that its [i.e. time's] distinguishing mark is its partlessness together with its insubstantiality.

Iamblichus, moreover, does not accept [the views of] those who consider the partlessness [of time to reside] in our flowing and generated time, and who say that it [i.e. the partlessness] is insubstantial on the ground that it never *is*, but is always *coming to be*: 'For everything coming to be,' he says, 'or what is moved in any way, is incapable of being partless: for every movement is endlessly divisible by virtue of its continuity. But what is indivisible as well [sc. as what is partless] automatically stands fast in its very being: if it eternally came to be, it would not preserve its form, but if it were expressly to be said to preserve its form,[453] it could not come to be eternally. And so[454] if [Archytas] wants to say (he continues) that the present instant is no sooner thought of and mentioned than it has fallen into the past, he should posit this sort of displacement [sc. only] among the *things which participate* in time.[455] For things that come to be cannot receive the indivisible essence [of time] motionlessly, but as they partake of it at different times with different parts of themselves, *their* undergoing is falsely ascribed to *it*. In consequence, too, the [sc. alleged] numerical diversity in constant alteration [of the instant] is [in fact] an indication of the differentiation of the participating *things*, while the permanence of the form indicates the stable identity of the partless *instant* [itself]. And this is well said, if we are to be able to comprehend in reasoning what is stable in the flux of generation.

'But when ([Iamblichus] goes on) Archytas says that the time at the present instant and the time to come are not the same as the previous [time] (for the latter has vanished and is no more, while the former, as soon as it is thought of and has become current, has gone), such [claims] ([Iamblichus] says) stand in need of a distinction for the sake of complete clarity: one should say that the whole of time is both the same[456] and not the same, just like the present instant too – for in respect of its essence and its form [the present instant] is one and the same, but insofar as it divides the past and the future it is many and different things. So too the points [sc. on a line] are each in some sense one, but in terms of their position and the division [which they

effect] they are [each] many and not the same: for insofar as we think
of the point as dividing, the single point becomes two – the one as an
end, the other as a beginning – and just so the instant, by becoming
successively different things in the division [which it effects], while
remaining the same in form, always joins up the whole of time within
itself and renders it continuous. And so when [Archytas] says that
the instant comes to be and is destroyed, one should understand here
not the generation and destruction of the instant itself, but that of
the things participating or not participating in it. For the rendering
continuous and joining up [of time] is the function of nothing other
than the partless [instant], but the coming to be successively different
things and being destroyed and the perpetual flowing is most appropriately [regarded as] a matter of the participation, in generation, in
the present instant.[457]

'Now how is it that the same thing both becomes successively
different things and remains the same in form, is both divided and
indivisible, is both altered and comprehends in one the limit [of the
previous time] and the beginning [of the next time]? Well, because
the instant which is participated in in nature, and which is inseparable from things coming to be, was [taken to be] different from the one
which is separate and [exists] *per se*: the latter [instant] stands fast
in the same form in the same way, while the former is observed in
continuous motion. But since these two aspects have been comprehended together in the instant's [role as an] origin rendering time
continuous, it was very clearly on this basis that [Archytas] likened
time's instant to the point about which there is a fracture when a
straight line is broken into an angle. For just as the point becomes
the beginning of one line and the limit of the other, so too the instant
comprehends in itself the beginning and the end of the whole of time:
it does not do this as an accident [of time], but as rendering it [i.e.
time] continuous and including its essence[458] within itself and sup-
plying it out of itself. One should not, therefore, expound [the nature
of time] as though the instant did not exist: for its oneness in respect
of form remains the same, and that is more important than its
numerical diversity.

'But, they say, it joins the limits of non-existents. We say, however,
that it is not *dispersed* among those non-existents, but both *contains*
in itself the non-existents and *exists* by itself, possessing a particular
individual essence. Time is continuous; it is not, however, rendered
continuous by a limit eternally coming to be and passing away, for
this [limit, i.e. the instant] stands fast in its own form, so that [time]
may both really be continuous and always be rendered continuous.
The [instant] which comes to be successively numerically different is
considered in connection with *another* instant, which has already
adopted a position and enjoys a combination with the things that

come to be. That is why, if one were to construe the instant as a part
of time, one would construe it as being naturally united with move- 30
ment; if, however, one were to represent[459] it not even as *time* [sc. let
alone as a part of time], then it would – as some have certainly judged
concerning it – be a separate *origin* of time, and would remain[460] the
same in form. And so when it is said that the past [portion] of time
no longer exists and that the future [portion] does not yet exist, it is
to be appreciated that this is said of the instants which issue forth
[sc. from the instant *per se*], are harmonised with movement, and are
altered together with this motion, whereas the things which are 35
included in the instant [*per se*] and defined in it, and which never
depart from their proper origin – these always remain in the instant.
That is indeed also why it was reasonable to define time as a moving 356,1
image of eternity, since the soul is modelled on the mind, its rational
principles on thoughts, and the instant on that which remains in one
thing. And the [instant] which is inclusive of time is modelled on the
[instant] of that [eternity],[461] which includes simultaneously and
eternally within itself the things that are, and the moved [instant] of 5
this [time[462] is modelled] on the stationary [instant] of that [eternity],
and the measurement of generation by number [is modelled] on the
[measurement] of essences by oneness.'

It is worth noting that Plato too said that time is the image of
eternity moving in accordance with number,[463] since he regarded time
as the number of eternity [taken] as a unit. And perhaps it is more 10
natural to understand Archytas' [definition] too in this way, namely
to the effect that [time] is the number of a certain movement, not in
the sense that the movement denotes one time and the number
another, but in the sense that everything[464] is said of the same [time].
For just as eternity possessed[465] unity enduringly, and there was not
one eternity in respect of its stability and another in respect of its
unity, so also time – both that which subsists primarily in the soul, 15
and that which issues therefrom into generation – was the number
in movement, and the same [time] was also the extension of the
nature of the universe. For again, just as eternity, considered in
respect of its indivisible and motionless total essence altogether,
coexisted with reality, so too time, considered in respect of its moved
and ever-changing dimension of generation, coexisted with the generated universe. And this further point is worth considering too, 20
namely whether time subsisted primarily *in* the soul or *from* the soul.
For if the soul is an intermediate between indivisible and divisible
being, then it will also possess a measure, naturally united [with it],
intermediate between eternity and time and coexisting with this
[soul] in its being; and strict time subsists proximately *from* that
[intermediate measure] *in* strictly generated things. But this needs
to be investigated further. 25

It is right to add a mention of the service which time performs for the universe. For just as reality, thanks to eternity, exists simultaneously as a whole, contracted in a single thing, so too generation, thanks to time, is differentiated in its order. If there were no time, there would be a confounding of generations[466] and of deeds, so that [for instance] the present times would be confounded with those of
30 the Trojan War. But, given that time has so much power, how can Archytas say that it either does not exist at all or that it exists obscurely and only just? Well, no doubt because he has condemned it to this fate after comparing it with the things that strictly and truly exist, since it has its existence in coming to be, and [because] the past no longer exists, the future not yet, and the present instant is partless
35 and indivisible: how, therefore, he asks, should this thing exist, never mind *simpliciter*, but [even] truly? For really existing does not accord with time, any more than it does with generation either. Archytas
357,1 seems to give it [i.e. time] a weaker reality even than the other continuous things, because the parts of a line and of a surface and of a place do exist all together, whereas of time part has been destroyed, and part does not yet exist. But perhaps the things which [merely] seem to exist – since they are generated and always in flux – [really] do exist as the same in form, though not in number, just like time's
5 present instant also. So much, then, for the [category of] when; it is time to turn now to the next thing.

On the Category of Where

The [category of] where seems to be arranged after the [category of] when on the basis of their kinship towards one another: for just as place and time are akin, since they are both measures comprising the
10 continuity of generation, the former in respect of size, the latter in respect of the dimension of being, and [just as] they both model eternity's partlessness, which is contracted together simultaneously, so too the [category of] when and the [category of] where have a relation of kinship to one another. The [category of] where has been arranged after [that of when], because (1) place both is a limit of things coming to be and is considered as containing the other things,
15 and because (2) acting precedes moved things, time is conjoined with moved things as their measure, and moved things finish up at a position in a *place*, 'since,' as Iamblichus says, 'as long as [a thing] is being moved, it is not yet *in* a place; rather, it is being moved *in respect of* place, but is not yet thereby *in* a place'. And in general what has already come to be and is contained [in a place] needs a *place*, whereas
20 *time* measures the journey itself which brings it into being. For even though what comes to be comes to be in a place, still what is in a place is what has in every case come to be.[467] But Archytas says that place

has prior existence to movement and that time obviously does so too, [this] in the passage where he says:[468] 'Since everything moved is moved in a particular place, and [since] acting and undergoing are particular movements, it is clear that place, in which the agent and the patient exist, must subsist first of all.' Hence he who says that moved things do not exist *in* a place will, it seems, disagree with Archytas, unless indeed each thing is *moved* in a place, but does not *exist* in a place except insofar as it *has been* moved.[469]

Now it has already been said (342,21ff.) that Archytas and Andronicus placed the [concept] when in the same class as time, and the [concept] where in the same class as place, and that is how they established the two categories, whereas Aristotle put time and place in the [category of] quantity for the reasons mentioned earlier, and set up separate categories of when and where. For just as the [category of] relative,[470] considered with regard to its reciprocating and balancing relation, was a natural offshoot of the other genera – such as substance and quantity – which serve as a foundation for it, so too even though both the [category of] when and that of where are constituted together with the other genera, there is nothing wrong in positing special categories for them, providing only that they have their own special significations. For just as time was not the [same thing as] the [concept] when, nor is place the [same thing as] the [concept] where, but rather, just as in the case of time, time was one thing and what is *in respect of* time or is something *belonging to* time another, so too place is one thing and what is *in respect of* place or is something *belonging to* place another. For indeed quantity is one thing and something's belonging to quantity another. So therefore just as it is wrong to say that double and equal *are* quantity, given that they are something *belonging to* quantity, so too one would be wrong if one called what is in respect of place, or is something belonging to place, place. Plotinus,[471] however, dispensed completely with the category of where, since he too assigned the [concept] where to that of place, just like Archytas and Andronicus, and he further allocated place as well as time either to the [category of] quantity or to that of relative.

The [category of] where signifies two things, *place* and what is *in place*, just as the [category of] when was also said (348,9ff.) to signify two things, *past time* and what is *in time*.[472] But the category of where has been defined [sc. by Aristotle] according to the second signification: for what is spoken of as a place will, on Aristotle's view, be a quantity, while what is in place belongs to the category of where. Even though the phrase 'in place' (and 'in time') is a certain composite, something simple should be gathered from the compound expression, just as we take one particular simple [meaning] out of the expressions 'Good spirit' or 'Holy city'.[473] And this twofold meaning [of the category

of where] also pervades all the differences of place: for indeed *above*
20   and *below, forward* and *back, right* and *left* are twofold – some
[figuring] as places, others as being in a place – and it is clear that
those denoting a place are quantities, while those [denoting] the
things in a place will be ranged under the category of where. And the
meaning of where also extends to *whence*, as for instance *from Athens*
(*Athênêthen*), and to *whither*, as for instance *to Athens* (*Athênaze*):
25   these too denote both place and the relation in place.[474] And things
said with prepositions (*sundesmoi*) signify the same [as things said
with suffixes], such as *from the Lyceum* and *to the Lyceum* and *in the
Lyceum*: for they have the same force as *from Athens* (*Athênêthen*), *to
Athens* (*Athênaze*) and *at Athens* (*Athênêsi*). Deictics too, such as *there*
and *here, far* and *near*, and suchlike are to be placed in the same class
as these. But *Athenian* and *Rhodian* do not exhibit place, but rather
30   origin, and a relation to the place [of origin] is signified, not the
place.[475]

      The [category of] where also admits of contrariety in respect of the
differences of place such as *above, below, forward, back, to the right,
to the left*. It admits too of more and less. For one thing is more above
or more below or more forward or less [above, below or forward] than
another – at least those that do not slant away to the side – and
likewise [more or less] to the right or to the left. Further, some things
35   are said [to be in a place] indefinitely, others definitely, for [things
are] either in place *simpliciter* or in some particular place. And some
[are said to be in a place] in a broad sense, such as in Athens, others
are defined by a boundary, as when [something is said to be] in the
Lyceum or in this particular place within the Lyceum. That is how
these things are.

359,1   Cornutus[476] wonders why indeed, if the [concept] where and the
[concept] when differ from place and time respectively in point of the
way the [corresponding] *expressions* are characterised, and so, given
that [Aristotle's] purpose concerns *linguistic* characteristics, have
been arranged in their own special categories, [Aristotle] did not add
the following too to the same category, I mean things like 'from Dion'
(*Diônothen*) and 'towards Dion' (*eis Diôna*), and the many other things
5   of this kind that there are. For they are similar to the expression 'from
Athens' (*Athênêthen*) and 'towards Athens' (*eis Athênas*). In response
to this it suffices to say that the division of the categories does not
have regard to the character of an expression: for in general they[477]
reduced linguistic[478] differences to name and verb or some such, but
not to any particular category. In the case of these [i.e. the catego-
ries],[479] however, while one must certainly adhere to the words, one
should not do so according to the form of inflection (*ptôtikon skhêma*)
10   of the *expression* ['*F*'], but rather do so by dividing up the meanings
in accordance with the differences among *the things that are* [*F*]. In

consequence neither does 'place', just because it has the same [lin-
guistic] character as the word 'horse', belong to the same category [as
'horse'], nor does 'time', just because it has the same form of expression as 'wolf ', belong to the same category [as 'wolf '], but rather they
[i.e. place and time] belong to the [category of] quantity, while the
others [i.e. horse and wolf] belong to the [category of] substance.[480]

Again, the same man [i.e. Cornutus] thinks one should refer *far*   15
and *near* to the [category of] relative, since they have a spatial subject,
whereas Andronicus places them in the [category of] where, since they
are indefinite in respect of place. And given that difference *of place*
manifestly predominates in their case, they are indeed to be referred
to the [category of] where rather than to another genus. For they do
not obviously evince a reciprocating relation, as do *farther* and *nearer*,
but rather separation of place. [Cornutus] also looks at *simultane-*   20
ous,[481] *apart, drawing together, separated, side by side* and *underly-*
ing,[482] to see whether these should be posited as belonging to the
category of where or to that of being-in-a-position or indeed to that of
relative instead – for they are [sc. partly] governed by this [latter
category], just as *double*, though a quantity, manifests it. Perhaps,
however, they do not all have a single account, but things which are
simultaneous and things which draw together manifest rather the   25
[category of] *relative* – for these too present impartially a common and
reciprocating relation – whereas things which are apart and separated [manifest] the [relation] of the [category of] *where*: for the
relation of things that are apart and separated towards the place
[where they are] is greater in them [than their relation to each other].
Things lying side by side and underlying, however, belong to the
category of *being-in-a-position*, for their position takes precedence in
their case, and their relation [to what they are beside/underlie]
supervenes [on them] from outside. And we should discriminate the   30
other things too in this way, in terms of what is greater and predominates and puts its concept forward in an obvious way, assigning to
this the prize of [being] the genus [to which the item belongs].

Plotinus[483] puts forward the [examples] *in the Academy, in the*
Lyceum, above and *below*, and asks whether these things denote
different places or some things in another. 'For if [they denote] places,
why should we seek another [category of] where apart from place?   35
But if [they denote] one thing in another, such a thing [will] not be a
single thing, nor simple either.' To this we should reply here too that
neither a place nor any composite is signified by these words *simplici-*   360,1
ter: for the objects[484] in a place and the place itself are not *combined*,
but simply the *relation* itself [of the objects to the place], and that
alone, is implied.[485] Nor indeed does the particle 'in' in the phrase 'in
the Lyceum' import a combination, but it exhibits just the relation
towards the place. 'But,' he says, 'if we say this, we are generating a   5

particular relation of this man in that place, of the recipient to what it has received. So why are these not relatives, given that they have their being on the basis of the relation of one thing towards something else?' To this it must be replied that there is a distinction between, on the one hand, a relation which is balancing and reciprocating and is of things said to be just what they are *of* or *than* other things, or [said] in some other way *in relation to* other things[486] – this [relation] is observed specifically in the case of the relatives – and, on the other

10   hand, the [relation] which is non-reciprocating but inclines in just one direction towards other things, producing its relation specifically towards time or place [sc. and not *vice versa*], and so which was not one of the things said specifically *in relation to* something, precisely because it did not reciprocate like the relatives. For in the cases of [the concepts] where and when the relation of place or time to what is in place or in time is not taken into account, but rather [just the relation] of what is in place to place [sc. and of what is in time to time].

15   But there is nothing remarkable if this [relation] sometimes assumes in addition the relation of the relative, as in the case of *on this side*, *on the further side*, and *on the upper side*, *on the underside*. So too in the case of things in time, the old and the young, the recent and the ancient are outside the category of the relatives, even though they have a relation to time or are specifically to do with time,[487] whereas

20   the older and the younger, the more recent and the more ancient and suchlike manifest the relation special to the relatives.

And additions of connectives do not create combination among the categories, because they are neither referred *per se*[488] to a category *qua* connectives, nor do they signify anything *per se*, but if [they signify] at all they *consignify* (*sussêmainousi*). The deictic words, too,

25   'here' and 'there' and similar, if characterised by a demonstration *towards* a place, indicate [that] place, but [if characterised] by a [demonstration] *in* a place will admit of the relation belonging to the [category of] where. But we must not become entangled in explanations of expressions, since in that way we shall think many of the simplest things to be composite. For some things manifest something [else] along with themselves,[489] which is not however referred to a special category, as for instance the [masculine and feminine] 'this' (*houtos kai hautê*): [masculine] 'this' signifies as a masculine, [feminine]

30   nine] 'this' as a feminine, but they do not evince a combination of genera. For [masculine] 'this' is not referred to a different genus from [feminine] 'this',[490] or male to a different genus from female. In the same way, too, in the case of the expression 'he walks around' (*peripatei*) both the present time and the person of the agent [i.e. the third person] have been embraced [sc. in the form of the verb], but it is nevertheless referred only to the category of acting. In consequence, also, even though the phrase 'at Athens' (*Athênêsi*) denotes 'is in

Athens', the 'is' is not additionally predicated (*proskatêgoreitai*) as   361,1
well as the place, as though creating a combination,[491] but is rather
additionally positioned so as to secure the existence in a place [of the
relevant thing], and as completing the phrase 'in Athens'. For it is
also the case that when we say 'Socrates discourses well', there are
not three categories as there are three expressions. Rather, the word
'well' concerns the manner of his discourse and is a way of charac-   5
terising that; it does not create some composite thing together with
that [discourse].

Iamblichus[492] adds to all these points an intellectual theory, and
he first asks whether the objects themselves which are in a place
define the place around them or with them, or whether the place
defines the objects, since it delimits them. And he says that if, as the   10
Stoics say, place subsists [merely] as an appendage (*paruphistatai*)
to bodies, then it will also adopt its definition from them, to the extent
that it is completed by the bodies [sc. on which it depends]. If, on the
other hand, place has being (*ousia*) *per se*, and no body can exist at
all unless it exists in place – as Archytas seems to want to signify –
then place itself defines bodies and delimits them in itself. For if place   15
were inert (*adranês*), having its being in infinite void and extension,
without any subsistent reality, then it would also receive its definition
from without. But if it too has an active potentiality and a determinate incorporeal being, and if it does not permit the separation of
bodies to proceed more or less indefinitely, but rather defines them
within itself, then plausibly it will also furnish bodies with their limit   20
from itself.

Archytas too made this clear when he said:[493] 'For since everything
moved is moved in a particular place, it is clear that place must
subsist first, in which the moving or undergoing thing is to be. And[494]
thus perhaps this thing [i.e. place] is indeed the first of all things,
given that all things that exist either exist in place or at least not
without place'. He clearly hypothesises place to be older than agents   25
and patients, and[495] since things in place always coexist with place,
he therefore says [that place is] 'perhaps first'. But if the things that
exist either exist in place or not without place, it is clear that place
does not subsist [merely] as an appendage to the things that exist.
And if one takes the substantial (*ousiôdês*) place, or the place of life,
or the specific (*eidêtikos*) place, or the place containing [things]
potentially, then all things that exist have their being in such a place.   30
But if one thinks of place as the bare limit of the containing thing and
as the incorporeal surface [of the contained thing],[496] then [even so]
the things that exist do not exist without place, not because the limit
is a random accident of them, nor because one- and two-dimensional
things are posterior to what has three dimensions, but because the
surface containing them is the originator of bodies and, supporting   362,1

them from itself, contains and defines them within itself. That is why indeed bodies have their being in place, as being contained by it and as confining their own dimension[497] within its dimensionless nature. For incorporeal being has been universally treated as prior to corpo-
5   real. Hence too place, being incorporeal, is superior to the things that exist in it: it is superior to the things which are deficient and need to be in place, since it is more self-sufficient than them. For place is the consummation (*teleutê*) not just of bodies, as some think, but also of the shape around them and of the life within them and of the forms around them and of all the potential and being there is in them. Place
10   is the common limit of all these things, so that we ought not to think of place as a *bare* limit – as we think of mathematical surfaces as being [bare] limits of mathematical bodies – but rather it is to be defined as being the physical bounds of physical bodies, as the life-supporting bounds of animate creatures, as the intellectual limits of intellectual beings, as the most potent [limits] of potential things, as the specific [limits] of specific things, and similarly for the other [limits], appropriately to each [domain], in order that the limits really
15   be akin to all those things that they delimit within themselves.

Following these points we ought to consider place in accordance with the [notion of] *containing* and in accordance with the whole genus of containment, and we ought to define the things in place in accordance with the [notion of] *being contained*. Now let no one think of the containment as a bare extension: for not even the extension of the universe is inactive (*argon*), but it is filled up, in the case of forms
20   with all manner of forms, in the case of living beings with all manner of living beings, in the case of potentialities with all manner of potentialities, and similarly in the other cases. Thus one should think of place not only as containing and situating within itself the things that are in place, but also as sustaining them by a single power, for in this way place will not only contain bodies from without, but it will
25   also fill them throughout their entirety with its uplifting power. The bodies sustained by that [power], left to their own nature, would fall away,[498] but once they are lifted up subject to the control of place they will exist in it in this manner. Hence the opinion of the many, which defines place to be the limit of the containing thing, insofar as it [i.e. that limit] has dimension, says that [the limit] is the extreme of the contained place[499] and is what supervenes on the end as a [mere]
30   accompaniment.[500] But the opinion which in its reasoning embraces the limit in accordance with the very cause[501] and origin [of things' being in place] does not speak of it as one of the accidents surrounding place, nor as one of the things which surround it [i.e. place] [merely] at the end, but conveys it [i.e. the limit, so understood] as its [i.e. place's] whole being and eldest cause.

From these remarks one may easily gather how it is that the

intellective[502] soul is said to be a *place* for the reasons (*logoi*) within
it: for it is clear how it comprehends within itself the many [reasons]   35
in a single reason and [under] a single head, not as some things
[comprehended] within a *different* thing, but as some things [compre-   363,1
hended] within the *same* thing [sc. as themselves]: here place is both
living and rational (*logikos*). And in just the same way too the place
for forms is [itself] a single form, inclusive of all forms. And let the
same account as applies to mind (*nous*) and thought (*noêsis*) also
apply to life and potentiality. For in their case too the manifest   5
relation of contained things towards containing things is [a relation]
as of things in place towards place. For even if – and especially in the
case of the incorporeals – the contained things are naturally united
with the containing things, still that does not confound the *order*,
which is of some things [contained] within *different* things.[503] 'Hence,'
says Iamblichus, 'the entire nature of place must extend – not homonymously, but in accordance with the very account of the genus –   10
to all things existing in any way at all as some things [contained]
within different things. For there is a single relation of contained
things towards containing things, which is the same everywhere, but
varying according to the different subsistent realities (*hupostaseis*) of
the participating things: for there is one variety [of this relation] in
the case of bodies and another which applies to incorporeals.'
      The following indeed is clear, that just as in the case of things
which are seen some things are contained in others – as for instance   15
the solid bodies [are contained] by the finer elements, such as earth
and water by air and fire, and these again by the heaven – so in the
case of other beings the secondary ones are contained by the primary
ones and are positioned in them: the world in the soul, the soul in the
mind, and similarly in the other cases. For the principal things have
always embraced the [position in the] order belonging to the eldest   20
place. Archytas too assigns this special feature to place, saying:[504]
'The distinguishing mark of place is that other things are in it, but it
itself is in nothing: for if it were [itself] in some place, then the place
[sc. containing it] would again itself be in some other [place], and the
process would go on to infinity. It is therefore necessary that while
other things are in place, place [itself] is in nothing, but rather   25
relates[505] to existents as limits relate to the things which are limited:[506] for[507] the place of the whole world is the limit of all things that
exist'. Iamblichus remarks: '[Archytas] clearly states here that the
special feature of place is to be the limit of things limited *in any way
at all*, unless, that is, by "things that exist" he means the bodies with
which the categories are concerned.'
      Now Iamblichus says the following: 'Let us not, as the account
[given by Archytas] suggests, apply these [marks of place] to the world   30
alone, but let us rather always refer the limit quite generally back to

the elder cause: for in this way the soul or mind, and the single and unified operation of this [mind], will be for us the limit of the whole world; and still higher up than this [mind] we shall descry the essence (*ousia*) of place as of a god, being a thing of one form and conserving everything within itself, and delimiting the whole according to a

364,1 single measure. And the same is to be concluded from the [nature of] containment too: for the principle (*aition*) of containment, ascending to the highest, draws us on to that divine place[508] which is itself the cause of itself and is itself inclusive of itself, which subsists in itself and which has a subsistent reality that is no longer not separate from

5 the things that are, but is indeed separate from them.' Let these, then, count as the doctrines of Iamblichus' intellectual theory concerning place.

But we,[509] investigating in a more balanced way the use and nature of place strictly and not metaphorically so called, say that since all ungenerated and indivisible things, on the one hand, possess their being and the continuation of their being in a unified way, they exist

10 as wholes simultaneously in themselves, and for this reason do not need either place or time; but eternity suffices for them, making them all persist in unity. Things which are generated, on the other hand, and which possess both their very being and the continuation of their being divisibly – these things need time: [a time] which does not permit the continuation of their being to be dispersed or confounded, but rather as far as may be unites and connects it in an order

15 according to before and after. Hence it is that the time of the Trojan War and of the present are not mixed together into the same one, and nor, on the other hand, are the parts [of time] altogether pulled apart from one another, but they maintain in [the right] order their continuity towards one another. In the same way, too, place on the one hand receives the parts of bodies – and thus these [parts] do not remain in a state of partlessness, but separate out into size and so

20 fall away from their partlessness – and on the other hand organises, arranges and defines them, in order that the hands neither be mixed up with the feet, nor that they [i.e. hands and feet] be altogether pulled away from one another, because each occupies its appropriate place.

Time is twofold, and place is twofold as well:[510] for [there is] a sort [of place] which is naturally united with and individual to each man, which conserves this hand and this organ on the right, that [hand]

25 and that [organ] on the left, the head up above the windpipe, and the feet below, under the groin. And [there is] common [place], some [places] being more common than others:[511] for the earth and air is a place for all land animals, and this or that particular part of the earth and air [is a place merely for some of them,][512] and to go still further [in narrowness, there is] the [place] immediately containing [each

thing],[513] which both Aristotle and Archytas assigned [sc. to place]. But it is not possible to find the [place] which is individual to and naturally united with each thing clearly conveyed.[514] And yet,[515] just 30 as we must specify a common time, so too [we must specify] an individual one, given that [we must do the same for] movement as well. And the commoner kind of place – that is, the limit of the containing thing – enjoys its status as being place not simply as a limit, but as what is active and receptive and definitional, as Iamblichus said too: for containing things always have a capacity which is active, containing, and definitional of the things in them. But let 35 this suffice for the present.

Concerning the Tenth Category, Having 365,1

In proceeding to the last category, that of having, let us again first ask about its [position in the] order [of the categories]. For Archytas places the category of having next after substance and the things which coexist with substance, quality and quantity, and after the relatives, saying:[516] 'After these things [comes] the possession (*skhe-* 5 *sis*) of acquired things: and it is clear that the control of whatever sorts of acquisitions there are[517] is also automatically [to be placed] under [the head of] this [possession].' For [Archytas] thought that the possession (*skhesis*) of acquisitions should appropriately be listed immediately after the relation (*skhesis*) balancing [two things] in relation to one another [i.e. the relatives], since in this respect it bears a kinship towards the latter.[518] Aristotle, on the other hand, thinking that everything [which derives] from a thing itself is more primary 10 than what accrues to it externally and is acquired, and since all the *other* genera,[519] existing either in substance or in certain conditions (*skheseis*) [of it], contribute a particular portion from themselves towards the existence [of a substance], whereas *having* comes about wholly externally and as something acquired [and placed] around us, on this account places having last. And that it is said in many ways is more manifest in the case of having than in the cases of the [category of] where or that of when – for these were said severally [merely] in respect of *place* and what is *in place*, and [in respect] of 15 *time* and what is *in time* – and this therefore provides a pretext for its[520] being positioned at the end. But it is clear that even though having is said in many ways, the genus is not the homonymous [having], but is rather the [having] which is differentiated from the homonymy.[521] In his specifications of the separate [categories], however,[522] Archytas too arranged having not [immediately] after the relatives but after acting and undergoing, thus assigning it seventh 20 place. Perhaps he thereby indicates that even if the genera have some particular order – which he conveyed in his account of their order –

still the latter ones, at any rate, are really in a sense indifferent in respect of their place [in the order], owing to the fact that substance (*huparxis*) is originative and generative[523] of all [the other genera].[524] But that is enough concerning order.

25   Archytas exhibited its [i.e. having's] nature nicely, saying:[525] 'What, being corporeal, is acquired and is separate from the substance [of the haver] is the distinguishing mark of the [category of] having. For[526] the cloak and shoes are different from the haver, and[527] are neither naturally united with him nor indeed an accident of him, as are brightness and blackness [of the eye][528] (for each of these is incorporeal[529]); rather, the acquired thing is just like the body [which acquires it].' Hence the distinctive feature of the [category of] having

30   is participation in some acquired thing which is separate from the substance [of the acquirer], which does not dispose that [substance] after its own manner, which does not bring it about that [that substance] is named after itself, and which is placed on [that sub-

366,1 stance]. Hence this [acquired] thing is thereby [itself] also bodily, but not an accident, because it is neither naturally united with the having thing nor capable of altering it, so that something is not said, [merely] by virtue of having either a quality or a quantity or a relation or an operation or an affection, to have [these things] *in the sense of this genus*, and nor is it possible to have [something in this sense] as a part (for [all of] these things are naturally united with that very thing itself [which 'has' them], and it with them). But if some acquired body

5 is placed on something which is *different* from it, then this is embraced in the category of having. Hence we are not said to *have*, in the sense of this genus, either possessions (*ktêmata*) or slaves or friends or fathers or sons, since these are not [things had] in the sense of their being placed around [one's body], even though they are possessions.

    That is also why Plato in the *Theaetetus* clearly differentiated having (*ekhein*) from owning (*kektêsthai*), saying:[530] 'Owning does not

10 seem to me to be the same thing as having. For example, someone who buys a cloak and is in control of it, but is not wearing it – we say not indeed that he has it, but certainly that he owns it. Consider then whether it is possible in the same way for someone to own but not have knowledge, just as, if someone were to catch wild birds – pigeons or whatever – and, having built an aviary at his house, were to nurture them, then we would say that in a certain sense, surely, he has them continuously, because of course he *owns* them, but that in

15 another sense he does not *have* any of them; rather, a certain power accrues to him with regard to them, since he has established them under his keeping in a special enclosure, namely [the power] to seize them and have them whenever he wants.' So in Plato's view too having comes about in just those cases where the haver is in control of the thing had, as for instance whenever he controls [i.e. holds

(*kratêi*)] a pigeon, just as one is said to have a ring whenever one places it on [one's finger]; and there is no independent operation [of the thing had] nor is there control [exercised] by *each* in relation to 20 the other *simpliciter*, but rather [only control exercised] towards the other thing in respect of the [having] thing itself[531] – [a control] which exceeds all the other categories by far.[532]

And it is further clear how the genuinely [so-called] genus of having differs from things which are homonymously said to have. For it is neither the case that having a state or [having] a quality or [having] a quantity are included in it [i.e. in the genus of having] – since these are incorporeal – nor is it the case that having a field, for example, or 25 having a son, or owning [material goods] [are included in it] – for although these latter things are certainly bodily possessions, they are not contained from without, nor do they [themselves] contain [anything else]. It looks as though having is in a way an intermediate between owning [a possession] and being disposed in a certain state: for in the sense in which [something] is had in the way whiteness [is 'had'], it is distinguished from external possessions, which we do not place on [our bodies]; whereas in the sense in which [what is had] is bodily and external, it is distinguished from states, which are accidents of us, being naturally united with us and not acquired.[533] Such, 30 then, is the special feature of the [category of] having, and in this way it has been distinguished from things said [to have] homonymously. 367,1

Since we must convey the species-forming differentiae of this genus too, as Aristotle himself did in the case of the other genera, and as we tried to follow him [in doing], and [since] this [genus] is said in 5 many ways, we must beware lest unawares we slide over into another signification.[534] For indeed even Archytas himself enumerates the many meanings [of having], instead of its species-forming differentiae, saying:[535] 'The [category of] having does not admit of several differentiae [constitutive] of species,[536] but is [instead] said in many ways: for those who know are said to have their knowledge, and thinkers [to have] their thought, and owners [to have] their owner- 10 ship.' And Aristotle says at the end of his book that the [category of] having is spoken of in several senses, and he there conveys *not* its species-forming differentiae but its many meanings.

Iamblichus, however, attempts to differentiate this [genus] too by species, specifying the differentiae of just the genus of having itself. He says: 'Things placed around part of the body, such as a ring round 15 a finger, and things [placed] around the whole body, such as clothes, are [species] of the [category of] having. Other [had things] are offensive implements, such as weapons; and yet other things are placed as coverings in front of the body, either to provide it with a certain ornament or for some other use. And it is also possible (he says) to divide up the differentiae of the [category of] having in

accordance with the conditions (*skheseis*) relating to life, as for in-
20 stance if some things are useful for peace, others for war (such as
ornaments and weapons [respectively]), and some things are placed
on us through our choice, such as clothes and weapons, others without
choice, such as fetters. And we control [i.e. hold] some [of these
things], such as a spear or staff, whereas we are controlled [i.e. are
held] by others, as for instance by shoes. And having [something]
25 either accrues to us through our exertion, or without any particular
effort.' These, then, are what Iamblichus enumerated as the specific
differences of the [category of] having. But it is worth asking whether
perhaps the majority of them are denotative of the differentiation not
of the [category of] *having*, but rather of the *haver* and of the *thing
had* and of the *manner* [of having]. For whether the haver is the whole
thing or just a part, and whether [he/it has] voluntarily or unwillingly,
and whether without exertion or with exertion, and again whether
30 [he has] ornaments or offensive [weapons], and [whether] the [hav-
ing] is in time of peace or in war – it is not of the *having*, but of the
particular *occasion* and the *circumstance* in which the haver has, that
[Iamblichus] is giving the differentiation. But the distinction between
controlling and being controlled does seem to me to denote a differentiation of the [category of] having itself. Iamblichus also attends to the
reason, on the basis of what is said about it, why this genus extends to
few things: it is that acquired bodies, and things cast around bodies, are
35 few; and further that [having] is considered as applying only to animate
things, as will be demonstrated [below] (370,21ff.).
368,1 Many people have raised puzzles in relation to this genus too.
Plotinus for one raises the question:[537] 'Concerning the [category of]
having, if having [is said] in many ways, why will not all the senses
be referred to the same category? So that the quantified thing,
because it *has* magnitude, and the qualified thing, because it *has*
colour, and the father, because he *has* a son, and the son, because he
5 *has* a father, and in general[538] [whatever has] possessions [sc. will all
be cases of having in the sense of the genus].' In response to this it
should be said that there cannot be a single category and a single
genus of things which are homonymous and vary in respect of their
genus. Despite the fact that the quantified thing *has* magnitude, or
that the qualified thing *has* colour, they are nevertheless not in *this*
[category of] having: for the qualified and the quantified thing are
incorporeals, but this category [of having] was of acquired bodies
10 [placed] around us. A father, though in one way [he meets the
criterion] insofar as he is a body, still was not *placed around* [anything
else], and though in another way [he meets it] insofar as he has a
relation to his son, still the relation was incorporeal.
Nicostratus[539] rebukes [Aristotle] in the words: 'Why did you not
put the eight significations of having, which you enumerated at the

end of the book, [here, in ch. 9], and why did you not separate off the improper (*allotria*) senses of the category before us, as do those who divide up a word with many meanings? For as it is we do not know   15
which of the enumerated [senses] this tenth genus is. For if one is to be pedantic, none of the [senses] expounded [in ch. 15] signifies having *in the sense of the genus*.

'Let us set out exactly what Aristotle says at the end. It runs as follows (15b17-30): "Having is said in several senses: either [having something] (1) as a state and a condition or some other quality (for we are said to have knowledge and virtue); or (2) as a quantity, such   20
as the size someone happens to have (for he is said [to be] three cubits [high]); or (3) as things around the body, such as a cloak or tunic; or (4) as on a part, such as a ring on the hand; or (5) as a part, such as a foot or hand; or (6) as in a vessel, such as a measure of corn; or (7) as a possession (for we are said to have a house and field). (8) And we are also said to have a wife and the wife [to have] a husband. But this last-mentioned seems to be a very improper sense of having. For we   25
signify nothing else by *having a wife* than that [the man] cohabits [with her]."

'Of these [senses of having], [Aristotle] himself rejected the eighth one – having a wife or husband – as not really concerning the having which is said homonymously, but rather denoting [merely] the being together [of husband and wife]. And the first [kind of having] clearly belongs to the [category of] quality: for to *have* a state and condition signifies (so Nicostratus) nothing other – if we transfer it into [the   30
terms of] what something *is* – than to be [say] knowledgeable and [in general] to be in a habitual state (*to hektikon einai*), which belong to   369,1
the [category of] *quality*. And furthermore having a size, and being three cubits [tall], belong to the [category of] *quantity*; and the third and fourth and seventh significations of having are each clearly in the category of relative: for (he says) having a cloak and having a ring are just like having a house and owning possessions, and belong to   5
the relatives, since the possession is the owner's and the owner is [the owner] of the possession. It is fairly clear that the fifth [sense] too, i.e. having a part, also belongs to the relatives, given that the part *relates* to the whole,[540] and in a different way it belongs to the category of substance: for if you express what it is to *have* feet and hands by transferring [the sense into the terms of what something *is*], you will speak, on a precise account – even if it is an unusual one – of *being*   10
footed and *being handed*, and in general of *being endowed with [a certain] substance* (*ousiousthai*), which is itself admittedly an uncommon [expression], but then the dialectician is interested not so much in usage as in accuracy. Hence ([Nicostratus] says), [Aristotle] erred in not separating off the other [sc., irrelevant] significations [of having], so that we might learn what the category of having really is.'

Iamblichus replies to this that '[Aristotle] differentiated the significations of having at the end for this very reason, namely that he
15   might separate them from the *category* of having, which[541] he denoted
by means of his examples at the beginning (2a3), and in the middle
when he spoke of the [sc. last] six genera together (11b13f.). And
indeed it is usual for dialecticians to define something as [i.e. in terms
of] an example, in order to separate off the things which are unlike
it. Thus when those from the Academy were defining the *haveable*
(*hekton*) as that which is capable of being *had*, in reply to people who
20   asked which signification of having they meant, given that having [is
said] in many ways (just as Aristotle too defined it) – well, in response
to these [questioners], they would furnish an example, saying that
the haveable is that which is capable of being had in just the sense in
which practical wisdom is had by the practically wise man, so producing a description of it by means of an example and simultaneously
separating off the improper significations of having [from the proper
sense]. Accordingly, too, given that having is said in many ways, when
25   Aristotle took up the sort of having in the sense of the genus which
being shod and being armed exemplify, he did away, by dint of an
example, with the whole crowd of other things homonymously said
[to be had].

'And [things that are had in the sense of the genus] are distinguished from states and from quantity:[542] for those are accidents and
at the same time are incorporeal. They are also distinguished from
things had as parts, because those things are naturally united [with
what they are part of], whereas these [i.e. things had in the sense of
the genus] are acquired. And they are further distinguished from
30   things [had] as possessions, because those are completely external
[sc. to the body] and not placed on [the body]. And they are distinguished from things in a vessel, because those are simply positioned
[in the vessel] as in a place. Only the third and fourth among the
enumerated cases belong to the category of having, that is, having a
cloak in the sense of [having it] around the whole of one's body, and
35   [having] a ring in the sense of [having it] on a part [of the body]. And
it is clear that these cases were easy to appreciate at a glance [sc. as
cases of having in the sense of the genus] owing to their likeness to
the cases of being armed and being shod, which Aristotle had already
put forward [in chs 4 and 9] as examples of the category of having.
370,1   'So Nicostratus is wasting his time when he rebukes [Aristotle] for
not separating off, among the significations of having, having in the
sense of the genus, unless, I suppose, [we admit the criticism] that
Aristotle did not append to [his mention of] the third and fourth
[senses] the point that *these* [kinds of having] are *in the sense of the
genus*, while the others are to be excluded from it. But such additions
are not in the usual manner of Aristotelian concision. And just to place

in the middle [sc. of the list of senses of having] the significations of 5
the category [sc. without glossing them as such] was, in my view,
appropriate for someone training his future readers in sharpness of
wit. Nicostratus, however, in reducing both the third and fourth
senses to the [category of the] relatives, buries the truth completely:
for even though clothes and a ring are possessions, they nevertheless
obviously differ from other possessions in virtue of their being placed
around [the body] and being had, so that even Plato thinks they 10
belong to the category of having.'[543]

'But,' says Plotinus,[544] 'if having bodily things around one's body
creates another category, but not [having] incorporeals, why does
there not also arise in the case of the [category of] acting, given that
there is a big differentiation [among actions], one category for cutting,
and another for burning or burying or throwing away?' Well, the 15
operation of acting is a single one, which has a single principle (*logos*),
and by no means needs a differentiated receptivity in the things
which receive the acting: for the cutter and the burner and the rest
do not differ in point of acting. The category of having, in contradistinction, possesses the entire feature that makes it special in the fact
that what is placed on [the receiving body] is not incorporeal, but is
[itself] a body – [a feature] which is not characterised by just any old 20
relation, but is considered strictly from the point of view of the
[relation] towards the other thing in respect of the [having] thing
itself.[545]

'But if the cloak which is placed on [the body],' [Plotinus] continues,
'creates another category, why will not the [cloak] positioned (*keimenon*)
on a bed create another [category] too?' Well, the cloak's lying on a
bed belongs to the category of being-in-a-position (*to keisthai*) or to
that of [something] in place:[546] for the bed exhibits no *operation* of
having. The category of having manifests a certain state of *possession* 25
and *control* – but [only] of *acquired* bodies. Now if this is so, having
will be true only of animate things, so that even if an ornament is
placed on (*perikeitai*) a statue, the statue, being inanimate, will not
be said to *have* it, but rather the ornament [will be said merely] to *be
positioned* (*keisthai*) on the statue. But if [the statue] were considered
as something animate, it could be said to have the ornament by
analogy with what is animate.

'But if ([Plotinus] says) having is characterised in terms of a 30
possessive condition (*kathexis*), it will be referred to a state of possession (*hexis*), and a state of possession is in the [category of] quality.'
Well, this state of possession is homonymous: for one sort was a
containment (*sunokhê*) of incorporeal things, but *this* sort [i.e. having
in the sense of the genus] is the control of acquired bodies. And the
[state of possession] belonging to *having* accrues by virtue of the
operation of the havers, whereas the [state of possession] of *qualities*

does not [accrue] by virtue of the operation either of the things that
are participated in or of the participating things. And they differ both
35   in respect of the things which are had – since in the latter case [the
had things] are incorporeal, whereas in the former they are bodies –
and in respect of the having things – since in the latter case [they
have what they have] *in* their substance, whereas in the former case
[they have it] *around* their substance externally.

371,1   'But if ([Plotinus] says) one is not to say that one *has* a quality,
because quality has already been accounted for, or that one *has* a
quantity, since quantity has been accounted for, or that one *has* parts,
since substance has been accounted for, why must we say that *having
weapons* belongs to another category despite the fact that we have
accounted for substance, to which weapons [are assigned]?' Well,
because it is not the case that weapons or shoes *per se* have been said
5   to belong to the category of having – nor even the ownership of them,
if whoever owned them does not make any use of them – but it is
rather the *control* of them, and the state of *possession* ascribed on the
basis of having them – this is what creates the category of having. It
was[547] one thing to have a quality and a quantity, and another to have
weapons and shoes: for in the former case the state of possession is
of incorporeals, and in the latter case it is of bodily things, and in the
former case the things which are participated in are capable of
altering the participating things, whereas in the latter case they are
10   merely placed on them.

'But how ([Plotinus] asks) can there be a genus for [such] a small
number of cases?' Well, because this genus obtains in the case of the
lowest things (*eskhatois*)[548] and exists *around* bodies and *on* bodies,
and in view of this it is contracted to a very small scope. But it is not
as if it could not be a genus on that account: for the phoenix too is just
one thing, and yet it contains the whole species in itself.

15   Now why did [Aristotle] not conjoin the account of having to the
[accounts of the] other categories, but as though by way of an after-
thought made mention of having after the account of opposites, of
simultaneous things and of movement? Well, on completion of his
account of the categories, since in that [account] he has mentioned in
passing several [extraneous] things, he [subsequently] elaborates
those things too. And since the category of having is last, having
20   regard to the order [Aristotle] reasonably mentioned the[549] homonymy of having last, thereby not only assigning the appropriate
order to the categories themselves, but also assigning the same
[order] to the matters extraneously appended and elaborated.

'But it is absurd ([Plotinus] says) for him to reject [from the proper
senses of having] the locution that a wife is had, given that this is
idiomatic.'[550] But if he had not mentioned it at all, it would have looked
strange to pass over what lies in custom, whereas in mentioning it

and classifying it he has performed the function of a dialectician, 25
whose particular concern is the distinguishing of the truth. So let
these, then, be our responses to the puzzles.

Aristotle tackled the significations of having more accurately in
book Delta of the *Metaphysics*.[551] For he says [there] that having is
spoken of in many ways: that which governs (*agon*),[552] according to
the nature and impulse in it, and in general [that] in which the 30
principle (*arkhê*) of the movement of the had thing [resides], [is said
to have], as for example the tyrant has the city [he governs], and the
fever or cough [possesses] some particular man. Contrariwise too: for
the city is said to have its tyrant, and in general a ruler, and the ship
[is said to have] its pilot, and the boy his tutor. These things are
indeed said to *have* in the sense that either they govern [something
else] according to their own principle (*arkhê*), or they are governed
according to the [principle residing] in that [other] thing; and they 372,1
belong to the category of acting or undergoing. In another sense the
matter is said to have the form, as for instance the bronze or the wax
[has] its shape, and the body its health or its colour, and Socrates
justice or temperance. For in general the capacity to receive [is spoken
of] in many ways: in one way, as mentioned, the matter [is capable of
receiving] the form, and in another way what [holds something else] 5
as in a vessel [is capable of receiving it] – in this way the jar is said
to hold wine, the flask oil, and the public baths a crowd. The former
cases belong to the category of quality, the latter to that of where. It
might look as if [we] are said to have a field, a horse and an ox[553]
differently [from any of the foregoing ways], but in fact these are said
in the first sense of having, for because we control and are masters
of the use of these things according to our own choice, we are said to 10
have them. And besides we are said to have our parts – hands and a
head – and the trees [are said to have] their roots. We are also said
to have a wife, a father, kin and siblings, though some of these too
will also fall under the first sense. For a man has a wife because he
governs her after his own principle (*arkhê*), and a wife [has] a
husband, because she is governed according to the [principle] in the
other. Of these [kinds of having] some will be referred to the [category 15
of] substance, others to that of acting and undergoing. And someone
is said to have his actions, because he acts and is engaged with them,
and to have reason, because he takes heed of it and does not slight it:
all of these belong to the [category of] acting. And we are said to have
shoes and clothes both as possessions and in virtue of being clothed
and shod; and these come under the category of having, by virtue of
the state of their possession.[554] And a state of possession [is spoken 20
of] in many ways too. For one sort is correlative with possessing
(having [*ekhein*]), as seizure is with seizing: hence just as we do not
seize the seizure, so too we do not possess the (state of) possession

(otherwise this would proceed to infinity).[555] And another sort is an enduring condition (*diathesis*), as we say for instance that virtue is a state and that skilled workmen are *in* a state [sc. constituted by their skill]. These [two kinds of possession] differ from one another in that we can have one but not the other, and secondly in that one sort admits of increase (for it is possible for someone in [such] a state, by practising, to come to be even more in that state), whereas the other sort does not so admit (for those who have something do not have it more or less). Furthermore, to the one sort [of state] another state is opposed, as for instance vice to virtue, while to the other sort [is opposed] not a state (of possession) but a state of privation.

It might appear that *being had* is contrary to *having* and [is therefore] another category, just as acting and undergoing are distinct [categories]. But one must appreciate that, since having is spoken of commonly,[556] one [species] of this is *specific* having, and another [species is] being had, while what is common [to both] is the category, under which [fall] both those things said to *have* specifically, such as [the subject of] the phrase 'he is underbound (*hupodedetai*) [i.e. shod]', and *being had* [sc. specifically] – and this too homonymously, for both the man and the shoe are [said to be] *underbound*.[557] And this too must be said, that having is in some cases spoken of homonymously with *having acted* (*enêrgêkenai*); for 'being shod' (*to hupodedesthai*) denotes both *having* shoes [on] and *having put* them on (i.e. the perfect of 'he has shoes on'). Opposed to having is privation, as for instance *naked, unshod, unarmed*: for to be in a state of deprivation is not to have [something] at the very time when it is natural to have it. Archytas too, first construing having something as just [having] *simpliciter*,[558] then tries to divide it up, and after arranging the *distinctive* sense of having,[559] which falls under [having] *simpliciter*, in the *category* of having, describes it, as we have already made clear (365,25ff.).

Boethus takes a contrary view to the Stoics, who think one should refer having to the [category of] *being a certain way (pôs ekhein)*,[560] and he contends that one should not reduce it either to what is a certain way or to the relatives, but that it is its own category. For [he says] that it is a *relatively dispositional (skhetikên)* [category],[561] and the relative disposition (*skhesis*) is spoken of in three principal ways, and homonymously: one sort is in the thing itself and *per se*, another is in relation to something else, and the third is of something else in relation to the thing itself. Now the first sort, which is in itself, is observed in the case of what is a certain way, as for instance the man who is standing with his guard up: for the relative disposition [here] is of the man towards himself. The second sort, which is in relation to something else, is the [relative disposition] of those things which are called relative: for the father and the right-hand man are spoken of in accordance with a relative disposition, but not that of some particular thing towards itself, but that towards something else. The 15 third sort [of relative disposition], namely from something else towards the thing itself, is for example that of the man who is armed or shod: for this is a relative disposition of something else towards the man himself – of the weapons towards the man who is armed, and of the shoes towards the man who is shod.

'But perhaps,' says Boethus, 'the sort [of having] which is equivalent to having *anything at all*, whether a part [of the body] or piece of land[562] – and this [i.e. the widest sense of having] is perhaps indeed signified by the expression put forward in itself – along with those 20 many and various things belonging to the class,[563] are significations of having: for the field which has been put forward [as a case of having] or the father or the part create the differentiation [of the class].' And [Boethus says that] under this [differentiation] there is another meaning of having, namely that applied particularly to the case of *control*. 'Now if one establishes the category in accordance with the first signification [i.e. having anything at all], being practically wise and being temperate and being healthy will be referred to this 25 category (for being practically wise is a matter of *having* practical wisdom), and the category of acting and [that of] undergoing will be done away by this [category]. But [this category] will be differentiated from the [category of] relative: for the *owner* will belong to the [category of] relative, but *owning* to the [category of] having, and the *father* [will belong] to the [category of] relative, but *being a father* [will consist] in *having* a son. If, on the other hand, [one establishes the category] in accordance with the second [signification, i.e. control], 30 the other significations of having will be referred to the other categories, and only all those to do with control of some acquisition [will be referred] to this [category].' Let such, then, be our additional narration of the noble Boethus' account.

Now if someone wants further to establish a division of the genus so defined,[564] let him say that things had in this sense are had either for the purpose of war or in peace, and of those [had] for the purpose of war some are things *placed on* [the body], while others are things 35 *controlled* [i.e. held], and of each of these [groups], some are defensive, such as a breastplate (placed on [the body]) and a shield (controlled [i.e. held]), whereas others are offensive, such as a sword (placed on [the body])[565] and a spear (controlled [i.e. held]). Of those things [had] in peace some are [had] for the sake of ornament in respect of different parts of the body, such as a fillet, necklace, or ring, while others [are 374,1 had for the sake] of a covering, and of these again some, such as a cloak, [go] round the whole body, whereas others, such as a shoe, [go] round a part. And some things are also had as implements, such as an adze, a rudder, or a staff, whereas others, equally, are [had as]

possessions, such as money, or whatever else we control by virtue of
5   having it. Every haver must, in my view, have as a matter of his
choice: that is why inanimate things are not said to *have* according to
the signification of the genus.

After the systematic treatment of the [category of] having Iamblichus takes up the intellectual theory of it, and first of all asks very
precisely where it draws its subsistence from, and what service it
performs in the universe. He says: 'Many things in the universe do
10   not coexist, and are not naturally united, with each other, but are
capable of deriving some benefit from each other. Accordingly, the
nature of the universe having devised acquired objects, it came about
that different men had different ones of these [acquired] things as
well [sc. as of other things], so that there might be intercourse even
among men living far apart from one another, and a potential for the
possession of things which were not present [to them] but which were
beneficial. For it was not fitting that the substance[566] which is in the
15   flux of generation,[567] and which is by itself in need of many things
owing to the uttermost (*eskhaton*) character of the division,[568] should
be bereft of those things and entirely lack participation in them. So,
once awoken, they [i.e. things in the flux of generation] gained some
means and strength to achieve control of the useful things, especially
as the possessed things gave themselves up readily into the hands of
those who took hold of them. And the primal cause of the universe,
long before nature, guides the things coming to be,[569] suitably harmo-
20   nising suitable objects of possession with the use [of those objects]
appropriate to their possessors, and raising up the possessors to that
[use]. That, then, is the kind of service which this genus renders the
universe, as it comes forth among existents for the self-sufficiency of
those in need and the potential union even of those who are altogether
separated.

'We should not (says Iamblichus) fix its [i.e. having's] entire nature
25   in terms of us and our body: for in that way[570] it will be confined to a
narrow [field of application]: but the [category of] having ought to be
considered in a yet higher sense, with regard to our soul and to nature,
in respect of exercises of control which are acquired and not naturally
united [with the controller]. For it is not as though bodies of the same
nature as it are placed on the body, whereas the soul, which has
multifarious powers, does not have certain acquired lives, some of the
30   same nature as it, others somewhat deficient in the appropriate
proportions [inhering] in it.[571] One can see what I am saying (he
continues) even from the most manifest of things: for if [a soul], on
descending into the body, projects some lives around itself as acquisitions, and receives others from the body – namely all those which
are observed to be in a process of change and displacement – how
should it not be said to *have* these? And indeed as [the soul] comes to

be present in each part of the world, it receives certain lives and   35
powers, some of which it itself projects, others of which it takes from
the world, and of suitable bodies in each part of the universe it takes
some from the world [sc. just as they are], and others it fashions as
instruments according to its own rational principles (*logoi*), and it
puts these powers and lives and bodies aside whenever it happens to   375,1
change to another assigned province (*lêxis*). It has clearly emerged
from these [considerations] that all these things were *acquisitions* for
it [i.e. the soul, when it descended into the body], and that it *had* them
as distinct things with a distinct existence: for it was not naturally
united with them in the manner of compounded bodies, but since it
was *per se* unmixed [with them] it *had* them as things placed on it.   5

'Likewise too in the case of the nature of the universe ([Iamblichus]
says), whenever, in accordance with its rational principles (*logoi*), it
contains many things which come to be through its agency, and of
these some perish, just as though they were particular acquisitions,
while it persists as the same thing, and, as it grasps the bodies and
animals and plants which are within itself[572] and releases nothing,
comes to rest – at that point the [category of] having will be being
considered in connection with the nature of the universe too, since   10
[that nature] contains[573] in itself all the acquired things, as many as
are not accidents [of the universe] nor naturally united [with it].

'And even more than [in the case of] these, the state of possession
currently in question is observed in the world as a whole, thought of
in respect of all its lives and the souls in it, the elements and natures
[in it], and the things which come into existence under their common
action. For since the entire world is perfect in itself (*autotelês*), having   15
been completed out of perfect parts, it possesses all the things in it as
complete and lacking a share in nothing that belongs to them. Hence
where these things are natural attributes it participates in them,
where they are acquisitions it exercises control over them too, and
where they are both, then it contains them too, as the earth has the
animals in it, which now come into being, now perish: you would say
that these are the earth's acquisitions, providing it [sc. while they   20
live] with a kind of participation [in themselves], and subsequently
departing from it; and the earth exercises control over them (as is
manifest to see), and the[574] sea likewise embraces the sea-animals in
it. But if in our case the things that are had are placed on us *externally*,
in the case of the universe they are rather enfolded into its *interior*
and are in this sense had, and this [difference] is not in disharmony[575]
with the particular and the general nature [sc. of these havers,   25
respectively]: for our bodies, being particular, have their had bodies
externally, while the universe, being complete and wanting nothing
external to itself, contains its had things in itself, and embraces them
from all sides within itself. The heaven too embraces the[576] four

elements within itself, and in another sense it also *has* the spheres
30   which are within itself, and all stars there are. Both the whole heaven
and the four elements *have* within themselves the animals in the four
elements,[577] and in general the containing things always *have* the
contained things. For the things in the world are differentiated in due
order one from another, and the higher and elder always embrace the
more deficient, and thus was the genus of having originally introduced.
35   'And if the world as a whole now has *these* things filling it, but will
hereafter [have] *other* ones – all those that the [process of] generation
376,1 puts into it – then its state of possession will be different, and [in
general] different at different times, owing to the change among the
things accruing to it. And if indeed the powers in the universe,
whether pertaining to spirits (*daimoniai*) or to gods (*theiai*), *have* the
parts of the world placed on them, and [if] this comes about unceas-
5   ingly in the universe, with assigned provinces, whether spiritual or
divine, *having* the parts of the world allotted to them,[578] then in this
way too everything will be full of the [category of] having. Further, if
the portions of life in the universe *have* parts of the world placed on
them, and [if] these [parts] are not naturally united with them, but
are as external acquisitions for them, then in this way too all these
things will be arranged in the [category of] having. And if the common
10   [kind] *animal* has smaller parts in connection with it and smaller
animals embraced within it,[579] in this manner too the whole such class
will be arranged in the [category of] having.' Iamblichus, then, in his
theoretical investigation looked into these matters [both] actually[580]
and intellectually.
        One should dare to examine carefully what [Iamblichus] says,
since he too is wont to receive what is said [by others] with close
consideration. And the things he says about the service performed by
the [category of] having seem to me to have been marvellously said,
15   as indeed also in a manner worthy of the man's greatness of mind:
but why does he say that the soul *has* the lives which are projected
by the soul, and the powers which are conferred on it by the body,
given that he too agrees that, in the sense of the category of having,
things which are had are *bodies* and are [placed] around *bodies* –
[namely] the ones which have them?[581] And why does he say that the
things which come to be through the agency of the whole of nature
20   are *had* by it? For having in a causal sense was not the same as having
in the sense of the genus of having.[582] And I question even more why
he says that the whole world, thought of in terms of all the lives,
elements and natures [in it], *participates* in these, if they are natural
attributes, and *exercises control* over them, if they are acquisitions.
For in the first place [the world] cannot *have* these things to the extent
25   that they are lives, since lives are incorporeal, but things had were to

be bodies; and in the second place if they are naturally united with, or in any way parts of, the universe, they could not, as he himself arranged matters,[583] be things *had* [by it], whereas if they are [its] offspring, the manner of their containment would be different. And whether the animals in the earth and in the other elements are considered as parts of the entire earth or as [its] offspring, they will not be said to be *had* by it. And how does the heaven *have* the spheres 30 within itself, if not as parts? For these [spheres] are naturally united [with it] and [so] not acquired. And how does the common [kind] *animal* embrace the smaller[584] animals within itself, if not as parts or as offspring? These, then, are objections one might raise, as well as others of the same sort lying read to hand.

It is in my view possible to say that while the thing had must be acquired and separate from the substance [of the haver], it is not necessarily a *body* (*sôma*), but [may be merely] *corporeal* (*sôma-* 35 *toeides*). Indeed Archytas too spoke not of [being a] *body* but of [being] *corporeal* (365,26), on the ground that this is what something acquired and separate is (for incorporeal things naturally unite completely [sc. with the things which 'have' them]). And so the corporeal life, being separate from the soul-substance and coming to be ac- 377,1 quired by that [substance] in such a way that it does not alter it nor create some single thing together with it, might be said to be had by it [i.e. by the soul-substance]. Insofar,[585] however, as the life is something capable of *altering* [the soul-substance], and insofar as it is productive of the *whole* substance [i.e. ensouled body], then it could not be said to be had [sc. by them]. The parts and offspring of wholes could not be *had* [by the wholes], although they too might with justice be said to be had as acquisitions and separate items and appendages 5 to the whole: for the parts of those [wholes] are not indivisibly naturally united [with them], as they are in our case, nor are their offspring dragged asunder from them in the same way as our [offspring are]. But these matters must be even further investigated.

CHAPTER 10

On the completion of his account concerning the ten categories, 378,1 Archytas adds that the subsistent reality (*hupostasis*) of all categories except substance is considered in connection with what is individual and perceivable and not in connection with what is general and intelligible.[586] He writes thus:[587] 'Since we have now reached the end of our account of the signifying and the signified things,[588] by means of which things *man* fulfils the complete system of sense (*logos*),[589] let 5 it be laid down in addition to what has been said, that it is not man as such but some individual man which admits of the coincidence of all these [categories].[590] For indeed the individual man is[591] necessarily

qualified, as well as *quantified*, and is a certain way *in relation to* something, and furthermore [necessarily] *acts* and *undergoes* and is *positioned* and *has* and is *in a place* and *at some time*. But man as
10   such, which admits of the primary meaning [of the word 'man']⁵⁹² – I mean the essence [of man] in accordance with the form (*to ti estin kata tan idean*)⁵⁹³ – is neither a *qualified* individual nor a *quantified* one, nor one which is a certain way *in relation to* something else,⁵⁹⁴ nor indeed one which *acts to bring about* something or *undergoes* something, nor one which *is positioned*, nor one which *has* something, nor one which exists *in a place* or *at some time*. For all those things are accidents of physical and bodily existence, and not of intelligible and motionless – not to mention partless – [existence].' He then makes a
15   few remarks about the composition of simple words, which Aristotle dealt with in his book *On Interpretation*, and at the end⁵⁹⁵ demonstrates the division of the genera into ten as being appropriate to first
379,1   principles and to knowledge – these being thereby determinate in number⁵⁹⁶ and [defined] in terms of the universal number.⁵⁹⁷

   Aristotle, on the other hand, examines after the categories the matters which particularly pertain to them, as we shall indeed find out forthwith: it is possible to call these [topics] 'On Opposites', 'On
5   Prior and Posterior', 'On the Simultaneous', 'On the Species of Movement' and 'On the Homonymy of Having'. But we must first investigate quite generally concerning these things exactly why they are appended at the end of the *Categories*, and what service they provide. For some, among whom Andronicus is one, say that these matters have been appended by someone against the purpose of the book,
10   namely by the man who inscribed the book of the *Categories* with the title *Preamble to the Topics*.⁵⁹⁸ But these people do not bear in mind the considerable service which the remarks [of *Cat*. 10-15] perform, not only for the treatise on the topics, but also for the account concerning the categories. Others, including Porphyry,⁵⁹⁹ opine that these investigations contribute to [the] clarity [of the work], because, among the names which receive mention in the *Categories*, those
15   which were not anticipated (*proeilêmmena*) by the common conceptions Aristotle took right at the beginning and analysed them, as for example in the account concerning homonymous and synonymous things, while those which were indeed anticipated in the common conceptions, but which required further analysis – of *these* Aristotle analysed [in each case] the confused [name] belonging to the preconception (*prolêpsis*)⁶⁰⁰ after the completion [of the *Categories* proper], in order not to chop up the continuity of the account by inserting the
20   analysis of these [names] into the midst [of the main account].

   Those who say this have a point, but they do not command the whole reason. For much more important than this, as Iamblichus says, is that these [appended chapters] include a *classification* (*epi-*

krisis) of all those [concepts] of which [Aristotle] made use, that is to
say of opposites and the rest. For since these [concepts] were useful
for the discovery and confirmation of the categories, but it was not
possible to classify them properly unless he gave full analytical   25
accounts of them, he appended these [accounts] at the end. And he
has set them out not in a disordered manner, but in due order. For
since he investigated, both in the account of substance and in the case
of the other categories, whether they admit of the contrary [i.e.
contrariety],[601] and, in the [accounts] concerning the [category of]
relative, whether the great is contrary to the small or rather is
opposed [to it],[602] and [since] in mentioning these things he did not   30
exhibit the respect in which contraries differ from opposites, after the
completion of the [account of the] categories he consequently produces
the account concerning the opposites, for the sake of a classification of
what generally coexists with, or does not belong to, all the categories.

   Again, after the [treatments of] substance and quantity, having
adumbrated the nature of the relative, he demonstrated that some
[relatives] are simultaneous in nature, while others are prior – that   380,1
is, in relation to other things which are posterior – as for example
what is knowable and perceivable is prior to knowledge and perception (7b15-8a12). So it was necessary, after the opposites, to adum-
brate the nature of the simultaneous, and of the prior and posterior.
And since he gave instruction on acting and undergoing next in order
(11b1ff.), and these categories include movements, he necessarily   5
conveyed, towards the classification of these, the species of movement, and assigned the third place to them [in chs.10-15], in the same
way as the [corresponding] categories too had had their order. And
he drew distinctions in connection with the homonymy of having last
of all, because he also mentioned the category of having last (11b12):
it is certainly necessary for the classification of this [category] to give
a separate definition of the large number of different ways in which   10
[having] is said, so that we are not in any way confused by them.[603]
In consequence the reception of these investigations [into his account]
became necessary for him, and their order was arranged in accordance
with the order of the categories.[604] In addition, these [investigations] are
useful for the whole of dialectic, and the profitable application of the
same to many areas was worthy of the capacity [i.e. intellectual abilities]
of the ancients. But let that suffice by way of general comment.   15

On the Opposites

Concerning opposites Iamblichus starts by asking on what basis we
have primarily come to think of them. Is it that, scrutinising the
plants and animals which are mutually obliterating, we have thus
discerned their *opposition*, or do we suppose that objects which do not

20   coexist are, insofar as they do not coexist, in conflict? But neither
obliteration nor non-coexistence[605] of things imports their opposition:
for [opposites] do actually coexist in some cases, as for example
opposites are observed in the case of the relatives (11b24-31).[606] In
fact the [class] of the opposites is *not* some common genus, as some
of the Peripatetics think;[607] rather, in taking the [name] of the
opposites to be a single common word, Aristotle arranged the ho-
25   monymy not only in respect of things which conflict and are not
compatible, but also in respect of some things which do coexist, but
which coexist in an opposed way to one another, like the relatives.
For when we talk of half in relation to double, the relation is in no
way one of conflict, but, if not a contrariety, at any rate a sort of
differentia of opposition – in the sense of an opposition of a particular
kind – is insinuated. Hence it is not the case that [the relatives] are
30   subsumed under a single genus in relation to the other three [pairs
of] opposites.[608] And nor is it even the case that while the relatives
are homonymous,[609] the other three [pairs of opposites] are arranged
under a single genus, namely that of non-coexistence[610] and conflict.
For the things sharing the common feature of being said to be opposed
do not have any common genus among themselves, but are opposed
homonymously.[611] That is also why Aristotle says '[We must talk]
381,1 about the opposites, and the various ways they are usually opposed'
(11b16). For the phrase 'the various ways they are usually opposed'
is [indicative] of their homonymy.
      But some of the Peripatetics have claimed that the opposite is a
genus,[612] 'because a common definition of the opposites is specified as
follows: "all those things are called opposites which cannot coexist
when examined in respect of the same simultaneous and common
5   signification of the same object and in relation to the same external
thing". This holds of the four species of opposition. For in the case of
contraries it is impossible for the same thing[613] to be white and black
simultaneously both in respect of the same [part of itself] and *qua*
itself. And with regard to the relatives, opposed [relations] are not
coexistent[614] when examined in relation to the same thing: for the
same thing cannot simultaneously be both bigger and smaller in
10   relation to the same thing, nor can the same man simultaneously be
both master and slave of the same man. And nor do the things
[opposed] in respect of possession and privation coexist simultaneously with regard to the same thing: for it is not possible to have both
sight and blindness in the same eye. Furthermore, the affirmation is
not coexistent with the negation: for if "It is day" is true, "It is not
day" is false. So if the account of the opposites fits all the species, then
15   the division is not of a word into its significations, but of a genus into
its species, since the opposite is not predicated homonymously but
synonymously.'[615]

Against this Iamblichus says that 'If the definition were not homonymous, then there would indeed be a common account and
common genus of all the opposites. But since (Iamblichus says) [their]
not being able to coexist in respect of the same thing and in relation   20
to the same thing is considered in one way in the case of the relatives,
in another way in the case of affirmation and negation, and in yet
another way in the cases of the remaining opposites, the original
account is correct – that the opposites are homonymous. Hence also
(he continues), Nicostratus went wrong in producing his disputation
against what he took to be a single genus of them [i.e. the opposites].'
But even Porphyry himself posits a *genus* [of opposites] rather [than
a homonymy], and I too incline rather in this direction, not having
heard any convincing account which obtains [as its conclusion] their   25
homonymy, and not being able to think of one myself, except Aristotle's remarking that '[We must talk] about the opposites, and the
various ways they are usually opposed'. And yet it was quite possible
[for Aristotle] to allude to 'various ways' even if there was a *genus* [of
opposites]: for if [the genus] contained three or if [it contained] four
species, it was true to say that things are opposed in three or four
ways, that is, in various ways. For 'in many ways' does not automatically denote the homonymity of a word:[616] only that something is *said*   30
in many ways, not however that [the corresponding things] *are* [in many
ways].[617] But let that suffice as a general account of the opposites; next
we must take up Aristotle's text and give an exegesis of it.

11b16-38 [We must talk] about opposites, and the various ways   382,1
they are usually opposed. [There are four ways in which things
are said to be opposed to one another, either as relatives or as
contraries or as privation and possession or as affirmation and
negation. And each of these sorts is opposed, to give a rough
sketch, as in the following examples: things opposed as relatives
– as double to half; things opposed as contraries – as good to bad;
things opposed in respect of privation and possession – as
blindness and sight; things opposed as affirmation and negation
– as *he is sitting – he is not sitting*. Now things opposed as
relatives are called just what they are *of* (or *than*) their opposites
or (are said) in some other way *in relation to* them. For example,
double is called just what it is (double) *of* the half. And knowledge is opposed to the knowable in the way the relatives are
opposed, and knowledge is called just what it is *of* the knowable,
and the knowable too is called just what it is *in relation to* its
opposite, knowledge: for the knowable is called knowable by
virtue of something, namely knowledge. Hence things opposed
as relatives are called just what they are *of* (or *than*) their

opposites or (are said) in some other way *in relation to* one another. Things opposed as contraries, on the other hand, are never called just what they are *in relation to* one another, but are called *contraries* of one another: for the good is not called good *of* the bad, but its contrary, nor is white called white *of* black, but its contrary.] So these oppositions differ from one another.

Just as in the other cases,[618] when he had conveyed the initial division by means of examples (1b25-2a10), [Aristotle] then expounded the account of each [category], so too here, having conveyed the division of the opposites, this being a fourfold one, and having adumbrated

5 their differentiae[619] by means of his examples in a way which makes them accessible to his audience, he introduces the account of each [opposition] and embraces them in definitions. Besides [the other material taken from Archytas], Aristotle appears to have transferred the material concerning opposites from Archytas' book entitled *On Opposites*, which the latter did not arrange together with the account

10 of genera, but deemed worthy to be a separate treatise.[620] For Archytas conveys the division of them [i.e. the opposites] thus:[621] '[Opposites] are said to be opposed to one another both by convention and by nature: some as[622] contraries, for example good to bad, healthy to sick, and true to false; others as possession to privation, for example life to death, sight to blindness, and knowledge to oblivion; others as things which are a certain way in relation to something, for example

15 double to half, ruler to ruled, and governor to governed; and yet others as affirmation to negation, for example that there is a man to that there is not [a man], and that he is morally excellent to that he is not [morally excellent].'

Aristotle defined the opposition in respect of the relative before the others because, it seems to me, it has a particular distinguishing mark lacked by the others, namely that things opposed in this way coexist with one another.[623] Archytas, however, placed relatives third,

20 as subsisting in respect of a relation (*skhesis*), and wrote the following about the opposition in respect of the relative:[624] 'The relatives necessarily come about and are destroyed simultaneously: for it is impossible for double to be, but not half, or for half to be, but not double. And whenever anything double comes about, a half too comes about simultaneously, and whenever anything double is destroyed, a half too is destroyed simultaneously.' Aristotle defines it [i.e. the opposi-

25 tion of relatives] in terms of the more general definition of the relatives, which calls them: 'The things which are said to be just what they are *of* or *than*[625] other things – namely their opposites – or [are said] in some other way in relation to something else' (6a36-7).[626] [The definition] needs this addition[627] because of the different specifica-

tions of relatives, as was said in the treatment of them.[628] And he very reasonably [makes use of the definition of the relatives], for this definition suffices too for their *opposition*, because it introduces them together, and clearly makes them mutually convertible,[629] and so does not need to be made in any other way precise for this [purpose]. At 30 the same time he will also show, using the following reasoning, that the relatives are not opposed in the same way as the other opposites: 383,1 for it holds of all the relatives that they are said in relation to *each other*. But how can relatives be *opposed*, if they are simultaneous and coexist with each other and reciprocate[630] towards one another? For opposites seem to be mutually cancelling. But perhaps it is not [mutual] cancellation that is the distinguishing mark of the opposites, but rather their not existing with regard to the same thing and in the 5 same respect,[631] and this does hold of the relatives too: for these do not coexist with regard to the same thing [sc. and in the same respect[632]].

Being 'called just what they are of or than' other things,[633] namely 'their opposites, or [being said] in some other way in relation to them' was possibly said [by Aristotle] not only because of the *inflected words* (*ptôseis*), in relation to which each of the relatives is specified, but also with regard to the chosen [relatives] *themselves* whose specification is being given. For not all [relative opposites] are said in such a 10 way as to be called just what they are in relation to something else in exactly the way that double and half and knowledge are. For each of *these*[634] is said to be just what it is in relation to something else in accordance with whatever *inflection* the specification of that [different thing] is given, but [there can be relatives][635] even if the specification is *not* given in terms of an inflection, as for example large and small, which are opposed to one another in respect of the relative, are not specified [as such] in terms of an inflection, nor is the one *of* or 15 *than* the other, but is only *said in relation to* the other, and nor are the knowable and the perceivable and the intelligible likewise, nor anything else of that nature, *of* those things in relation to which they are said: for the knowable is not itself *of* something different, but rather something different [i.e. knowledge] is *of* it, for it is said in relation to knowledge not because it is of knowledge, but because knowledge is of it.

Archytas wrote about the reason for this in the place where he 20 conveys the differences among things opposed as the relatives are, and it is better to transcribe his entire text:[636] 'Of the relatives some reciprocate towards one another from both sides, as for example the larger and the smaller, the sibling and the similar. Others do indeed possess reciprocation, but not from both parts [of the relation]. For knowledge is said *of* the knowable and perception *of* the perceivable, 25 but not, contrariwise, the knowable of knowledge and the perceivable of perception. The reason for this is that what is judged can exist without the judger, as for instance the perceivable [can exist] without perception and the knowable without knowledge, but it is impossible for the judger to exist without the judged, such as the perception

30   without the perceivable and the knowledge without the knowable. Now of [relatives] which possess reciprocation from both parts [of the

384,1 relation], some reciprocate towards each other identically (*adia-phorôs*), such as the similar, the equal, and the sibling. For this is similar to that, and contrariwise that to this, and this is equal to that, and contrariwise that to this, and this is sibling to that, and contrari-wise that to this. But other [relatives], while they reciprocate towards

5   each other from both parts [of the relation], do not do so identically (*adiaphorôs*): this is *bigger* than that, but that is *smaller* than this, and this man is *father* of that, but that is *son* of this.'

It is to be understood that while Aristotle did not convey a mean between the relatives, Archytas wrote the following about them:[637] 'The relatives admit of means: for between the master and slave is

10   the free man, and between the greater and less is the equal, and between the broad and narrow is that which fits.' If Aristotle had [considered and] not accepted this mean, he would have said that the opposition in respect of the relative differs from that in respect of the contrary in the additional respect that it [i.e. the former] does *not* admit of a mean.

The relatives differ from the contraries in the manner of their

15   predication.[638] For relatives are called just what they are *in relation to one another*, in some way or other, whereas although contraries are opposed, they do not reciprocate towards one another. For the good is not called good[639] *of* bad, nor the bad bad *of* good, but they are merely contraries to each other. We must beware not to slip from the relatives into the opposition of the contraries or some other. For the relatives

20   are not conflicting or mutually cancelling, but rather indeed [mutu-ally] entailing, since their mere diversity introduces a *coexistent* opposition.[640] For clearly knowledge bears a coexistent opposition towards the knowable, namely the [opposition] in respect of the relative, while [it bears a] conflicting and incompatible opposition towards ignorance: for knowledge is not called [knowledge] of igno-rance, but rather [called] knowledge of the knowable on the one hand, and the contrary of ignorance on the other. So it is necessary to think

25   of the opposition of the relatives as uniting its subjects together with a certain opposition which derives its difference[641] from [the subjects' relation to] *one another* and not from [the subjects taken in] *them-selves*. For because of this, while contraries repel one another, rela-tives unite their diversity on the basis of their kinship to one another. Hence too some [relatives] manifest their diversity to a greater extent, such as the double towards the half, others to a lesser extent, such as

knowledge towards the[642] knowable, and still others almost not at all,   30
such as men who are equals towards one another.

Now all those things which, in bearing an opposition, are called
just what they are *of* or *than* their opposite – all these belong to the
relatives, as for example the greater is called just what it is[643] [i.e.
greater] *than* its opposite, and the same thing [is said to be] greater
in relation to one thing,[644] but smaller in relation to another: hence
such an opposition is not conflicting.[645] And the active [verb] 'to strike'
is opposed to the passive [verb] 'to be struck' as a relative. That is also   35
the reason why Aristotle, in saying that acting and undergoing admit
of contraries (11b1), did not say that they themselves are contraries   385,1
of one another, but demonstrated contrariety within each of them,[646]
as for example in the case of whitening and blackening, and being
whitened and being blackened. Andronicus, however, claimed that
acting and undergoing are not merely opposites but also contraries.

It is also worth noting the following point,[647] that while the rela-   5
tives are said in relation to each other, contraries are not called just
the contraries they are – that is, the things which are included in the
contrariety, such as white and black – in relation to one another.[648]
But the contrary *itself*, not the things included under it, *is* said in
accordance with the relatives, and not in accordance with the contrary: for they[649] mutually introduce one another and coexist. And
perhaps the reason for this is the common coexistence in contrary   10
things of contrariety.[650] But Nicostratus thinks he can show that the
contraries[651] are said in relation to each other, producing his argument not on the basis of the things [falling] under the contrary, but
on the basis of the contrary itself. But we know that in all cases each
thing itself is one thing, and what is arranged under it and participates in it is a different thing, as for example the equal itself is one
of the relatives, but the things [falling] under it are quantities in
which the equal is present. So in the same way too the *contraries*   15
themselves, *qua* coexisting things, are *relatives*, but the things [fall-
ing] *under* the contraries, *qua* things participating in the contraries,
are *contraries*.[652] And it is indeed remarkable how contraries insofar
as they are contraries are *not* contraries but relatives. There would
be nothing remarkable if, *in addition* to their being contraries, being
relative also held in their case. What looks like a miracle is if they,
being contraries, are, insofar as they are contraries, not contraries at   20
all. But in fact there is nothing remarkable if, when the contraries
are set up in accordance with their common and single special feature,
they coexist with each other, whereas [when they are set up] in
accordance with their separating and conflict-engendering [special
feature] they bring it about that the things which *participate* in them
conflict. And indeed since the very division and conflict [between the
contrary things] is a single one it is united in relation to itself,

whereas the things participating in the conflict and division are
25 separated from one another.[653] That will suffice on this subject.

In setting out examples of affirmation and negation Aristotle did
not specify the whole statements, but [just] the predicated terms,
because the statements are characterised in accordance with them,
the negating particle being attached to the predicate. But we must
proceed to what comes next in order.

30 **11b33-12a25** Things opposed as contraries, on the other hand,
are never called just what they are *in relation to* one another
[but are called *contraries* of one another: for the good is not called
good *of* the bad, but its contrary, nor is white called white *of*
black, but its contrary. So these oppositions differ from one
another. All those contraries which are such that it is necessary
that one or other of them belong to the things they naturally
come about in or of which they they are predicated – these have
nothing intermediate. For example, sickness and health naturally come about in the body of an animal, and it is indeed
necessary that one or the other belong to a given animal's body
– either sickness or health. And odd and even are predicated of
number, and it is indeed necessary that one or the other belong
to a given number – either odd or even. And now there is nothing
intermediate between these – neither between sickness and
health nor between odd and even. But in the case of all those
things where it is not necessary that one or the other belong, in
these cases there is something intermediate. For example, black
and white naturally come about in body, and it is indeed not
necessary that one or the other of them belong to a given body
– for not every body is either white or black – and bad and good
are predicated both of man and of many other things, but it is
not necessary that one or other of them belong to those things
of which they are predicated: for not all such things are either
bad or good. And now there is something intermediate between
these, as for instance between white and black there is grey and
yellow and all the other colours, and between bad and good there
is the neither bad nor good. In some cases, furthermore, names
have been established for the intermediates, as for instance grey
and yellow between white and black. But in some cases it is not
straightforward to specify the intermediate by means of a name,
and the intermediate is defined rather in terms of the negation
of each of the extremes,] as for instance the neither good nor bad
and neither just nor unjust.

After the relatives [Aristotle] proposes to talk about contraries, because, of the opposites, the contraries are both species, whereas in

the case of possession and privation [only] one [is a species],[654] and in
the case of affirmation and negation the whole [consists] in a sentence   386,1
and composition.[655] So it is appropriate that contraries were accorded
higher esteem than the latter [two oppositons].[656] At the beginning of
the account of contraries [Aristotle] immediately conveyed the difference between them and the relatives: they are not called just what
they are *of* or *than* other things, sc. their contraries. For white is not
called <white *of* black, but *contrary*> to black.[657] They differ from the   5
rest of the opposites, as mentioned, in that *both* contraries [of any
given pair] are species.

[Aristotle] next conveys the differentiation of the contraries themselves, and says that some contraries – [those] of which one [contrary]
necessarily belongs to the thing capable of receiving it – are without
an intermediate. Examples given are 'health and sickness', and 'odd
and even' – for the even-odd and the odd-even [numbers], as well,
although they might seem to be in some way between the two, namely   10
between odd and even, are nevertheless even in species.[658] (Whereas
Aristotle says that there is nothing intermediate between health and
sickness, although as a philosopher he sees a mean between virtue
and vice, the medical men, who are experts on the body, have also
established many means between health and sickness, [means] which
move between [health and sickness] in the broad area of the condition
called *neutral* by these men.[659]) But some contraries – those of which   15
it is not necessary that one [contrary] is in the thing capable of
receiving them – have intermediates. Examples given are 'white and
black': for it is not necessary in every case (*pantôs*)[660] that [something
capable of being white or black] is either white or black, since there
are grey and yellow things, and things having other intermediate
colours.

Of [contraries] having intermediates, or *mediated* [contraries] as
they are also called, some have several intermediates – those perhaps
which differ more from each other by nature, as has been said in the   20
case of white and black: for there are many colours in the middle of
these. Other [contraries have] just one [intermediate], owing to their
proximity to one another, as for example lukewarm is the sole
intermediate between hot and cold. And of contraries with an intermediate some have named intermediates, as in the mentioned cases,
others unnamed ones, which are denoted by the negation of both the
extremes: for what is between good and bad was not given a name [by   25
Aristotle], but is called 'neither good nor bad' (for the name 'indifferent' has been established by more recent [thinkers]),[661] and the
intermediate between just and unjust is nameless, but is named by
the negation of the extremes. It is clear that the [intermediates] which
have become familiar through usage have also received a usual name,

whereas those which are unfamiliar to usage have remained nameless.

30   Now since some of the contraries are *in* a subject, such as white
and black (for they belong *in* body, which receives them affectively),[662]
while others are said *of* a subject, such as even and odd (for these are
said *of* number as subject, because they are differentiae, and differentiae, as [Aristotle] himself showed in his account concerning substance (3b1), are said *of* subjects, namely of the species), for this
387,1 reason [Aristotle] denoted the things [which are] *in* a subject by
means of the phrase 'in which they naturally come about' (12a1), and
the things [which are said] *of* a subject by means of the phrase 'or of
which they are predicated' (ibid.).[663] For indeed even though number
is certainly *in* a subject,[664] still, whenever the subject is not taken into
consideration, even and odd are said *of number* as of a subject.[665] That
5   health and sickness do not belong to body in the same way as odd and
even [belong] to number is clear from the fact that health and sickness
belong to the same body by turns, but even and odd in no way belong
to the same number.

It is worth considering whether even and odd are differentiae of
number or are species of number. If in our definition of even number
10   we call it 'number divided into two [equal parts]', and if [even number]
were a species of number made up of (*ek*) the genus of number plus a
differentia, how is it then said to be *of* number as subject (12a6-7)?
For the species could not be said of the genus as subject, given that
what is said *of* a subject is more general than that of which it is said.
Well, even and odd, *qua* species, are not predicated of number, *qua*
genus, but the *differentia* – being divisible into two [equal parts] – is
15   predicated of even number *qua* species; perhaps he called this [differ-
entia] 'even' because it forms the species of even [number].

But since Aristotle's text achieved clarity, let us also look at the
points which the more famous of his interpreters[666] have treated of in
addition on the topic. For since the Stoics pride themselves on their
treatment of logical matters both in the other areas [of logic] and in
20   the case of the contraries,[667] [these interpreters] are intent on showing
that *Aristotle* provided the starting points for everything in a single
book, which he entitled *On Opposites*,[668] in which there is also a
perplexing multitude of puzzles, of which they [i.e. the Stoics] have
cited [only] a small part. Now the other areas are not sensibly
incorporated in an introduction, but we must mention those things
which the Stoics arranged in agreement with Aristotle. So then,
25   having set down the old definition regarding contraries, which we
have also mentioned already (148,31ff.), namely that they are those
things which differ most from one another in the same genus,[669]
Aristotle corrected this definition in his book *On Opposites*, after
examining it in multifarious ways. For he considered whether things

which are different are contraries and whether difference can be contrariety; whether the total separation (*diastasis*) [between contraries] is the one differing the most;[670] whether things' being furthest apart[671] is the same as their differing the most; what is the nature of the contrast (*apostasis*) [between contraries] and how the [notion of] being furthest apart is to be understood. In view of the emergence of these untoward matters, [he considered] that something must be added to the [definition of the] genus, so that its definition is '[Contraries are] the things furthest apart in the same genus'. And [he considered] what untoward things follow from this [new definition]; whether contrariety is a kind of diversity;[672] whether things which are especially other are contrary; and he set down many more arguments.

[Aristotle] made use of this definition in his account of quantity notwithstanding,[673] with a reference to the fact that the definition is an ancient one (6a11-18), and the Stoics adopted it and made use of it, demonstrating its unsoundness, but trying nevertheless to solve the difficulties appearing in it. Nicostratus, however, alleges that <contraries exist>[674] not merely in the same genus, <but also in contrary ones: in the same genus,> colour, [there exist] black and white, and sweet and bitter in the [genus of] taste, but justice and injustice are from contrary genera, for the genus of the former is virtue, but that of the latter is vice. In one sense virtue and vice themselves are from the same genus (for the genus [i.e. category] of both is state (*hexis*) and quality), but in another sense they are from contrary genera: for the genus of virtue is the good, and of wickedness the bad, and the good and [the] bad appear themselves to be genera (unless indeed they too are in quality as their genus). Aristotle, however, in many places[675] manifestly posits the good and the bad not as genera but as homonymous words.

This is but a tiny part[676] of the matters which Aristotle puzzled over in his account concerning contrarieties, and it is fitting in the case of all such questions to engage in advocacy as the ancients do, and even if a particular description is under suspicion, to make use of it when it does no damage in its domain of application. Hence, in his [inquiries] concerning the [category of] quantity, wishing to show that *down* is the contrary of *up*, [Aristotle] made use of the definition, since the older philosophers expounded it on the basis of contrariety of place (6a15-18). But here (11b33ff.), in his teaching concerning the contraries, he has not make use of it as it was specified above, since it is not beyond suspicion.

Now the Stoics made use of all these points and followed in the footsteps of Aristotle's other definitions concerning contraries, after he had given them the starting points in his book *On Opposites*, [points] which they developed in their own books. Above all they took

388,1

5

10

15

20

30

25   *states* (*hexeis*) to be contrary, just as he did, as for example *practical wisdom* and *folly*, and *predicates* (*katêgorêmata*), such as *being practically wise* and *being foolish*,[677] as well as *means* (*mesotêtes*),[678] such as *wisely* or *foolishly*. They did not also, however, take the men who are qualified (*poioi*) and who are a certain way (*pôs ekhontes*)[679] to be contrary, but to be contrarily related, and they say that this man is not [contrary] to that man, but that the practically wise man [is contrary] to the foolish man *mediately*.[680] And if we do sometimes also say that this man is contrary to that one, we establish our meaning,

30   so they claim, by having regard to[681] the *immediate* [contraries].[682] Contrariety is, accordingly, principally observed in the case of states, relations and operations, and similar things; but predicates and the things which are in some way connected with them are spoken of in

389,1 a secondary sense as contraries; and they[683] in some manner or other add to the contraries the [means] *wisely* and *foolishly*. But contraries are considered *generally* in objects (*pragmata*),[684] and thus practical wisdom and folly are said to be contraries immediately, not this *particular* [wisdom] to that *particular* [folly]. This being the Stoic

5   teaching, let us see how they extracted it from Aristotle's instruction.

       For he says in his [book] *On Opposites* that justice is contrary to injustice; he says that the just *man* is not said to be *contrary*, but to be contrarily *disposed*, to the unjust man. He says: 'If these things too [i.e. the men] are contraries, then "contrary" will be being said in two different ways: things will be called contraries either *per se*, as for example virtue and vice, movement and[685] rest, or by *participating in* [*per se*] contraries, as for example the thing moved [will be contrary]

10   to the thing at rest, and the good thing [will be contrary] to the bad thing.' In these words he has told us why he did not call the qualified *men* contrary. For since it is by virtue of *participation*[686] that the qualified men are different,[687] the participating thing will not be spoken of in the same way as[688] what it participates in, but rather [will be said] to participate in that, and, if anything, to be derivative[689] from it, as is the white thing from whiteness.[690] Since, then, practical wisdom is contrary to folly, the men participating [in them] will not

15   be said to *be* contrary, but rather to *participate in* contraries. But if someone is going to call these [participating] things contraries too, he ought to draw a distinction, [Aristotle] says, and say that the one set of things are contraries *simpliciter*, and that the other things are called contraries by virtue of participation in contraries [strictly so called].

       Since it is possible to say the same thing both by virtue of an uncompounded word, such as 'practical wisdom' (*phronêsis*) [or] 'folly' (*aphrosunê*), and by means of a definition, such as [that practical wisdom is] knowledge of the things that are good and bad and neither,

20   and that folly is ignorance of the same, they ask whether only those

things [said] in virtue of simple [words] are contraries,[691] or whether those things [said] in virtue of definitions are [contraries] as well.[692] And Chrysippus, for one, raises the question whether perhaps the appellatives (*prosêgorika*)[693] and simple [words] alone are contraries, and their [definitions] not. For in the case of these [definitions] we bring many elements together with the help of connectives and with conjunctions and other explanatory particles, each of which it would be improper to bring into the account of contraries. Hence he says that practical wisdom is contrary to folly, but he says[694] that the *definition* [of the one] is not uniformly contrary to the *definition* [of the other] – but, by establishing a reference to the former,[695] people set the definitions also in pairwise (*kata suzugian*) opposition to one another. These matters were first defined by Aristotle, who did not deem that an uncompounded [term] is contrary to the *definition* of its contrary – for example [he deemed] that practical wisdom is not contrary to ignorance of things that are good and bad and neither – but, if [definitions can be contraries] at all, [he deemed that one should] set definition in pairwise opposition to definition, and call them contrary by virtue of being of contrary objects. He makes further refinements concerning these matters, such as that a definitional account is contrary to [another definitional] account if the genus[696] has something contrary to it, or the differentiae, or both.[697] This is so in the case of the definition of the beautiful, if the following is right, namely the due proportion of parts towards one another: to this [definition] the contrary is ill-proportion of the parts towards one another, and here the genus has the contrariety. Elsewhere the differentiae [have it], as for example white, [defined as] a colour which dilates the stream of sight, and black, [defined as] a colour which compresses it.[698] In this case the genus [i.e. colour] is the same, and the contrariety is in respect of the differentiae. It has been explained, therefore, how an account can be contrary to an account; accounts which are explanatory of the essence [of something] will also be [capable of being] contrary.[699] But let it suffice that these matters have been brought to this point.

Since Aristotle divides the contraries into those without an intermediate and those with an intermediate, and calls those without an intermediate those of which necessarily one or the other [contrary] belongs to the thing capable of receiving them, and is present by turns to the subject, so long as it is not one of the things naturally united [with it], as heat is with fire, but rather is one of its accidents, his account of [contraries] without an intermediate becomes the following: that contraries are without an intermediate in the cases where one or the other [contrary] belongs necessarily in connection with the thing capable of receiving them,[700] whereas [those contraries] of which it is not necessary that one or the other [belong] have an intermediate.

25

30

390,1

5

10

Nicostratus contradicts Aristotle's assertion that the intermediates are characterised by the negation of the extremes, saying that: 'If the
15 negation [of the extremes] denoted the intermediate, then the "not-man and not-horse" would denote a mean. Hence (he says) "the intermediate being taken in the same genus as that in which its extremes lie" must be added.' But one who says this does not take into account the fact that horse and man are neither extremes nor contraries – but the discussion was about extremes and contraries.
20 In his book *On Opposites* Aristotle asked whether, if when one discards one [contrary] it is not necessarily the case that one adopts the other, there is then an intermediate between these [contraries], or not in every case: for one who discards the true opinion does not necessarily adopt a false opinion, nor does one [who discards] a false [opinion necessarily adopt] a true [opinion], but sometimes one changes from [having] this [true or false] opinion either to supposing nothing at all, or to [a state of] knowledge – and there is nothing
25 intermediate between true and false opinion, assuming neither ignorance nor knowledge is.

There are other differentiae of contraries, too, which [Aristotle] will also touch on as he proceeds (14a15-25). He made special mention of these ones – namely being without an intermediate and having an intermediate – because he exhibits what differentiates contraries from the other opposites on the basis of these features. For his purpose is not to go through all the properties of the opposites
30 individually, but only their principal ones, in order to demonstrate their comparative differences in relation to each other. He will show that the four genera of the opposites differ from each other, and he has already made clear how things [opposed] as relatives differ from the contraries. He will make clear how both of the these differ from things [opposed] as privation and possession, by setting out the distinguishing marks of each, and then he will demonstrate the difference between all
35 these and the things [opposed] as affirmation and negation.[701]
391,1 It would be good next to quote also what Archytas says concerning the differentiation of the contraries. It is as follows:[702] 'Each of these oppositions is also divided into neighbouring species to one another. For of contraries some are without intermediates, but others have an intermediate: between health and sickness there is nothing intermediate, nor [is there anything between] rest and movement, nor [be-
5 tween] waking and sleeping, nor [between] straight and bent, nor [between] the other contrarieties [without an intermediate]. But between much and little [there is] the moderate, and [between] high and low [there is] unison, and [between] swift and slow there is the equally fast, and [between] greater and less [there is] the equal. In general, therefore,[703] of those contrarieties of which it is necessary that one [contrary] be present in the thing capable of receiving them

– these do not admit of an intermediate. For between health and
sickness there is nothing intermediate, and it is necessary that every   10
animal be either sick or healthy, nor [is there an intermediate
between] waking and sleep, and it is necessary that every animal be
either awake or asleep, nor [is there an intermediate between] rest
and movement, and it is necessary that every animal be either at rest
or in motion. But of those contrarieties of which it is not necessary
either that both or that one of them [i.e. the contraries] be present in
the thing capable of receiving them – these do admit of a mean. For
between white and black [there is] the grey, and it is not necessary   15
that every animal be either white or black, and [between] great and
small [there is] the equal, and it is not necessary that every animal
be either great or small, and [between] hard and soft [there is] the
comfortable to touch, and it is not necessary that every animal be
either hard or soft.

'Further, there are three differentiae of contraries: some are opposed as good to bad, as for example health to sickness, some as bad
to bad, as for example meanness to profligacy, and yet others as   20
neither [good nor bad] to neither [good nor bad],[704] such as white to
black, heavy to light. Further, some contraries occur in *genera of
genera*: for good is contrary to bad, and the good is the genus of the
virtues, the bad [the genus] of the vices. Others [occur] in *genera of*   392,1
species: for virtue is contrary to vice, and virtue is the genus of
practical wisdom and temperance, vice that of folly and licence. Yet
others [occur] in *species*: for courage is contrary to cowardice and
justice to injustice, and[705] justice and courage are species of virtue,
injustice and licence of vice. Now the first genera, the ones which we   5
are calling genera of genera, <only> admit of division <into gen-
era>,[706] and the last-mentioned species, being also <the things most
proper> to perception [admit of division] <only into individuals,[707]
whereas the [contraries dealt with] in the middle> are not only genera
but also species.[708] For triangle is the genus of equiangular and
isosceles and scalene, <but a species of plane figure, and virtue is the
genus of practical wisdom, courage, temperance and justice,> but a
species of the good.'[709] In these remarks the other points are consonant
with Aristotle's instruction, but the last differentia, according to   10
which some contraries are in genera of genera, others in genera of
species, and yet others in species, has perhaps been omitted by
Aristotle here as being rather insubstantial.[710] But now we must turn
to the third opposition, namely that[711] of things [opposed] in terms of
possession and privation.

12a26-b5 Privation and possession are spoken of in connection   15
with the same thing, [for example sight and blindness in con-

nection with the eye. To put it generally, each of them is spoken
of in connection with whatever the possession naturally comes
about in. We say that each of the things capable of receiving the
(relevant) possession is deprived of it whenever it is in no way
present to the thing in which it is natural for the possession to
come about, and at the time when it is natural to have it. For
we do not call what does not have teeth (*simpliciter*) toothless,
nor do we call what does not have sight (*simpliciter*) blind, but
rather what does not have them at the time when it is natural
for it to have them: for some things do not have either sight or
teeth from birth, but are not (thereby) called toothless or blind.
Being deprived and having the possession are not (identical
with) privation and possession: for sight is a possession and
blindness a privation, whereas *having* sight is not sight, and
being blind is not blindness either. That is because blindness is
a particular privation, but being blind is being deprived, not a
privation. Further, if blindness were the same thing as being
blind, they would both be predicated of the same thing. But man
is called blind: in no sense is man called blindness. These – being
deprived and having a possession – do seem, however, to be
opposed as privation and possession are. For the manner of
opposition is the same one: for just as blindness is opposed to
sight,] so too is being blind opposed to having sight.

[Aristotle] sets down the third species of opposites, that in respect of
possession and privation, since this naturally precedes that in respect
of affirmation and negation, because the latter has its subsistence in
words, the former in objects. Privation is said in many ways, but the

20   sort which [Aristotle] has mentioned here is a certain complete
absence [of a property] from a thing which naturally possesses it, in
the [part] in which it naturally does so, when and where[712] it naturally
does so. '[From] a thing which *naturally* [possesses]',[713] because one
would not call the wall blind, since it is not at all its nature to see. '*At
the time when* it naturally [possesses]', because one would not call
newly born puppies blind, because it is not yet natural for them to
see, nor would one call newly born children toothless, because they

25   [naturally] do not yet have teeth. The phrase '*in the [part] in which*
[it naturally possesses]' is added so that we may get hold of the
appropriate part [of the body] in which the possession occurs: for it is
not if someone does not have eyes in his feet that he is deprived of

393,1 eyes, but [only] if someone has not received his share of eyes in the
appropriate place. [Aristotle] himself conflated all these points together, denoting the thing naturally [possessing] and the part [of the
body] in which the possession occurs both together by means of the
phrase 'in which it is natural [for the possession to come about]'

(12a30);[714] and he conflated together the time, the place[715] belonging to [the thing], and the other co-manifestations [of the possession] in 5 the phrase 'at the time when it is natural' (12a30) [for the possession] to belong. For whenever [a property] entirely fails to obtain, which it befits [something] to possess, and in the way in which it befits [that thing] to possess it, then [the thing] is said to be in [a state of] privation. Hence some people add to the account given of privation the phrase 'and in the way in which it is natural [for the possession to belong]'. For it is also the case that we call people with short necks 'neckless',[716] since the necks they have are not in accord with nature, and we call the pomegranate pipless, since it has smaller pips than 10 is natural, thereby referring to the natural defect as though it were a privation of the whole.

[Aristotle] does not simply say that the possession and privation are said about the same thing, but about the 'same *particular* thing' (*peri tauton ti*, 12a26),[717] thereby showing, through the addition of the word 'particular' (*ti*), *how* one says them about the same thing. For contraries too [are said] about the same thing, if, that is, the same thing is capable of receiving contraries, but in the case of contraries the contraries are not necessarily about *numerically* the same subject 15 (for if one part [of something] is white, such as the teeth, there is nothing to stop another [part] being black, such as the area of the pupil). In the case of privation, however, this is not possible, but the privation [occurs] in the very same part where the possession [occurs].[718] And that is plausible, for privation is just absence, and it is necessary[719] that the absence obtain in exactly the same place where 20 the presence also obtains, whereas contraries, being species, are in no way prevented from sometimes being in numerically different subjects as well, while preserving the principle of contrariety. So it is clear from these [considerations] that the things thus opposed [as possession and privation] bear both a certain likeness towards the contraries and an unlikeness. For contraries naturally come about in connection with the same subject;[720] for example sickness concerns just what health concerns: for these do not concern inanimate things, 25 but concern animals. And likewise too things opposed in respect of privation and possession: for sight concerns [what is an] animal, and does not concern [the] inanimate; hence blindness as well concerns [what is an] animal, for no one would call a pillar blind. Things opposed in respect of privation [and possession] have, then, this feature in common with contraries. But they differ from them, as I have said, in that contraries, even if they are in the same species, 30 nevertheless do not necessarily also [occur] in the same [individual] part of the species, whereas things [opposed] in respect of privation and possession tend also to obtain in the same part.

Aristotle next goes on to demonstrate that 'being deprived' or

having a privation is not the same thing as the privation [itself], and
nor is 'having a possession' the same thing as the possession [itself].[721]
He demonstrates this on the basis of the fact that sight is a possession,
35   but that having sight is not the sight [itself], so that having the
possession is not the possession [itself] either. And likewise being
blind is not blindness. He also shows this on the basis of the fact that
if they were the same, whatever the one were predicated of, the other
[would be predicated] of the same thing too. But that is not how it is:
394,1   for man is said to be *blind*, but not said to be *blindness*, and he is said
to *have* sight, but not to *be* sight. The arguments seem to differ from
one another in that the first proves the proposition (*to prokeimenon*)
on the basis of *being*, whereas the second [proves it] on the basis of
being predicated. Having demonstrated that the privation [itself] and
having a privation <are different, as are the possession and *having* a
5   possession,>[722] [Aristotle] reasonably added that, even though they
are different, nevertheless just as the possession is opposed to the
privation, so also are having a possession and being deprived [opposed
to one another], and the same manner of opposition exists, because
the latter are opposed in virtue of a reference to the former, and [so]
'the manner of opposition is the same one' (12b3) in the case of the
predications as the one which also [obtains] in the case of the possession and privation. 'For just as blindness is opposed to sight, so too is
10   *being blind* opposed to *having sight*' (12b3-5). These remarks suffice
for the elucidation of the text.
    Iamblichus conveys the more substantial aspects of these matters
somewhat as follows: 'One doctrine which is common to the ancients
and the moderns is that the things said in respect of privation and
possession are not contraries, although the ancients did not go as far
15   as to arrange them in a special genus of opposition, that of privation
and possession, as Aristotle does. But that it is a different [opposition]
becomes clear to those who distinguish the many ways in which
possession and privation are said, and the main kinds of signification
in accordance with which the opposition of things [said] in respect of
possession and privation comes about. They say, accordingly, that in
one way the *operation* (*energeia*) of the possessor and the possessed
is called (a state of) possession (*hexis*): one talks of the possession of
20   a cloak when someone possesses it, and it is possessed by the possessor, and Plato spoke somewhere of the possession of weapons in
connection with someone's having weapons.[723] In another way we call
acquired qualities which have become enduring states of possession
– both natural [qualities] and those in respect of skills, and states of
knowledge – in virtue of which those who are in them are also said to
be 'in a habitual state' (*hektikoi*).[724] And the perfect virtues, too, are
said in this sense to be states of possession: for an acquisition of
reason is observed in their case.

'Further, the natural constitution is said to be a state of possession, 25
when it is enduring, as for example we observe states of possession
belonging to the body and to the soul, and natural virtues or vices in
some people. And they say that a natural capacity is itself called a
state of possession, and that a privation is opposed to it as being a
disabling of it. But some say that it is not the natural capacity which
is included in the opposition of possession and privation, but rather
the [state of possession] said in accordance with the first significance 30
[of possession], which is the one called possession by derivation from
the [verb] "to possess, have" (*ekhein*). And moreover [they say] that
Chrysippus too, following Aristotle, calls those things privative
which, while intimating (*paremphainonta*) the nature of the possessing, obliterate [the state of possession] – not *simpliciter*, but when the
thing which naturally [possesses] manifests [that nature], and at the
time when it is natural [for it to possess], as was said before
(392,15ff.). And opposed to the state of possession which is called after
the [verb] "possess, have" is its privation – and the privations are not
merely of qualities, but also of operations, such as blindness, [being 35
the privation] of the operation of seeing, and lameness, [being the
privation] of the [operation] of walking. In another sense the absence
of what something is capable of possessing, considered in the sense
of its potential, is called privation; Aristotle mentiones this in the
Physics (191b15ff.). For a thing which is capable of having [some-
thing], and which potentially is [something] but does not yet have it[725] 395,1
operationally, is said to be in a state of privation from it.

'But perhaps (says Iamblichus) we ought not to construe its opposition towards privation in terms of [just] one particular signification
of possession, but in terms of all [its senses]. In this way there will be
a complete opposition of all states of privation towards all states of
possession, and thus too, in general, of each one opposed to each one, 5
such as of this particular privation to this particular possession in
accordance with their own special manner [of opposition]. For generally the non-possession [of some property] by a thing which naturally
possesses it, and at the time when it naturally does so, is to be termed
privation, and since possessing is said in many ways, so too non-possession and privation will be [said] in many ways.

'There is another sort of privation apart from the natural one – I
mean the one about which we spoke in connection with things
naturally [being in states of possession or privation], and at the time
when they are naturally [in such states] – which Chrysippus calls 10
"pertaining to custom" (*ethikos*). For *uncloaked, unshod* and *without
lunch* signify on the one hand a bare cancellation (*anairesis*), but they
also, on the other hand, signify a certain intimation (*paremphasis*),[726]
when they are spoken of in the sense of a privation. For we will not
say that an ox is uncloaked, nor that we ourselves are unshod when

we are bathing, nor that the birds have gone without lunch, nor
ourselves at break of day, but [in these cases] the privation of one who

15 is *accustomed* [to wear a cloak, shoes etc.], *at the time when* he is
accustomed to do so, is necessarily implied. For since it is a matter of
custom to take lunch at a certain established hour, whenever one who
is a party to the custom does not take lunch at the established time,
he cancels, by virtue of his privation, a manifestation not of nature
but of custom. So some states of non-possession are of things [pos-
sessing] by nature, others of things [possessing] in virtue of a custom,
and [there are] cancellations [of possession] in both cases, where the
things [possess] by nature and where they do so by custom. Often the

20 privation manifests a deviation not from custom but from what is
seemly, as in the case of someone who comes *uninvited* to dinner –
when we intimate that it is unseemly and not in accord with what
belongs to the customs that he has arrived.

'And, besides, privation is one of the things said homonymously.
For whenever some whole genus is not by nature such as to possess
some particular thing, we say that it is "deprived" of that thing which
it does not naturally possess. Thus we say that plants are deprived

25 of perception by virtue of their not naturally having perception. And
when some of the things in the genus are naturally such as to possess
[something], whereas others are not naturally [such as to possess it],
those which are not naturally [such as to possess it] are said to be
deprived of it, as for example in the genus of animals the mole [is
deprived] of sight, and we even prefer to say this than in the case of
removal by force [of the possessed feature].[727] But privation is strictly
said in the case of things which are by nature such as to possess
[something], but which do not possess it at the time when they would

30 naturally do so, and [at the time] when they are accustomed and have
begun to possess it, [all of] which is considered to be opposed to
possession. And the opposition in such cases is called the [opposition]
in respect of possession and privation.'

Archytas, however, divides privation three ways, saying:[728] 'Privation and being deprived are said in three ways: either in virtue of not
possessing at all, such as the blind [not possessing] sight, the toothless [not possessing] voice, and the ignorant [not possessing] knowledge; or in virtue of possessing less, such as the hard of hearing

35 [possessing less] hearing, and the sore-eyed [possessing less] sight;
or in virtue of not possessing in the way that one ought, such as the

396,1 bow-legged [not possessing] legs [in the way that it ought], and the
harsh-voiced [not possessing] a voice [in the way that it ought].'

One should be aware too that sometimes names which are not
privative [in form][729] denote a privation, as for example *poverty*
[denotes] the privation of money and *the blind man* the privation of

5 sight. Sometimes too privative names do not denote a privation: for

immortal, which has a privative form of expression, does not signify a privation, since we do not apply the term to something whose nature it is to die, but which subsequently does not die. Much confusion arises over the privative words. For if they are introduced by the [prefixes] *a-* and *an-*, as in [the Greek words for] 'homeless' (*aoikos*) and 'hearthless' (*anestios*), then it happens that they get assimilated sometimes to *negations* [i.e. contradictories], and sometimes to *con-* 10
traries. For just as cowardice (*deilia*) is the contrary to courage (*andreia*), so also is injustice (*adikia*) to justice (*dikaiosunê*), since it is contrary to justice. Often something bad is denoted [by the privative prefixes], as for instance we call an actor with a bad voice (*kakophônos*) voiceless (*aphônos*).[730] But it is also the case that negations are denoted by privative words, as for example 'different/ not-different' (*diaphora/ adiaphora*), 'profitable/ unprofitable' (*lusitelê/ alusitelê*). And often [privative words] signify more than one thing, so that negation and privation and contrariety are denoted by them, as 15
in the case of the word 'voiceless' (*aphônos*). Other [privative words] signify contraries [which are simply] different,[731] as for instance 'the wrong moment' (*akairia*) denotes the contrary of 'the right moment' (*kairos*), but does not at all express anything privative, while it is also the case that even though baseness is the contrary of uprightness, and lack of baseness (*aponêria*) is the privation of baseness, it sometimes also expresses uprightness.[732] Such being the wealth of irregularity [in this field], Chrysippus examined it in his writings called *On* 20
Privative [Words],[733] but Aristotle did not set himself that task, but merely that of going through matters relating to things [said] in respect of possession and privation. Hence even if many both of the contraries and of the negative [words] are said privatively, one should still construe the privative oppositions of states of possession in the way appropriate to them: this amounts to taking, in the opposition, the appropriate privation of the possession which belongs [to some- 25
thing]. Such a state of possession and the privation opposed to it come about in connection with the same subject – though not simultaneously – as for example, blindness [comes about] in connection with the eye, and sight too [comes about] in connection with that [subject].

12b5-16 Nor is what is under an affirmation or negation itself an affirmation or negation. [For an affirmation is an affirmative sentence and a negation is a negative sentence, but none of the things under an affirmation or negation is a sentence. These things too are, however, said to be opposed to one another as affirmation and negation: for in these cases too the manner of opposition is the same. For just as, at a time, an affirmation is opposed to a negation, such as 'he is sitting' to 'he is not sitting',]

30   so also the object under each of these is opposed (to the object
        under the other) – *that he is sitting* to *that he is not sitting.*[734]

        Having shown that possession is distinct from *having* a possession,
        and that privation is distinct from *having* a privation,[735] and that
        nevertheless what has a possession and [what] has a privation fall
        under the same opposition – that, namely, of possession and privation
        – <[Aristotle] says the same about affirmation and negation>[736] and
397,1   proves the point with an example. For the object (*pragma*) denoted
        by the affirmation is not [itself] an affirmation, and that [denoted] by
        the negation is not [itself] a negation, since the affirmation and
        negation are sentences, while the [objects] signified by them are not
        sentences. But even though the [signified objects] are not the same
        [as the corresponding sentences], they too nevertheless fall under the
5   same opposition – that, namely, of affirmation and negation – exactly
        as[737] the things which *have* possession and those which *have* privation
        [fall] under the [opposition] of possession and privation. For when I
        think of Socrates sitting, I suppose him to be a rational animal
        operating thus in accordance with the object itself (*auto to pragma*).[738]
        But the sentence which says that Socrates sits, assembled [as it is]
        from a noun and a verb,[739] is different from the object itself.[740]
10   Whether, indeed, statements consist in words or in the [correspond-
        ing] thoughts or in the incorporeal sayables (*lekta*) which subsist as
        an appendage (*paruphistamenois*),[741] these [statements] differ from
        the qualified bodies. And the former things are said to be opposed as
        statements, as negation and affirmation, whereas the latter things
        under the statements are also themselves opposed in just the same
        way.
          But, they say, no one would say that Socrates is opposed to himself.
15   Well, in point of fact we do not say that the opposition comes about
        concerning one or the other [*individual* in the opposition],[742] but in
        respect of the *operation*[743] of the sitting or not sitting. And the
        opposition comes about for these [i.e. the sitting/the not sitting] in
        virtue of the opposition [consisting] of the contradictory pair,[744] for[745]
        the way in which these [objects] signified [by the statements] are
        mutually cancelling is just how the contradictory pair also is op-
        posed.[746] And, contrariwise, corresponding to the manner in which the
        sentences are thus and so, the [signified] objects are also mutually
20   cancelling, and the proportion[747] comes about in the same way [in each
        case]: just as the [one] denoted object relates to the [other] denoted
        [object], so the [one] denotative sentence relates to the [other] deno-
        tative [sentence], and contrariwise. And even if we should take as
        opposites the things signified[748] by the words – and these are the
        rational discursive thoughts about Socrates seated or not – they too
        are said to be opposed in a similar way to the affirmation and

negation: for they too are *under* the negation and affirmation. Having 25
shown thus far which are the things opposed in respect of possession
and privation, [Aristotle] consequently raises the question how they
differ from the opposition of the relatives and from that of the
contraries, and first he raises the question how [they differ] from
those things opposed as relatives, making clear that:

> **12b16-25** It is clear that privation and possession are not
> opposed as relatives. [For neither is called just what it is *of* (or
> *than*) its opposite: for sight is not sight *of* blindness, nor is it said
> in any other way in relation to it. And similarly blindness would
> not be called blindness *of* sight, either: rather, blindness is called
> a privation of sight; it is not called blindness of sight. Further,
> all relatives are spoken of in relation to reciprocating correla-
> tives, so that if blindness too were one of the relatives, that in
> relation to which it is said would also reciprocate: but it does not
> reciprocate,] for sight is not called sight of blindness. 30

Since there are four oppositions which differ from one another, the
number of all the differences amounts to six. For in general, whatever
the number of the differing things, one must multiply their number
by that number minus one, take half of the resulting number, and 398,1
say that there are so many differences between the differing things.[749]
Now in this case the opposition of relatives differs from that of the
things [opposed] as contraries, and from that of things[750] opposed as
possession and privation, and from that [of sentences opposed] as
affirmation and negation: three relations [of difference] come about
from each one, since there are [in each case] three things in regard to
which there is [such] a relation, which is why we multiplied the 5
original number [i.e. four] by that [number] minus one. Again,[751] the
opposition of contraries differs from the remaining two: [there are just
two remaining,] for the difference in respect of relatives has already
been accounted for. So the [number of] differences becomes five.
Finally, the [opposition of things opposed] as possession and privation
differs from the [opposition] in respect of negation and affirmation:
[this is the only remaining difference,] for the [differences of each] in
relation to the other two have already been accounted for. In order
that the same differences are not taken into account twice, if we 10
sometimes begin from the first [differences], and sometimes from the
last ones, we are accordingly[752] instructed in the procedure to take
half of the number yielded by the multiplication. In this way, then,
according to this order too,[753] six differences come about. Aristotle,
however, does not arrive at them in this way, but first demonstrates
that the relatives differ from the contraries, as we have said; and now 15
he will show how the things opposed as possession and privation

differ from those [opposed] as relatives; and subsequently how the things [opposed] as possession and privation [differ] from those opposed as contraries; then, after this, [he will show] how the things opposed as affirmation and negation differ from those opposed as contraries, and from those [opposed] as relatives, and finally from those [opposed] as privation and possession. Thus [Aristotle] will
20   have conveyed the six differences, proceeding, within the [remaining] five differences,[754] on the basis of the second manner [of ordering them] and not on the basis of the first, as we did.

So he now shows how the things opposed as possession and privation differ from those opposed as relatives, establishing his demonstration on the basis of the definition of the relatives, as he also did before (11b32ff.), when he distinguished the relatives from the con-
25   traries. Hence he says that relatives are called just what they are *of* (or *than*) their opposites, but that sight is not sight of blindness (and this is clear in advance), and nor is blindness blindness of sight. They are both *of* the eye – both the possession and the privation. And that blindness is not called blindness *of* sight, in the manner of relatives, is demonstrated by appeal especially to a second dialectical proof (*epikheirêma*):[755] for if blindness were spoken of as a relative in
30   relation to sight, then since 'relatives are said in relation to reciprocating [correlatives]' (12b21-2), sight would also be called sight *of* blindness; but it is not so called. There will also be a difference, as we have said (380,18ff.), in virtue of the fact that the relatives are simultaneous by nature, whereas possession and privation, in addition to not entailing each other, are actually mutually cancelling. Having said that 'sight is not sight *of* blindness', [Aristotle] added 'nor
399,1 is it said in any other way in relation to it' (12a18-19), because even though the contraries were not called just what they were *of* (or *than*) their opposites,[756] the one [contrary] was said in *another* way in relation to the other [contrary]: for it is said to be *contrary* to it. Now it is true that privation, though it is not said to be just what it is [e.g. blindness] of possession, is nevertheless said to be the *privation* of
5   it;[757] the possession, however, is not put into any kind of relation to the [corresponding] privation.[758] Hence by means of these [arguments Aristotle] has shown the opposition of possession and privation to differ not only nominally but also objectively from the [opposition] of the things opposed as relatives, and proceeding in due order he now compares the same [opposition] [i.e. possession/privation] to the [opposition] of contraries.

12b26-13a36 That things said in respect of privation and possession are not opposed as contraries either [is clear from the following. In the case of contraries with nothing intermediate it is necessary that one or other of them always belong to things in which they naturally come about or of which they are predicated: for there was nothing intermediate between them in those cases where it was necessary for one or the other to belong to the thing capable of receiving them, as in the case of sickness and health and odd and even. But in the cases where there is something intermediate, it is never necessary that one or the other belong to everything (capable of receiving them). For it is not necessary that everything capable of receiving (black or white) be black or white, nor hot or cold, for nothing prevents something intermediate between these (states) belonging to them. Furthermore, there was something intermediate between them in those cases where it was not necessary that one or the other belong to the thing capable of receiving them, except in those cases where one of them belongs by nature, as for example being hot (belongs by nature) to fire, and being white to snow. But in these cases it is necessary that determinately one of them belong, and not as chance has it: for it is not possible that fire be cold or that snow be black. Hence it is not necessary that one or other of them belong to everything capable of receiving them, but only to those things where one belongs by nature, and determinately one belongs to these and not as chance has it. But in the case of privation and possession neither of these accounts is true: for it is not necessary that one or other of them always belong to the thing capable of receiving them, for what does not yet naturally have sight is not said either to be blind or to have sight. Hence these would not be among the sort of contraries that have nothing intermediate; but nor are they among those that do have something intermediate. For it is necessary that, at some time, one or other of them belong to everything capable of receiving them. For as soon as a thing naturally has sight, at that point it will be said to be blind or to have sight – not determinately one or these, but as chance has it: for it is not necessary either that it be blind or that it have sight, but (it will be) as chance has it. But in the case of contraries which have something intermediate it was (held to be) never necessary that one or other belong to everything – but only to some things, and to these determinately one of them. Hence it is clear that things opposed in respect of privation and possession are not opposed as contraries in either of the ways (in which contraries are opposed). Further, in the case of contraries it is possible, while the thing capable of receiving them is present, for a change from one to the other to come about, unless one (contrary) belongs to something by nature as being hot does to fire. For it is possible for what is healthy to fall sick

and for what is white to become black and for what is cold to become hot; and it is possible to become bad from good and good from bad. For if the bad man is led into better ways of living and reasoning he will improve, even if only a little, in the direction of being better; and if he once achieves even a little improvement it is clear that he might either change completely or achieve a very great improvement. For he becomes ever more easily changed towards virtue, even if the improvement he initially achieved was ever so small, so that he is likely to achieve still greater improvement. And if this goes on occurring it will shift him completely into the contrary state, as long as it is not prevented by time. In the case of privation and possession, on the other hand, it is impossible for a change from one to the other to come about: for although change comes about from possession to privation, it is impossible for it to do so from privation to possession. For neither does a man who has become blind see again, nor does a man who is bald recover his hair,] nor does a
10   toothless man grow teeth.

In this passage Aristotle shows that things said to be opposed in respect of possession and privation differ from things opposed as contraries – both those [contraries] without an intermediate and those with an intermediate, the difference between which he has necessarily anticipated, in order to demonstrate for both [types of contrary] the difference between the contraries and the other opposi-tions. And in first of all distinguishing things [opposed] in respect of
15   possession and privation from the contraries without an intermediate he mentions both varieties of [contrary] without an intermediate – those which are *in* a subject and those which are *said of* a subject – in the words '[the subjects] in which they naturally come about or of which they are predicated' (12b28-9). As examples of things in a subject he cited 'health' and 'sickness', which come about in body, and of things [said] of a subject 'odd' and 'even', which are said of number,
20   or rather, as I suggested above (387,10), being divisible into two equal parts [is said] of even number: for the species are not said of the genera as subjects, but the differentiae [are said] of the species as subjects. He distinguishes things [opposed] in respect of privation and possession from both these sorts of contrary [without an intermedi-ate], on the ground that of these [contraries] it is always necessary that one [contrary] belong to the thing capable of receiving them. For a body is either healthy or sick, and the number which is in the
25   species[759] is either divisible by two or not. But of privation and possession it is not always necessary that one of them belong to the thing capable of receiving them. For they were not opposed *simplici-ter*,[760] but [only] when it was natural [for one of them to apply]. For

clearly, at the stage when it is not yet natural for puppies to have sight, they are not said either to have sight or to be blind. And children who have not yet reached the stage at which it is natural for them to have teeth will not be said either to have teeth or to be toothless. But from whatever time it is natural to have [sight or teeth], from that 30 point the former are said to see or to be blind, and the latter to have teeth or to be toothless. Hence the difference has come about depending on whether [the opposition belongs] always, or [only] at some time. For contraries without an intermediate maintain their separation from the moment of generation;[761] privation and possession, on the other hand, [do] not [belong] right from the beginning, but rather from the time at which it is natural to have [the possession or the 400,1 privation]. But if any things *do* have the possession right from the beginning, in the way for example that all animals possess the sense of touch, and if it happens that they are deprived of that [sense] from the beginning, then they also have the privation from the beginning. But this is not true in all cases: where it obtains at all, it does so [only] in the case of those things which naturally [have the possession or privation] from the beginning. But *all* contraries without an intermediate naturally [belong] thus from the beginning, so that this very 5 point constitutes the difference, namely that contraries without an intermediate all [belong] thus [from the beginning], whereas of things [opposed] in respect of privation and possession some [belong] thus, whereas others do not [belong] thus.

In the case of contraries with an intermediate, the manner of opposition which comes about is not the same between these [contraries] and the things [opposed] in respect of possession and privation, because of contraries with an intermediate it is *never* necessary that one or other of them belong to everything capable of receiving them:[762] for it is not necessary that everything capable of receiving [white and 10 black] should be white or black (for there is also room to be yellow), nor [must be] hot or cold (for there is also room for everything capable of being hot or cold to be lukewarm). But in the case of possession and privation it is *at some time* necessary that one or other of them [obtain]:[763] for from the moment at which it naturally has [one or the other], from that moment the thing of necessity either is deprived or has the possession. And while there are also some contraries with an intermediate of which one [of the contraries] belongs by nature, as for instance heat to fire, things [opposed] in respect of possession and 15 privation will differ from these [contraries] as well. For in the case of these [contraries] determinately one of them[764] [belongs], such as whiteness to snow, and it necessarily does so always, and it is quite clear in advance which [contrary will belong]. But in the case of things [opposed] in respect of possession and privation it is not the case that determinately one of them, nor one of them at all times, [belongs], and it is unclear [in advance] which [will belong]. For neither sight nor blindness accrues [to creatures] determinately always.[765]

So the difference between things [opposed] in respect of possession
20   and privation and the contraries comes about in respect of [whether they belong] always or [only] at some time. For [privation and possession] differ from the contraries without an intermediate by virtue of the fact that of those [contraries] necessarily at all times[766] one or other of them belongs to the thing capable of receiving them – for example, it is either healthy or sick – whereas of these [i.e. possession and privation] it is not necessary [that one or other of them belong] at all times for all cases [of possession and privation]; but for some cases [of possession and privation, one of them belongs only] at some time: for a puppy has neither.[767] And [privation and possession differ] from contraries with an intermediate in that of those [contraries] it is never necessary that one or other of them belong to the thing capable
25   of receiving them,[768] whereas of these [i.e. possession or privation] it is at some time necessary that one or other of them belong[769] [to a thing capable of receiving them], namely from the moment when the thing naturally [receives the possession or privation], and of some cases [of possession and privation one of them necessarily] even [belongs] from the beginning. But [possession and privation] will also differ from those [contraries[770]] to which one [contrary] belongs by nature, in terms of [whether the belonging occurs] *at some time*,[771] and in terms of [whether the belonging occurs] *determinately*.[772] For of the latter,[773] in every case at all times one of them belongs, whereas, of some of the former,[774] [one belongs only] at some time; and of the latter determinately one [of the contraries belongs], whereas in the case of the former it is not so that determinately [one belongs], but [it is] whichever it chances to be. When Aristotle says that 'it is necessary
30   that one or other [of the contraries] belong to everything [capable of receiving them]' (13a14), the addition of the phrase 'to everything' seems to some people to import an unclarity. But this is not so, for he clarifies the contrast by reference to the necessity [of belonging] 'to some things', i.e. to those having one of the contraries naturally inhering in them, not to all things [capable of receiving them].[775]

What if it were [generally] the case that sight accrued [to creatures] from birth, as it always does in the case of men? Would not either
35   possession or privation obtain in the case of these [creatures] too, and would then [possession and privation] in no way differ from contraries
401,1 without an intermediate? What if someone were to say that in the case of [creatures] which have not reached maturity things [opposed] in respect of possession and privation are opposed in the same way as the contraries *with* an intermediate (for neither [belongs] necessarily[776]), whereas in the case of [creatures] which have reached maturity [they belong] in the same way as the [contraries] *without*

an intermediate (for one of them necessarily [belongs]⁷⁷⁷)? Well, [Aristotle] solves such disputes too by adding another difference between them, namely that contraries [can] change round in the things capable of receiving them, but it is not possible 'that a change' from possession or privation 'to the other one come about' (13a19).⁷⁷⁸ For although blindness comes about from sight, [change] does *not* [occur] in the reverse direction as well. And because of this Chrysippus raised the question whether those suffering from a cataract but able to recover sight after a couching of the eye should be called blind, and [he raised the same question] in the case of those whose eyelids are [naturally] shut: for since the capacity [to see] exists, they resemble someone [voluntarily] keeping his eyes shut, or someone prevented by a screen from seeing, since if this [screen] is removed he is in no way prevented from seeing. So it is not from privation to possession that such a change comes about. But [Aristotle] is here considering the kind of privation which consists in a *disability*. For from such a [privation] there is no return to the [corresponding] possession.

There was another sort of privation, which he mentions in the *Physics*,⁷⁷⁹ and which he says is an accidental cause of things that come about, [there] considering the absence in the primary matter of the forms which naturally come about in it as being, no less than the presence of the form, in accordance with nature for the matter of generated things. But *here* privation in composite things has been construed in accordance with its condition *contrary* to their nature. Furthermore, privation is to be construed [here] as that in respect of *nature*, and not in respect of *custom*. For a return to the state of possession from the [corresponding] privation in respect of custom does indeed come about, for example from nakedness to being clothed. But Aristotle does not at this point mention these [privations] which pertain to custom, but rather those which are natural and are observed in the case of disabilities. He says that a change of contraries into one another can come about, when the thing capable of receiving them is present, unless one of the contraries belongs to something by nature, as heat does to fire. As examples of such [changes] he partly chooses agreed cases, such as health and sickness, and partly disputed ones, such as 'good' and 'bad'. [The latter example is controversial] because some think⁷⁸⁰ that while a good man can come about from a bad, it is impossible for a bad man to come about from a good. And [Aristotle] himself proved the former of these [possibilities] more thoroughly [than the latter], saying that if the bad man is led 'into better ways of living' (13a23-4) he will keep improving by small degrees and, by continuously achieving a small improvement and becoming more practised, in the end 'he might change completely' (13a26) and be brought into the contrary state, 'as long as he⁷⁸¹ is not prevented by time' (13a30-1), whether by completing his [allotted] time and dying, or by becoming very old (for that sort of man is not capable of complete improvement). That is how he proved this point.

But the Stoics do not admit the reverse process: for they deny that
35 virtue can be lost. So either [Aristotle] took the good man in a more ordinary sense, not the man in possession of the complete virtues, but the man who is good only in respect of [having] a good disposition, or [showing] assiduity and progress, or in reasoning;[782] or else [Aristotle]
402,1 perhaps means that virtue can be moved in the way he has mentioned in the foregoing (8b25ff.), by great suffering or bodily disease, forget-fulness thereby setting in, although it is only with difficulty and not at all readily that these circumstances coincide. For indeed he him-self, in his [*Nicomachean*] *Ethics* (1100b12ff.), bears witness to the fact that virtue is very stable. But anyway the result of all these points
5 is that if 'in the case of contraries it is possible, while the thing capable of receiving them is present, for a change from one to the other to come about, unless one [contrary] belongs to something by nature, whereas in the case of possession and privation it is impossible for a change from one to the other to come about' (13a17-20, 31-2), then it is clear that the[783] opposition of the contraries is different from that in respect of possession and privation. And the following has also become clear, that things opposed in respect of possession and priva-tion are the same neither as the contraries without an intermediate
10 nor as those [contraries with an intermediate] which have one deter-minate [contrary] by nature.

With these points established it is an easy matter next to solve Nicostratus' puzzles as well. He says that this difference [sc. between the opposition of contraries and that of possession and privation] has not been specified accurately: for neither do contraries change in all respects into one another – since a bad man does not come about from
15 a good one – nor is every privation unchangeable into a state of possession. 'For indeed out of the illuminated, armed or clothed there may come to be the darkling, unarmed or naked, and contrariwise the state of possession [may come to be] out of the privations. So it is absurd to differentiate among the things which [in fact] belong to both [oppositions], and assign some to the one [opposition] and the others to the other one.' Against this it is easy to say that the [claim] that
20 virtue cannot be lost has been too readily assumed. For Theophrastus indeed gave sufficient demonstration regarding [the possibility of] this change, and Aristotle's view is that what cannot be lost is not human.[784] Further, even the Stoics concede that in cases of torpor, depression and lethargy, and in cases of drug-taking, a loss of virtue itself along with the entire rational state comes about; vice does not
25 supersede it, but the firm hold [of virtue] is loosened and slips into a

state which the ancients called intermediate. Thus [we can deal with] that point.

But [Nicostratus] produces arguments, absurdly, on the basis of privations in respect of custom and claims that privation can change into possession as well [as *vice versa*]. For the man going without lunch and the unarmed man, being in a state of privation [merely] by virtue of a practice, readily change into the [corresponding] states of possession, the former by taking lunch, the latter by arming himself. But Aristotle employed the [opposition of] possession and privation   30 not in the case of those [states deriving] from custom, but in the case of those [which come about] by nature, and it is in the case of these that the opposition in respect of possession and privation is indeed principally said. Let us then employ Aristotle's own [words] against Nicostratus. For he says in his [book] *On Opposites* that some privations are said to be [privations] of the things [which belong] by nature, others of the things [which belong] in virtue of a custom, others of material possessions, and still others of other things: blindness [is a privation] of things [which belong] by nature, whereas nakedness is   35 [a privation] of things[785] [which belong] in virtue of a custom, and privation of money [is a privation] of things accruing to one in practical dealings. And there are several further kinds of privation, and from some privations there is no escape, while from others there   403,1 is. Given that there are many varieties of privation and that one of these is [privation] of things [belonging] by nature, since the difference from the contraries comes about [only] in the case of the things [belonging] by nature, [Nicostratus] should not have thought he could refute [Aristotle's] account by adducing [examples] from the other varieties.

It is possible to extract the full account of privations from Aris-   5 totle's [book] and Chrysippus' book, and Iamblichus too wrote some things [on the subject], which run as follows: 'Possessing being said in many ways, as we have already demonstrated, privation extends to all the significations of possessing, but not thereby also to all the contraries. For privation is equivalent to loss, so that privation of the bad could not be said, because loss of the bad or of the harmful could   10 not come about, but [only] of the good or of the beneficial: for the man rid of sickness or poverty could not be said to be deprived of sickness or poverty, but rather the[786] man robbed of health or wealth [is said to be deprived of these things]. Blindness is a privation of a good: for sight is a good. Nakedness, on the other hand, is [the privation] of an indifferent [property]: for a cloak is an indifferent thing, neither good nor bad. Hence no privation is a good thing, but either a bad or an   15 indifferent one. And there can be privation either of all goods or of the majority. But Aristotle says that privation of the goods which are in the soul and connected with choice come about least of all. For no

one talks about being deprived of justice, and he who said that no one
carries off knowledge spoke from the same conception.[787] Privations,
20   then, are rather of wealth, good opinion, honour and such things, and
especially of so-called goods in connection with material possessions.
That is why expressions of pity and compassion accompany most
privations. Aristotle, however, has here compared the opposition of
natural privations with that of the contraries.' But that will suffice
on this matter. [Aristotle] proceeds next to the opposition of affirma-
25   tion and negation,[788] and in conveying the difference between it and
the other oppositions he speaks as follows:

> **13a37-b35** Things opposed as affirmation and negation [are
> obviously not opposed in any of the aforementioned ways: for in
> their case alone is it necessary always that one of them be true
> and the other false. For in the case of contraries it is not
> necessary always that one be true and the other false, nor in the
> case of the relatives, nor in the case of possession and privation:
> for example, health and sickness are contraries, and certainly
> neither is either true or false; likewise, the double and the half
> are opposed as contraries, and neither of them is either true or
> false; nor indeed are things opposed in respect of privation and
> possession, such as sight and blindness. And in general none of
> the things said *without* any combination is either true or false:
> but all these cases are said without combination. Not but what
> it might easily seem that some such thing does occur in the case
> of contraries said *with* combination – for *that Socrates is well* is
> contrary to *that Socrates is sick* – but even in these cases it is
> not necessary always that one be true and the other false. For
> although if Socrates exists one will be true and the other false,
> if he does not exist both will be false: for neither *that Socrates
> is sick* nor *that he is well* will be true if Socrates himself does not
> exist at all. In the case of privation and possession, if he does
> not exist at all neither will be true, while if he does exist it will
> not always be so that one or the other is true. For *that Socrates
> has sight* is opposed to *that Socrates is blind* as privation and
> possession, and if he exists it is not necessary that one or other
> be true or false[789] – for at the stage when it is not yet natural for
> him to have it both will be false – while if Socrates does not exist
> at all then likewise both will be false, both *that he has sight* and
> *that he is blind*. But in the case of an affirmation and negation
> the one will always be false and the other true, regardless of
> whether he exists or does not exist: for it is clear that one or
> other of *that Socrates is sick* and *that it is not the case that
> Socrates is sick* is true or false if he exists, and if he does not

exist likewise. For *that he is sick* will be false if he does not exist,
and *that it is not the case that he is sick* will be true.] Hence its
always being the case that one or other of them is true or false
will be a distinguishing mark of these alone [– i.e. of the things
that are opposed as affirmation and negation].

That these too [i.e. affirmation and negation] are among the opposites, and are the things which are most of all opposed, is clear in
advance. For they above all are mutually cancelling and not coexis-   30
tent, the universal negative [being opposed] to the particular affirmative, and the universal affirmative to the particular negative:[790] thus
the Stoics consider that only negatives are opposed to affirmatives.
[Aristotle] conveys clearly the difference between them and the[791]
other varieties of the oppositions on the basis of the fact that alone in   404,1
the case of this opposition consisting of a contradictory pair is one of
the statements true and the other false. The statements to be taken
are the ones which are *strictly* opposed, as the matter is defined in
the *de Interpretatione* (17b16-20).[792] But in the case of the other
opposites these [truth-values] are not divided [between the members
of the opposition]: for it is not the case either of contraries or of things
said in relation to each other or of things opposed in respect of   5
possession and privation that the one [member of an opposed pair] is
true and the other false. [Aristotle] proves this both by means of his
examples, and he also proves it apodeictically, thus: things opposed
in accordance with the [other] three varieties [of opposition] are said
'without combination' (13b12), and nothing said without combination
signifies either truth or falsehood. For the true and the false are
invariably in a statement, and every statement is a sentence (*lo-*   10
gos),[793] and the sentence [consists] in a combination of certain things.
But none of the other [oppositions] is said in combination: rather, they
are simple, as for example white/black, double/half, sight/blindness.

    In saying that 'in the case of the contraries it is not necessary
always that one be true and the other false' (13b3-4), [Aristotle] did
not primarily say that this was not necessary in the sense that the   15
contraries *sometimes* divide the true and the false *per se*;[794] rather,
[he said it] because of the objection which he subsequently raised,
namely that 'it might seem that some such thing does occur' – dividing
the true and the false – 'in the case of contraries said with combination' (13b12-14). Of this sort are the ones where the contraries are
predicated of the same thing, such as *that Socrates is sick* and *that
Socrates is well*: for being well and being sick are contraries without   20
an intermediate.[795] But these [expressions] *per se* signify objects and
are mere *phrases*;[796] a true *sentence*, on the one hand, and a false
[sentence], on the other, come about [only] if they are *combined*.[797]
And it is possible that these [expressions] do not even, in the first

instance, refer to contraries, but that contraries are *predicated of the same thing*: for the same thing is capable of receiving contraries.⁷⁹⁸

25   Hence if nothing is capable of receiving *that Socrates is sick* or *that Socrates is well*, these will not be contraries.⁷⁹⁹ But even if one should agree that these *are* contraries, it is still not necessary that one of them be true and the other false: 'for although if Socrates exists one [statement] will be true and the other false, if he does not exist both will be false' (13b16-18). For someone who does not exist could not correctly be said to be either sick or in health. But a contradictory

30   pair *always* partitions the true and the false, whether Socrates exists or not. For of the *non*-existent [Socrates] the negation 'It is not the case that Socrates is well' is true as well as 'It is not the case that Socrates is sick'.⁸⁰⁰ For not being sick is not the same thing as being well, just as it is not the case, either, that not seeing is the same thing as being blind. For it is clearly true to say in the case of a wall that 'It is not the case that it is healthy and nor is it the case that it sees',

35   but false [to say of it] 'It is sick and blind'.

These points must also be applied to the things which have privation and possession in combination.⁸⁰¹ For the true and the false

405,1   indeed *appear* in their case too to be divided; but in point of fact they are not really partitioned. Rather, if [the subject] does not exist, both the [statement] that it sees and the [statement] that it is blind are false, while if it does exist it is [still] not necessary that one of them [be true], [either] when it is not naturally such as to receive [either the possession or the privation], as in the case of the wall, or [when] it is not *yet* naturally such [as to receive the possession or the privation], as in the case of the puppy. In the case of a contradictory

5   pair, however, whether [the subject] exists or not, and whether it naturally [can receive the property] or not, it is always the case that one or other [member] is either true or false,⁸⁰² as was said before. This, then, has been accurately shown.

What does [Aristotle] mean when he says of Socrates that 'at the stage when it is not yet natural for him to have' sight, 'both' [statements] are 'false' (13b24-5), i.e. the [statement] that he sees and the [statement] that he is blind? For as soon as he is born it is natural for Socrates to see, and [so] one [statement] is immediately true in his

10   case, and the other false. But against this they say that since Socrates was adduced as an example both in the case of the contraries⁸⁰³ and in the case of things [opposed] in respect of affirmation and negation,⁸⁰⁴ when [Aristotle] turned to privation and possession he made use of the same [example] again instead of the puppy, transferring to this [example] that disposition which applies to things which have neither [the possession nor the privation] at the moment of birth. [He does this] both because he wishes to prove everything on the basis of

15   the same [example], this being the more scientific [method], when it

is possible,[805] and because as usual he treats the examples as of no importance, when the state of affairs truly obtains. But perhaps, they say, man does not have sight from the beginning either,[806] in the way that he has a sense of touch, nor does he appear to use it [i.e. the sense of sight] immediately, until the midwife opens his eyelids and wipes [the eyes][807] clean: as far as the sense of touch is concerned, as soon as the infant falls from the womb,[808] and as it perceives the outside air filling it, it wails.[809] But if that [is correct], it will be appropriate   20
to say in the case of this [infant] too that at the moment of its coming about both [the statement of possession and the statement of privation] are false in his case. So it is clear that only [statements] which are opposed as affirmation and negation divide the true and the false. But if this [is correct], they will differ from the other three species of opposition.

The Stoics, too, affirm that none of the things said with a negation   25
is contrary to anything. For then non-virtue would be contrary to virtue and non-vice contrary to vice, and since under non-virtue falls not only vice but many other things (a horse, indeed, and a stone, and everything except virtue), while under non-vice [falls] not only virtue but everything else too, it will follow that everything [else] would be   30
contrary to [any given] one thing,[810] and that the same things [will be] contrary to virtue and to vice. And further, if the contrary of vice is not virtue, but non-vice, it will result that intermediates[811] are contrary to the morally excellent and to the wicked.[812] But that is absurd, especially if even the same things [are contrary to the morally excellent and the wicked].[813] And indeed the [postulation] of two contraries such that all the things falling under the one are qualities
– as for example under virtue and vice – whereas [the things falling]   406,1
under the other are both qualities and qualified *things* – as for example under non-virtue and non-vice (for under these are not only qualities but also qualified things, and operations and everything whatsoever) – well, this too is incongruous. Thus among the Stoics too a difference was drawn between contraries and things opposed contradictorily.   5

But Nicostratus censures [Aristotle] here too, saying that dividing the true and the false is not the distinguishing mark (*idion*) of things opposed as a contradictory pair. 'For [dividing the true and the false] belongs neither exclusively to [contradictory oppositions] nor to all of them:[814] not to them exclusively, because the necessity of one or the other's [being true or false[815]] also belongs to sentences containing positive and negative oaths, such as "Yes by Athena, I did that!", "No by Athena, I did not do it!";[816] and indeed (he says) the same holds for   10
expressions of wonder, such as[817] "How beautiful the Piraeus is!", <"The Piraeus is not beautiful">,[818] and of blame, such as "How[819] worthless he is!", "He is not worthless". So this [i.e. dividing the true

and the false] does not belong exclusively to those things [opposed] as a contradictory pair; but nor (he says) [does it belong] to all of them. For those statements which are inclined towards the future time are neither true nor false owing to the nature of the contingent. For

15   neither "There will be a sea battle" nor "There will not be a sea battle" is true, but it will be as chance has it.'[820]

In response to these points it is possible, they[821] say, to reply that given that there are four sorts of opposition, [Aristotle] has specified this[822] as the distinguishing mark of one of them not in relation to everything, but in relation to the [other] three [oppositions]: for someone who says that of the four [oppositions] one partitions the true and the false has not declared this in an absolute sense, but has

20   done so only in the case of the opposites.[823] And apart from this, they say, these matters were solved long ago in the explanations of the definition of the proposition (*axiôma*), which defined the proposition as that which is true or false.[824] For an oath cannot be true or false; rather, it is plausible that in oaths one swears truly (*euorkein*) or one forswears oneself (*epiorkein*), but it is not possible to make a true assertion (*alêtheuein*) or a false assertion (*pseudesthai*) in them, even if one swears concerning true or false things.[825] And an expression of

25   wonder, in going beyond a [mere] proposition by the addition of the wonderment, and an expression of blame, [exceeding a proposition] by its rebuke, are neither true nor false, but they are like true or false [propositions]. Let these be the solutions of the Stoic exactitude.

But perhaps one should approach the issue more simply: for the oath[826] 'By Athena!' does not denote anything true or false, but certainly, when it is combined with a statement which is either true

30   or false, brings it about, if the statement is true, that one *swears truly*, but not that one *speaks the truth* (for the statement [rather than the oath] had the truth), whereas if it is combined with a false [statement] it compels one to *forswear oneself*, not to *speak falsely*. And the [word] expressive of wonderment, namely 'How!', is joined to the statement 'The Piraeus is beautiful', and the [word] expressive of blame likewise,[827] and it is the *statements* which have the truth or falsity. Concerning the contradictory pairs having regard to future time the

35   Stoics, on the one hand, think the same as [they think] in the case of the other [sorts of proposition][828] too. They say: 'As are the oppositions

407,1   concerning present and past things, so too are future ones – both the [oppositions] themselves and their parts. For either "It will be" is true or "It will not be", since it is necessary that [future propositions] be either false or true (for according to them [i.e. the Stoics] future things have [already] been made determinate).[829] And if there will be a sea battle tomorrow, then it is true to say that there will be one; but if there will not be one, it is false to say that there will be one. But either

5   there will be or there will not: so one or the other member [of the

contradictory pair] is true or false.'[830] The Peripatetics, on the other hand, say that the sort of contradictory pair which has regard to the future is indeed true or false,[831] but that which part of it[832] will be true and which false is ungraspable in its nature and unstable.[833] For while there is nothing to prevent a contradictory pair being said in respect of any time you like, [such as] the [pair] 'Either there will be or there will not be',[834] each of the component parts in it – such as 'There will   10 be' or 'There will not be' – is already, in the case of the present or past time,[835] determinately either true or false, whereas those [parts of contradictory pairs] which are specified as being about the future are not yet either true nor false, but it will turn out one way or the other (*estai de ê toia ê toia*). Let these remarks, then, suffice in response to Nicostratus.[836]

Now that Aristotle's account of the difference among opposites has   15 been completed, it would be a good idea to append too Archytas' [remarks] on them in his book *On Opposites*, since these are the model for the things said [by Aristotle],[837] and especially because even the divine Iamblichus[838] did not insert anything from this book into his commentaries, and perhaps it did not fall into his hands: for no one examining *Aristotle's* book *On Opposites* would have passed it[839] over   20 [sc. if he had read it]. The account is as follows:[840] '[Opposites] are said to be opposed to one another both by convention and by nature: some as contraries, for example good to bad, healthy to sick, and true to false; others as possession to privation, for example life to death, sight to blindness, and knowledge to oblivion; others as things which are a certain way in relation to something,[841] such as double to half, ruler to ruled, and governor to governed; and yet others as affirmation and   25 negation, such as that there is a man to that there is not [a man], and that he is morally excellent to that he is not [morally excellent].'

Having set out the four oppositions in this way, he adds the following on the difference between them:[842] 'These things differ from one another, because contraries do not necessarily come about at the same time or get destroyed at the same time: for health is contrary to sickness and rest to movement, but neither does health coexist with sickness nor rest with movement, nor indeed does either of them come   30 about at the same time, nor get destroyed at the same time, [as the other]. Possession and privation[843] differ from these[844] [i.e. the con- traries], because contraries naturally change into one another, for   408,1 example the healthy into the sick and the sick into the healthy and the high-pitched to the low-pitched and the low-pitched to the high- pitched, whereas possession and privation do not do so, but rather, although possession goes over to privation, privation does not go over to possession: for the living dies, but the dead will never live. And in   5 general possession is a containment of what is natural, whereas privation is a deficiency of what is natural. The relatives necessarily

come about and are destroyed simultaneously: for it is impossible for double to be, but not half, or for half to be, but not double, and whenever anything double comes about, a half too comes about simultaneously, and whenever anything double is destroyed, a half too is destroyed simultaneously. Affirmation and negation are,
10   rather, forms of sentence,[845] and also are, rather, significative of true and false. For *that a man is* is true, when it obtains, and false, when it does not obtain. And the same account holds of the negation too: for it too is true or false depending on the signified object – it is true when that obtains, and false when that does not obtain.[846]

'Further, something is intermediate between good and bad, namely
15   what is neither good nor bad, and [between] much and little, namely the due measure, and [between] slow and fast, namely the equally fast, but nothing is intermediate between possession and privation: for there is nothing between life and death or sight and blindness, unless someone were to say that the animal which has not yet come to be but is in the process of coming to be is between life and death, and that the puppy which does not yet see is between a state of having
20   been blind and seeing. But one who says this will be specifying the mean accidentally, not according to the proper definition of the contrarieties. The relatives admit of means: for between the master and slave is the free man, and between the greater and less is the equal, and between the broad and narrow is that which fits. And something intermediate will be found for the other contraries,
25   whether named or unnamed. But there is nothing between affirmation and negation,[847] such as [between] the [statement] that there is a man and the [statement] that there is not a man, or that he is musical and that he is not musical.

'Besides, too, it is necessary for someone talking about something
409,1   to affirm or deny: to affirm, when he makes clear that something is, such as a man [or] a horse, and that[848] something coexists with this, such as that being musical [coexists] with man[849] or [being] a charger with a horse; to deny, when it is made clear that something is not, such as that a man is not or that a horse is not, or that[850] something
5   does not coexist with this, such as that the man is not musical or that the horse is not a charger. There is nothing between the affirmation itself and [the] negation.' This, then, is what Archytas as well wrote about the difference of opposites in relation to one another, at the same time too demonstrating their nature rather accurately, and what Aristotle says is faithful to this account, as has become clear
10   from what has been said. Aristotle next subjoins a division of the contraries (13b36–14a6) which Archytas too conveyed, and after it he adds some other points concerning the contraries. The remarks of Aristotle's[851] are as follows:

CHAPTER 11

13b36-14a6 The contrary of a good thing is necessarily bad. [This is clear by induction from particular cases: for example, sickness (is contrary) to health and injustice to justice and cowardice to courage, and similarly in the other cases. But the contrary of a bad thing is sometimes good and sometimes bad: for excess is contrary to deficiency, which is bad, and is itself bad, but the mean is equally contrary to each of these, and it is good. But while one can see this kind of thing in a few cases,] in the majority of cases the contrary of a bad thing is always a good thing.

[Aristotle] subjoins these remarks to the ones he has already made   15
about the contraries, since they are useful both in relation to the general theory of the categories and in relation to the devising of topics.[852] These remarks are [to the effect] that the contrary of the good is in every case bad, whereas [the contrary] of the bad is sometimes good, and sometimes bad; secondly, that it is not necessary, if one of the contraries [of a pair] exists, that in every case the other exist too – indeed in the case of individual [contraries the other one] in every case does *not* exist; thirdly, that the contraries concern   20
the same subject either in genus or in species; and fourthly, that the contraries are either in the same genus, or in contrary genera, or are themselves genera. He established the proof (*pistis*)[853] for the first of these, namely that the contrary of the good is necessarily bad, by means of induction (*epagôgê*):[854] for he proved the general [proposition] on the basis of 'health' and 'sickness', 'justice' and 'injustice'. That the contrary of the bad is sometimes good and sometimes bad   25
he reasoned from the cases of things [existing] in respect of 'deficiency' and 'excess' and 'mean': for both the mean and the excess are contrary to the deficiency, as for example both courage and recklessness [are contrary] to cowardice,[855] and both a balanced temperament (*krasis*) and a too warm one [are contrary] to a too cool imbalance of the body.[856] In his book *On Opposites* [Aristotle] also subjoined to these   30
varieties of the contrarieties that of the things which are neither good nor bad towards things which are neither good nor bad, thus saying that white is contrary to black, sweet to bitter, high-pitched to   410,1
low-pitched and movement to rest.

But how is it that (1) *one* thing seems to be contrary to one thing, whereas [Aristotle] here says that there are *two* contraries of the bad, namely the good and the opposite bad – as for example both courage and cowardice [are contrary] to recklessness – and (2) it appears that *two* bad things are contrary to the good,[857] as for example both recklessness and cowardice to courage, and [in general] both the   5 excess and the deficiency to the mean?[858] (1) In response to the first point one should say that if each [of courage and cowardice] were opposed to recklessness in the same respect, the account would indeed be absurd. But if the good is opposed to [its contrary] *qua bad*, and the balanced to [its contrary] *qua imbalanced*, as one thing to one

10 thing, and if the deficiency consisting in cowardice is opposed to recklessness *qua excess*, there is nothing absurd in this.[859] (2) In response to the second point, [one should say] that both to [the mean] *qua* good there is one opposed thing, namely the bad, and to [the mean] *qua* balanced thing there is one [opposed thing], namely the imbalanced, which is considered [as consisting] in both the excess and the deficiency *together*: for it is not opposed *qua excess and deficiency* to the balanced, but *qua imbalance*. But the deficiency is opposed to

15 the excess in respect of the [category of] quantity:[860] and indeed the affections, insofar as they are divisible, are quantity.[861] And Aristotle indeed indicates two distinct kinds of opposition, saying: 'But the contrary of a bad thing is sometimes good and sometimes bad' (14a1-2). For this is not the same as 'both good and bad [are contrary to bad]' but rather [the same] as 'in one respect good [is contrary to bad], and in another respect bad is'. In consequence there are two contraries to [each of] the extremes, the other extreme in respect of

20 the [category of] quantity, and the intermediate in respect of the [category of] quality, [opposed to each extreme] as balanced to imbalanced (for the intermediate quantity is not contrary *qua* quantity to the extreme: for they [i.e. intermediate and extreme] are not separated from each other the most in respect of quantity), and both the extremes are, taken as one, contrary to the intermediate. For taken as imbalanced [they are contrary] to balanced and taken as vice [they are contrary] to virtue.

25 Nicostratus censures [Aristotle] firstly on the grounds that the division of the contraries is incomplete: for he has not added that indifferent (*adiaphoron*)[862] is opposed to indifferent. [Aristotle] did add this in his book *On Opposites*, saying that there is a particular variety of opposition of things which are neither good nor bad towards things which are neither good nor bad, as has already been said (409,30). (He did not call them indifferents because, I suppose, the

30 name 'indifferent' is more recent, since it was established by the Stoics.) But he did not mention them here [i.e. in the *Categories*] because it was controversial whether indifferent is not only opposed to indifferent, but also indifferent to bad – since the skilled, which is an intermediate (*meson*),[863] seems to be contrary to the unskilled, which is bad, and being sober [is contrary] to drinking (*methuein*) – and again, contrariwise, [it is controversial whether] an intermediate [can be] contrary to a good, such as imbibing (*oinôsthai*) to being

411,1 sober.[864] But this construal is incongruous. For the unskilled is also

an intermediate, since is it said too in the case of children,[865] and being sober is of two kinds, the one good, the other intermediate (when it denotes not imbibing), and drinking [is also of two kinds], the one bad, the other intermediate (when it denotes imbibing),[866] and thus it is fitting to oppose intermediates to intermediates and good things to bad [after all]. If [Aristotle] mentioned these matters at all he would   5
either create an absurd [effect] if he left them unexamined, or if he examined them he would introduce a disproportionate length into this introduction.

The same man [i.e. Nicostratus] censures [Aristotle] on a second ground by trying to show also that good is contrary to good: for he says that a prudent walking[867] is contrary to a prudent state of rest, and prudent pleasure to prudent pain, and all other such things which appear to be said contrarily too. But these things are *not* contraries, since they harmonise with one another in relation to the one aim and   10
the one end of the man who does both wisely (*emphronôs*).[868] If there is additionally contrariety in these [examples] at all, it is not [the contrariety] of a good towards a good, but of an intermediate towards an intermediate: for [walking] is opposed *qua* walking to a state of rest, and [pleasure is opposed] *qua* pleasure to pain.

But someone might ask how it is that bad is contrary to bad and intermediate to intermediate, but not good to good. [In reply] we should say that the good is one thing and simple, whereas the bad is   15
various. So just as it is everywhere the case that hitting the mark (*tukhein*) comes about in virtue of [just] one thing, namely by a throw onto the target, whereas missing the mark (*apotukhein*) [comes about] in virtue of many things, for [it comes about] in virtue of excesses and deficiencies, so the good, being [just] one thing, is not contrary to itself, whereas the bad, being various, is [so] contrary. And the intermediate is not itself *qua* intermediate contrary [sc. to   20
another intermediate] either, but [only] in virtue of that nature possessing which it is an intermediate: for [it is] *qua* white [that it is contrary] to black, and *qua* sweet [that it is contrary] to bitter. The bad, however, is not [contrary] in virtue of something else, but [only] in virtue of excess and deficiency, in virtue of which [bad] things are both imbalanced and bad.[869] And just as two true [statements] are not opposed, whereas two false ones are, as for example in the case of a contingent subject-matter the 'all' [statement] and the 'no' [statement] [are both false],[870] so good does not conflict with good, whereas bad conflicts with bad. Hence it is that husbandry and generosity do   25
not conflict, even though the former strives to preserve resources, the latter to give them away; but both, in aiming at the right measure, are joined at the point of the good.[871] But recklessness and cowardice conflict [with each other].

Aristotle has put forward this difference, too, among the contraries

30   in reliance on Archytas. For the latter writes as follows[872] in his book
      On Opposites:[873] 'Further, there are three differentiae of contraries:
      for some are opposed as good to bad, as for example health to sickness,
      some as bad to bad, such as meanness to profligacy, and yet others
      as neither [good nor bad] to neither [good nor bad], such as white to
412,1 black, heavy to light.' He himself calls what is [termed] 'indifferent'
      among the more recent [philosophers] 'neither', just as Aristotle, by
      dint of the negation of the extremes, calls it[874] 'neither good nor bad'.
      'But [only] in a few cases', [Aristotle] says (14a4-6), is it possible to
      see the contrariety of the bad towards the bad: for [it is possible] only
      in those cases where the good is observed in [the] mean, and the bad
5   in excess and deficiency.[875] And in these cases too both of them [i.e.
      the extremes] are opposed as one bad thing to the good. But I think
      it is worth asking whether it is not perhaps the case that *every* good
      thing which has an opposed bad is observed [to consist] in balance,
      and *every* bad thing [to consist] in imbalance – if this is so, the
      opposition of bad to bad, as well,[876] will arise not just in a few cases:
      for imbalance comes about in respect of excess and deficiency, which
10   are opposed to one another as bad things – or [whether there are] also
      many [goods and bads] which are not so [observed].

> **14a6-14** Further, of contraries it is not necessary, if one of them
> exists, that the other exist too: [for if everyone were well then
> health would exist, but not sickness, and similarly if everything
> were white then whiteness would exist, but not blackness.
> Further, if *that Socrates is well* is contrary to *that Socrates is
> sick*, and if it is not possible for both to obtain simultaneously in
> respect of the same man, then it will not be possible, if one of
> the contraries exists, that the other exist too: if *that Socrates is
> well* is the case,] then *that Socrates is sick* will not be the case.

      [Aristotle] conveys a second theorem concerning the contraries, which
      we previously employed when making clear the difference between
      the contraries and the relatives (384,19ff.), namely that, on the one
      hand, in the case of the contraries without combination[877] 'it is not
15   necessary, if one of them exists, that the other exist too' (14a6-7) – for
      it is not necessary, if health exists, that sickness also exist – whereas
      the relatives coexist simultaneously; and, on the other hand, in the
      case of the contraries taken together (*suneilêmmenôn*) [with mat-
      ter][878] – and these are the individuals, as when I say *that Socrates is
      well*, [or] *that Socrates is sick* (14a10-11) – in these cases (not contin-
      gently but) necessarily only one of these [contraries] obtains.[879] Aris-
20   totle took up the first of these points on the strength of the hypothesis
      that everyone is well and that everyone has become white, thereby
      making clear that the contraries do not depend on one another as the

relatives do. All those who set up the contraries as first principles will disagree with this, both the Heracliteans and the others: for [on their view] if one of the contraries were to be wanting, everything would evanesce and vanish. Hence too Heraclitus criticises Homer for say- 25 ing 'Would that strife might be done away with from among gods and men':[880] for then, he says, everything would vanish.[881] However, in what follows, [Aristotle] does not demonstrate this [claim] – namely that the contraries do not [necessarily] obtain simultaneously in the world – but rather that Socrates cannot be sick and well simultane-ously, although if one man is sick nothing prevents another man's being well. And if someone demanded that this account harmonise 30 also with the first point, he would be answered thus: just as it is not possible for Socrates to be simultaneously well and sick, [so] nothing else either can be sick, if it is well [sc. at the same time]. So if everyone were well, in accordance with our hypothesis, there would be no sickness anywhere.

In response to his saying that contraries cannot come about [sc. 413,1 simultaneously] with regard to numerically the same thing, some counter that pleasure and pain come about simultaneously in the case of one who drinks something hot [and] sweet. But, in the first place, this does not happen in respect of the same thing: rather, the sense of *touch* is distressed, while the sense of *taste* is delighted. What is more, from the fact that pleasure and pain coexist with one another in the man who is thirsty and drinks Plato shows,[882] if I remember 5 rightly, that these things are not good and bad: for they are not even contraries.

Iamblichus, in extending the [Aristotelian] account to all the contrar-ies, says that some contraries are mixed, such as white and black in grey, and sweet and bitter in absinthe, whereas others are unmixed, such as health and sickness, though the doctors do mix even these in the case of the so-called 'neutral' condition.[883] 'Further,' he says, 'of those contraries 10 which [together] generate some one thing, this generated thing is in some instances more than one of the generating [contraries] and less than the other, such as grey,[884] and in other instances is greater than both, such as what is added together from a greater [quantity] and a lesser [quantity], and in yet other instances is less than both, as for instance the [sum] of straight and bent: for it is less straight than the straight [parent] and less bent than the bent [parent].' 15

14a15-19 It is clear that contraries naturally come about in connection with the same thing – the same either in species or in genus. [For sickness and health come about in an animal's body, but whiteness and blackness do so in body *simpliciter*,] and justice and injustice do so in a soul.

Since, in speaking of the contraries with and without an intermediate, [Aristotle] made use of the phrase '*in* which [the contraries] naturally arise or *of* which they are [naturally] predicated' (12b28-9), he informs

20   us which are the things *in* which contraries naturally arise. And since 'the same' is said in three ways – either in genus or in species or in number – he says that they come about in things which are the same 'in genus' and the same 'in species'. For when we take body *simpliciter*, in connection with which the contraries whiteness and blackness [obtain], we have taken the same thing to be the *genus*; if, on the other hand, [we take] the body of an animal, in which sickness and health [obtain], we have taken it to be a *species* under the genus [of body].

25   And if [we take] all souls as the same in genus, the rational and the non-rational will be contraries in connection with them; if, on the other hand, [we take] human souls as a species,[885] virtue and vice will be [contraries] in connection with them. [Aristotle] has not, however, added that the contraries arise in connection with what is the same in *number*: some do indeed say that determinately this [instance of] practical wisdom, say Solon's, is contrary to his folly, were that [folly]

30   to come about, and that this man's health [is contrary] to that very man's sickness, but not just any [health] to any [sickness]. But Aristotle does not seem to establish the matter in this way. Hence he said that the contraries come about only in [the same] genus and in the same species.

414,1   And Iamblichus, following him, says that it is not the case that *this* [instance of] practical wisdom is demonstratively (*kata deixin*) said to be contrary to *that* [instance of] folly, but that practical wisdom [is said to be contrary] to folly immediately.[886] And even if the contraries are applied determinately to a particular one among individuals, still [that is so] by reference to the immediate [contraries]: for how is folly contrary to the [instance of] practical wisdom in *this* man rather than

5   to the [instance] in *that* man? But perhaps there is some sort of opposition even in these [instances], given that both the virtues and the vices are individualised (*idiotropountai*)[887] in relation to the souls which have them, and healths and sicknesses in relation to the bodies which have them. And why should Aristotle not say that the contraries come about in connection with numerically the same thing as well,[888] given that he himself defined the distinguishing mark of substance as this very thing, namely that it, while remaining numeri-

10   cally one and the same thing, is capable of receiving contraries (4a10ff.)? Well, it is not that Aristotle wants the underlying subject for the contraries *not* to be one in number: rather, [the fact that they *can* be one in number] has perhaps been omitted here as having been said clearly in the account concerning substance; but, if contraries[889] do indeed come about in individuals too, [he wants] them not to possess contrariety *in respect of the individual*: for it is not because

it is *this* [individual] practical wisdom and *this* [individual] folly [that they have contrariety], but because they are practical wisdom and folly. And that is also the way in which Iamblichus' point is to be properly accommodated. It is clear that in connection with what is the same in genus and in connection with what is the same in species the contraries not only come about simultaneously, but also exist simultaneously, since they can come into existence together in different [sc. individual] things. But it is impossible for them to exist in connection with numerically the same thing, other than by turns.[890]

14a19-25 It is necessary that all contraries [either be in the same genus, or in contrary genera, or be themselves genera. For white and black are in the same genus – for their genus is colour – and justice and injustice are in contrary genera – for the genus of the former is virtue and of the latter vice – while good and bad are not in a genus,] but actually are themselves genera [of certain things].

[Aristotle] conveys the fourth theorem that all the contraries are either under the same genus – such as 'white and black' (14a20-1) under the [genus of] colour – or under contrary genera – such as 'justice and injustice' (14a22), since the genus of the former is virtue, and of the latter vice – or else they are themselves genera, such as the 'good' and the 'bad', which 'are not in' another 'genus, but actually are themselves genera' (14a24-5).[891] Nicostratus criticises this division, saying that the third section in it is non-existent: for there are no contraries which are [themselves] just genera and not also species of some one or more [genera]: 'For clearly the good and the bad, for example, are arranged under the [category of] quality, and either [under] *condition* or *state*. Moreover, every contrary will either be arranged under one of the ten genera – and then it will certainly be *under* a genus and the statement that [contraries] themselves are genera was wrong – or it is outside the ten categories and then the division into ten [categories] will be incomplete.'

This well-urged difficulty the students of Porphyry solve by saying that some of the contraries are homonymous, and others not homonymous, and that '[Aristotle] has divided the non-homonymous [contraries] into those arranged under one genus and those [arranged] under contrary genera, while he says that those [contraries] which are [said] homonymously, since they are not under one genus but are said of many things, are themselves genera, on the ground that the genera resemble things which are homonymous on the basis of one thing.'[892] And such are the good and the bad.[893] For the good is homonymous, since indeed it is in substance, as god, and in quality, as virtue, and [it occurs] as quantity too, as the balanced, and in the other categories.' But the people who say this kind of thing say, in the first place, that 'genus' is being improperly said of a homonymous word, and secondly they do not admit that the good and the bad are qualities.[894] Others interpret [Aristotle's] text in a peculiar way,

10   saying that what is made clear in the words 'good and bad are not in a genus, but actually are themselves genera of certain things' (14a23-5) is nothing other than that the good and the bad are not under contrary genera, but are themselves contrary genera: for although they are under the [genus of] quality, the [genus of] quality is not contrary to another genus. This solution is also forced: for the third differentia will not then differ at all from the first, since the good and

15   the bad, which are contraries, are under one genus.

Theophrastus wrote the following remarks in his *Topics*, and they render the account even more intractable: 'Since the principles of contraries are contrary [to each other], it is clear that these [principles] are not in a single genus,[895] just as the good and the bad and movement and rest are not [in a single genus] either. Now both excess and deficiency will be not only contraries but also principles, as will be both form and privation.' In response to this Iamblichus says that

20   'If [there are] ten genera of the things that are, and all the contraries [are] under these, then either all will be arranged under a single genus, or some under one and some under another, or contraries will be [things said[896]] in many ways, each one being arranged under several genera.'[897] Well, [Theophrastus] does not simply say that the [sc. principles of] contraries are 'not in a single genus', referring to the categories as genera, but he also denies that there are *further*

25   genera of them which are themselves contraries. For these [principles][898] are indeed *principles* of contraries, and [sc. all] other [contraries] are arranged under these[899] – though [Theophrastus] too regarded excess and deficiency as arranged under one genus (namely quantity) as under a single category – and he does not want them, as contraries and principles of contraries, to be [themselves] arranged under *other* contraries. Well, the primary contraries[900] too[901] are not genera, strictly speaking, and this is [the force of] the remark that 'these are not in a single genus'.[902] For the examples which they

30   use in these cases[903] are such as have the prior and posterior in them.[904]

'Perhaps, therefore,' says Iamblichus, 'Aristotle is here following the Pythagorean disposition concerning the co-ordinate series (*sustoikhia*) of the good and bad,[905] calling their [i.e. the Pythagoreans'] contrary first principles[906] "genera", so that this third differentia of the contraries is put forward[907] rather by way of opinion[908].[909] But someone might perhaps raise the question how the account of con-

35   traries which says that contraries are what differ most from one another *under the same genus*[910] can still be true, if they are indeed

not only under the same but also under contrary genera, so that I   416,1
pass over the third point[911] as having been put forward by way of
opinion [only].' But the account included the reference [of contraries]
to one [genus] *of some sort or other*, whereas the differentiation [given]
here has been construed in respect of the *proximate* [genus], since
some [contraries] are arranged proximately under a single genus –
as for instance white and black under colour – whereas others [are   5
arranged] proximately under contrary [genera] – as for instance
justice and injustice under virtue and vice, but through these under
the one thing, either state or condition or the [category of] quality
itself.[912]

Now Archytas does not pass over this [fourth] difference among
the contraries either, and seems to expound it more securely by saying
the following:[913] 'Further, some contraries occur in *genera of genera*:   10
for good is contrary to bad, and the good is the genus of the virtues,
the bad [the genus] of the vices. Others [occur] in *genera of species*:
for virtue and vice are contrary, and virtue is the genus of practical
wisdom and temperance, vice that of folly and licence. Yet others
[occur] in *species*: for courage is contrary to cowardice and justice to
injustice, and justice and courage are species of virtue, injustice and
licence of vice.' In these words Archytas says that some contraries are   15
genera of genera, notwithstanding that they may themselves be
ranged under one genus, as for instance the good and the bad under
the [genus of] quality,[914] whereas others [he says] are genera of
species, and yet others are species. And he adds that even the primary
genera[915] are certainly also species. For he says: 'they are not merely
genera, but also species'.[916]   20

But since we have now concluded the account concerning contraries and the opposites as a whole, it would be appropriate not to omit
consideration of a question of such magnitude [as the following].
Aristotle everywhere in these discussions[917] – and before Aristotle
Archytas[918] – puts forward as examples of contraries the good and
bad, health and sickness, true and false, justice and injustice, virtue   25
and vice or moral excellence (*spoudaiotês*)[919] and baseness (*phau-
lotês*), while as examples of possession and privation [they give] sight
and blindness.[920] I think, therefore, that it is worth investigating
whether one ought to posit the good and bad and justice and injustice
and health and sickness as contraries or as states of possession and
privation. For[921] if the contraries tend to be[922] equipollent[923] and
equally primary and both according to nature, but *these* ones – I mean   30
the bad and injustice and sickness and suchlike – are rather failures
(*apotukhiai*),[924] deviations (*parallaxeis*) and perversions (*paratropai*)
away from what is according to nature, and appendant subsistences
(*parupostaseis*),[925] how could *both* [contraries][926] be primary or
equipollent or equally according to nature? For if there is such a thing

417,1 at all as the counternatural, it is to be found in these things and not in anything else. And that they are failures[927] is made clear firstly by the fact that they are not the end (*telos*) of anything, and also by the fact that those who choose injustice are lured by the false tinge (*parakhrôsis*)[928] of the good in it, and succumb to it as a result of a failure, while seeking self-sufficiency and adequacy and what is foremost. And who doubts, in the case of sickness, but that it is a
5 counternatural condition? That is how all doctors up to the present day continue to define it. Hence if these things[929] are opposed as what is in accord with nature and what is against nature, the[930] opposition [between them] will not be as of *contraries* (for both of those[931] are in accord with nature and are forms, as for instance white and black and hot and cold), but rather as of possession and privation – both [the privation consisting] in being currently deprived (*to steriskesthai*),
10 and that [consisting] in having been deprived (*to esterêsthai*). For indeed being sick is a privation, and so is having died, and having ophthalmia and having been blinded [are also privations], but the former[932] [consist] in being currently deprived, the latter[933] in having been deprived.

Now although [privation] is of two kinds, these men call *privation* only the kind [which consists] in *having been deprived*,[934] owing to its being completely incapable (*adunamon*), while they posit those [conditions consisting] in *currently being deprived* as *contraries*, on account of the continuing presence in them of a certain capacity deriving
15 from the admixture of a bit of possession,[935] and yet Archytas knew about this differentia[936] in his book *On Opposites* – and not only this one, but he also put forward a third, distinct [differentia]. He writes as follows:[937] 'Privation and being deprived (*to esterêsthai*)[938] are said in three ways: either in virtue of not possessing at all, as for example what is blind [not possessing] sight, and what is toothless [not possessing] voice, and what is ignorant [not possessing] knowledge; or in virtue of possessing less, as for example what is hard of hearing
20 [possessing less] hearing, and what is sore-eyed [possessing less] sight; or in virtue of not possessing in the way that one ought, as for example what is bow-legged [not possessing] legs [in the way that it ought], and what is harsh-voiced [not possessing] voice [in the way that it ought].' It appears that even if [Archytas] as well [sc. as Aristotle] would not have gone so far as to regard having sore eyes[939] *not* as a sickness, still [he did regard] this [condition] too as being in the [classification] *being deprived* (*to esterêsthai*): for after all the whole division was of the [classification] *being deprived* (*to esterêsthai*).[940]

Furthermore, the contraries, by progressing and reaching the goal of their generation become *purely* contrary, whereas when
25 ophthalmia progresses to a great extent and reaches its goal it becomes blindness, and sickness [becomes] death, so that ophthalmia

and sickness were [after all] not contraries. In general both the contraries [in a pair] are functions of nature, whereas sickness is a failure of nature and a privation, not merely in the sense of being an *absence* of the natural but in the sense of being its *failure*. Now the privation [mentioned] in the *Physics*[941] was just absence of the form, which does not manifest the counternatural anywhere, but rather   30 diversity: for, clearly, although the matter of an ox has been deprived for a while of the form of bees,[942] and that of bread of the [form] of flesh,[943] the counternatural is nowhere present in these instances, as it is in the case of the privation which is opposed [to possession]. So wherever the   418,1 counternatural [is present], we ought rather to say that there a privation [is present] and not a contrary, for in this way our account in response to those who posit the bad as a first principle[944] will also be expedited.

What reason, therefore, can one give for such a disposition of these godlike men,[945] and for the fact that not even Iamblichus objected to it, although he laid out many and excellent reasons why we ought to   5 regard the bad [as consisting] in appendant subsistence (*paruposta-sis*) and failure? Well, it appears that they [i.e. Archytas and Aristotle] followed the instruction of the Pythagoreans, which sets out the two co-ordinate series,[946] the worse [series] and the better, as *contrary*; and the good and the bad were arranged in these [contrary series]. But this needs to be investigated at greater length. If what has been said was correctly said and we then investigate the differences between the oppositions – namely the [opposition] of things [opposed]   10 as contraries and that of things [opposed] as possession and privation – we shall no longer mention the following [as a point of difference], namely that while the contraries change into one another, things [opposed] as possession and privation do not change [into one an-other], given that, as has been said, even though they change into one another sickness and health and justice and injustice and the good and bad are opposed not as contraries but as possession and privation. Rather, we shall say what [I said] just now (416,29), namely that both   15 the contraries are equipollent and primary and in accord with nature and are forms, whereas privation is incapacity and appendant sub-sistence and against nature and is a failure of the form [to be present]. But we should proceed to what Aristotle takes next in order.

CHAPTER 12

On Prior and Posterior

14a26-b23 One thing is called prior to another in four ways.   20 [Firstly, and most strictly, (something is prior) in respect of time, in accordance with which one thing is said to be older or more ancient than another: for it is called older or more ancient in

virtue of the fact that the time is longer. Secondly, what does
not reciprocate in respect of the entailment of existence (is
prior), as for instance one is prior to two: for if there are two it
automatically follows that there is one, but if there is one it is
not necessary that there be two, so that the entailment of the
other's existence does not hold reciprocally from one; and the
thing which is such that the entailment of existence does not
hold reciprocally from it is held to be prior. Thirdly, something
is called prior in respect of some order, as in the cases of
branches of knowledge and of speeches. For in the case of the
branches of apodeictic knowledge there exist the prior and the
posterior in terms of order: for the elements are prior in order
to the diagrams – and in the case of grammar the elements are
prior to the syllables. And it is the same in the case of speeches:
for the exordium is prior in order to the exposition. Further,
apart from the mentioned ways (of being prior), what is better
and more valued is held to be prior by nature: even the many
are accustomed to assert that the people who are more valued
and especially loved by them are prior. This one of the ways (of
being prior) is really the least proper. Thus there are as many
as these mentioned varieties of the prior. There might seem,
however, to be yet another variety of priority apart from the ones
mentioned. For in the case of things which reciprocate in respect
of the entailment of existence, the one which is in some way the
cause of the other's existence could legitimately be called prior
by nature. And it is clear that there are examples of such things:
for that there is a man reciprocates in respect of the entailment
of existence with the true sentence about him: for if there is a
man, then the sentence by means of which we say that there is
a man is true. And it indeed reciprocates: for if the sentence by
means of which we say that there is a man is true, then there is
a man. The true sentence is in no way the cause of the object's
existence; the object, however, does appear in some way to be
the cause of the sentence's being true. For the sentence is said
to be true or false in virtue of the existence or otherwise of the
object.] Hence there are five ways in which one thing might be
said to be prior to another.

[Aristotle] has also[947] made use in the foregoing of the [concept of]
prior, both in the account of substance (2a12ff.) and in the case of
relatives, saying: 'The knowable seems to be prior to knowledge'
(7b23-4).[948] Because of this, accordingly, and since the prior is said in
many ways, he produces its division, though he does not convey all
25   the ways [in which the prior is said]: for both he himself in other
[writings][949] and Strato in his monograph *On the Prior and Posterior*

add several other [varieties] as well.[950] But he thinks that the ones he sets out here are sufficient for an introduction.

He says that the first and strictest variety of the prior is that 'in respect of time' (14a25-6), in accordance with which we call the first   30
in time 'older or more ancient', establishing these names as marks of   419,1
honour. 'Older' (*presbuteron*) is applied, strictly speaking, to animate beings and especially to men, in accordance with which we call Pythagoras older than Socrates, whereas 'more ancient' (*palaioteron*) [is applied] to inanimate things and to events, as for instance we say that the Trojan War is more ancient than the Persian War, and in this sense prior.[951] It is clear that, in establishing[952] the comparison,   5
one must compare [what is prior] to something *else*: otherwise someone will be found to be older than himself in respect of his youth, because that was prior in time. In these discussions we should ask first how, if the prior is homonymous, there can be something in it which is its strictest [application]: for in the case of things which are said in many ways and are homonymous it is [surely] not possible for one to be the strict [instance] and another [to be so called] metaphori-   10
cally, as was said in the account of homonymous things.[953] But[954] the individual substance was called [substance] in the strictest sense, primarily and most of all (2a11-12), because the secondary substances are said synonymously of it. Hence we should say that it *is* possible to speak of the 'strictest sense' in the case of homonymous things as well,[955] when one [case] is posited as the foremost, and another [as deriving] from that, as in the case of the animate animal and the depicted one: the former is an animal in the strictest sense, the latter   15
secondarily so in virtue of its likeness to the former, but both are homonymous. Secondly we should ask why the [prior] in respect of *time* is the strictest signification of the prior. Well, it seems that the other kinds of prior have been so called on the basis of those things which are prior in respect of time. And this signification is quite familiar to usage: 'since I was born earlier' says Homer.[956]   20

The second variety of the prior is, he says, 'what does not reciprocate in respect of the entailment of existence' (14a30), when it follows from the positing of something else, but the something else does not follow from the positing of it, as for example if there are two things there is at all events one, but if there is one thing it is not necessary that there be two. Hence that thing is prior from which the entailment [to the other] does not follow, and that thing posterior from the   25
positing of which the other follows. The more recent [philosophers][957] are wont to call what is prior in this sense 'what is implied [by the other] but does not imply [it] and what [if cancelled] cancels [the other] but is not cancelled[958] [if the other is cancelled]'. Aristotle conflated these points in his phrase 'not reciprocating in respect of the entailment of existence'. He said that [the prior in this sense] does

not reciprocate in respect of the entailment of existence because it is
30   not the case that just as if there are two things there is one, so also if
there is one thing there are two. So the one does not rank equally with
the two in respect of the following of the two's existence from the one's
existence in the same way as the one's existence follows from the two's
existence. Hence what does not reciprocate in respect of the entailment of existence is prior.

In this way it is also shown that the genus is by nature[959] prior to
the species, since [if the genus is cancelled] it cancels [the species],
420,1   but is not [itself] cancelled [if the species is cancelled], and it is implied
[by the species] but does not imply [the species]. For if animal is
cancelled man is cancelled, but if man is cancelled animal is not
cancelled, and in respect of the entailment[960] of existence man neither
coexists with, nor is implied by, animal in the way in which animal
5   [coexists with and is implied by] man. But why did [Aristotle] not say
that the genus is prior to the species and the species to the individual
and the cause to the caused?[961] Well, he established a more general
specification, which is appropriate to the case of both genus and
species and also to some causes which by nature precede the things
they cause,[962] as for example the one is cause of the two.

[Aristotle] enumerates as a third variety of the prior the one 'in
10   respect of order' (14a35), and he proves this one both on the basis of
the branches of apodeictic knowledge, as in the case of geometry – for
in it the definitions are prior to 'the diagrams', as are the axioms, the
postulates and the hypotheses, these taking pride of place in the order
– and 'in the case of grammar' [where] 'the [sound] elements' are
likewise prior in order to 'the syllables'. And the same thing is
demonstrated in the case of a speech, whether forensic or political:
15   for the 'exordia' are prior to the 'expositions' and the expositions to
the proofs. And perhaps this example strictly indicates priority just
in respect of order: for, in the case of the others, they were also prior
as causes, whereas in this case the exordium [to a speech] is not the
cause of the exposition, but has prior existence by virtue of order
alone.[963]

20   [Aristotle] posits a fourth variety of the prior, according to which
we say that what is 'better and more valued' (14b4) is prior both in
terms of its capacity and in terms of its superiority, as for example
divine things [are prior] to mortal. Thus too in cities and among
friends the more valued men are called prior. He says that this variety
is the 'least proper' (14b7) of the meanings in respect of what is first,
not because the better and more valued things are not in reality first
25   by nature, but because the [name] 'prior' is not altogether customary
in the case of such things: for clearly we do not customarily call our
fathers and teachers, even though they *are* more valued, 'prior' in that
sense, and the name 'prior' has not [here] become naturalised in the

way it has in the case of the other varieties. But perhaps it is not because of usage that [Aristotle] says that this variety of the prior and posterior is the least proper (for as a matter of usage we do in fact quite often call what is more valued 'first'), but because the prior 30 and posterior in this kind of nature tend to be as [they are] in the case of time, or [as] the one and two [are] in the case of number, or [as] the exordium and exposition [are] in the case of a speech. The [variety of prior] to be introduced next [by Aristotle],[964] on the other hand, is posited in the case of things which rank equally, and not things which are, as such,[965] better and worse. Although those things which are causally prior *are* better, they nevertheless do not hold their priority in virtue of being better, and [those which are] posterior [contrari- 35 wise], but it is in virtue of the fact that, while being in some sense of the same nature,[966] they are [respectively] prior and posterior.

[Aristotle] adds a fifth variety of the prior to what has already been 421,1 said, according to which in the case even[967] of things which reciprocate in respect of the entailment of existence and which seem to obtain simultaneously, the one which includes the cause is nevertheless said to be prior, as in the example he has cited. For the 'object' (*pragma*) is the cause of the 'true sentence', but not the sentence of the object.[968] And in the case of things which reciprocally entail one another [the 5 prior] sometimes comes about as a *productive* [cause] – as for instance both in the case of the mentioned example and of course if there is a father, there is a son and contrariwise, but the father is a productive cause [of the son] – and sometimes as a *material* [cause], as for example clay: for [clay] is simultaneously water and earth, but mixed, since it is mud (*pêlos*) made out of earth and water,[969] but the water and the earth are a *material* cause [of the clay], whereas the mixture is a *formal* [cause] of this.[970] 10

Consequently [Aristotle] has set out here five varieties of the prior: in respect of *time*, in respect of *nature*, in respect of *order*, in respect of *capacity* and in respect of *cause*. And it is clear that what is posterior will be said in as many ways as what is first. Anyone who defines what is first in terms of *position*, as for instance if we were to say that the eastern one of the columns [of a temple] is the first one – if it has a [merely] notional primacy, there is no reason [for the 15 choice]: for the same thing will be first and posterior.[971] But if, further,[972] it has [priority] by nature, then it will be ranged under the [priority of] *order*. But what is first in notion, such as the end (*telos*) – since we excogitate the end in advance, as for example [we think of] the shelter before the walls, the foundations and the digging – that will accordingly be ranged under the first in time: for the conception of the end is prior in time, whereas its existence is posterior in time, 20 although first in being, since the more complete things (*ta teleiotera*) are first in being. And this latter signification of the first[973] seems to me not to have been omitted [by Aristotle], as Iamblichus asserts, but to be included in the fourth variety, in which what is more valued and best was called first. Elsewhere[974] [Aristotle] also calls part of the

25 definition of an object prior, and this, I think, when taken as a material cause will be included in the fifth variety [of priority], being consequential on the whole thing in the same way as matter is, and of course it does *not* reciprocate in respect of entailment of existence. And he says[975] that the end is both prior and more familiar to us, even if it is posterior by nature.

30 In the *Metaphysics*[976] the prior and posterior are divided as follows: 'The primary,' he says, 'is what is nearer a certain origin, defined either *simpliciter* and by nature or in relation to something or somewhere or by certain men, as for instance the [prior] in respect of place [is prior] by virtue of being nearer to some place defined either by nature (such as the middle or the extreme), or in relation to some

422,1 given thing, and what is further away is posterior. And [there are] things prior in respect of time, these being in the case of what has come about the things more distant from the present moment, and in the case of what is to come the things nearer [the present moment]: for in this sense the Trojan War came about before the Persian War, and the Nemean Games will come about before the Pythian Games, since we make use of the present moment as an origin. Other things

5 [are prior] in respect of movement: for what is nearer the first mover is prior, as child [is prior] to man, and this too is a kind of origin [taken] *simpliciter*. Other things [are prior] in respect of capacity: for what rules by dint of its capacity and is most capable is prior. Something is of this kind if it is necessary that another thing – namely what is posterior – follow according to its choice, so that if this thing moves [the latter] moves, and if it does not move [the latter] does not

10 move: for choice is also an origin. Other things [are prior] in respect of order: these are the ones which differ from some one defined thing by virtue of their account, as for example the man next to the chorus leader is prior to the next but one, and the next lowest string to the lowest: for where in the first case the origin is the chorus leader, in the latter case it is the middle string. Accordingly these things are called prior in this sense.

'In another sense what is prior in the [order of] knowledge is also prior [taken] *simpliciter*. But of these [what is prior] in respect of its

15 account differs from [what is prior] in respect of perception: for universals are prior in respect of their account, whereas in respect of perception particulars [are prior]. Furthermore,[977] the affections of prior things are said to be prior, as for instance straightness is prior to smoothness, since the former is the affection of a line, the latter of a surface. Things are also called prior by nature and substance when they can themselves exist without other things, but those [other]

things cannot [exist] without them: Plato employed this variety [of 20
the prior],'[978] – and [Aristotle] himself [does so] here. So that is how
he enumerated the varieties of the prior and posterior in that text,
and it is clear that the ones mentioned in the *Categories* are included
in them: that in respect of time, that in respect of order, and that in
respect of capacity[979] in the first [sense],[980] those in respect of nature
and cause[981] in the last [sense].[982]

Now the five varieties [of the prior] in the *Categories* will be 25
referred to the highest genera as follows: that in respect of time to
the category when; that in respect of nature, which cancels without
being cancelled, that in respect of capacity and that in respect of cause
under the relatives; that in respect of order under the [category of]
being-in-a-position. It is clear that the posterior too will be in the same
categories as those in which the prior is. 30

Strato of Lampsacus too, in his monograph *On the Prior and* 423,1
Posterior, enumerated many varieties [of priority], which I think it is
possible to reduce to the five specified here, being as it were a division
of them. (1) For the incomplete, being called [prior] to the complete,
will be arranged under the prior in time, because the end is the last
thing in all matters. The same thing [will] also [be arranged] under 5
order. (2) Furthermore, something comes under both of these,[983] as
well as under the[984] prior by virtue of worth and capacity and by virtue
of nature,[985] if knowledge of it is prior, as for example [knowledge] of
the unit [is prior] to [knowledge] of the dyad, and [knowledge] of
plurality [is prior] to [knowledge] of even and odd: for these things do
not reciprocate in respect of the entailment of existence,[986] just as
knowledge of them does not do so either. (3) And things whose
function is prior, as for example the good [is prior] to the bad,[987] are 10
also first in time and worth: for the former is the cause of preserva-
tion, the latter of destruction, and being is before being destroyed,
both in time and in worth. (4) And whatever can exist while something
else does not exist is first by nature, since it does not reciprocate in
respect of the entailment of existence, as for instance place [is prior]
to body and body to colour, and likewise if one thing naturally comes
about *in* another[988] [then the latter is prior to the former], as for
instance substance [is prior] to quality and quantity (*poson*). In this 15
way too what is in accord with nature is prior to what is against
nature, and the law [is prior] to transgression of the law, and possession to privation. (5) Under what is prior in worth and capacity will
be arranged the things which are more akin to what is more valued,
as for instance quantity will be arranged before quality, given that
quantity is part of substance, whereas quality is not. And [so too]
where one thing partakes of generation and destruction, as time does,
and another does not, as place [does not], and where one thing is 20
separable, and another not:[989] for without perception it is impossible

for there to be a soul, but without desire it is possible for there to be one.⁹⁹⁰ And the partless [is prior in worth] to the divisible into parts: for it is more similar to an origin, so that the centre is also [prior] to the circle. And what partakes more of the prior [is itself prior in worth], as for instance the eternal [partakes more] of the good, whereas the transient [partakes more] of the bad,⁹⁹¹ and the even [partakes more] of the dyad, whereas the odd [partakes more] of the triad.⁹⁹² And where one thing remains for a certain time, and another

25   does not remain, [the former is prior in worth to the latter,] as for instance body [is prior] to movement and time. (6) Under what is prior in order will come what is prior to something in between, and [under what is] posterior [in order will come] what is posterior to something in between. (7) Under the prior in the sense of being causally [prior] in the case of reciprocating things,⁹⁹³ the element will be prior. For again, the part too [is prior in this sense] to the whole, as the finite [is prior] to the infinite, and if something is [made] out of something else [then the latter is prior], as for instance the bronze [is prior] to

30   the statue: for this [bronze] too is a (material) cause [of the statue].⁹⁹⁴ And that the⁹⁹⁵ same thing can in one respect be prior and in another respect posterior, Strato himself also indicated, by showing that time and place are prior and posterior to each other.

<h1 style="text-align:center">CHAPTER 13</h1>

<h2 style="text-align:center">On the Simultaneous</h2>

14b24-15a12 Those things are called simultaneous [*simpliciter* and in the strictest sense whose generation is at the same time: for neither is prior or posterior. These things are said to be simultaneous in respect of time. Those things are called simultaneous by nature which reciprocate in respect of the entailment of existence and where neither is in any way the cause of the other's existence, as for instance in the case of double and half: for these reciprocate – for if there is a double there is a half, and if there is a half there is a double – but neither is the cause of the other's existence. And things taken from the same genus which are contradistinguished from one another are said to be simultaneous by nature. Now things are said to be contradistinguished from one another if they are yielded by the same division, as for instance the winged (is contradistinguished) from the terrestrial and the aquatic. For these are from the same genus and are contradistinguished from one another: for animal is divided into these – i.e. into the winged, the terrestrial and the aquatic – and none of these is prior or posterior, but rather things of this sort are held to be simultaneous by nature. Each of these – I mean the terrestrial, the winged and the aquatic – may be further divided into species, and it follows that those (species) too will be simultaneous by nature – all that are from the same genus and are yielded by the same division. But genera are always prior to species: for they do not reciprocate in respect of the entailment of existence. For example, if there is an aquatic animal there is an animal, but if there is an animal there is not necessarily an aquatic one. Hence both those things which reciprocate in respect of the entailment of existence, where neither is in any way the cause of the other's existence, and those things taken from the same genus which are contradistinguished from one another, are called simultaneous by nature.] And those things are called simultaneous *simpliciter* whose generation is at the same time.

Having made additional use of the simultaneous in the account of the relatives, [Aristotle] appropriately proposes to give instruction about it as well.[996] He arranges the simultaneous after the prior and 5
posterior because they are opposed to one another, as the fact that [the simultaneous] is denoted by virtue of the negation of them [i.e. the prior and posterior] makes clear.[997] Hence he also enumerated as varieties of the simultaneous roughly those opposed to their varieties,[998] and [enumerated them] to some extent in the same order.

He sets down the first [variety], in respect of which, he says, those things 'whose generation is at the same time' are called simultaneous 10
'*simpliciter* and in the strictest sense' (14b24-5). [He takes this variety first], for in the preceding discussion[999] he also arranged before [the other kinds of priority] the prior in respect of time, in accordance with which one thing was said to be older and more ancient than another. And he says that this [sense of] simultaneous – the one in respect of time – is also what is called [simultaneous] '*simpliciter*' and 'strictly', as being well-worn in usage.

[Aristotle] sets down the second signification of the simultaneous, which he reasonably opposed to the second and fifth significations of 15
the prior and posterior.[1000] For the former of these was what does not reciprocate in respect of the entailment of existence, and in this sense had priority, while the latter did reciprocate, but the reciprocation was as of cause and caused, and in this sense again the first of these was prior and the second posterior. But in the case of the simultaneous, insofar as it reciprocates, it is opposed to the non-reciprocating [variety of prior and posterior]; and insofar as it is of things [taken] as ranking equally, [it is opposed] to the[1001] [prior and posterior taken] as cause and caused, as are for instance 'double' and 'half'. It was in 20
respect of this signification of the simultaneous that the relatives

were called simultaneous: for indeed the double and the half always
entail and cancel one another, and neither is cause of the other.

    [Aristotle] conveys a third signification of the simultaneous, calling
simultaneous 'things taken from the same genus which are contradistinguished from one another; ... and those things are said to be
contradistinguished' which are yielded by one and 'the same division'
(14b34-5). [The proviso is necessary], for it can sometimes happen
that several [distinct] divisions of a single genus come about, some
co-ordinately (*isostoikhôs*), as when we say that of bodies some are
hot and some cold, or some animate and some inanimate – and they
call these additional divisions (*epidiaireseis*)[1002] – while others contain
priority and posteriority, as when we [further] divide the animate
(that is to say, the [genus] animal) into the winged, the terrestrial
and the aquatic, and they call this a subdivision (*hupodiairesis*)[1003] of
the [genus] animal. But a contradistinction (*antidiairesis*) is an
opposition of the divided things (*diairêmata*) which arises by virtue
of one and the same split (*tomê*), so that the inanimate is contradistinguished from the animate, since they come about from the same
split, and the terrestrial and aquatic [are contradistinguished] from
the winged. And each of these is further split into species (15a1-3),
and those species will likewise be simultaneous by nature (14b33ff.),
since they are contradistinguished things taken from the same genus.[1004] For none of them[1005] is considered to be prior or posterior, as
in the case of the other divisions the things [coming about] by virtue
of the first division *were* prior to the things in the posterior [divi-
sion],[1006], since they[1007] cancel [those others] without themselves being
cancelled, and are implied [by the others] without themselves implying [them] – which is as much as to say that they do not reciprocate
in respect of the entailment of existence. For if there is an animal
there is not necessarily an aquatic one, but if there is an aquatic one
there necessarily is an animal; and if animal is cancelled, the [species]
aquatic [animal] is cancelled, whereas if aquatic [animal] is cancelled
the [genus] animal is not cancelled.

    Now nothing prior and posterior opposed to this [variety of the]
simultaneous[1008] seems to have been conveyed [by Aristotle]. But
Iamblichus says that the things which come about by virtue of a prior
and a posterior division are opposed to this [variety of the simultane-
ous], as for instance the animate taken from the prior division [sc. of
body] is prior to the winged which is taken from the posterior division
[of the animate]: for these do not reciprocate in respect of the entailment of existence either,[1009] so that this signification of the simultaneous too[1010] is opposed to the second variety of the prior and posterior,
in which the genera and species are arranged.[1011] Moreover, having
divided the [genus] animal into rational and non-rational, and the
non-rational into winged, terrestrial and aquatic, Iamblichus posits

the rational as prior to the winged.[1012] 'And thus,' he says, 'in the case 20
of propositions too some have produced the division by dividing the
simple and non-simple into simultaneous [species],[1013] whereas others [have divided propositions] into the simple, the conditional and
the disjunctive – incorrectly: for the conditional and the disjunctive
[propositions] are species of the non-simple [proposition] which is
contradistinguished from the simple[1014] [proposition].[1015]

'But there seem also to be some things simultaneous in order, 25
([Iamblichus] says), which are opposed to things prior and posterior
in order, as for example things of equal value and equal worth.[1016]
And indeed it may be that contradistinguished things taken from the
same genus were said [by Aristotle] to be simultaneous in a more
general sense, both by nature and in order: for these things are *rather*
simultaneous in order than by nature, assuming that it is things
which coexist with each other[1017] and are cancelled by [each other's
removal][1018] which are simultaneous by nature, as is the case with the
relatives. But contradistinguished things taken from the same genus 30
do not relate in *this* way to each other.' But it is worth noting that
neither what is of equal worth nor what is of equal value will possess
their simultaneity in virtue of *order*. For nor were the prior and
posterior in respect of order said to have their priority or posteriority
in virtue of an excess or deficiency of *worth* or *value*, but rather in 426,1
virtue of the chief rank of the *position* [of the prior], as for instance
the exordium was said to be prior in respect of order to the exposition.
Rather, what is of equal worth and of equal value is opposed to the
fourth variety of the prior and posterior, namely that in respect of the
better and more valued, and this point has no doubt been omitted by
Aristotle as being clear. Things simultaneous in respect of order
would be those things having the same position, as for instance 5
several exordia would be said to be arranged simultaneously prior to
the exposition, and there is a certain kind of order in them too.[1019] But
perhaps it is [rather] *these contradistinguished things*[1020] which are
opposed to the prior and posterior in respect of order, since they are
both co-ordinate and have the same order. Iamblichus, however, says:
'But perhaps the simultaneous will not, strictly speaking, tolerate an
order either: for order [consists] in distinction.[1021] But it is to be noted 10
(says Iamblichus) that in every genus it is necessary that *some* species
be contradistinguished and be simultaneous by nature – which is not
so in cases where one thing is prior and another posterior – and that
the winged, the terrestrial and the aquatic are species of the [genus]
animal.'[1022]

Also simultaneous are those things which come to be in the same
place as each other, just as prior and posterior were spoken of in
respect of place as well.[1023] For things which are in the same place 15
and in the same receptacle we call simultaneous (*hama*) and together

(*homou*), and 'simultaneous' is spoken of in the same way as 'together': '[Let us return home], since the war and the plague are simultaneously going to destroy the Achaians', says Homer.[1024] And we say that things positioned in the same place are simultaneously
20   positioned, and that those dwelling in the same house dwell together. And people also use 'simultaneous' in the case of men acting in common to some practical effect, as in the case of governing simultaneously. But perhaps it is not possible, strictly speaking, to call any of these mentioned cases simultaneous, unless indeed in a broad sense: for it is not possible for two bodies either to be or to be positioned in the same place, in such a way as to be called strictly simultaneous as well. And that is also why Aristotle passed over these points.
25   Iamblichus says: 'One must also note the following point, that to the simultaneous in respect of time we oppose the prior and posterior in respect of time, whereas in the case of things [simultaneous] in respect of place the [notion of] *separate* (*khôris*) is opposed. And this is of two kinds: the one kind [is of things] in different places, the other kind [is] in respect of one [place], to which the [notion of] *in concert* (*koinêi*) is opposed – as in "Let us lift this in concert" (we are not saying "in concert" in respect of place or in respect of time, but in respect of
30   the operation).'[1025] And perhaps, given that in the *Metaphysics* [Aristotle] also defined the prior and posterior in respect of place,[1026] calling what is nearer in respect of place to a defined origin *prior* in respect of place as well, and [calling] what is further off posterior, there is indeed also some kind of simultaneity in respect of place which is opposed to this priority and posteriority, and [perhaps] there is also some other kind of simultaneity in respect of place which is opposed to what is separate in respect of place.
35   But if anyone wonders why Aristotle did not go into all these matters, it suffices to reply that he analysed as many[1027] of them as
427,1   was convenient to him for the purpose of the clarity of the things which have been discussed in the foregoing, missing out abstruse matters to maintain the balance of the introduction.[1028] For example, the point that things taken from the same genus which are contradistinguished from one another are simultaneous contains a reference to those things '[taken] from different genera and not arranged under one another' (1b16), and [to the claim] that in the case of substances
5   none of them are any more substances than the others (3b33-4a9).[1029] And the point about reciprocating, without one [of the members] being a cause [of the other], was said in the case of the relatives (6b28ff.),[1030] where [Aristotle] also said that they [i.e. the relatives] are simultaneous by nature (7b15). That is why he has here (14b27-34) given instruction in the simultaneous by means of the [concept of] being

simultaneous by nature, as being appropriate to what has already been said. But these remarks [will suffice] on this matter.

CHAPTER 14

On Movement

15a13-33 There are six species of movement:[1031] [generation,   10
destruction, increase, diminution, alteration, change in respect
of place. That the other movements (apart from alteration) are
distinct from one another is obvious – for generation is not
destruction, nor is increase <or> diminution, nor is change in
respect of place, and likewise the others (are not identical with
each other) – but there is a puzzle in the case of alteration,
whether what is altered is necessarily altered in respect of one
of the other movements. But this is in fact not the case. For with
just about all the affections, or most of them, it happens that we
are altered without our sharing in any of the other movements:
for what changes in respect of an affection is not necessarily
increased or diminished, and similarly in the other cases. Hence
alteration will be distinct from the other movements. For if it
were the same, something being altered would automatically
have to be increased or diminished, or some one of the other
movements would have to ensue. But this is not necessary.
Similarly, too, what is being increased, or moved in respect of
some other movement, would have to be being altered. But there
are some things which are increased and which are not (thereby)
altered, as for instance a square has been increased when a
gnomon has been placed around it, but in no way has it (thereby)
undergone alteration. And similarly in other such cases.] Hence
the movements are distinct from one another.

[Aristotle] has mentioned movement in the account concerning quantity (5b3), and the categories which involve acting and undergoing
are so akin to movement that it has even seemed to some not
inconsiderable philosophers[1032] that movement is the genus of them
both. Hence he reasonably enough discourses about movement by   15
distinguishing the species of movement (*kinêsis*), that is to say of
change (*metabolê*): for he speaks more generally of 'movement' instead of change. For since in the account concerning substance he said
that the individual substance receives contraries by virtue of a change
of [the substance] itself (4a29-34),[1033] he reasonably divides up
change. And he has spoken in a rather general sense of 'species': for
change, which he divides up in the fifth book of his *Physics* (224b35ff.)   20
into generation (*genesis*) and destruction (*phthora*), and into the other

changes which he calls *movements* – increase (*auxêsis*), diminution
(*meiôsis*), alteration (*alloiôsis*) and change in respect of place (*kata
topon metabolê*) – is not considered by him to be a genus. But what
the nature of movement is, what its definition is, whether it is a genus
or not and the other exact theorems concerning it have been examined
thoroughly elsewhere [i.e. in the *Physics*], as being appropriate to the
25   physical treatise. But [Aristotle] has conveyed some of its divisions
[here], as is customary in introductions, and we must examine these,
with the proviso that the present account of movement does not
concern [movement] of the intellect or soul, but physical and bodily
[movement].

Now since the thing moved, *qua* body, is displaced from the state
in which it was before, and [since] some things are displaced in respect
30   of substance, others in respect of quantity, others in respect of quality,
while yet others produce a change in respect of place, and when the
[process of] changing is considered in general and everywhere, four
differentiae come about, of which some are duple: for[1034] the [differ-
entia] in respect of substance is 'generation' and 'destruction', that in
respect of quantity is 'increase' and 'diminution', that in respect of
428,1 quality is 'alteration', and that in respect of place is motion (*phora*),
this latter being further divided up into the circular, the rectilinear
and the mixed [motion]. But Nicostratus lodges the criticism that in
the *Physics* (225a20ff.) [Aristotle] does not want generation and
destruction to be movements, whereas here he enumerates them
5   too[1035] among movements. But[1036] it was easy [for Nicostratus] to see
that in the first place it was reasonable [for Aristotle] to employ here
the name 'movement' rather than 'change', since here,[1037] as befits an
introduction, he employed the name in accordance with the usage
that has come to be dominant; and, in the second place, in the *Physics*
he establishes his primary account of this matter, sanctioning what
satisfies him, and [there] he does not think it right to say that things
10   which come to be and are destroyed are *moved*, given that movement
is of subsistent things.[1038] But both the former and the latter things[1039]
change, which is why in the *Physics* he posited the common term
change, and defined generation and destruction not as movements
but as changes.

It is to be appreciated that when Democritus hypothesised that
atoms are first principles of beings he admitted only movement in
15   respect of place. For he indeed considered that even things which are
altered are moved in respect of place, but that this escapes our notice
in virtue of the fact that not *all* the parts exchange places, but rather
some of them do so, and these are invisible to us – which is why, he
says, only perceivable compounds seem[1040] to be moved in respect of
place, by changing from one place to another, either all together or if
their perceivable parts are moved successively, receiving each other's

places in exchange, such as the parts of a semicircle and of a sphere
when a rotation about an axis comes about. But Plato realised that   20
many things which are moved are not moved in respect of place, as
for example things which are heated up or whitened, and so he
introduced, as a second [kind of movement], alteration, as being
distinct from [movement] in respect of place, and one which comes
about neither by transposition of the parts, nor by displacement of
the whole.[1041] And Aristotle added [movement] in respect of quantity
too, which in the view of some people is mixed out of alteration and   25
motion, but which is in fact simple. For it differs from alteration to
the extent that quantity differs from quality, and from motion, in that
it does not lose its place as things in motion (*ta pheromena*) do; and
even if what increases in size acquires a larger place than it originally
had, and what decreases in size loses [some of its original place], the
acquisition or loss of place comes about accidentally, and what primarily comes into existence is the movement in respect of quantity.   30
Plato, however, called every difference in respect of form, so long as
the underlying subject remains, an 'alteration', since it renders [the
subject] different in kind, but not a different thing, and under this [on   429,1
his view] fell both increase in size and change in respect of quality.

But perhaps increase and diminution are [really] constituted as an
intermediate between generation and destruction [on the one hand]
and alteration [on the other]. For insofar as a gain or loss of *substance*
comes about, they resemble generation and destruction; but insofar   5
as change of *form* comes about while the [underlying] thing remains
the same, the result is rather an alteration. And in fact Plato is aware
of increase and diminution even before Aristotle, writing thus in the
tenth book of the *Laws* (893E): 'And moreover things which are
compounded, too, increase in size,[1042] while if they are separated they
become diminished, provided that the constituted order of each is
preserved.'[1043] Indeed he [i.e. Plato] makes the species of physical   10
movement not merely six but eight, adding to these [six Aristotelian
ones] the combination (*sunkrisis*) and separation (*diakrisis*) of bodies,
since these accompany movement in respect of place but are distinct
from it.[1044]

Nicostratus censures Aristotle on the ground that he was not
correct to demonstrate the difference between increase in size and
alteration by means of the example with the 'square' and the placing
of the 'gnomon' around it (15a30-1), as [an example] of [something]   15
increased in size but not altered. For he says that there are two kinds
of figure, 'on the one hand the bodily and enmattered, and on the other
hand the mathematical and immaterial, and if [Aristotle] is talking
about the immaterial square, that is neither altered nor increased in
size, such things being unmoveable (*atrepta*) and unalterable (*anal-
loiôta*), since they are beyond quality[1045] and matter. But if he is

talking about the enmattered [square] ([Nicostratus] continues), then
to the extent that this is increased in size it will also have been
altered.' But one who makes these points does not seem to be defining
alteration in terms of change in respect of quality, and increase in
size in terms of [change] in respect of quantity, as Aristotle does, but
instead, as I put it earlier (428,31), he is calling every change in
respect of form, so long as the underlying subject remains, an 'alteration', because he is claiming that even something increased in size is
automatically (*euthus*) altered. He ought to have borne in mind that
it is indeed possible [for something] to be increased in size while
remaining in the same shape and the same quality, the difference
coming about solely in respect of size (*megethos*), as when the form of
Alexander comes to be present both in the stone of a ring and in Mount
Athos shaped into a colossus of Alexander. That is also why the
peculiarly qualified [individual] is said[1046] to remain the same from
infancy to old age: its quantity is changed, but its form remains. And
contrariwise, there is nothing to prevent the size [of something]
remaining the same while it changes in respect of quality, as for
instance wine which has gone sour has changed in respect of its
quality, while remaining the same in quantity.

But for the sake of the non-mathematical we ought to say more
clearly what the gnomon is, and how the square is increased in size
by the placing around it of a gnomon.[1047] A figure is called a square
when it has its four sides and four angles equal to one another, such
as ABCD [below]. Let the diagonal of this, BC, be drawn, and let any
point, E, on the [line] AB be taken, and let [the line] EF be drawn
through E and parallel to each of the [lines] AC and BD, and let the
[line] GH be drawn parallel to each of the [lines] AB and CD through
I, which is the common point of intersection of the diagonal and the
drawn parallel [i.e. EF].

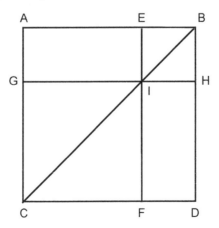

Now in the area ABCD there are four four-sided figures, namely AI
and also BI, IC and ID,[1048] and BI and IC[1049] are squares, while AI and
ID, which are called complements – since they complete the whole   20
figure when taken together with the two squares, which hold the
primary place on account of the defined [figure][1050] – these two
complements AI and ID, I say, taken together with either of the
squares,[1051] is called a gnomon, both because the figure resembles the
letter Gamma (G), and because it discriminates (*gnômateuei*) and
picks out (*krinei*) the remaining [square]. For if it is removed, it
renders the remaining [square] congruent (*homoioskhêmon*) with the   25
whole, and if it is added, [it renders] the whole congruent with the
[square] one began with. So since what remains when the gnomon is
removed is a square, it is clear that when a gnomon is also *added* to
a square, the [resulting] whole becomes a square: the quality remains   431,1
(for it is a square), while the quantity is changed (for a larger [square
comes to be] from a smaller one). If, therefore, the square is not, either
in being increased or in being diminished, subject to an alteration, it
is clear that movements in respect of increase or diminution are
different from those in respect of alteration.   5

Having said with regard to the rest of the changes that they clearly
differ from one another [Aristotle] says that there is 'a puzzle in the
case of alteration' (15a17-18) over whether what is altered necessarily
also undergoes some other kind of movement in virtue of the very fact
of being altered: for example some say that it is moved in respect of
place.[1052] And these people, following Democritus, maintain concerning the other movements (*kinêseis*)[1053] too that one ought to reduce   10
them all to [sc. spatial] motion (*phora*). But even if those who say this
are allowed to fashion alteration in terms of the exchange of parts,
even so there will be a difference between the change in respect of
place that is of the *parts*, and the alteration belonging to the *whole
thing*, which does not change in respect of its place. And likewise in
the case of increase in size there is a difference between the motion
of the parts, and the movement of the increased thing, which does not   15
change its position to anywhere else.[1054] So if the motion is of different
things from what is altered or increased or diminished, the motion
[of the parts] will not be the same as movements like these.

But [Aristotle] quite reasonably says that the puzzle applies especially to the case of alteration, because alteration is usually a concomitant of the other movements: for [it is a concomitant of] things
which are increased and diminished and come into existence and are
destroyed (for it is by the alteration of certain things that each of these   20
[movements] comes about), and things which are moved in respect of
place or are at rest are warmed up or cooled down, and have differences of colour. If therefore alteration is always a concomitant of some
other movement or movements, it will not be, so they would say, a

determinate movement *per se*. And the followers of Democritus, and
subsequently those of Epicurus, in hypothesising atoms to be unaf-
25   fected and unqualified by other qualities apart from the shapes [of
the atoms] and the way they are composed (*tên poian autôn sunthe-
sin*), say that other qualities – whether simple, such as temperatures
(*thermotêtes*) and textures (*leiotêtes*), or those in respect of colours and
tastes – *supervene*.[1055] And if these latter things[1056] [consist] in the
way atoms are composed, alteration too will consist in change in
respect of them[1057] [i.e. the atoms]. But the way they [i.e. the atoms]
are composed, and their transposition and order, derive from nowhere
30   else than from their motion and spatial movement, so that alteration
is the same thing as their motion, or at least is a concomitant of this
and is something belonging to this.[1058]

But now, [Aristotle] says, if alteration were indeed the same thing
as some one of the other movements, what is altered would necessarily have to be moved in respect of that movement too: but in point of
fact we see many things being whitened or heated or changing in
432,1 terms of the other qualities, and which are *not* being increased in size
or diminished or coming into existence or being destroyed, and
moreover are not changing their place either. And similarly, [we
would] also [see] what is moved in respect of another movement, as
for instance what is increased in size, being automatically altered too,
if [alteration] is the same thing as increase in size: but many things
which are increased in size are not altered, such as the square which
5   is increased in size by the placing around it of the gnomon. It was a
remarkable discovery [of Aristotle's] that in the case of increase in
size alteration is not even in general coexistent [with that in-
crease],[1059] for in the case of the other movements it is difficult to deny
that it coexists [with them]. For what is moved in respect of place is
warmed up, and a different colour is consequent upon the warmth,
and it is because certain things are altered that what comes to be or
is destroyed is moved in respect of those movements. That was indeed
10   why there was room for a puzzle in the case of alteration. But even if
[alteration] does coexist [with the other movements], that does not
mean that it is the same as them. Rather, it has been shown that
alteration is distinct from motion, since even according to those who
posit it as the same the motion is held to be of a different thing –
namely of the parts, as they say – from what the alteration is of,
namely the whole. And that [alteration] is distinct from increase in
15   size has been sufficiently shown from the increase in size of the
square. And alteration is different from both generation and destruction: for it comes about while the underlying subject is preserved,
whereas generation [consists in a transition] from what is not to what
is, and destruction from what is to what is not. In this respect
generation and destruction differ from the other [movements] as well.

And in general, in the sense in which the four categories *substance*,
quantity, *quality* and *where* differ from one another, in that sense   20
the[1060] movements in respect of these [categories] will also differ.

> **15b1-15** Taken *simpliciter* movement is contrary to rest: [but to
> particular movements (particular movements are contrary) –
> destruction to generation, diminution to increase, while rest in
> respect of place is plausibly most opposed to change in respect
> of place. And perhaps change to the opposite place (is also so
> opposed), as for instance (change of place) upwards (is opposed)
> to (change of place) downwards, and downwards to upwards.
> But to the remaining one of the specified movements it is not
> easy to specify what the contrary might be. Indeed it seems as
> if nothing is contrary to it, unless in this case too one were to
> oppose to it rest in respect of quality or change to the contrary
> of the (relevant) quality, just as in the case of change in respect
> of place, too, (we opposed to it) rest in respect of place or the
> change towards the contrary place. For alteration is change in
> respect of quality, so that to movement in respect of quality is
> opposed rest in respect of quality or change towards the contrary
> of the (relevant) quality, as for instance becoming white (is so
> opposed) to becoming black.] For something is altered when a
> change comes about to the contrary of the (relevant) quality.

Noticing that movement too, just like some of the categories, is
capable of receiving a contrary, [Aristotle] says that while 'taken
simpliciter' rest (*êremia*) is contrary to movement – what he calls 'rest'   25
is not permanence (*stasis*), but rather the negation and privation of
movement[1061] – 'to *particular*' movements particular movements [are
contrary] – destruction to generation, diminution to increase: for
these were also previously produced in opposed conjunctions. But
what contrary could [movement] in respect of place, which seems to
be just one thing, have? Well, insofar as it is movement in respect of   30
place, [it has as its contrary] rest in respect of place, whereas insofar
as contrarieties can be spatial (for up is contrary to down), in this
sense a contrary movement will also be found towards the contrary   433,1
place, as for example movement down [is contrary] to movement up.
 'But to the remaining one of the movements' – that is, to alteration,
which is movement in respect of quality – 'it is not easy', [Aristotle]
says, 'to specify' its contrary, not because there are no contrary
qualities or movements in respect of these, but because the concept   5
of an opposition in this case is not usual, and in addition because
movement in respect of alteration is not as distinctive as [movement]
in respect of place, but it will be evident to those who give the matter
a little attention. Hence [Aristotle] decides to transfer by way of

analogy what he has said in the case of spatial movement to the case of [movement] in respect of quality, and to oppose to movement in respect of quality *both* (1) the state of rest, in the same quality, of the

10   changing thing[1062] *and* (2) the change from the contrary quality to this [quality], as for example to the [change] from white to black, which they call blackening, [Aristotle opposes] *both* (2) the [change] from the black to white, which they term whitening, <*and* (1) the state of rest, in white: for the state of rest, in black, is opposed to whitening,>[1063] but to the movement from white to black one should oppose the state of rest in white: for [the movement] must retreat from the contrary and not arrive back at it. 'By "state of rest",' says Iamblichus,

15   'we must understand the privation of movement, which [Aristotle] has solecistically called its contrary.' And people ask in the case of generation and destruction, as well, what states of rest are to be opposed to these, and they reply that to generation [one should oppose] the [state of rest] consisting in non-being – obviously that *prior to* being[1064] – whereas to destruction [one should oppose] the [state of rest] consisting in being. And likewise to increase in size is opposed rest in respect of what is *imperfect*, to diminution [rest] in respect of what is *perfect*.

20   Plotinus notes[1065] that rest is the negation of being moved: hence[1066] rest is not in another genus either.[1067] He then asks why movement is not also the negation of permanence, and replies: 'because movement comes bringing something [with it],[1068] and because movement [is] a function,[1069] and is [something] effecting something else and pushing the subject, as it were, and working it in countless ways and [ultimately] destroying it, whereas the state of rest of each thing is

25   nothing other than that thing itself, and signifies merely that it does not possess movement. But (he says) in the case of the intelligibles there is not the same manner [of opposition], in that the one does not cancel the other, but both exist simultaneously, both movement and permanence.'

Boethus, however, does not think that the state of rest opposed to movement in respect of quality is a quality,[1070] nor that the [state of rest opposed to movement] in respect of size is a size, nor that the [state of rest opposed to movement] in respect of substance is a

30   substance,[1071] claiming that this is clear from the case of [rest] in respect of place: for it is unreasonable to call the state of rest in a place [itself] a place. Moreover, he does not agree either that the states of rest are *negations* of movements in respect of these things,[1072] but [says that] rest and movement are a *relation* (*skhesis*) towards the

434,1   time and the form in respect of which a thing is actually being moved or is at rest. 'For,' he says, 'time seems to be of such a nature as to be always flowing and changing into other kinds of thing, and because of this it accompanies every movement and state of rest. But now movement is *similarly* related to time and place (for instance, in the case of motion, he says that it is similarly related [to time and place] on account of its continuously coming about in respect of different places[1073]), whereas rest (he says) is *contrarily* related to place and time, for the time is never the same, while the place is always the same, so that this relation to time and place, being differentiated, becomes sometimes a state of rest, and sometimes a movement. And in the other cases (he goes on) we shall say, in the same way, that whenever there is the same relation of the subject to time and size[1074] there is movement, but whenever [the relation to time] is contrary to that in respect of size,[1075] there is rest. And the same has to be said about alteration too, so that it is clear from these considerations ([Boethus] claims) that rest is neither the size *itself* nor the form *itself* nor the place *itself*, but is rather the simultaneous relation towards each of these and towards time. And so the varieties of states of rest are the same as those of the [corresponding] movements, for in each instance a contrariety of the relation itself was shown applying to things which are moved and things at rest.'[1076] These are the differentiations Boethus makes, thanks to his sharpness of mind. But perhaps neither movement nor rest is a *relation* towards time, since time is the *number* of movement.[1077]

But I think it is worth asking why we do not oppose permanence (*stasis*), as a form, to movement (*kinêsis*), as a form. For both movement and permanence are included among the genera of being in Plato's writings,[1078] and just as movement is among[1079] the genera mentioned [by Plato], so too must the permanence which is opposed to movement necessarily be [among them]. For substance not merely comes into being and is destroyed; it also *exists*, and has this [existence] by virtue of its permanence. And bodies are not merely *moved* in respect of place: they also *stand fast*. And this permanence is not the negation of movement: for the earth does not stand fast about its centre by virtue of a negation of movement, and similarly nor is the sky moved in a circle by virtue of a negation of permanence. For permanence too possesses an operation no less than does movement, as is made clear by the fact that if permanence is completely obliterated, movement itself ceases to exist too. But now given that this is so, we ought to posit the state of rest (*êremia*) *qua* negation of movement in things which are by dint of force unmoving, as for example in the case of a clod of earth forcibly held in the air. For this is not permanence, but is at best a negation of movement and a [mere] state of rest, which is why we will be right to oppose this to movement as its *privation*. As the *contrary* form [to movement], however, I think we should oppose both the permanence [which obtains] *before* movement, and [that obtaining] *after* movement, and perhaps also that [obtaining] *in* movement itself.

435,1   Let us not omit to ask the following as well: why, given that among
generated objects change exists in respect of each of the categories,
have they[1080] defined changes in terms of just the four: *substance,
quantity, quality* and in addition the [category of] *where*? For why do
we not also change in respect of the [category of] *when*, when out of
young men we become old and out of boys we become adults, and in
5   respect of the *relatives*, when out of enemies [we become] friends, or
out of left right, or out of unequal equal? And it is clear in advance
how in the case of *acting* and *undergoing* we change on each occasion
to the contrary [conditions]. And *being-in-a-position*, too, accepts
many changes: the [case of a] bed bears witness to this, especially
when one tosses oneself about on it.[1081] And often when we *have a ring*
or *are armed*, do we not change into [a state of] not having, or having
10   other things instead of these? So why is it that we change from a
downwards place to an upwards one, and from a white colour to a
black, by means of a *movement*, whereas we do not posit further forms
of movements to cover the aforementioned changes? For I don't
suppose anyone will say that the aforementioned [forms of changes]
can be reduced to the four [official] forms of changes, since on that
basis he will also be reducing the [corresponding] six categories[1082] to
the four.[1083]
15   But the point which surprises me most of all is why, given that
they[1084] have noticed movement in respect of place, they have not
taken cognizance of [movement] in respect of time – unless indeed the
reason is that anyone positing *movement* of time will also be forced
to speak of *time* of time.[1085] And why does Aristotle himself, though
he says clearly in the third book of the *Physics* 'so there are as many
forms of movement and change as there are of being' (201a8-9),
nevertheless both in the fifth book of that treatise (224b35ff.) and here
20   [in the *Categories*] enumerate not ten but four forms of movement?
Since in the fifth book of the *Physics* (225b10ff.) Aristotle undertakes
to specify in addition the reasons why he denies that there is movement or change in the other genera, I have tried in my comments on
that treatise to say something in response to the statement there of
his reasons,[1086] but lest anyone think me too bold, 'singing vainly
25   against the divine bird of Zeus', as Pindar has it,[1087] I want to
demonstrate that even Theophrastus, the best of Aristotle's pupils,
concurs with my suppositions. For he speaks as follows in the first
book of his *Physics*: 'It is not difficult to specify the common and
universal account of movement, and say that it is a certain incomplete
operation of what is potential, *qua* such, in respect of each genus of
30   the categories, and this is also more or less apparent from perception.'
But these matters, which are widely the subject of puzzlement in the
436,1   practice of philosophers, need to receive a fuller inquiry both from us

and from others. Perhaps, however, they do not really deserve to have [the status of] a puzzle.

Now the Stoics think that there is a difference between remaining (*menein*), being at rest (*êremein*), being quiet (*hêsukhazein*), being unmoved (*akinêtein*) and being unmoving (*akinêtizein*): for remaining would not be said in relation to a single time, but in relation to the 5 present and the future, for we say that something *remains* if it is and is going to be in possession of the same place, and something which has been in possession [of the same place] we say *has remained*. 'And,' [the Stoics] say, 'we also make use of "remaining" in the case of not being moved, so that someone might solecistically even ascribe the [property of] remaining to the incorporeals, instead of the [property of] not being moved. Now remaining is common to all bodies, but perhaps, they say, being at rest is an accident (*sumptôma*) of *animals*: 10 after all, a stone does not *rest*. Being quiet is also [an accident] of animals. And being unmoved and being unmoving are said in the case of bodies whose nature it is not to be moved; it is said [of them] instead of not being moved.'

CHAPTER 15

On Having

15b17-32 Having is said in several senses: [either as a state and a condition or some other quality – for we are said to have knowledge and virtue; or as a quantity, such as the size one might have – for one is said to have a size of three or four cubits; or as the things around the body, such as a cloak or a tunic; or as (what is) on a part, such as a ring on a hand; or as a part, such as a hand or foot; or as in a vessel, such as the measure (having) the corn or the jar the wine – for the jar is said to have the wine, and the measure corn, so that these are said to have as in a vessel; or as a possession, for we are said to have a house and a field. We are also said to have a wife and a wife to have a husband, but this sense of having under consideration appears to be a very improper sense: for we signify nothing, by saying that one has a wife, than that he cohabits with her. Perhaps some other senses too of having might emerge, but those in common parlance have more or less all been enumerated.]

[Aristotle] reasonably gives instruction also on having, because in 15 discussing the other genera he mentioned this genus briefly in passing. He has placed it last, because he also assigned it the last place among the genera, whereas Archytas arranged the category of having after the first four [categories], as has been said (365,3). [Aristotle]

says that having is homonymous and that it is said in eight ways. For
20   (1) someone qualified in any way – whether in terms of a 'state' or in
terms of a 'condition' or in terms of a shape or (obviously) a colour or
an affection of any sort whatever – is said to have the quality in virtue
of which he is [so] qualified. (2) And what is quantified is said to have
a quantity, such as 'a size of four cubits'. 'And he who has eight
household slaves,' adds Iamblichus, 'is said to be served by eight'. But
perhaps this belongs to the seventh signification [of having], namely
25   [having] as possession.[1088] (3) We are also said to have 'the things
around the body' as a whole, such as 'a cloak', though that every part
of the body be covered is not necessary, but certainly the greater part,
so that [the statement] may thus be true as applied to the *whole*
[body]. (4) Further, one is said to have what is 'on a part' [of the body],
as for instance a necklace or armlet or 'ring'. (5) Further, we are said
to have the parts [of the body] themselves, as for instance 'hands' and
437,1   'feet'. (6) And for something to be stored in a vessel [is a kind of
having]: for 'the measure' is said to have 'the corn', and 'the jar the
wine'. (7) And [there is having something] 'as a possession', as for
instance we are said to have 'a field' and 'a house'. (8) That the
husband 'has a wife' and the wife a husband is, we say, a 'very
improper' [sense of having], both because it reciprocates (for neither
5   *has* any more than it is *had*),[1089] and because this sort of having
signifies 'cohabiting'. And indeed Homer applies having to dwelling:
'They who had hollow Sparta; and they who had Arcadia'.[1090] And
'perhaps', [Aristotle] says, 'other senses too' of having might be found.
For indeed he himself in the *Metaphysics* (5.23) investigated [having],
10   and I mentioned him[1091] in the [section on the] category of having
(371,28ff.).

  We ought to ask *how* [Aristotle] has established the division of
having as something which is said in many ways: for if this is what
it is, how can having be a genus? And furthermore, indeed, [we ought
to ask] what is the reason why he has conveyed this division at the
end and not in the place of the genus.[1092] Well, it is clear that what is
15   here divided up is *not* the [having] *qua* genus. For as examples of *that*
[Aristotle] introduced 'he is shod', 'he is armed', whereas the [exam-
ples given] *here* are ranged under the same category as the things
which are had – for he who has a quality is *qualified* and he who has
a quantity is *quantified*.[1093] Furthermore, these things are cases of
having only in combination, for having *on a part* or having *a part* are
[cases of having] *with combination*, as is containing inanimately[1094] –
20   in the way that the [corn] measure and [wine] jar contain[1095] – but
having in the strict sense is without combination, such as *he is armed*,
he is shod and *he is clothed*,[1096] which are contained in the third and
fourth senses [of the homonymy of having] only. So [Aristotle] has
enumerated the things together with which having is customarily

arranged, and of which it is customarily predicated, but he has not established a division of the genus called 'having' – not unless, indeed, there is nothing to prevent us speaking both of having become white (*leleukanthai*) and of having become long (*memegethunthai*) under one name, and the other things too, even if no names are available. Perhaps, then, it is better to recall what was said before (365,25ff.), that the category of having was a placing, which manifests the control of the haver, of an acquired body around the body of an animal. For on this account both incorporeals and the divisible and detached parts of bodies, as well as those things which are placed on inanimate objects, will be excluded [from the category of having]. It was certainly reasonable, then, for [Aristotle] to make the division not at that [earlier] place but at the end.

Iamblichus says: '[Aristotle] did not divide having, in the sense of the genus, into species, because he would have divided it in the same way as the [category of] acting, that of undergoing and that of being-in-a-position. For the acting or undergoing things, as animate or as inanimate, would be species of acting and undergoing, to take that case, and of these things some actings and undergoings would be [as] general things, others as individual and particular. And in the case of being-in-a-position (he says), the same might be said: for something is positioned either as an animate or an inanimate thing, and in respect of the [other] differentiae mentioned. Hence having, taken as a genus, might be divided into species in just the same manner as those; but (says [Iamblichus]), [Aristotle] did not establish this division either in the case of those [genera] or in the case of this one, in order not to have anything superfluous [in his account].' In these remarks of Iamblichus I am surprised that he ascribes the same differentiae and the same species to genera which are distinct and not arranged under one another – I mean acting, undergoing, being-in-a-position and having. For in general the sort of division [he proposes] does not apply to genera but to the things which partake [of them] – and not even insofar as they do partake [of them].[1097] In fact he himself arranged the matter better in his discussion of having taken as a genus, where he attempted to convey its own particular differentiae, and where he said that of things which are had some provide ornament, others are weapons, and others are coverings, and [these are] either around the whole body, such as a cloak, or around part of it, such as a shoe; and all the remaining such things he says there we too collected from his discussion (367,13ff.) as our division [of the category]. But it is [still] worth asking what the divisions by species of these genera[1098] are.

We should append here what Iamblichus says next: 'For perhaps,' he says, 'the fact that having is said in several senses does not signify that it is said in many ways *and homonymously*. For (he says) all the

25

30

438,1

5

10

15

20   senses which [Aristotle] lists are arranged as though under having taken as a *genus*. But just as he said in the case of quality "Quality is one of the things said in many ways" (8b26) – *not* [thereby] calling it homonymous – so too [here] he sets out some of the differentiae of having *qua* genus. For both what is qualified does indeed *have* the quality, and what is quantified the quantity, but differently and not

25   in the same sense.[1099] So [Aristotle], seeing the presence of differentiation within the [category of] having as well, thought that he ought not to pass over this one undefined, either, at the same time too showing that it *is* a genus, since it is predicated of several different things. For [having] *seemed* [at first glance] to be something simple, but if it really *were* like that then there would not be a genus of having.'[1100] But neither incorporeals nor parts should be adopted [into the category]: for what has whiteness or a height of three cubits or has feet is a unity with the things which are had.[1101] And neither the

30   son nor the field, nor what is placed on an inanimate object, is under the control (*krateitai*) [of the haver].[1102] And that is why Archytas too, in his precise investigations concerning [having] *qua* genus, says that having signifies a certain control over acquired things.

Since this is also as far as the divine Iamblichus reached, I too cease here my account, entreating the guardians of my words both to render a more accurate scrutiny of these matters [than I have] and to bestow

35   this on me as a resource on my journey towards the sublimer theories, and [thereby] to grant me relief from the distractions of life.[1103]

Notes

Abbreviations

Anonymous Paraphrase = M. Hayduck (ed.), *Anonymi in Aristotelis Categorias Paraphrasis,* Berlin 1883 = *CAG* 23.2, pp. 1-85

Bonitz = H. Bonitz, *Index Aristotelicus,* Berlin 1961

DK = H. Diels and W. Kranz, *Die Fragmente der Vorsokratiker,* Zurich 1992-93

FDS = K. Hülser, *Die Fragmente zur Dialektik der Stoiker,* Stuttgart 1987-88

Kalbfleisch = K. Kalbfleisch (ed.), *Simplicii in Aristotelis Categorias Commentarium,* Berlin 1907 = *CAG* 8

SVF = J. von Arnim, *Stoicorum Veterum Fragmenta,* Leipzig 1905-1924

Szlezák = T. Szlezák, *Pseudo-Archytas über die Kategorien,* Berlin/New York 1972

Thesleff = H. Thesleff, *The Pythagorean Texts of the Hellenistic Period,* Åbo 1965

William of Moerbeke = A. Pattin (ed.), *Simplicius Commentaire sur les Catégories. Traduction de Guillaume de Moerbeke,* vol. 1, Louvain/Paris 1971, vol. 2, Leiden 1975

1. Note that this heading, along with the other such headings which occur in the commentary, is not present in our text of Aristotle, as Simplicius notes elsewhere (208,5). Cf. Philoponus, *in Cat.* 166, 31-2, who takes the heading to be Aristotle's own. On Simplicius' treatment of acting and undergoing, see in general N. Vamvoukakis, 'Les catégories aristotéliennes d'action et de passion vues par Simplicius', in P. Aubenque ed., *Concepts et catégories dans la pensée antique,* Paris 1980, pp. 253-69.

2. There is a crux concerning the accentuation and consequently the meaning of *pote* and *pou*. Kalbfleisch follows the MS tradition in accentuating *pou* as if it were an interrogative, though in fact he regards it as an indefinite adverb (cf. his index, p. 522), as well as *pote* which, following the MS tradition, he accentuates as such. In his text of Aristotle's *Categories* (*Aristotelis Categoriae et Liber De Interpretatione*, Oxford 1949), L. Minio-Paluello accentuates *pou* as an indefinite adverb, justifying this policy (p. xxiii) on the basis that the names of the categories of when (*pote*), relative (*pros ti*), quantity (*poson*) and quality (*poion*) are all accentuated in the MSS and incunabula as indefinite adjectives, not as interrogatives; and there is no reason to treat *pou* as a special case. P. Hoffmann asserts ('Les catégories POU et POTE chez Aristote et Simplicius', in P. Aubenque ed., *Concepts et catégories dans la pensée antique,* 217-45, at pp. 218-24) that the traditional accentuation of *pou* should be retained, but so far as I can see he offers no convincing support for his claim, and it is surely *a priori* quite implausible that *pou* should be treated differently from *pote, pros ti, poson* and *poion.* The senses of *pote* and *pou* (at least for Simplicius) are clearly brought out at 297,29-30 where I have rendered them 'somewhen' and 'somewhere'. These would be the best renderings of the corresponding category names in English, if only the word 'somewhen' existed. In its absence I have retained the traditional renderings 'when' and 'where', to be understood as 'somewhen' and 'somewhere' respectively.

3. 1022b15ff., 1023a8ff., 1045b26ff., 1068a8ff.

4. i.e. in the *Categories*.

5. cf. Philoponus *in Cat.* 163,24-164,5.

6. cf. Philoponus *in Cat.* 165,22-5.

7. The translation of *energeia* in Peripatetic texts is a vexed matter. Normally it is rendered by either 'actuality' or 'activity', and both of these senses are indeed relevant to Simplicius' use of the term. The former is especially relevant in contexts where a contrast with potentiality is intended (as e.g. at 304,28ff. below), but it is not suitable as a translation where the subject-matter is the category of acting: hence I have avoided it, reserving 'actuality' for *entelekheia*. 'Activity' has the disadvantage that the corresponding verb in English, 'activate', is transitive, whereas *energein* is normally intransitive in Simplicius. I have adopted 'operation' as my translation of *energeia*, since the cognates of the one term match reasonably well with those of the other, but the reader should bear in mind that in some contexts the sense 'actuality' may be relevant.

8. i.e. acting and undergoing.

9. cf. Philoponus *in Cat.* 165,22-166,26 on the question whether acting and undergoing are reducible to the relatives.

10. Simplicius, following Iamblichus, identifies this source with the Pythagorean Archytas (2,15-25; 13,21-4). But in fact the texts which Simplicius treats as deriving from the fourth-century BC Pythagorean come from a much later Peripatetic treatise on the categories, *peri tou Katholou Logou* (*Codex Ambrosianus* 23 A92 sup.), estimated to have been written in the first or second century AD: see P. Moraux, *Der Aristotelismus bei den Griechen*, vol. 2, Berlin/New York 1984, pp. 608-23. The treatise, fragmentarily reported by Simplicius in its original Doric, is preserved independently from Simplicius in a Koiné version, available in H. Thesleff, *The Pythagorean Texts of the Hellenistic Period*, Åbo 1965, at pp. 21-32, and in T. Szlezák, *Pseudo-Archytas über die Kategorien*, Berlin/New York 1972; Szlezák re-edits Thesleff's text from the original MS and supplies a commentary. The treatise is given various titles in the tradition: see Thesleff, 21,7-22,5. In employing this treatise to supplement the exposition of Aristotle's text, Simplicius is following Iamblichus, and it is likely that the passages from Archytas quoted by Simplicius have been taken from Iamblichus' lost commentary on the *Categories*.

11. = Thesleff 24,7-10.

12. cf. Philoponus *in Cat.* 166,3-8.

13. The constructions in lines 14 and 15 are not parallel, and it may be that we should either change *kai to psukhein* in line 14 to *tôi psukhein*, or change *tôi psukhesthai* in line 15 to *to psukhesthai*. But nothing affecting the sense hinges on this.

14. If A and B are contraries in the category of acting, the effects they produce in the category of undergoing are contrary to each other.

15. Reading *gar* instead of *kai*, as suggested by Kalbfleisch.

16. cf. Philoponus *in Cat.* 166,33-167,9.

17. Aristotle discusses affective qualities (*poiotêtes pathêtikai*) at 9a28ff. Cf. Simplicius *in Cat.* 228,26ff.

18. 6b2-3, 11-14, 11b10-11. The point is not that the word *keisthai* is derived from the word *thesis*, but that, case by case, words for being-in-a-position are derived from words for positions, as the next sentence makes clear.

19. Their names are *anakeklisthai* (corrected at 6b12 from *anakeisthai*, read by most MSS of Aristotle: Simplicius also has *anakeisthai*), *hestanai* and *kathêsthai*, which are derived, so Aristotle claims, from *anaklisis*, *stasis* and *kathedra*.

20. The reference is probably to 2a2-3.

21. I read *ouden allo peri autôn <legetai>* following Aristotle, who has *ouden huper autôn allo legetai*. Cf. 300,18 below.

22. i.e. in ch. 15.

23. In fact Aristotle's text is probably lacunose at this point.

24. Porphyry wrote two commentaries on the *Categories*, one of which (dedicated to Gedalius) has not survived, and the other of which is only partially extant: its remaining portion (*CAG* 4.1, pp. 55-142) breaks off just where Porphyry begins to discuss the points mentioned here by Simplicius.

25. Iamblichus' commentary on the *Categories*, relied on heavily by Simplicius, is lost.

26. On the dependence of the later categories on the earlier ones, cf. Philoponus *in Cat.* 163,4-164,5 and Ammonius *in Cat.* 92,6-12, though their account of the dependence is somewhat different from Simplicius' here.

27. Kalbfleisch registers a lacuna and suggests *khthes <Dionusia. ou>*, which I translate.

28. See preceding note.

29. cf. Philoponus *in Cat.* 164,23-165,19.

30. I follow LKv in omitting the second *kai* in 298,2, and Kv in inserting *ton* before *kata* in 298,3.

31. I read *to en khronôi on* instead of Kalbfleisch's *to en khronôi einai*. Cf. 297,30 and Philoponus *in Cat.* 164,22-3.

32. cf. Philoponus *in Cat.* 164,22-3.

33. cf. 301,15-16.

34. Porphyry and Iamblichus: on the latter see 374,7ff.

35. Acting, undergoing, being-in-a-position, when, where, having.

36. This phrase introduces not a further objection to Aristotle, but an alternative response to the puzzle, one which concedes its main point (that the last six categories are not 'said of' species) but resists its conclusion (that they are not genuinely categories). On 'perhaps' a scholiast comments aptly that Simplicius' solution of the puzzle is oblique (see Kalbfleisch p. xxi).

37. i.e. in the category of substance.

38. Reading *legontes <hôsperanei>* as suggested by Kalbfleisch. But it is possible that more should be supplied.

39. i.e. the separate natures (of acting, undergoing, being-in-a-position, when, where and having).

40. The last six categories signify genuinely distinct natures, not distinct species of a single nature, as do predications within the category of substance.

41. cf. Philoponus *in Cat.* 165,22-166,26, where a different ground is offered why acting and undergoing cannot be reduced to the relatives: acting and undergoing have one underlying subject (*hupokeimenon*), namely movement (*kinêsis*), whereas the relatives have at least two such subjects, namely the relata of the relation.

42. sc. in these categories.

43. sc. when it was discussed at 10a27-32. There Aristotle says that grammar is a quality.

44. cf. 6b34f., 11a23ff. The term 'genus' is not restricted by Aristotle to the categories: see 1b16-17 with Simplicius' commentary ad loc. (56,30-57,3).

45. sc. and not in virtue of their *relation* to the agents which cause these states.

46. This is explained below at 385,4-29.

47. cf. *Cat.* 4b22-35.

48. It may be right to delete *deka* at 299,27, given that the objection is supposing that there are really only eight categories, and given also that the example of loving can hardly be made to fit *all* categories (not the category of having, for instance, as that is defined). It is easy to see how *deka* might have intruded (and note that *decem* is missing from most of the William of Moerbeke MS tradition).

49. This point, that acting and undergoing are as such relatives, while the particular cases of acting and undergoing each get assigned to some other category, appears to accommodate Simplicius' answer to the original objection, and is left standing.

50. It might seem difficult to reconcile this claim with 301,15-16 below, but the point is that, just as being-in-a-position includes the relation between positioned thing and position, so too having already includes the (oppositely oriented) relation between had thing and haver, and so is not *itself* relative to anything. The claim would be more cogent if the category were called not *having* but rather, on the model of being-in-a-position, *having something*.

51. It is impossible to give a definition (*horismos*) of the highest genera, since definitions proceed by specifying genus and differentia. But it is possible to give a description (*hupographê*) characterising their special features: see further 29,16-20; 45,23-4; 92,7-10; 159,9-12.

52. i.e. the primary substance, substance in the sense of the *Categories*.

53. i.e. the categories of when and where.

54. i.e. substance, quality, quantity, relative, acting and undergoing.

55. The MSS have *pollakis* ('often'), but this makes little sense, and Kalbfleisch suggests *pantôs*, which I adopt.

56. i.e. in chs 10-14.

57. i.e. in ch. 15.

58. Including Porphyry: see 379,12ff.

59. i.e. in ch. 9.

60. On homonymy, see *Cat.* 1a1ff. Homonymous things share a common name, but 'the account of their being' is different. The various cases of having treated in ch. 15 are not, in Simplicius' view, cases of having in the sense of the *category* of having, but are cases of having in name only. See 437,12ff. Note that Simplicius, like other commentators, uses 'homonymous' both of ambiguous words and of the things designated by such words (so the word 'homonymous' and homonymous things are themselves homonymous): see, e.g., 25,4-5, where both usages occur.

61. i.e. being-in-a-position and having. I delete *ta pros ti* with Kalbfleisch.

62. i.e. there is an asymmetry in the particular relations of being-in-a-position and having which is not present in the concept of a relation as such, so that to that extent these categories are not reducible to the category of relative, nor indeed to each other since (apart from other differences) the relations of being-in-a-position and having (sc. something: see n. 50 above) are oppositely oriented.

63. sc. of the last six categories.

64. Kalbfleisch suggests adding '[and] concerns substance' (*peri tên ousian*). 'Comes after substance' = 'is a property of substance'.

65. Reading *tautêi* instead of *tautês*, as suggested by Kalbfleisch (p. 574).

66. To make sense of the comparison we have to take both occurrences of 'or' in the question in an inclusive way. Cf. here Plotinus *Enn.* 6.1.15.

67. The thought is: a phrase denoting a doer (e.g. 'the runner') both denotes a substance and refers to the activity of that substance, whereas in words referring to activities (e.g. 'running'), in either their nominal or verbal-nominal aspect, no such denotation of a substance is present. They refer to the universal 'pure'.

68. The ambiguity of the Greek is impossible to reproduce in English. The word *poiêsis*, which I elsewhere render by 'action', is the standard word in Greek for a work of art; hence 'creation' here. On the lexicography of *poiêsis*, see C. Brink, *Horace on Poetry: Prolegomena*, Cambridge 1963, pp. 76-8.

69. cf. Philoponus *in Cat.* 166,27-33.

70. *Enn.* 6.1.15.

71. *Phys.* 258b10ff. But Aristotle also in a number of places treats *movement* as a category: see e.g. *Metaph.* 1029b25, 1069a22. In their defence of the doctrine of categories as it is presented in the *Categories*, however, the commentators ignore such passages: see Szlezák, p. 115.

72. Pupil of Andronicus and his successor as head of the Peripatetic school: see Moraux, *Aristotelismus* vol. 1, pp. 143-64.

73. sc. and encompassing them both.

74. But Porphyry is going to *distinguish* movements like throwing and pushing on the one hand, where the undergoing is continuous with the acting and forms a single transaction, from striking (*plêttein*) on the other, where the affection is distinct from the action. Hence one might suspect *plêgê* here. But there is no need to emend it: the point is that movements like throwing and pushing involve a different kind of impact from striking. Kalbfleisch's comma after *kinêseôn* is therefore misleading – for the ensuing relative clause is a defining one – and should be deleted.

75. i.e. the spatial separation of agent and patient plays no role in the transaction. There is not a chain of causes and effects bridging the gap: it is genuinely action at a distance.

76. sc. by the fact that the agent and patient are spatially separated.

77. I read *sunêkhousin* instead of Kalbfleisch's *sunekhousin*. The latter, if retained, would imply that the strings touch, but that is the opposite of the sense required, which is that we have a case of action at a distance: vibrating one string causes a suitably tuned neighbouring string to vibrate. Cf. Aristides Quintilianus *de Musica* 2.18 (89,23-90,5 Winnington-Ingram), where there is a description of this phenomenon, as well as a relevant use of the verb *sunêkhein*. (I am grateful to Donald Russell for suggesting this change to me.)

78. Bringing a flame close to liquid naphtha causes it to ignite: cf. Strabo 16.1.15. Simplicius here uses the form *ho haphthas*, attested (along with three other forms of the word) by the so-called *Chrestomathiai* (16.9) compiled on the basis of Strabo.

79. i.e. the capacity of the one to affect the other, and of the other to be affected by it.

80. i.e. in the cases of action at a distance mentioned in the previous paragraph.

81. This is Iamblichus' own conclusion, not that of the view he has just rejected.

82. *Enn.* 6.1.16.

83. *huphesis* (decline from a superior into an inferior nature) is an important part of the Neoplatonic doctrine of procession from the One: see A. Lloyd, *The Anatomy of Neoplatonism*, Oxford 1990, ch. 4.

84. i.e. movement will not be a species of operation.

85. Plotinus says this not of movement *per se*, but of particular quantified movements: *Enn.* 6.1.16.

86. Pupil of Aristotle, and his successor as head of the Peripatetic School.

87. i.e. all movements are operations but not all operations are movements.

88. Deleting *tên* with Kalbfleisch and reading *hê* instead with Brandis. William of Moerbeke has *ea*.

89. i.e. the perfection of operation, which Theophrastus is identifying with the perfection of realised form.

90. The appeal to Theophrastus seems not quite to fit the Iamblichan context: for Theophrastus' remarks imply that movement is one species (among others) of operation.

91. The following, though not expressly labelled as such, represents a typical piece of Iamblichan 'intellectual theory' (*noera theôria*): cf. 2,9-15 and 327,6ff., 339,34ff., 350,10ff., 361,7ff., 374,7ff. below, with J. Dillon, 'Iamblichus' *Noera Theôria* of Aristotle's *Categories*'.

92. Reading *autôn*, as Kalbfleisch suggests, instead of *hautai*.

93. i.e. by admitting non-separate as well as separate operations in the sense of the previous paragraph.

94. i.e. generatings of enmattered things.

95. sc. as opposed to the things that come to be.

96. See below 312,22ff.

97. i.e. involve the agent's being affected, as in the examples given above at 306,7-8. On affective actions, see further below 321,21ff. esp. 323,3.

98. With the following cf. Origen *de Principiis* 3.1.2-3, with Long and Sedley, *The Hellenistic Philosophers*, vol. 2, Cambridge 1987, p. 310.

99. Reading *te* instead of *de*, as Kalbfleisch suggests.

100. Reading *idiaiteron* instead of *heteron*, as Kalbfleisch suggests.

101. Reading *prattein* instead of *plattein*, as suggested by Kalbfleisch (p. 574).

102. Kalbfleisch's text reads: *dia tês energeias gar auton apodidoasin*. If we retain *energeias* the sense is presumably that the Stoics are being said to offer a circular definition of *energeia* ('for they expound it [i.e. the definition of operation] in terms of *operation*'. But this text is implausible for two reasons: (1) if circularity were in question one would expect something like *dia tês energeias gar <autês> auton apodidoasin* ('for they expound it [i.e. the definition of operation] in terms of operation *itself*'); (2) it is much less likely that circularity is here in question than the Stoics' alleged confusion of operation with movement (with *sunkekhumenos* at 306,31 cf. 306,15-16). Accordingly I conclude that *energeias* is wrong and I replace it with *kinêseôs*, to yield *dia tês kinêseôs gar auton apodidoasin*.

103. The expression suggests that even in the intervening passage 306,13-307,1 Simplicius is reporting Iamblichus.

104. The following is in fact a quotation from Plotinus, *Enn.* 6.1.16.

105. i.e. in accordance with *natural* number. Cf. *Cat.* 4b23ff. and Simplicius at 124,5-8.

106. Omitting *ou*, along with JLKv.

107. i.e. operation itself (*energeia*): cf. 305,5ff.

108. i.e. what was called simply *entelekheia* at 305,5ff., where Iamblichus identified it with the operational (*to energeiai*), which is contrasted with the potential and is to be distinguished from operation itself.

109. sc. of whatever lies at the end of the transition: *kinêsis*, which I translate throughout as 'movement', also means 'change' (I am reserving this latter word for the translation of *metaballein* and cognates).

110. *Phys.* 201a27-9.

111. Although the piece of bronze is not in itself formless (it has the form of bronze), it is considered formless with respect to what it becomes, a statue. Matter and form are relative terms in the Aristotelian tradition.

112. *Enn.* 6.1.16.

113. As if one were to say it is perfectly imperfect.

114. Possibly one should emend *gegonos* to *gegonuia*.

115. *Parm.* 163A.

116. Possibly we should read *tina* instead of Kalbfleisch's *tên.*

117. 407a6ff, 424a27.

118. DK B.2.

119. *Phys.* 186a10ff.

120. See here *de Anima* 418b20-6.

121. i.e. change in the sense of having changed.

122. The change which is constituted by the *onset* of illumination (a state of having changed) is an instantaneous matter, and therefore does not involve movement; it is imperceptible in the sense that one cannot notice it happening (for there is no process of its happening), only when it has happened. But (on the current hypothesis) it has been prepared for by, and depends upon, a change which does involve movement (and is perceivable), namely the motion of the sun as it rises (the *process* of illumination).

123. sc. whichever hypothesis is correct.

124. sc. of discrete units.

125. i.e. which are dense (have the order-type of the rational numbers) or continuous (have the order-type of the real numbers).

126. i.e. the followers of Plotinus.

127. Deleting *ho* with Kalbfleisch.

128. And of course motion is, for the Aristotelian, continuous.

129. *Enn.* 6.1.17. Simplicius does not retain Plotinus' precise wording or word order; but the divergences are not significant.

130. i.e. prior to being relatives.

131. Being *in* something is the converse relation to participation: to say that movement is *in* the thing moved is to say that the thing moved participates in movement.

132. i.e. do not create that category in the first instance: Simplicius is not denying that participations do, in a secondary sense, exhibit the category of relative.

133. The text is lacunose at this point. I translate Kalbfleisch's suggested supplement: *alla dia ti, phasin, ho Aristotelês oukh hen etheto genos to poiein kai paskhein;.*

134. The noun *katêgorêmata* is to be understood.

135. The Stoics distinguished 'active' (*orthos*), 'passive' (*huptios*), 'neuter' (*oudetera*) and 'reflexive' (*antipeponthota*) predicates. Active predicates are signified by active verbs and construed with an oblique case (e.g. 'he sees him'); passive predicates are signified by passive verbs, and construed with the passive particle (i.e. *hupo*) and an oblique case (e.g. 'he is heard by him'); a neuter predicate would be, for example, 'he walks'; and a reflexive predicate is passive in form but active in sense (e.g., 'he has his hair cut': *keiretai*). See here D.L. 7.64. Active and passive predicates import a relation to something else, respectively a patient and an agent. Simplicius' point is that not all cases of acting are predicated using 'active' predicates, and not all cases of undergoing using 'passive' predicates: so not all cases of acting involve a patient, nor all cases of undergoing an agent.

136. The terminology is Stoic: according to their tripartite semantic theory words (*phônai*) signify (*sêmainousi*) not physical objects, but incorporeal *lekta*, which are then correlated with physical entities in the world, objects such as Socrates, and properties such as wisdom (about which the Stoics took a materialist line). Such incorporeal *lekta* include at least predicates (*katêgorêmata*), and possibly also cases (which do not figure here). For discussion of Stoic semantics, together with further reference to relevant primary and secondary texts, see now

A. Schubert, *Untersuchungen zur stoischen Bedeutungslehre*, Göttingen 1994, and my 'The Stoics on Cases, Predicates and the Unity of the Proposition', in R. Sorabji ed., *Aristotle and After*, London 1997, 91-108.

137. i.e. coexist with the primary predicates, these being those which indicate the primary substance of a thing (in the Aristotelian sense).

138. According to Simplicius' earlier report (66,32-67,2), and in agreement with our other sources (e.g. Plotinus *Enn.* 6.1.25), the Stoics recognised four categories, of which 'being a certain way' (*pôs ekhon*) was one; the others were 'subject' (*hupokeimenon*), 'qualified' (*poion*) and 'being a certain way in relation to something' (*pros ti pôs ekhon*).

139. Stoic discussions of the categories frequently employ the masculine gender when no restriction to human beings is intended.

140. Presumably here the thing struck, rather than the underlying matter of the striker.

141. Reading *to* instead of *ta*, as suggested by Kalbfleisch.

142. Again, the masculine gender here implies no restriction to human beings.

143. i.e. being-moved (or 'being-moved') is ambiguous as between genus and species.

144. i.e. it is not what they, as such, really are.

145. I read *auto* instead of *autên*, following Kalbfleisch's suggestion.

146. sc. as defined by Aristotle.

147. It is true that the first solution does at one point claim that being-moved is not predicated of actions at all (311,20). But this was qualified by the phrase 'in their being', and the main point of the first solution is that being-moved does not extend to 'pure actions'. Since these pure actions are just the 'operations' of the second solution, the two solutions come to the same.

148. Deleting *hê* with Kalbfleisch.

149. i.e. a category.

150. The passage shows the influence of Stoic terminology: the Stoics distinguished between the linguistic level (the level of *lexis*, expression), the lektical level (the level of *lekta* – things said – or, as they were also called, *pragmata*, which I have rendered here as 'objects [meant]'), and the level of physical objects in the world. See n. 136 above.

151. i.e. grammatically passive.

152. sc. out of acting and undergoing.

153. *Enn.* 6.1.18.

154. i.e. Aristotelians.

155. Simplicius' text is lacunose at this point and needs to be eked out from Plotinus. I follow Kalbfleisch's supplements: <*tas men energeias legontes einai tas athroas, tas de kinêseis*>, *hoion to temnein:* <*en khronôi gar to temnein*>.

156. I combine Kalbfleisch's text and the Plotinian text to obtain: *ê pasas poiêseis kinêseis ê meta kinêseôs*.

157. 'Both sorts are of each sort': some actions defined in relation to a patient are movements, and some are operations (i.e. some are in, others are out of, time); some absolute actions are movements, and some are operations.

158. Reading *apolelumenon* <*on*> from Plotinus' text.

159. That there are absolute operations, and that there are movements defined in relation to patients, is uncontroversial. Plotinus, in Simplicius' version, now confirms that the other two permutations envisaged by 'both sorts are of each sort' are indeed also realised: there are absolute movements and operations defined in relation to patients. Plotinus has *oukh ekhon to paskhon kai auto* in place of *kaitoi ekhon paskhon to nooumenon*, which yields an opposite sense to

Simplicius' text ('although [thinking] does *not* have a patient either'). If that is the right reading, only the first of the other two permutations would be admitted.

160. At least, movements are not in the category of acting in the *primary* sense of acting: 311,13ff.

161. i.e. in the sense of *taking* time.

162. Heating and cooling are Aristotle's examples (11b2-3). But earlier (310,8ff.) Simplicius claimed (somewhat implausibly) that for Aristotle even heating and cooling carry a primarily absolute sense.

163. sc. of operation and movement.

164. = Thesleff 28,17-29,1. As Szlezák notes (p. 136), the distinguishing marks of acting and undergoing have been borrowed – in the absence of any guidance on this matter in the text of the *Categories* – from Aristotle's characterisation elsewhere of the difference between nature (*phusis*) and potential (*dunamis*).

165. sc. as well: for the subsequent discussion makes clear that Pseudo-Archytas thought – and Iamblichus interpreted him as thinking – that the distinguishing mark of the patient is that it has the cause of the undergoing *both* in itself *and* in something else: 314,20 and 25-7. The text is not in question, as comparison with 315,25 and the Koiné version shows (the discussion of the case of anger at 314,20ff. below also forgets to mention the causal basis of the emotion in the angered man himself), but one would have preferred at least *to <kai> en heterôi* at 314,18.

166. cf. *EN* 1135b26.

167. i.e. who metes out the contemptuous treatment etc.

168. Reading *to paskhon* instead of *to paskhein*, following Kalbfleisch's suggestion.

169. sc. taken as wholes.

170. sc. because the capacity has to be activated by something external.

171. Of course the patient does *partially* have the cause of the undergoing in itself: presumably (unless he is confused: perhaps he is being misled by Pseudo-Archytas' rather austere wording: see n. 165 above) Simplicius means to rule out the case in which the *entire* cause resides in the patient, for then the patient would, absurdly, be the agent.

172. *Enn.* 6.1.20-1.

173. Plotinus' example is a bad one, as Simplicius goes on to point out: we wanted an example of something which is influenced externally in some way, without thereby undergoing an affection, but the example explicitly states that the cause of the swan's turning white is an *internal* principle. The next example maintains the same confusion.

174. With Kalbfleisch I read *<hup'> allou* and delete *ou*.

175. Kalbfleisch rightly notes (p. 574) that some words must have fallen out after *kat' energeian* at 316,8. He offers no conjectural supplement, but suggests that the missing words would probably have dealt with the cases of rotting and rusting. A bare supplement which yields the required sense (cf. 325,8-10), and which I translate, would be: *kat' energeian <tou enontos logou. to de kai sêpesthai kai iousthai kaitoi en tôi paskhein onta ouk estin apoluta pathê, all' ekhei tên tês kinêseôs aitian exôthen, hôs> hupo aerôn* etc.

176. *Enn.* 3.6.1,4; 4.6.2.

177. sc. but not from outside the thing as a whole: cf. above at 316,4-7.

178. i.e. something external to the matter.

179. sc. and the answer is that the affection does originate externally to the matter. So, either way (whether matter is *identical* with its suitability to receive a form or *undergoes* it), the affection by which the matter becomes informed originates externally to it.

180. The MSS have *auto to*, which Kalbfleisch transposes to *to auto*. But I conjecture that *auto* has crept in by dittography after *oute*, and delete it.

181. Kalbfleisch follows b in inserting *eis* before *ho de poiei*; but I think the text makes better sense without it, and follow the other MSS (as does William of Moerbeke).

182. Kalbfleisch notes that in A there are three erased letters, the first of which was *t*, after the word *kai*. I conjecture that an elided *tina* has dropped out, and adopt as my reading *kai <tin'> oukh hupotattei*.

183. = Thesleff 25,18-26,2. As Szlezák remarks (p. 124), the following division relates not to acting in general, but only to acting which involves the use of intellect. Pseudo-Archytas himself notes at the end of the citation that the division does not cover the activity of unreasoning animals. The division is based on similar ones at D. L. 3.84 and Aristotle *Metaph.* 1025b25.

184. Reading *hoion <geômetren>* with Kalbfleisch (the Koiné version has *geômetrein*: Thesleff 25,20).

185. i.e. common to the three species defined (to the first of which Simplicius will add a subdivision: 317,24-9).

186. i.e. not the overall genus, action, but the species of that genus, namely theorising: species of the overall genus, which themselves have sub-species, can be regarded as themselves genera in respect of those sub-species, as here.

187. The word translated here and elsewhere as 'productive' (*poiêtikos*) is cognate with the word *poiein*, which I translate as 'acting' when the general category is in question, though here it also signifies one of the three species of acting identified by Pseudo-Archytas, namely making.

188. Reading *houtôs <hê>* with v, as suggested by Kalbfleisch.

189. A view which can claim to have good Aristotelian credentials: see *EN* 1140b6-7.

190. In all probability the whole preceding discussion of Archytas has been taken from Iamblichus: cf. n. 10 above.

191. Reading *ta sômata* instead of *to sôma tas*, as suggested by Kalbfleisch.

192. Reading *theôrountai <kai>* with Kalbfleisch.

193. i.e. they are an effect of movement; they do not initiate it.

194. *Enn.* 6.1.22.

195. A reference back to the discussion at 312,22ff. But the phrasing here is hard to understand, especially in conjunction with the immediate sequel. We might perhaps eke out the sense as follows: 'Not all operations are absolute, as for example in the case of thinking (of), because <although thinking (of) itself perhaps *is* absolute (cf. 319,25-8; Plotinus *Enn.* 6.1.21-2), *being-thought-of* is not, and> being-thought-of is <indeed an operation, whether we place it in the category of> acting <which is where I have argued it should go> or undergoing <as its superficial grammatical appearance suggests>.' If that is the right reconstruction of Simplicius' thought, he has expressed himself very badly, since the 'since' clause purports to cite as a reason something which is in fact quite irrelevant (the issue of the precise categorial allegiance of being-thought-of), while omitting to mention the real point (that being-thought-of, though not absolute, is an operation).

196. *Enn.* 6.1.18.

197. ibid.

198. *Enn.* 6.1.18-19.

199. i.e. in addition to making a more essential differentiation of the genus of movement.

200. i.e. active movement, from which Simplicius is about to distinguish acting.

201. sc. in his characterisation of acting.

202. sc. in his characterisation of undergoing.

203. sc. if one fails to observe this distinction.

204. i.e. the two distinct origins of acting and undergoing.

205. The noun *tmêsis* can mean not only a cut, i.e. the result of an act of cutting (also expressed by *hê tomê*), but also the act of cutting itself, in which case its sense is hardly distinct from that of the verbal noun *to temnein*. But in this context *to temnein* is reserved for 'the act of cutting', and *tmêsis* is not relevantly distinguished from *tomê*.

206. *Enn.* 6.1.19.

207. The expression is back to front: Simplicius means to say that, as the cutting and the being-cut are, so too is the cut. But no doubt he means this latter to be understood by an appropriate principle of symmetry.

208. This possibility is also suggested by Plotinus, ibid.

209. sc. even though the movement of the hair exactly follows that of the hands.

210. Deleting *ê engus* with Kalbfleisch.

211. *Enn.* 6.1.19-20.

212. Simplicius appears to think that Plotinus embraced the alternative account instead of the 'Pythagorean' one (i.e. Pseudo-Archytas' account given above at 314,17-24): but Plotinus recognised that there are difficulties with the alternative, as Simplicius is forced to acknowledge below (325,3ff.), and did not clearly abandon the 'Pythagorean' definition.

213. *Enn.* 6.1.21-2.

214. Simplicius is allowing that the just man who dies for his country in a sense undergoes, and the unjust man who obliterates the whole of mankind in a sense acts. This point will be clarified at 322,11ff. Here he gives another example.

215. i.e. in both cases against the natures of fire and earth themselves.

216. As Plotinus remarks, ibid.

217. i.e. supporters of the alternative account.

218. sc. as opposed to his proper end.

219. The thought is that if *he* were the cause of his dying for his country, by suicide or by handing himself over to the enemy (see below), then he would act not only in the sense of achieving his proper end, but also in the sense of being the active cause of his own death. If, on the other hand, he dies for his country at the hands of others, while he is the agent in respect of his proper end, he is the patient in respect of the active cause of his death, which resides in the hands of his slayers. ('Being in possession of the operation which preserves and safeguards himself' is elliptical for: 'being in possession of the operation which preserves and safeguards himself (as opposed to his proper end), *or not*, i.e. which determines whether he lives or dies'.)

220. 'Destroys himself' in the sense of destroying within himself his principle of humanity.

221. Kalbfleisch has *hôs hup' allou heautou diaphtheiromenos*, but his app. crit. indicates that the tradition had difficulty with *heautou*, which is certainly a little awkward on its own. I read *hôs hup' allou <huph'> heautou diaphtheiromenos*. William of Moerbeke has *et patitur etiam tamquam ab alio a seipso corruptus*.

222. i.e., in this case, fire and earth.

223. i.e. the action by which the elements are forced, by the 'cause operating in them' applied by the creator, to constitute the forms of animals and other gross objects.

224. The language alludes to *Timaeus* 28A6ff. Cf. *Republic* 596B7.

225. i.e. they rebel against the cause which produces the animal.

226. sc. in being so constrained to constitute the animal.

227. Hence the impulses and movements by which the elements are constrained by the creator to constitute animals are not only, regarded from the point of the view of the elements, affections creative of the animal, but also actions destructive of the elements themselves. So there are undergoings in accordance with nature and actions against nature.

228. sc. as opposed to a case like that of the elements, which are constrained by the creator of animals against their own nature.

229. i.e. so far we have no coalescence.

230. Reading *aph' heautou* as suggested by Kalbfleisch (p. 574).

231. i.e. the merely acoustic phenomenon of hearing.

232. *Enn.* 6.1.21.

233. i.e. what if a better outcome eventuates from an ill-intentioned action?

234. Reading, with Kalbfleisch, <*ê*> *ei* from Plotinus.

235. The last sentence is not in Plotinus.

236. Not in these exact words, but they give the sense of some of the questions Plotinus raises.

237. Stoic terminology: see n. 135 above.

238. *de Anima* 405b31ff.

239. But cf. 316,14f. above.

240. *Enn.* 6.1.21.

241. Again, not in these exact words.

242. Reading *ou deêi* instead of *oude êi* (A has *ou deê*). William of Moerbeke has *non oportere*.

243. *Enn.* 6.1.21.

244. Strictly, Simplicius ought to claim that this *either* (i) does not tell us what the cause of the affection is, *or* (ii) leads to the opposite of what Plotinus wants. For, Simplicius goes on to argue, *either* the affection is causeless (in which case (i) holds) *or* the cause is external (in which case (ii) holds, since Plotinus wished to allow for internally caused affections).

245. So Simplicius opposes to both Iamblichus and Plotinus the point that only a substance can be affected. He further contends against Plotinus that (qualitative) alteration is not a distinguishing mark of affection (i.e. does not attach to all and only cases of affection).

246. ibid.

247. i.e. towards the better and towards the worse.

248. But the point of Plotinus' remark is precisely to question that supposition, which is already waived in allowing that affections may lead to a better state: the addition of 'or neither' merely adds to the respects in which undergoing need not lead to a worse state. Iamblichus' criticism makes little sense.

249. *diaphoron.* What is in question is what the Stoics called an *adiaphoron*, i.e. an indifferent thing. But there is no need to consider emending the text, which makes good sense as it stands.

250. *Enn.* 6.1.21.

251. i.e. that substance must already be present if anything is to receive affection: 325,19-20.

252. This is the solution Plotinus offers, ibid.

253. *Enn.* 6.1.22

254. *Enn.* 6.1.22.

255. Plotinus adds here: 'The same thing, if regarded in one way, is acting, if in another way, it is undergoing. And each is considered not in itself, but along with the agent or [respectively] the patient, in the case where this thing moves ...' etc. (as in Simplicius). One MS to Simplicius supplies something similar to Plotinus' text. But the first sentence of this addition introduces an irrelevancy at this point in the argument, so Kalbfleisch is right not to include it in Simplicius' text.

256. This last clause is not in Plotinus.

257. This sentence is not in Plotinus.

258. *badizein*: the action of walking (William of Moerbeke has *ambulare*).

259. *badisis*: the state or condition of walking (William of Moerbeke has *ambulatio*).

260. e.g. 167,4ff.

261. cf. Aristotle *Cat.* 11a37-8.

262. This is Iamblichus' 'intellectual theory' (*noera theôria*).

263. Kalbfleisch registers a lacuna, and suggests that a word like *paradidôsi*, which I translate, has dropped out.

264. *Philebus* 26E1ff.

265. i.e., in Neoplatonic metaphysics, the Demiurge's transcendent intellections.

266. Reading *pros alla* instead of Kalbfleisch's *pros allêla*. (He records the variant *pros allên*.) William of Moerbeke has *in alia*.

267. I read, with Kv, *energein <kai> poiein*: this reading is tentatively endorsed by Kalbfleisch (p. 574), and supported by William of Moerbeke, who has *operari et facere*. The omission of *kai* is no doubt to be accounted for by Simplicius' subsequent use of the singular *pan auto* to refer to operating and acting taken together as a single idea.

268. After his 'intellectual theory' (*noera theôria*) concerning the category of acting, Iamblichus turns to his 'intellectual theory' of the category of undergoing.

269. Reading *kata tina diadokhon* with Kalbfleisch (p. 574). (William of Moerbeke has *secundum motum quemdam successivum actus*.)

270. i.e. not just operations.

271. i.e. matter, of which we have just had three different characterisations.

272. sc. of things in the category of undergoing.

273. Reading Kalbfleisch's conjecture of *to poiein te* instead of *tôi poiounti*.

274. Deleting *hê* with Kalbfleisch.

275. sc. let alone possess the cause of the acting.

276. = Thesleff 26,2-7. In the Koiné text this passage follows immediately upon the passage Simplicius quotes at 317,13-17. As Szlezák notes (p. 125), the distinction between affection (*pathos*) and passive undergoing (*peponthenai*) is not true to Aristotle's practice in the *Categories*, where these expressions are correlatives (9b32). Stoic influence is detectable here: cf. Plutarch *de Stoicorum Repugnantiis* 1042E (= *SVF* 3.§85).

277. Deleting the first occurrence of *ta* with Kalbfleisch.

278. i.e. a form of self-awareness during perception. See next note.

279. In the Anonymous Paraphrase (64,18-19), these phrases are expanded with *kai mê lanthanein heautou alloioumenon kai trepomenon*, i.e. 'and which is aware of itself *as* being altered and changed'.

280. *hôs gar ekeino en tôi theôrein proetatteto*. But the sense is awkward, and one might well suspect that *theôrein* has intruded as a gloss on *ekeino*: the balance of the sentence, as well as the syntax of this clause, seems to demand *poiein* rather than *theôrein*, yielding 'just as the latter [i.e. theorising; cf. 317,6ff.] was placed foremost in the [category of] acting'.

281. i.e. the self-conscious kind of affection.

282. i.e., not the whole category of undergoing, but the genus (in a loose sense) within the overall category which houses undergoings involving some kind of consciousness.

283. Kalbfleisch suggests *kai hosa* <, *kai hosai*>, but I prefer the *kai hosa. hosai te gar* of the Anonymous Paraphrase (64,29).

284. sc. within the overall category of undergoing.

285. Presumably, Iamblichus' thought is that, since we are dealing with a sub-class of the category of undergoing, a production does indeed derive from something else.

286. 330,36-331,17 constitutes a discussion of the final part of the Pseudo-Archytas quotation: the claim that something can also passively undergo by virtue of a deficiency and a privation. Whereas Pseudo-Archytas suggested that this sort of undergoing does not involve a correlative acting, Iamblichus now argues that we can regard privation and deficiency themselves as agents. But his reasoning is questioned by Simplicius at 331,11ff. This whole passage breaks the connection of thought between 330,36 and 331,17; there is no equivalent in the Anonymous Paraphrase, where the discussion of *poiêma* proceeds uninterrupted at 64,33, the point at which the train of thought is broken in Simplicius' treatment. In view of this, and in view of *touto* at 331,17, which has no referent in the immediately foregoing text but must be taken to refer back to the discussion before 330,36, it seems likely that the whole passage is a later addition, not properly integrated into its context.

287. *Phys.* 199a7.

288. Reading *hê* instead of *kai*, following Kalbfleisch's suggestion.

289. This is the point Simplicius will query at 331,11.

290. i.e. the preceding cause of the fact that the thing is deprived, this cause being identified by Iamblichus with the privative principle itself. (The expression is contorted, but I do not think that *tês stereseôs* at 331,8 can be a subjective genitive. If it were, that would yield the desired sense: 'the preceding acting cause *consisting* of the privation'. But that sense would have been much more naturally expressed by a prepositional construction with *kata* or the like. Parallel considerations apply to the phrasing at 331,11: see n. 292.)

291. This case is irrelevant to the argument: the important point is the following one.

292. Again, the point is that there is an independent principle of deficiency which causes the state of deficiency in the deficient thing. Iamblichus' expression is misleading, since on the view under consideration the cause is strictly to be located in the principle of deficiency itself, not in the deficient thing. (The right sense would be obtained by taking *tên aitian* as subject of *enapergazesthai* and *tês endeias* as a subjective genitive, but I do not think the Greek is naturally taken in that way.)

293. Simplicius is questioning whether it makes sense to posit a separate privative principle to function as the cause of particular deprivations in particular things.

294. This sentence picks up from 330,31-6, repeating the claim of that sentence that productions contribute to substance. See n. 286 above.

295. The text has *prôtoi*. Kalbfleisch obelises and suggests that *deuteroi*, found in the margin of b, gives the right sense. The reference is to the threefold classification of actions at 317,6ff. (especially 318,6ff.). I adopt *deuterôi* instead of *prôtôi* as my reading.

296. *Metaph.* 1022b15-21. But Simplicius' version does not in all points agree with our Aristotelian text.

297. As in the case of the English word 'suffering', *pathos* can mean not merely undergoing, but the undergoing of pain or misfortune (so at 402,2 below).

298. = Thesleff 26,8-10. In the Koiné text this passage follows immediately upon the passage cited by Simplicius at 330,3-8. As Szlezák notes (p. 125f.), the immediate source of the present passage is Stoic doctrine: cf. D. L. 7.134 = *SVF* 2.§300. On the elements, see *SVF* 2.§§ 415-8. For parallel passages elsewhere in Pseudo-Archytas and the Pseudo-Pythagorean tradition, see Szlezák ad loc. Szlezák speculates that the point of introducing god and matter into a discussion of acting and undergoing might have been to resist the attempts of Platonists and Stoics to assimilate these categories to a single category of movement; and if that is right the use here of Stoic terminology to keep the categories apart would have had a serious polemical value. Boethus was the first commentator to insist on the distinctness of acting and undergoing, and he did so by adducing the Aristotelian doctrine of the unmoved mover (see above 302,5ff.). Perhaps, then, at 332,7 we should read, in line with the Koiné text, *to men enti poieon <monon>*, i.e. 'One thing is an agent <alone>'. But this *monon*, even if not read, is clearly implied.

299. An early Aristotelian commentator and head of the Peripatetic School, active in the first century BC, whose writings Simplicius probably did not know at first hand. See Moraux, *Aristotelismus* vol. 1 (1973), pp. 45-58, 97-113.

300. Reading *holên* instead of J's *allên*, adopted by Kalbfleisch. William of Moerbeke has *totum*.

301. Reading *ekhei <ti>*, as suggested by Kalbfleisch (p. 574).

302. sc. in virtue of the fact that the quality of heat is contrary to that of cold.

303. On the 'neutral condition' in Galen see R. Durling, *A Dictionary of Medical Terms in Galen*, Leiden 1993, p. 118, under *diathesis oudetera*.

304. i.e. the shape of the painting is the form at the limit of the action of painting.

305. Reading *ethesan <to peras> tou poiêin* with Kalbfleisch.

306. Kalbfleisch wonders (p. 574) whether we should emend so as to read 'in *most* cases'. Simplicius may perhaps intend us to understand 'in a secondary sense': cf. 310,32ff. and note 336,10-13, where it is again confirmed that acting and undergoing, like being-in-a-position, are relatives as well as belonging to their own categories.

307. Reading *<en> tôi pros ti* as suggested by Kalbfleisch (p. 574). They are reckoned in to the category of relative *as well* as being in their own categories.

308. Reading *de <kai>* with Brandis.

309. The suggestion is that there are two possible models of the point, not that the point is confined to just these two cases. The type of undergoing which is 'considered in respect of its condition' would still count as a sub-class of the first type, if we could detect the influence of an agent, whether acting by means of a surrogate implanted in the patient (the imagination case), or acting at a distance (the case of the fire).

310. i.e. an agent places; a patient is placed.

311. i.e. it acts in the former case, and undergoes in the latter.

312. sc. including acting and undergoing.

313. i.e. being-in-a-position and having.

314. It is crucial to the category of having that the haver and had thing do not coalesce to produce a single reality.

315. = Thesleff 30,22; 31,2-3. The passage is quoted in full below at 378,4-15.

316. *hupographein*: see n. 51 above.

317. Reading *tina* with the Anonymous Paraphrase (65,37) instead of *tên*. William of Moerbeke has *quamdam*.

318. i.e. reclining is a stabler position than sitting: see Anonymous Paraphrase 68,5-6.

319. Reading *hotan* <*tis*> *huptiôteros* with the Anonymous Paraphrase (68,8). Cf. Kalbfleisch, p. 574.

320. i.e. the parts of the heavens are continuously moving into positions formerly occupied by other parts.

321. Reading *eskhen* instead of *eskhon*. Cf. 336,35.

322. In this passage Simplicius is expounding the doctrine of his teacher Damascius: see Simplicius *in Phys.* 624,37ff.

323. DK B.57.

324. *Iliad* 18,20: *'keitai'* is the word which I elsewhere translate as 'is positioned'.

325. Accepting, with Kalbfleisch, J's correction of *dioti* ('because') to *dio* ('which is why').

326. A fixed star is not in place because it is located at the outermost rim of the universe and so is not *surrounded* by body.

327. *Phys.* 212a5ff. Cf. Simplicius *in Phys.* 601,28-9.

328. cf. *Phys.* 212a31ff.

329. Proclus, *in Timaeum* 3.266,18-23 = fr. 130 R. Majercik, *The Chaldean Oracles*, Leiden 1989.

330. cf. *Phys.* 212b27-8.

331. = Thesleff 29,8-10.

332. Reading <*ananka*> *toigaroun* with Kalbfleisch.

333. But do not the parts of something which has shape and dimensions also themselves have shape and dimensions? Simplicius may have in mind a sense of 'part' according to which it is not determinate what the parts of a thing is, because there is any number of ways of dividing a thing into parts.

334. = Thesleff 25,17-18. Instead of the *stasei* of the Simplicius MSS (A has *diastasei*) Thesleff reads *ktasei*, following the reading *ktêsei* found in the MS of the Koiné version of Pseudo-Archytas' treatise. But that reading is incorrect, and should be emended to *stasei* on the basis of Simplicius' text: see Szlezák, p. 123. Szlezák remarks (p. 124) that the point of Pseudo-Archytas' division is rather obscure, given that Aristotle divided the category of being-in-a-position into lying, standing and sitting (6b11). Boethus, we are told (339,18ff.), sought to exclude acting and undergoing from the category of being-in-a-position taken *per se*, and thereby restricted its range to inanimate objects in the first instance, given that the being-in-a-position of a living being involves activity (339,22-3): Szlezák speculates that Pseudo-Archytas may have sought, in conscious opposition to Boethus, to divide the category of being-in-a-position in such a way as to include *per se* the activity-involving positions of living beings: these are embraced by the subdivisions 'operating' and 'undergoing', themselves ranged, not altogether happily, under the division 'being-in-a-position *in potentiality*'.

335. This term is here used loosely, for strictly speaking acting and undergoing (and moving and being moved) are not contraries.

336. Deleting the *kai* before *epeidê* with Kalbfleisch.

337. *Enn.* 6.1.24.

338. sc. elsewhere in the system of categories.

339. Kalbfleisch registers a lacuna and suggests inserting *phônai*, which I translate.

340. sc. the straightness of a line.

341. *Enn.* 6.3.14.

342. This is the word I elsewhere translate as 'reclining', the sense it plausibly has at *Cat.* 2a2. But in this passage and below at 339,24ff. the force of the prefix *ana-* (= upwards) is felt and needs to be registered in translation by selecting another meaning from the word's semantic range.

343. i.e. that these things belong to the category of being-in-a-position does not prevent them from also belonging (and perhaps primarily so) to other categories, a point Simplicius frequently stresses.

344. i.e. with what configuration.

345. i.e. nor is something positioned necessarily in a place.

346. Reading *eite sômatôn <eite asômatôn>* with Kalbfleisch. Presumably the word *askhêmatistos* ('lacking configuration'), as applied to bodies, means the same here as it does at Aristotle *Phys.* 191a2, where bronze is said to lack configuration (i.e. in advance of being shaped into a statue): a lump of bronze may be, as we say, 'shapeless', where this does not mean that it has no shape at all, but that it lacks a conventionally recognised shape.

347. sc. as such a thing as being-in-a-position without place.

348. ibid.

349. Reading *anapim<p>latai*.

350. sc. in the case of predications in the category of being-in-a-position.

351. i.e. standing, sitting etc.

352. sc. along with being-in-a-position.

353. cf. Simplicius *in Cat.* 174,14–30.

354. *Enn.* 6.1.17, where Plotinus discusses (and rejects) a proposal to absorb the other categories into the category of the relatives.

355. Reading *mia kai <hê> autê* with Kalbfleisch.

356. = Thesleff 24,7-10.

357. But in what way has place ever come into existence? If the point is that place has existed, exists, and will exist without place (i.e. it is not ever *in* place), then a corresponding point holds of time: there is no second-order time series. This point is well made by Simplicius below (342,6ff.).

358. i.e. time measures not merely the movement of things that have become substances, but also the movement of the processes by which they become substances.

359. And so to the extent that rest is prior to movement place will be prior to time.

360. i.e. in which place comes before time.

361. On the apparent conflict between the present passage and *in Cat.* 63,21–4, where Andronicus is said to have reduced the number of categories to two, see Moraux, *Aristotelismus* vol. 1, p. 103-4. Cf. too *in Cat.* 134,5-11.

362. Reading *epeita <hoti>* with Brandis and Kalbfleisch.

363. *Enn.* 6.1.13.

364. *Enn.* 6.3.3. These five categories apply to the sensible world only: In *Enn.* 6.2 Plotinus had argued that the appropriate categories for the intelligible world are the five 'Greatest Kinds' of Plato's *Sophist*.

365. Reading *<ou> bouletai* with Kalbfleisch.

366. *Enn.* 6.1.5.

367. Reading *ê gar psukhê ê to nun*, from Plotinus, instead of the reading found in the Simplicius MSS, *ê gar psukhên ê ton noun*.

368. Reading *kata men*, following Plotinus, instead of the reading found in the Simplicius MSS, *ei men kata*.

369. sc. but time does partake of something else, namely quantity.

370. Reading *en de tôi tritôi tôn peri tôn*, as suggested by Kalbfleisch, instead of *en de tôi tritôi tôi peri tôn*.

371. *Enn.* 6.3.11.

372. Reading *autês* instead of *autois*, as suggested by Kalbfleisch (p. 574).

373. *Enn.* 3.7.12.

374. Reading *ôn* instead of *on*, as Kalbfleisch tentatively suggests.

375. i.e. telling us the measurement of something does not tell us what the measured thing is.

376. *Timaeus* 37D.

377. *Enn.* 3.7.1.

378. The expression is loose, and strictly incorrect: it is not the case that *both* Plotinus' characterisations of time fail to give *either* a *per se* account of it *or* to assign it to the category of relative. Simplicius ought to say instead that if time is characterised as a measure or as what is measured then, while it can indeed, so understood, belong to the category of relative, the characterisation of it is not a *per se* but merely an accidental one, whereas if time is characterised as the moving image of eternity then, while such a characterisation can indeed count as a *per se* one, it involves abandoning the assignment of time to the category of relative.

379. i.e. time includes the things which *come to be* (things that have life and movement), as opposed to the things that *are* (thoughts and forms).

380. i.e. as a separate category.

381. *Phys.* 219a10ff.

382. i.e. from movement. Reading *autês*, conjectured in b, instead of *autou*, adopted by Kalbfleisch.

383. *Phys.* 219b1-2.

384. *Phys.* 221b7.

385. e.g. *Phys.* 219a9-10.

386. *Phys.* 221b8.

387. Reading *hen* instead of *hena*, as suggested by Kalbfleisch.

388. i.e., in modern parlance, 'man' is a count noun rather than a mass term.

389. Reading *gar* after *hôsper*, as suggested by Kalbfleisch.

390. Reading *autêi ekhei kai autê* from b, tentatively endorsed by Kalbfleisch, instead of *autôi ekhei kai auto*.

391. Hence time is measured in both of the ways detailed above at 344,17-21, in terms of natural units and in terms of conventionally and arbitrarily established units.

392. Reading *kai* from b, instead of Kalbfleisch's conjectured *ê*.

393. Reading *hê ousia autou* from the margin of b, instead of *autos*. Cf. 345,12.

394. *Phys.* 220b23.

395. Reading *<hê> kinêsis*, as suggested by Kalbfleisch.

396. *Phys.* 221b20f.

397. 'Motionless' in the sense that such things are not the sort of thing of which it makes sense to say either that they are in motion or that they are at rest.

398. *Phys.* 219b1f.

399. A pupil of Theophrastus and his successor as head of the Aristotelian school (third century BC).

400. *Phys.* 223a18, 251b28.

401. The thought is: the occurrence of the word 'number' (*arithmos*) in the Aristotelian definition of time as the number of movement is actually strictly incorrect, for it implies discreteness, whereas time is the measure of continuous motion. So 'measure' (*metron*) would have been the right word, and we should regard Aristotle as having in effect used 'number' in this context in the sense of 'measure'.

402. Note that the word I am translating as 'continuous' (*sunekhês*) does not just mean uncountably infinite (having the order-type of the real numbers), as it does in modern usage, as opposed to countably infinite (having the order-type of the natural or rational numbers): it covers both these possibilities.

403. sc. if he had addressed the question of their categorial allegiance.

404. Reading *proêgoumenois* with v, instead of Kalbleisch's *proêgoumenôs*. William of Moerbeke has *tamquam principalissimis generibus utitur*.

405. *Enn.* 6.1.13.

406. i.e. the parts of time and a relation towards time.

407. Presumably the point is that *next year* does not yet exist, and *this year* does not yet exist completely. Cf. below 358,13, and see P. Hoffmann, 'Les catégories POU et POTE chez Aristote et Simplicius', in P. Aubenque ed., *Concepts et catégories dans la pensée antique*, pp. 217-45, esp. p. 239 n. 1.

408. *arti*, which can refer to the immediate future or the immediate past, here probably refers only to the immediate past: see last note.

409. There is no *rate* at which time flows: so it does not flow.

410. sc. which have the form of acting (they are active in grammatical form), but are in the category of when.

411. cf. 46,5ff. The list is reproduced here, with differences. (8) is missing from the earlier list, and (1) from the first version of it; in their place we find being in the end or goal of something, as everything is said to be in its own good, and being in the mover. (1) is subsequently added to the list, which then has twelve items.

412. 'Species' is in both these occurrences plural.

413. *Enn.* 6.1.14.

414. Reading *meresi* from Plotinus instead of *merei*. William of Moerbeke has *partibus*.

415. This is a further objection to Iamblichus' response to Plotinus.

416. The latter would count as an instance of being in a place, but not the former (cf. 350,3).

417. A body must be located in *some* place and time: hence a body is not separate from place and time, the universals, though it is separate (as Simplicius goes on to say) from a particular place and time.

418. cf. *Cat.* 1a24ff., where 'this particular white' (e.g. Callias' individual white) is *Cat.* given as an example of what can be *in* a subject.

419. i.e., names special to the categories of when and where, as opposed to names relating to time and place *simpliciter* and so introducing the category of quantity.

420. = Thesleff 24,15-16. On this definition and Simplicius' discussion of it see in general P. Hoffmann, 'Jamblique exégète du Pythagoricien Archytas: trois originalités d'une doctrine du temps', *Les Études Philosophiques* 1980, 302-23, and Moraux, *Aristotelismus* vol. 2, pp. 594-7; cf. also E. Sonderegger, *Simplikios: Über die Zeit*, Göttingen 1982, pp. 87-102, 183-4. The Koiné version of Pseudo-Archytas' tract has *kinêseôs* instead of Simplicius' *phusios*: i.e., 'time is the extension of the *movement* of the universe', which seems to make better sense, since otherwise time would not be properly distinguished by the definition from space: cf. 337,27ff. above and Szlezák, pp. 117-8. But there is no doubt that Simplicius read *phusios*: see 351,19ff. below with Hoffmann, 'Jamblique exégète du Pythagoricien Archytas', p. 312. However, as Moraux remarks (ibid., p. 595 n. 13), Iamblichus and

Simplicius both interpret Pseudo-Archytas' definition, in their version of it, as treating specifically of the *movement* of the universe.

421. Iamblichus took the Archytas of his source material to be the Pythagorean of that name (cf. n. 10 above); but according to Boethius Themistius questioned the identification (*in Cat.* 1, 162A Migne), and may be the source of this objection: see I. Hadot, P. Hadot and P. Hoffmann, *Simplicius: Commentaire sur les Catégories I*, Leiden 1990, p. 7 n. 18. In spite of Simplicius' protestations to the contrary, it is evident that Pseudo-Archytas' definition of time is indeed a conflation of Aristotle's and Chrysippus' definitions: Hoffmann, 'Jamblique exégète du Pythagoricien Archytas', p. 310ff.

422. *Phys.* 219b1f.

423. cf. Stobaeus *Ecl.* 1.8.40e (Wachsmuth p. 104,7ff.) = *SVF* 1.§93.

424. cf. Stobaeus *Ecl.* 1.8.42 (Wachsmuth, p. 106,5ff.) = *SVF* 2.§509.

425. i.e., the Aristotelian and the Stoic definition (the two Stoic definitions being taken together). On the correct translation of this sentence, see Hoffmann, 'Jamblique exégète du Pythagoricien Archytas', p. 311 n. 21. (*SVF* 2.§510 wrongly implies that the subject of the sentence should be understood to be 'Chrysippus'.)

426. The temporal language is to be understood in a logical sense.

427. I emend *auton* to *autou*.

428. *Phaedrus* 245C7-D1.

429. See e.g. *Phys.* 258b10ff. For other references see Bonitz, *Index Aristotelicus*, Berlin 1961, 25a11ff.

430. On this Neoplatonic doctrine of projection, or emanation, of the soul's principles see L. Siorvanes's note on Simplicius *in Phys.* 633,11, in J. Urmson, *Simplicius: Corollaries on Place and Time*, London 1992, p. 64 n. 88. There is no explicit basis in Pseudo-Archytas' text for Simplicius' Neoplatonising interpretation of it (an interpretation which Simplicius evidently draws from Iamblichus).

431. Kalbfleisch prints *ou polu diestêken* ('does not differ much') with no indication of variation, but two William of Moerbeke MSS, B and C, omit *non*, and the text only makes sense without the negative (cf. Hoffmann, 'Jamblique exégète du Pythagoricien Archytas', [n. 420] p. 315 n. 52), which I accordingly delete.

432. sc. as well as Archytas, on the above Neoplatonising interpretation of him.

433. *Phys.* 223a25.

434. On these Stoic principles see D. L. 7.148.

435. Cornutus was a Stoic active in Rome during the first century AD, who held the view that the categories are purely linguistic (and are consequently more than ten in number): see here Porphyry *in Cat.* 59,6-14; 86,20-4; Simplicius *in Cat.* 18,26-19,1; 62,24-7; 359,3. On Cornutus in general see Moraux, *Aristotelismus* vol. 2, pp. 592-601; the present passage is discussed at pp. 594-7. The parenthesis here tells us that Cornutus tentatively embraced a Pythagorean doctrine about the nature of time, rather than a traditionally Stoic one: the point of 'later on' (*opse*) is almost certainly not to indicate that Cornutus came to insight late in life or late in the period of his philosophical activity, for it is unlikely that Simplicius would be sensitive to such a shift, but rather, as Moraux suggests, that Cornutus' Pythagoreanism about time was a later development in the history of Stoicism.

436. What is wrong with the Stoic account, in Simplicius' view, is not so much the replacement of Archytas' *phuseôs* (nature) with *kinêseôs* (movement) – as I have noted (n. 420 above), Simplicius seems anyway to interpret Pseudo-Archytas as if he had written *kinêseôs* rather than *phuseôs* – but rather the omission of the specification that it is the movement of the whole *universe* which is in question, for this omission has the consequence that the Stoic account is insufficiently fundamental.

437. The following passage should be compared with Simplicius' commentary on the *Physics*, 786,11ff. There are a number of significant divergences between the two passages, but except in the case of 352,6-8 I have not altered the version of the *Categories* text given by Kalbfleisch.

438. The version in the *Physics* commentary (786,31) has 'a dance of the present instant' (*khoreiai tini tou nun*).

439. I have not been able to make sense of the text Kalbfleisch prints, and in particular the *hôs ... houtôs* construction (which leaves the verbs *theôreitai* and *sumplêroi* without a satisfactory subject). Comparison with the parallel passage in Simplicius' *Physics* commentary (786,25-9) suggests that we should replace this construction with *hò ... touto*. Accordingly I read here: *hò gar epi tôn en genesei touti to nun para to prosthen nun kai hautê hê kinêsis para tên prôtên kinêsin metabolên epideiknusin, touto polu* etc.

440. The version in the *Physics* commentary has 'in comparison with the previous (*prosthen*) movement'.

441. The *Physics* commentary adds: 'and which contains the principles of nature' (*tou sunekhizontos tous tês phuseôs logous*), 786,29.

442. i.e. Pseudo-Archytas' definition of time falls into two distinct parts. Simplicius will seek to unite them by deriving the first part ('the number of a certain movement') from the second ('the extension of the nature of the universe').

443. = Thesleff 29, 11-30,16; cf. Simplicius *in Phys.* 785,16ff.

444. This is not quite accurate: time, being a continuum, is not partless (*Phys.* 233b31-2), but the instant, being extensionless, is. The sequel makes clear that Pseudo-Archytas appreciates this point. See here Szlezák, p. 139, who conjectures that Pseudo-Archytas' use of the non-Aristotelian concept of time's 'insubstantiality' (*to anupostaton*) may be directed against the Stoic position, according to which the past and the future do indeed subsist, though not exist (*SVF* 2.§509).

445. Kalbfleisch obelises, and suggests reading *on*, which I adopt. I also delete the first occurrence of *legomenon* (cf. 353,18 and 354,20), and hence read *to gar nun ameres on hama nooumenon kai legomenon*. Cf. the *Physics* commentary at 785,17. (A similar garbling occurs in the Anonymous Paraphrase at 54,20.)

446. cf. Aristotle *Phys.* 219b12-21 and Hoffmann, 'Jamblique exégète du Pythagoricien Archytas', (n. 420) p. 321.

447. See Szlezák, p. 139, for relevant Aristotelian passages.

448. Number = natural number. The following is loosely based on Aristotle *Cat.* 4b25-5a14.

449. Reading *hopoka khronos <ouk ên>* from the version in the *Physics* commentary (786,2) and on the basis of the Koiné text.

450. The Koiné text adds here: 'those which are coming to be are being destroyed'.

451. i.e. these interpreters take partlessness and insubstantiality to be both features of the present instant, the view Iamblichus rebuts in the sequel.

452. cf. Simplicius *in Phys.* 787,10ff.

453. sc. as indeed it has been expressly said to preserve its form.

454. cf. Simplicius *in Phys.* 787,17ff.

455. sc. and not as holding for time itself.

456. Reading *<ton> auton* with Kalbfleisch.

457. i.e. is a matter of the participation of generated things, during the process of generation (sc. and that of destruction), in the present instant.

458. i.e. time's essence: reading *tên <ousian>*, as Kalbfleisch suggests. William of Moerbeke has *essentiam*.

459. Reading *apophainoito* with Kv, tentatively endorsed by Kalbfleisch, instead of *apophainointo*.

460. I alter the accentuation on *diamenei* from an acute on the third syllable (present tense) to a circumflex on the final syllable (future tense).

461. I follow Kalbfleisch, who supplies *pros to ekeinou* from the parallel passage of the *Physics* commentary at 793,16ff. In line 5 I also supply, following Kalbfleisch's suggestion, *ta onta* from the same source.

462. i.e. our time, the time of things which come to be and pass away.

463. *Timaeus* 37D.

464. i.e. both movement and number.

465. i.e. in the Neoplatonic story which Simplicius has found in Pseudo-Archytas.

466. i.e. a confounding of the *processes* of generation.

467. Hence place is posterior to time, which measures the process of coming to be.

468. = Thesleff 24,7-10.

469. i.e. Iamblichus is invited to accept that moved things *do* exist in place – insofar as they have *been moved*. (And, since time and place are continuous, anything which *is* moving *has* moved.)

470. Reading *hôs <gar> to*, as suggested by Kalbfleisch, instead of *hôs ta*. Cf. Simplicius *in Cat.* 174,14-30.

471. *Enn.* 6.1.14; 6.3.11.

472. cf. n. 407 above.

473. On the references of these expressions see I. Hadot ed., *Simplicius: Commentaire sur le Manuel d'Epictète*, Leiden 1996, pp. 43-6. The 'Good spirit' (*Agathos daimôn* here, *Agathodaimôn* at 43,23) is a divinity mentioned in contemporary Hermetic writings notable for their currency among pagan circles at the Mesopotamian city of Carrhae; the 'Holy city' (*Hiera polis*) is likely to be the Syrian city of that name (Hierapolis), lying on a major trade route midway between Aleppo and Carrhae. Accordingly Hadot, following Tardieu, argues that these allusions support the hypothesis that Simplicius wrote the *Categories* commentary (along with his other extant works) at Carrhae, to which (it is hypothesised) he had fled after the closure by Justinian of the Neoplatonic school at Athens in 529. (Hadot gives the *Categories* commentary a *terminus post quem* of 538: p. 5.)

474. As the Greek words in brackets indicate, the expressions I have translated using two English words are each a single word in Greek, the orientation being indicated by a suitable suffix. The point that one can indicate orientation by use either of a suitable suffix or of a preposition will be made by Simplicius in the next sentence. To make the point effectively in English one would be restricted to the cases of 'here', 'there' or 'where', e.g. here/ at this place; hence/ from here; hither/ to here. Moraux (*Aristotelismus* vol. 2, p. 598 with n. 21) conjectures that this extension of the Aristotelian doctrine concerning the category of where – for which Simplicius unfortunately cites no authority – derives from the teaching of the grammarians.

475. sc. where the Athenian/Rhodian is.

476. On the following see Moraux, *Aristotelismus* vol. 2, p. 597ff.

477. Presumably Simplicius has in mind writers of grammatical handbooks.

478. Reading *lektikas*, with Kalbfleisch, instead of *dialektikas*. William of Moerbeke has *locutionales*.

479. i.e. in deciding how to allocate items to the different categories.

480. The Greek words for 'place' (*topos*), 'time' (*khronos*), 'horse' (*hippos*) and 'wolf' (*lukos*) are all masculine nouns of the second declension. But this linguistic similarity among the words does not bring them any closer in meaning, and it is their meanings which decide the categorial allegiances of them and their referents. Simplicius here reiterates his adherence to Porphyry's understanding of the nature of Aristotle's categories: see 9,4ff., especially 10,20-3 and 13,11-15.

481. sc. in a spatial sense.

482. Inserting *kai hupokeimenon* with Kalbfleisch.

483. *Enn.* 6.1.14.

484. Reading *ta pragmata <ta> en*, as suggested by Kalbfleisch.

485. i.e. is indicated by both parts of the compound phrase 'in the Lyceum' (*en Lykeiôi*).

486. The 'other things' being the opposite poles of the relations in question.

487. The MSS have *tôn*, which makes little sense, and Kalbfleisch suggests replacing it by *ta*, but I prefer to delete it.

488. Omitting *kai* with A (it is not translated by William of Moerbeke).

489. We might say (putting it in linguistic terms): they have a connotation as well as a denotation.

490. Reading, with Kalbfleisch, *<ê hêde>* from b.

491. sc. of the categories of substance and where. The verb 'predicate', *katêgorein*, is cognate with the word 'category', *katêgoria*: the categories are the basic predicative items. Simplicius here is answering the point raised by Plotinus (359,35-6).

492. On the following see R. Sorabji, *Matter, Space and Motion*, London 1988, ch. 12.

493. = Thesleff 24,7-11.

494. This additional sentence is not present in the Koiné text and is transmitted by Simplicius only here, whereas the first sentence is quoted by him also at 296,5-8, 340,30-3, 357,23-5. Furthermore, since its sense stands in virtual contradiction with that of the first sentence – which envisages a location for the category where before acting and undergoing, but after substance – Szlezák conjectures (pp. 115-7) that it represents a later addition to the treatise.

495. Reading *epeidê <de>* with Kalbfleisch.

496. In *Physics* 4.4 Aristotle treats the place of three-dimensional bodies as a two-dimensional surface surrounding them. (By analogy, the place of two-dimensional plane figures will be their one-dimensional outline, a case which Simplicius, reporting Iamblichus, perhaps has in mind below at 361,33.)

497. Or separation (*diastasis*). Cf. 361,18 above and Sorabji, *Matter, Space and Motion*, p. 205 n. 14.

498. i.e. would degenerate into prime matter: Sorabji, *Matter, Space and Motion*, p. 205.

499. The MSS have *to periekhomenon eskhaton tou topou*, but as Kalbfleisch notes this is unsatisfactory. The Anonymous Paraphrase's *to tou periekhomenou eskhaton ton topon* (58,15) is no better, for as the sequel indicates the 'opinion of the many', as Iamblichus is interpreting that (see next note), must be to the effect that the limit is an accident of place, and supervenes on it, not that *place* itself is a supervening accident. The requisite sense is yielded by changing *to periekhomenon eskhaton tou topou* to *to eskhaton tou periekhomenou topou*.

500. i.e. is an accident of place conceived as already fully constituted, not a contributor to the constitution of place. It is hard to see how Iamblichus feels himself entitled to extract this implication from the 'opinion of the many', which, since it *defines* place as a limit, seems to have precisely the opposite purport.

501. Reading *kat' autên* from the margin of b instead of *kata tautên*, adopted by Kalbfleisch.

502. Accepting Hayduck's conjecture of *noêtikê* for *noêtê* at Anonymous Paraphrase 58,20.

503. i.e. different from the contained things. Although, as we have been told (363,1), in the case of incorporeals the containing and contained things are really the same, nevertheless in some sense the *order* of containment found in the case of corporeals, where container and contained are distinct things, is preserved in the case of incorporeals too.

504. = Thesleff 29,5-11.

505. Reading *houtôs <ekhen>*, as suggested by Kalbfleisch (p. 574).

506. cf. 337,25-7 above.

507. Again, as in the case of 361,23-4, this clause is missing from the Koiné text, and we therefore probably have to do with a later addition. On the connection between this addition and Aristotelian doctrine concerning heaven, see Szlezák, pp. 137-8.

508. Presumably the allusion is to the Neoplatonic One: cf. Dillon, 'Iamblichus' *Noera Theôria* of Aristotle's *Categories*', p. 77.

509. In this paragraph Simplicius is again heavily dependent on the doctrine of his teacher Damascius, who is in turn dependent on Theophrastus: for an account of these influences, together with references to relevant parallel passages from Simplicius' *Physics* commentary, see Sorabji, *Matter, Space and Motion*, ch. 12, esp. pp. 207-8.

510. See here again Sorabji, *Matter, Space and Motion*, pp. 209-10.

511. The sense is: common to more things, in a sense to be explained (see next note).

512. The whole of the earth and air is 'commoner' (ie. is inhabited by more animals) than this or that particular part of the earth and air.

513. As we progressively shrink the dimensions of common place, we eventually arrive at a kind of place (namely that immediately containing each thing) which is no longer common (*koinos*) but individual (*idios*).

514. sc. in Aristotle's or Archytas' writings. The problem with the notion of an 'individual' place is that it seems partially to duplicate the notion of a thing's essence: Sorabji, *Matter, Space and Motion*, p. 210.

515. sc. as far as time is concerned (and the cases of time and place are presumably parallel).

516. = Thesleff 24,5-7.

517. The sense is clear, though the presence of the word *tinôn* is awkward (but comparison with the Koiné version of Pseudo-Archytas' tract shows that it is correct).

518. i.e. they are both *skheseis*.

519. sc. apart from having (and substance).

520. i.e. having's: possibly *autês* should be emended to *autou*, as Kalbfleisch tentatively suggests.

521. Having is 'said in many ways', i.e. is homonymous, but this homonymy, which Aristotle deals with in the last chapter of the *Categories*, is not to be confused with the category of having, which is restricted to the having of something (e.g. a garment or a piece of armour) placed around the human body. Simplicius explains this point in the sequel and again in his discussion of *Cat.* 15 below at 436,13ff.

522. i.e. contrary to his official ordering of the categories.

523. Reading *gen<nêt>ikên*. But see next note.

524. 'The latter ones' here means all the genera at the end of the list, and that, as the rest of the sentence makes clear, really amounts to all the genera other than substance, the point being that the only thing that matters, as far as order is concerned, is that substance should be placed first. Substance should be placed first because it is presupposed by each of the other genera, though not, in each case, *vice versa*. Kalbfleisch prints *genikên* ('generic') in line 24. I do not see that this can stand with *hapantôn*, and have emended to *gen<nêt>ikên*; but another possibility worth considering is *genik<ôtat>ên*: with that reading the claim would be that substance is the most generic of all the genera (i.e. has the best claim to be a genus), which is very much to point here.

525. = Thesleff 29,1-5.

526. Reading *to gar lôpion* from the Koiné text, instead of Kalbfleisch's *to te lôpion*.

527. Reading *<kai> oute* from the Koiné text.

528. Reading *melanotas* with Szlezák (p. 48,4, cf. p. 137) on the basis of *melanotês* in the Koiné text, instead of *manotas* (or *manotês*) of the Simplicius MSS. Cf. 298,15.

529. This parenthesis is no doubt aimed at the Stoics, for whom properties were material: see, e.g., Plutarch *de Stoicorum Repugnantiis* 1084A and Seneca *Ep.* 117.

530. 197B8-D1.

531. i.e. the haver controls (holds) the thing had, and not *vice versa*.

532. The other accidental categories involve *configurations* of substance, the basic category; only the category of having involves the *control* exercised by one substance over another substance.

533. Simplicius' point would more naturally be expressed the other way round: in the sense in which had things are distinguished from external possessions (such as a field), which are not worn, they are like states such as whiteness; in the sense in which had things are distinguished from such states, they are like external possessions in being bodily and not accidents or things which are naturally united with the haver. Had things are intermediate between external possessions and internal states in the sense that they are closer to the body than external possessions, but further away than accidental states. ('Accidental' is not being used in this context in contrast to 'essential', but in contrast to 'substantial', i.e. it carries the sense 'pertaining' to all categories other than that of substance.)

534. As usual, no precise distinction is observed between the category as thing and the category as word.

535. = Thesleff 25,13-16.

536. i.e. it does not admit of *any* species-forming differentiae. Szlezák has a useful note on this passage (p. 123).

537. *Enn.* 6.1.23.

538. Reading *holôs* from Plotinus' text instead of Kalbfleisch's *hoti*.

539. On Nicostratus see Moraux, *Aristotelismus*, vol. 2, pp. 528-63. The reference is probably to the second-century AD Platonist of the same name. Nicostratus, whose views are only known to us through the objections cited by Simplicius in his *Categories* commentary, rejected the tendency of (other) Platonist philosophers (e.g. Albinus) to make Aristotle's category theory fundamental to Platonic philosophy – a tendency which triumphed, however, in the Neoplatonic curriculum.

540. This is rejected by Aristotle, *Cat.* 8a13-b24.

541. Reading *hên en*, as suggested by Kalbfleisch, instead of *en men*.

542. Kalbfleisch has *kai gar khôrizetai apo ktêmatôn: ou gar perikeimetha ekeina: kai apo tôn hexeôn* etc. ('And [things that are had in the sense of the genus] are distinguished from possessions: for we do not place those on [our bodies], and from states ...'). But the point about possessions is repeated three lines later, where its occurrence corresponds to the Aristotelian order: its occurrence here is out of order, and the use of *apo* with *khôrizein* does not fit with the construction of that verb elsewhere in this passage: so I surmise that the words *apo ktêmatôn: ou gar perikeimetha ekeina: kai apo* are a later insertion, and delete them.

543. cf. 366,8ff.

544. *Enn.* 6.1.23.

545. cf. 366,20f.

546. i.e. to the category of where.

547. sc. when the categories were established.

548. i.e. material beings, lowest in the Platonic hierarchy of beings.

549. Reading *<tês> tou ekhein* with Kalbfleisch.

550. This sentence does not occur in *Enn.* 6.1.23, nor, so far as I am aware, elsewhere in Plotinus' work.

551. The following paragraph is loosely based on *Metaph.* 1023a8ff., with the addition of much extraneous material.

552. Reading *kai gar <to agon>* with Kalbfleisch.

553. Reading *boun* from the Anonymous Paraphrase (69,2) in place of *noun*.

554. i.e. by virtue of the manner of their possession (external inanimate bodies placed on the human body).

555. Possession is the internal accusative of the verb 'to possess (have)': if we treat it as an external accusative, another internal accusative will spring into existence; if we externalise that too, we are launched on a regress.

556. i.e. commonly to several species, in the way to be explained.

557. i.e. the man is shod; the shoe is on. In Greek *hupodedetai* can be used in both senses.

558. i.e. having in any sense at all.

559. i.e. having in the sense of placing some corporeal thing on one's body.

560. On the Stoic categories, see n. 138 above.

561. i.e. it is in some sense a mixture of being a certain way and the relatives.

562. But having in this widest possible sense also includes having incorporeals, as the sequel will make clear.

563. i.e. the class of eight senses set out by Aristotle in ch. 15.

564. i.e. in terms of the second sense, control of acquired articles.

565. i.e. in its scabbard.

566. Reading, with Kalbfleisch, *pheromenên <ousian>* from the Anonymous Paraphrase (70,3).

567. cf. Plato *Theaetetus* 177C7.

568. i.e. allocation of goods to them. This allocation is said to be 'uttermost' because it is undertaken last and in respect of the lowest beings in the Platonic hierarchy, i.e. material things in flux. In consequence of their being relegated to last place in the metaphysical allocation of goods, material beings in flux each end up with only a selection of the goods they need, and have to go out and acquire the things in which they are deficient.

569. i.e. material substances in the flux of generation.

570. Reading *houtô* instead of *autôi*, as suggested by Kalbfleisch.

571. i.e. souls as well as bodies meet the requirements for *having* in the sense of the genus, in that they possess acquired things which are of the same nature as them (*homophueis*) – i.e. are lives (just as the things had by bodies are bodies) –

but are distinct entities which are not naturally united (*sumphuseis*) with them. But this extension of the theory of having does not fit the official Aristotelian doctrine, as Simplicius has expounded that, for according to that doctrine the category of having arises when inanimate artefacts are placed on *animate* bodies, whereas (among other points of difference, some of which are noted by Simplicius below, 376,13ff.) the extended theory envisaged by Iamblichus involves treating the human body as not essentially alive (that characteristic has been transferred to the soul), with the consequence that wearing a cloak, say, would not differ essentially from the placing of a cloak on a statue.

572. Reading *heautêi* with JLK instead of *autêi* (cf. Kalbfleisch, p. 574). The word-order in the text Kalbfleisch prints (*peridrassomenê ta en <he>autêi kai apheisa mêden pauêtai sômata te kai zôia kai phuta*) is strained: one would prefer *peridrassomenê ta te sômata kai zôia kai phuta en heautêi kai apheisa mêden pauêtai*.

573. Reading *periekhousês* (sc. *autês*) with v instead of *periekhousêi*.

574. Reading *<hê> thalassa* with the Anonymous Paraphrase 71,5.

575. I read *apaidei ... merikês ... merika* following Hayduck (at Anonymous Paraphrase 71,8), instead of the MSS' *apodei ... meristês ... merista*. The universe is 'general' in the sense that it is complete.

576. Reading *<ta> tettara* with Kalbfleisch.

577. i.e. animals living in the earth, water, fire and air.

578. Reading *autais* instead of *autois*: cf. Kalbfleisch p. 574.

579. 'Smaller' in the sense that they are particulars.

580. i.e. concretely, in the sense in which Aristotle defined the category of having.

581. i.e. at 367,13ff. and 373,33ff.

582. Reading *to ekhein kat' aitian kai to ekhein* from the Anonymous Paraphrase (71,30) instead of *to kat' aitian kai to ekhon*.

583. Iamblichus has agreed that things had are not naturally united with the haver.

584. Reading *ta mikrotera* as suggested by Kalbfleisch, instead of *mikrotera ta*.

585. Instead of the MSS' *ei ... hê* Kalbfleisch suggests reading *ei ... ei* ('if ... if'), but I follow the attractive alternative suggestion, made by Hayduck (at Anonymous Paraphrase 72,11), of reading *hêi ... hêi*.

586. Only in the case of substance does Aristotle expressly admit the existence of what he calls 'secondary substance', i.e. genera and species of particular substances: *Cat.* 2a11ff.

587. = Thesleff 30,17-31,5.

588. i.e. the categories, taken in both their linguistic and ontological roles.

589. i.e. the example of man illustrates the whole gamut of the categories, among which all intelligible words and concepts are divided: cf. Thesleff 22,8-10. With Szlezák I read *tô logô* (i.e. *tou logou*) at 378,5 instead of *tôn logôn*. 'Complete' (*teleion*) is intended to ward off the charge either that Aristotle has included too many items in his list of categories, or that he has included too few: see Szlezák, p. 141.

590. With the following cf. Thesleff 23,2-16.

591. Reading *poson <êmen>* as suggested by Kalbfleisch.

592. See here Szlezák, p. 142.

593. The Platonic form is meant.

594. Reading *pot' heteron ti pôs* instead of the MSS' *pote gerontikôs* as Kalbfleisch suggests (p. 574).

595. cf. Thesleff 32,10-23.

596. The text is awkward at this point. In his addenda Kalbfleisch suggests *hôs oikeian tais arkhais kai tên epistêmên hôrismenên ousian* instead of the text he prints, *hôs oikeian tais arkhais kai têi epistêmêi hôrismenais ousiais.* But that fails to deal with the phrase *kai dia touto en arithmôi,* which cannot stand. Instead I read *ousais* instead of *ousiais* (that is in any case what is suggested by 68,23-4: cf. Thesleff 32,17f.), and delete the first *kai* of 379,1, hence obtaining *hôs oikeian tais arkhais kai têi epistêmêi hôrismenais ousais dia touto en arithmôi kai tôi panti arithmôi apodeiknusin.*

597. i.e. ten. Number is, according to Pseudo-Archytas, based on the decad: see Szlezák, p. 97. Cf. 68,22-31, and Iamblichus, *in Nicomachi Arithmeticam Introductionem* ed. H. Pistelli, Leipzig 1894, 118,9-18.

598. Adrastus (active in the second century AD) recommended placing the *Topics* after the *Categories* in the ordering of Aristotle's works (cf. 15,26-16,30), and he may also have favoured naming the *Categories* 'Preamble to the Topics' (*pro tôn Topôn*), but for reasons of chronology cannot be the originator of this name. See Moraux, *Aristotelismus* vol. 1, pp. 99-101.

599. And cf. Philoponus *in Cat.* 167,21-168,3; Ammonius *in Cat.* 93,9-12.

600. i.e. in each case he examined the various senses of the name according to the common preconception of its meaning.

601. 3b24-32, 5b11-6a18, 6b15-19, 10b12-25, 11b1-4.

602. sc. as a relative. This discussion occurs rather at 5b14ff., i.e. in the section on quantity. Cf. Ammonius (who makes the same mistake as Simplicius) at *in Cat.* 93,12-14, and Philoponus (who identifies the Aristotelian source correctly) at *in Cat.* 168,10-12.

603. i.e. so that we do not confuse the various homonymous kinds of having with having in the sense of the category.

604. sc. which had occasioned their subsequent treatment.

605. Here I adopt *asunuparxia* instead of *anuparxia,* at 380,31 I adopt *asunuparxias* instead of *anuparxias,* and at 381,8 I adopt *asunuparkta* instead of *anuparkta,* in all cases following Kalbfleisch's suggestion (p. 574). *asunuparxia* is unattested elsewhere, but *asunuparktos* is found at e.g. Sextus Empiricus, *PH* 2.202, as well as here at 381,13. The readings are supported by William of Moerbeke's translation: he has *incoexistentia* at 380,21, *non coexistentiae* at 380,31, and *incoexistibilia* at 381,8.

606. There appears to be a gap in the logic: from the fact that non-coexistence is not necessary for opposition it does not follow that it is not sufficient.

607. See below, 381,2ff, and Boethius *in Cat.* 264C-D Migne.

608. i.e. contraries, privation/possession and affirmation/negation. But Simplicius will express a reservation about the claim that the opposites do not form a genus (and that Aristotle did not think they did), at 381,24ff.

609. i.e. are not the same kind of opposition (in the sense of being under the same genus) as the other three (taken together).

610. Reading *asunuparxias,* as suggested by Kalbfleisch (p. 574): see n. 605 above.

611. i.e. 'opposition' is an ambiguous term, as between the various kinds of opposition.

612. Although Nicostratus is not expressly named as holding this view, it is probably an implication of Iamblichus' criticism of him below (381,17ff.) that he did so. But whether the following quotation is taken from his writings, or is based thereon, cannot be settled with certainty: see here Moraux, *Aristotelismus* vol. 2, p. 553 with notes 116-7.

613. Reading *to auto,* as Kalbfleisch suggests, instead of *ta auta.*

614. Reading *asunuparkta*, as suggested by Kalbfleisch (p. 574): see n. 605 above.

615. i.e. since the definition applies to each thing which the general term 'opposite' applies to: *Cat.* 1a6ff.

616. A case in point is the genus of quality, of which Aristotle remarks that it is 'said in many ways' (8b26) without intending a homonymy: cf. 438,18ff. below.

617. i.e. that they are genuinely different kinds of things covered by one ambiguous name.

618. i.e. the case of the categories.

619. I so translate *diaphorai* in view of Simplicius' considered inclination (381,24ff.) to treat the opposites as a genus after all.

620. On Pseudo-Archytas' *de Oppositis*, which is in fact dependent on the Peripatetic treatise *de Oppositis* (this work is not certainly by Aristotle himself: see further n. 668 below) rather than *vice versa*, see Moraux, *Aristotelismus* vol. 2, pp. 623-8. The fragments are collected by Thesleff at pp. 15-19.

621. = Thesleff 15,14-20.

622. Reading *ta men <hôs> enantia* with Kalbfleisch.

623. cf. Philoponus *in Cat.* 169,4-11.

624. = Thesleff 16,3-6.

625. I employ this phrase to cover both the relevant senses of the genitive case.

626. The wording at 11b24-5 differs: 'Things opposed as relatives are called just what they are of or than their *opposites* or in some other way in relation to *them*' (emphases indicate the variation).

627. i.e. 'or [are said] in some other way in relation to something else'.

628. 6b6-11. That is, relatives can be specified in Greek not only by employing the genitive case (translated by *of* or *than*), but also by employing the dative case (translated by *to* or *for*), or by using suitable prepositions.

629. i.e. if *a* has *R* to *b*, then there is an 'opposite' relation *R** (not necessarily distinct from *R*: see further 383,22ff. below) such that *b* has *R** to *a*.

630. In the sense of the previous note.

631. As was suggested by 'some Peripatetics', 381,2ff.

632. This proviso is necessary, for of course something can be both big and small, in relation to different objects of comparison. But it has to be admitted that Aristotle himself shows some confusion on this point at 5b33ff.: see Ackrill's note ad loc in his *Aristotle's Categories* and *De Interpretatione*, Oxford 1963.

633. This phrase is not found at 11b24-5, but is imported from 6a36-7: see n. 626 above.

634. i.e. double and half and knowledge.

635. Some such apodosis to the ensuing protasis ('even if ...') needs to be supplied.

636. = Thesleff 18,21-19,2.

637. = Thesleff 16,19-21.

638. cf. Philoponus *in Cat.* 171,18-24; Ammonius *in Cat.* 95,2-7.

639. Reading *ou legetai tou kakou <agathon>* as suggested by Kalbfleisch. Cf. *Cat.* 11b35-7.

640. i.e. an opposition both members of which coexist.

641. sc. from the other three kinds of opposition. Relatives are *constituted* by their mutual opposition in a way in which the other opposites are not.

642. Reading *<to> epistêton* with Kv.

643. Reading *esti* in place of *legetai*.

644. *pros men to meizon*: i.e. *pros men heteron meizon*.

645. i.e. the relative opposites such as greater and smaller can coexist in the same thing (in relation to different further things).

646. i.e. there are contrarieties between certain cases of acting, and between certain cases of undergoing, but not between (a case of) acting and (a case of) undergoing.

647. cf. Philoponus *in Cat.* 188,20-9; Ammonius *in Cat.* 102,2-5.

648. This is the point that has already been stressed, that the good is not called the good *of* the bad etc. Cf. *Cat.* 11b33ff.

649. i.e. contraries *per se*, taken as relatives: see next note.

650. The point (to be explained in what follows) is this: two contrary terms *A* and *B*, just *qua* contraries, reciprocate (if *A* is the contrary of *B*, *B* is the contrary of *A*), are said to be just what they are (namely, *contraries*) *of* one another, and coexist. So, just *qua* contraries, they are relatives. But as soon as we specify them as *particular* contraries, this relativity disappears. Suppose *A* is white and *B* is black. Black and white do not reciprocate, are not said *of* one another (*A* is not white *of B*), and do not necessarily coexist. The thesis that 'the contrary itself is not said in accordance with the contrary' means that *contrariety* is not a *contrary*: the contrariety which *A* has towards *B* is not the *contrary* of the contrariety which *B* has towards *A*, but its *relative*.

651. i.e. the 'things included under' a contrariety (e.g. black / white, good / bad etc.).

652. Nicostratus' mistake is not the claim that 'the contrary itself' (i.e. contrariety) is a relative – Simplicius is arguing precisely that it is – but his attempt to *transfer* this relativity from the level of contrariety to that of things participating in contrariety.

653. What unites them is that they are *contraries*; what divides them is the nature of the property in respect of which they are contrary (colour, moral character etc.).

654. i.e. possession, *hexis*, also translated as 'state', which is a species of quality: 8b26-7.

655. sc. and so neither is a species (which is necessarily simple).

656. For an alternative explanation of the principle behind the ordering of the four oppositions, see Philoponus *in Cat.* 169,2-170,16 and Ammonius *in Cat.* 94,4-28.

657. The text is lacunose at this point. I have translated Kalbfleisch's supplementation: *to gar leukon ou legetai <tou melanos leukon, all' enantion> tôi melani.*

658. Even-odd numbers are factorisable as 2 x (2m + 1), i.e. they are even numbers which, when halved, leave an odd number as quotient; odd-even numbers are factorisable as 2^{n+1} x (2m + 1), i.e. they are even numbers which can be halved twice or more times successively, but the quotient left at the end of this process is an odd number greater than 1. See here T. Heath, *Greek Mathematics* vol. 1, Oxford 1921, p. 72.

659. cf. above 332,25-6.

660. This word is very much in point here, for, as will subsequently emerge in Aristotle's text (12b26ff.), the characterisation of contraries with an intermediate, as being those contraries of which it is not necessary that one contrary be in the thing capable of receiving them, needs to be tightened so as to read: contraries with an intermediate are those contraries of which it is not necessary that one contrary be in *every* thing capable of receiving them. (It is necessary that *snow* be white, or that *fire* be hot.)

661. i.e. the Stoics: see e.g. D.L. 7.101ff.

662. cf. *Cat.* 1a23-9.

663. cf. Philoponus *in Cat.* 173,3-6. Ackrill, on the other hand, asserts (*Aristotle's Categories and De Interpretatione*, p. 109) that the distinction at 12a1 is not the same as that at *Cat.* 1a23-9. There is indeed a difference: for here the class of things *in* a subject is restricted to just those things which are *naturally* in a subject. But Simplicius and Philoponus are surely right that 12a1 does intend to draw on the earlier distinction. The point, I take it, is that the class of things *in* a subject can be further divided into those which are *always naturally* in their subjects, such as health and sickness, and those which are not always naturally in their subjects. Those which are always naturally in their subjects are such that one or other (though not any particular one) of the contraries must always be in *every* subject capable of receiving them (every body must at any given time be either healthy or sick); those which are in a subject but not always naturally so are such that it is not the case that one or the other contrary must always be in every subject capable of receiving them. Contraries of the former variety do not have an intermediate, those of the latter do.

664. 'Subject' here and at the next occurrence means specifically an individual, or individuals, in one of the categories.

665. i.e. even and odd are predicated essentially of the species of number, but not of the individuals in the various categories (e.g. the class of horses does not have to have some particular number).

666. cf. above 1,3-2,31.

667. Kalbfleisch places a comma after *exergasiai*, but I follow Hülser (*FDS* 941) in shifting it to after *enantiôn*.

668. The fragments of this work are collected in Ross, *Aristotelis Fragmenta Selecta*, Oxford 1958, pp. 105-110. On the question of its authenticity, which Simplicius does not question, see Moraux, *Aristotelismus* vol. 2, pp. 557-9 with n. 134 (Moraux rejects its authenticity).

669. cf. *Metaph.* 1018a25ff.

670. i.e. is the one in virtue of which the contraries differ the most.

671. Reading *ei tauton <to> ta pleiston apekhonta*, with Ross, p. 107.

672. The reading and sense here are doubtful. I read *heterotêtos* with Kalbfleisch, but it might be right to read *heterotês*, as Brandis suggested (and note that William of Moerbeke has *diversitas*), which yields: 'whether contrariety *is* diversity'. Possibly better than *heterotêtos*, while carrying much the same sense, and requiring only a small change, would be *heterotês tis*.

673. i.e. in spite of its difficulties.

674. I have translated Kalbfleisch's first suggested supplementation of the lacuna he registers here: *hoti mê monon en tôi autôi genei <ta enantia huphestêken, alla kai en enantiois: en men gar tôi autôi genei> tôi khrômati*. Note that 'genus' is being used loosely here, as Simplicius immediately observes.

675. For references see Bonitz, *Index Aristotelicus* 3b26ff.

676. *polloston meros*: this seems the likely sense, in view of 387,22-4, though in itself the phrase can also mean the opposite ('a large part'), which is how William of Moerbeke takes it.

677. *to phronein/aphrainein*. On the terminology see my 'The Stoics on Cases, Predicates and the Unity of the Proposition', §5 with n. 15.

678. i.e. what correspond at the level of *lekta* to adverbs: cf. Dionysius Thrax *Ars Grammatica* p. 74,3 (Uhlig). Cf. also above 37,12-13 and 208,18.

679. 'Qualified' and 'being a certain way' are two of the four Stoic categories (cf. n. 138 above). I have retained the masculine form in translation, both here and below, of the word *poioi*, but in fact Stoic texts regularly employ the masculine of this word when there is no particular stress on gender (and where one would therefore expect the neuter *poia*).

680. I read *kai* <*ou*> with von Arnim (*SVF* 2.§173) and *alla mesôs* with Lvb instead of Kalbfleisch's *all' amesôs*. On my reading, the second part of the sentence mirrors the first part both structually and in sense. Since qualified men (*poioi*) are not contraries, it follows *a fortiori* that *this man* and *that man*, who on Stoic teaching are peculiarly qualified (*idiôs poioi*: see here the passages collected by Long and Sedley, §28), are not contraries either. But qualified individuals can be contrarily *related* or, as Aristotle puts it below (389,7), contrarily *disposed* towards one another, and so the practically wise man and the foolish man will be so related. And though such individuals cannot be *immediate* contraries – because, on Stoic teaching, according to this report, and in agreement with Aristotle, it is not *individuals* which are immediate contraries, but (principally) *states* (388,29-389,7; cf. 413,16ff. below) – they can, nevertheless, be *mediate* contraries, and that is what, on my reading, the Stoics here tell us they are, thereby rendering precise the sense in which they are contrarily related: they are so related by virtue of the *immediate* contrariety between the relevant corresponding states. On my reading the pairs *contrary / contrarily related* and *immediate / mediate* are precisely correlated, with the consequence that two items are contrarily related if and only if they are mediate contraries. Accepting Kalbfleisch's text, on the other hand, would involve admitting a further distinction within the class of contrarily related things between those which are immediately and those which are merely mediately so related (the practically wise man / the foolish man being a case of the former, and this man / that man a case of the latter). This refinement seems to me needlessly complicated, as well as objectionable on the ground that it renders the use of *amesôs* at 388,28 implausibly divergent from that of *amesa* at 388,39 and of *amesôs* at 389,3 (where in each case we have to do with immediate *contraries*, i.e. contrary states); I also agree with von Arnim that the second *alla* in 388,28 requires a preceding *ou*. I conjecture that the reading *amesôs* arose from an infiltration of the superficially similar but here entirely irrelevant point that virtue and vice are, on strict Stoic ethical theory, *amesa* in the sense of having no *inter*mediate state (D.L. 7.127). (The confusion, as I take it, is present in Hülser's translation of the passage at *FDS* 944.)

681. Reading *epi ta amesa* <*blepontes*> as suggested by von Arnim.

682. i.e. states, predicates and 'means'.

683. i.e. the predicates.

684. *Pragmata* may here carry the sense which it regularly has in Stoic writings, i.e. *lekta*, as distinct from objects in the world (which are called *tunkhanonta*): see, e.g., D.L. 7.57.

685. Reading *kinêsis* <*kai*> *stasis* with A.

686. sc. in qualities which are *per se* contrary.

687. i.e. are contrary to one another.

688. Reading <*hôs*> *hou*, as suggested by Kalbfleisch.

689. Reading *parônumon*, as Kalbfleisch suggests, instead of *parônuma*.

690. On things so called derivatively (by paronymy), see *Cat.* 1a12-15.

691. Reading *poteron* <*enantia*> *estin* with Kalbfleisch.

692. Reading <*kai ta*> *kata tous horous* with Kalbfleisch and von Arnim.

693. i.e. common names. Chrysippus wrote a work on appellatives: D.L. 7.192. See also Dionysius of Halicarnassus, *de Compositione Verborum* ch. 2.

694. Reading *phêsin* with Kv and Ross (p. 107) instead of *phasin*, adopted by Kalbfleisch.

695. i.e. to practical wisdom and folly. The sense is that the definitions are ordinarily allowed to count as contrary to one another by reference to the contrariety of the defined things.

696. Again, the word is used here in an extended sense, rather than in the narrow sense in which genus = category.

697. With this discussion cf. 106,28-108,4 above.

698. See here Plato *Timaeus* 67D-E; Aristotle *Metaph.* 1057b8ff.

699. Reading *kai ... enantioi esontai* with Kv and Ross (p. 108), instead of *kan ... enantia estai* with Kalbfleisch.

700. i.e. it is necessary that one or the other belong (not: whichever belongs does so necessarily).

701. Reading *ta hôs kataphasis kai apophasis*, as Kalbfleisch suggests, instead of *tên hôs kataphasin kai apophasin*.

702. = Thesleff 17,3-18,1.

703. The text is damaged at this point. Following Kalbfleisch's suggestion I read: *to katholô <ôn, hôn> men* [delete *anagkaiotaton*] *<enantiotatôn> anagkaion*. I take the *men* of this clause to be answered by *de* at 391,13, and the *de* of 391,9 to be apodotic (cf. Kalbfleisch's entry under *de* at p. 461).

704. Reading *oudeteron <oud>eterôi* on the basis of 411,33.

705. Reading *<kai> enti eidea* with Kalbfleisch.

706. The text is lacunose here and in the next few lines. Here I read Kalbfleisch's suggested supplement: *epidekhetai <monon tan eis genê> toman* (omitting *men*). The sense of this supplement is that these genera of genera only admit of *being themselves divided* into genera, i.e. they are not also *products* of such a division. In other words, these genera of genera are not themselves also species.

707. i.e. only into things which cannot be further divided. Hence these species are not themselves also genera.

708. Kalbfleisch's suggested supplement (p. 574), which I translate, is: *ta d' eskhata eidea kai poti tan aisthasin <oikeiotata tan eis atoma monon, ta de mesa> ouk an genê ge monon enti, alla kai eidea*.

709. Again, we have a lacuna. I follow Kalbfleisch's supplement: *skalênos genos, <tô de epipedô eidos, kai ha areta tas men phronasios kai andreias kai sôphrosunas kai dikaiosunas genos,> tô de agathô eidos*.

710. But Aristotle does mention a rather similar division at 14a15-25.

711. Reading *<tên> tôn*, as suggested by Kalbfleisch.

712. The MSS have *hopou*, but there is a clash between this reading and *tropon*, read by most MSS, at 393,4, for on that reading the criterion of time is there put together with a criterion of manner, not of place. Kalbfleisch therefore suggests reading *hopôs* instead of *hopou* at 392,21. Alternatively, it would be an option to read *topon* with Kv at 393,4 instead of *tropon*. Neither place nor manner figures in Aristotle's discussion at this point, so that recourse to the base text will not settle the issue. Perhaps Kalbfleisch rejected the alternative strategy of keeping *hopou* and adopting *topon* on the ground that the criterion of appropriateness of place has apparently already been dealt with at 393,4, having been taken together with that of appropriateness of part and subsumed under the phrase 'in which it is natural ...' (392,25-393,4), while the criterion of appropriateness of *tropos / topos*, whichever it is, is taken together with that of appropriateness of time and subsumed under the phrase 'at the time when it is natural to belong' (393,4-5). But this reasoning seems to me mistaken. If we read *topon* at 393,4, we can suppose that the 'appropriate place' figures in Simplicius' discussion in two distinct roles: as the appropriate *part* of the animal's body (393,2), and as the appropriate *location* of the animal itself (393,4) – for example, if it is in a desert it might be deprived of food. The latter sense of *topos* will be marked off from the former by the epithet *epiballonta*: we have to do with the place which *belongs to the whole animal*. What settles the issue, however, in favour of the alternative strategy is the fact that at 393,6-11 the criterion of appropriateness of manner, which is initially mentioned by Simplicius in a broad sense by way of summary of the foregoing (393,6), is then subsequently developed by him in a narrower sense, in connection with the views of 'some people', in such a way as to imply that, thus narrowly construed and illustrated by the examples of 393,8-11, it is a *new* considera-tion. Hence *hopou* at 392,21 is correct, and the right reading at 393,4 is *topon*.

713. This phrase is not in Aristotle: see next note.

714. Simplicius probably misinterprets Aristotle here. The phrase 'in which [it is natural for the possession to occur]' plausibly refers to the *sort of thing* in which it is natural etc., not to the *bodily part* in which it is natural etc. Aristotle does not have the phrase '[From] a thing which naturally [possesses]' (*apo tou pephukotos*), which Simplicius included at 392,21: its inclusion prompts Simplicius to find in the phrase 'in which [it is natural for the possession to occur]' a reference to the part of the body in which the possession occurs, rather than a second, otiose, reference to the thing which, as a whole, has the possession or privation. Cf. Philoponus *in Cat.* 175,3-16 and Ammonius *in Cat.* 96,11-28: their accounts coincide with Sim-plicius' on this and other points, indicating that this interpretation of Aristotle was part of the tradition.

715. Reading *topon* with Kv instead of *tropon* with Kalbfleisch. See n. 712 above.

716. i.e. as well as the other criteria of deprivation listed, we should add a criterion of appropriateness of manner: see n. 712 above.

717. i.e. numerically the same thing, as Simplicius goes on to make clear.

718. Possession and privation are, unlike contraries, individuated by numeri-cally particular bodily parts, so that while different parts of the same body (and different bodies) can have opposed contraries, it would not be right to oppose such parts in respect of possession and privation.

719. sc. in any given possession/privation opposition.

720. i.e. the same *kind* of subject.

721. cf. Philoponus *in Cat.* 175,19-176,27 and Ammonius *in Cat.* 97,3-8.

722. Kalbfleisch offers the supplement *ekhein <hetera onta>*, but I think a longer phrase must at some stage have been suppressed: *ekhein <hetera onta, kai tên hexin kai to hexin ekhein,>*. The contraction could have occurred by eyeskip: omission of the words in between the two occurrences of *ekhein*.

723. *Laws* 625C.

724. *hektikos* is a Stoic term: see *SVF* 2.§458 and 3.§510.

725. sc. or is not yet that thing (i.e. *ê on*, which has perhaps fallen out after *ekhon*).

726. i.e. they intimate the nature of the possessing (that only human beings are uncloaked etc.).

727. i.e. we prefer to use the language of deprivation in this case than in the case of forcible removal of a natural feature. I am accepting von Arnim's correction of the MSS' *hôs*, which makes little sense, to *ê* (the change is also accepted by Kalbfleisch and by Hülser at *FDS* 936).

728. = Thesleff 18,12-17.

729. i.e. lacking a privative prefix, *a*- or *an*- in Greek (= *un*-, *in*-, *-less* etc. in English).

730. cf. Dionysius Thrax, *Ars Grammatica* 12,3-4 (Uhlig).

731. i.e. neither contrary is a state of possession or a privation.

732. By the figure of speech known as litotes. The point is that privative words are capable not only of denoting non-privative conditions, but even states of possession.

733. cf. D.L. 7.190.

734. Simplicius' discussion of this passage is fraught with exegetical difficulty, partly because of the involvement of Stoic thought. In the notes which follow I restrict myself to essentials: for a full exegesis of the text I refer the reader to my 'Simplicius on the Meaning of Sentences: a Commentary on *in Cat.* 396,30-397,28', *Phronesis* 43, 1998, 42-62. It is unclear to me why in his text of *Cat.* 12a14-15 Minio-Paluello did not adopt the readings of n, the earliest MS, namely *to kathêtai pros to ou kathêtai*, and *to kathêsthai tina pros to mê kathêsthai*. I conjecture these readings to be correct, but in the latter case instead of *tina pros to* Simplicius simply has *tôi*.

735. Reading *kai <allo> to sterêsin* with L.

736. Kalbfleisch registers a lacuna, and supplies *tauto palin eipôn kai peri tês kataphaseôs kai apophaseôs*, which I translate.

737. Reading *hôsautôs <hôs>* as suggested by Kalbleisch.

738. i.e. in accordance with the operation of his sitting. The 'object' underlying an affirmation or negation is thus a possible state of affairs, a sense often borne by the word *pragma* in Aristotle's writings (for references, see my 'Simplicius on the Meaning of Sentences', n. 7), and probably also borne by it at *Cat.* 14b19-20 (see 421,4-5 below with my note ad loc.).

739. Reading *onomatos <kai rhêmatos>* with Kalbfleisch. William of Moerbeke has *ex nomine et verbo*.

740. i.e. is different from the (possible) state of affairs of Socrates' sitting (cf. 397,11-12, where 'the object itself' is replaced by 'bodies [sc. like Socrates] qualified [as e.g. sitting]').

741. On the terminology see Sextus *AM* 8.12. Sextus tells us that *lekta* subsist appendantly to our *thought* (*dianoia*), and Simplicius may intend this point to be understood here.

742. *ou kata tou heterou phamen ginesthai tên antithesin*. The expression is odd, for (1) the important point, as the supplement in my translation indicates, is that the opposition does not come about concerning the relevant *individual*, just as such, but 'individual' is not contained in the Greek, and has to be supplied; further, (2) *heterou* is inapposite, given that in the considered example ('Socrates is sitting'/'Socrates is not sitting') the individual is the same on each side of the opposition. I wonder whether *kata tou heterou* has been corrupted from *kata tou hupokeimenou* ('concerning the underlying subject of predication'). But the overall point is clear.

743. cf. Clement of Alexandria *Stromateis* 8.9.26.2 = *FDS* 763.11.

744. sc. composed of the two corresponding statements.

745. Reading *tôi <gar>*, as Kalbfleisch suggests.

746. i.e. is just how its component statements are opposed. 'Contradictory pair' is my rendering of *antiphasis*, i.e. a pair of statements which contradict one another. An *antiphasis* is not usually itself thought of as a statement in its own right, but simply as a list of its components. At 407,9 below, however, the example given of an *antiphasis* has itself the form of a (disjunctive) statement.

747. sc. between the mutually cancelling components.

748. In my 'Simplicius on the Meaning of Sentences' (above n. 734) I argue that there is a strong case for emending the text here so as to read: *kan ta <a'>* [i.e. *prôta*] *sêmainomena*. The sense of the whole clause would then be: 'And even if we should take as opposites the *primary* things signified by the words'. An allusion would thereby be made to the opening chapter of *de Interpretatione* (16a1ff.), where, according to the traditional interpretation of that passage, a distinction is drawn between the primary significance of words (thoughts) and their secondary significance (extra-mental things).

749. So in this case the computation is: $4 \times 3 \times \frac{1}{2} = 6$. Cf. Philoponus *in Cat.* 184,21-185,2. At 379,33 I read *kai <tou>* with Kalbfleisch.

750. Reading *tês <tôn>* with Kalbfleisch.

751. Simplicius will now explain the rationale for halving the product of the original number n and $n - 1$.

752. Deleting *tôn* with Kalbfleisch.

753. sc. as well as the order, about to be described, which Aristotle follows. The distinction between the method Simplicius has described and Aristotle's is that the former starts with A, enumerates its differences with B, C and D, then takes the differences of B with C and D, and finishes with the difference between C and D, whereas the latter starts with the A-B difference, proceeds to the C-A and C-B differences, and finishes with the D-B, D-A and D-C differences.

754. Both methods start with the A-B difference (that between relatives and contraries); they then diverge in the order they take the remaining five differences.

755. cf. *Top.* 162a16.

756. e.g. white is not said to be white *of* black etc.: 11b33-7.

757. cf. Philoponus *in Cat.* 177,26-180,27.

758. Blindness is the privation of sight, but sight is not the possession – or anything else – of blindness.

759. i.e. the species of number, even and odd: cf. 387,8-16.

760. i.e. the opposition of possession and privation does not apply at all times to things to which it at some time applies.

761. i.e. one or the other applies from the start. Reading *apo prôtês ge<neseôs>* as suggested by Kalbfleisch (p. 574).

762. 'Everything' has wide scope with respect to 'one or other': it is never necessary that, for everything capable of receiving the contraries, one or other contrary belong to it. ('Never necessary' means 'not necessary that ... ever'.)

763. The sense is that for *each* thing capable of receiving the possession or privation it is necessary that one or other of the possession or the privation obtain *at some time*.

764. i.e. one *rather than* the other.

765. i.e. neither determinately sight nor determinately blindness accrues to *all* creatures (some are sighted, some are blind), nor does one or the other belong throughout the entire life of each creature (at birth neither belongs).

766. Deleting *pantôs*, which is not read by William of Moerbeke, and which has plausibly been added by way of false symmetry with *pantôn* in the next line (in Ja it is found in the margin).

767. i.e. neither possession nor privation in respect of sightedness.

768. Simplicius should have said: '... to *everything* capable of receiving them'. (Perhaps we should read: *<panti> tôi dektikôi*.)

769. i.e. it is necessary that at some time one or other of them belong.

770. i.e. among the ones which have an intermediate.

771. i.e. whether the relevant properties belong *only* at some time, or whether they belong always.

772. i.e. whether determinately one of the items (one *rather than* the other) in the relevant opposition belongs.

773. i.e. contraries which belong naturally.

774. i.e. oppositions of possession and privation.

775. What is the difficulty here supposed to be? The quotation (400,30) must be from 13a14 rather than, say, 13a8-9, both because that is what its wording requires and because the point concerns contraries with an intermediate (the subject of 13a14), not possession and privation (the subject of 13a8-9). But at 13a14 the word *panti* ('to everything') does not import an unclarity which then has to be sorted out by *tisin* ('to some things') in the same line, but is governed by *oudepote* ('never'), a word crucially omitted by Simplicius from his quotation, and is accordingly part of the perfectly perspicuous thought that 'it is never necessary that one [such contrary] belong to *every*thing, but it does to *some* things ...'. At 13a8, on the other hand, *panti* might just be said to import an unclarity if one reads *pote* in a restricted sense, so that the claim is that it is necessary, concerning everything able to receive a possession or privation, that at some time *subsequent* to its coming into existence have one or the other. Now this claim would indeed not allow for the case, mentioned by Simplicius (though not by Aristotle), where a thing has the possession or privation *from the start* (400,1-3), and so in that sense Aristotle's text might be said to leave things unclear. But if there is an unclarity, Aristotle does not sort it out, and certainly does not do so by inserting the word *tisin*, which belongs to the later discussion of contraries with an intermediate. It might be suggested that there is an unclarity in the scope of *panti* at 13a14: is Aristotle saying that it is never necessary for everything etc. ..., or that it is, for everything, never necessary etc. ...? The inclusion of the *alla tisin* clause settles this question in favour of the former interpretation. Perhaps, then, we can interpret Simplicius as merely pointing this out. But what was the problem? That the *oudepote* clause is ambiguous taken on its own, i.e. without the *alla tisin* clause? But the *alla tisin* clause is there! It seems hard to avoid the supposition that confusion is present somewhere, either in the minds of the objectors Simplicius is reporting, or in his response to them, or both. In particular, Simplicius' omission of the crucial *oudepote* is suspicious. It is possible that there has been a garbling, at some point in the tradition, of the commentaries on 13a14 and 13a8-9.

776. i.e. it is not necessary that either possession or privation belong.

777. i.e. it is necessary that one or the other belong.

778. The claim is too wide, as the sequel (in Aristotle as in Simplicius) shows.

779. *Phys.* 191b13-15. Cf. Simplicius *in Phys.* 209,5-212,15.

780. Deleting *phêsin* with Kalbfleisch.

781. Simplicius has changed Aristotle's construction so that the morally improving man rather than the process of change is the subject of the verb 'is prevented'.

782. For the threefold division of the elements of virtue, see 237,7-14 and 287,33-288,2. The doctrine is represented by Simplicius as Aristotelian, and is broadly speaking so, but his immediate source will probably have been Hellenistic manuals containing an eclectic mixture of Stoic and Platonic as well as Peripatetic tendencies: see here Stobaeus *Ecl.* 2.7.3g (= Wachsmuth vol. 2, p. 51,1-6) and *Ecl.* 2.7.13 (7) (= Wachsmuth vol. 2, p. 118,5-6).

783. Reading *estin <hê>* as Kalbfleisch suggests.

784. Perhaps Simplicius has in mind the point that, in the tenth book of the *Nicomachean Ethics*, Aristotle argues that true *eudaimonia*, which alone is characterised by perfection (*teleia*) and self-sufficiency (*autarkeia*), is a divine state towards which men can and should strive, but which they cannot completely attain. Hence the best that men can in practice achieve will lack perfection and self-sufficiency, and so will be unstable.

785. Reading *<tôn> en ethei* with Kalbfleisch and Ross (p. 109).

786. Deleting *hôs* with Kalbfleisch and Ross (p. 109).

787. When Demetrius asked Stilpo what he lost in the sack of Megara, Stilpo reportedly gave the answer quoted by Simplicius: Plutarch *Demetrius* 9, *de Tranquillitate Animi* 17, *de Liberis Educandis* 9; Seneca *de Constantia Sapientis* 5.6-7, *Epistulae Morales* 9.18-19; D.L. 2.115.

788. Reading *kataphaseôs <kai apophaseôs>*, as Kalbfleisch suggests (p. 574).

789. The sense of this phrase is that one of the contrasting pair is true and the other false. Cf. 13b31 and 13b33-4 below where Aristotle again uses the phrase 'one or other is true or false', where the required sense is again that one be *true* and the other *false*. If this were not the sense, the contrast between affirmation / negation oppositions on the one hand, and predications of opposed contraries or of possession and privation on the other, would fail, since Aristotle's point is that in these latter cases *both* limbs of the contrasting pair may be *false*.

790. i.e. respectively, 'No *F*s are *G*s' is opposed to 'Some *F*s are *G*s', and 'All *F*s are *G*s' is opposed to 'Some *F*s are not *G*s'. The locus classicus for this division is *Int.* 17b16-20. Simplicius presents the division in the reverse order from Aristotle's, possibly because he is using other sources as well – perhaps a Stoic text, as his next remark may indicate.

791. Reading *pros <tous> allous tropous* as suggested by Kalbfleisch (p. 574).

792. Aristotle strictly opposes *all* to *not all* and *none* to *some* (i.e. *not none*). In general, statements are strictly opposed only if the pair is of the form: *p* / it is not the case that *p*.

793. But not *vice versa*: *Int.* 16b26ff.

794. They never divide the true and the false, taken in uncombined form ('primarily' is thus misleading and would have been better omitted). Simplicius' claim is that Aristotle's 'not ... always' is not supposed to leave room for 'sometimes', in the case of contraries taken in uncombined form: Aristotle selects the weaker form of expression because he is already thinking of the fact that contraries, taken in combined form, do sometimes – but not always – divide the true and the false. Cf. Philoponus *in Cat.* 185,26-8 for a similar interpretation.

795. And so *one* of health and sickness must apply to Socrates: *Cat.* 12b27-32.

796. 'These expressions' refers to *that Socrates is sick* and *that Socrates is well*. 'Objects' (*pragmata*) here means *non-propositional* objects (but not necessarily substances), presumably Socrates' sickness and Socrates' health respectively, but the word may also carry Stoic connotations here, for expressions like *that Socrates is sick* and *that Socrates is well* refer, on Stoic theory, to *lekta*, which the Stoics also call *pragmata* (see here my 'The Stoics on Cases, Predicates and the Unity of the Proposition').

797. i.e. only if these expressions are each combined with suitable further components.

798. This is of course only true of substances: *Cat.* 4a10-11.

799. In question is *not* the point on which Aristotle insists, and which Simplicius is about to come to, that if Socrates does not exist neither 'Socrates is well' nor 'Socrates is sick' will be true, but rather the more general claim that since *statements* like 'Socrates is well' (or states of affairs like *Socrates' being well*) do not inhere in anything, they cannot, strictly speaking, be contraries. But Simplicius places no weight on the point, and immediately abandons it to consider Aristotle's own argument.

800. The form of expression is paradoxical but the sense clear.

801. i.e. the same goes for sentences expressing possession or privation.

802. Simplicius here follows Aristotle's manner of expression (see n. 789 above), the sense of which is that the distinctive feature of a contradictory pair is that its members both not merely take truth-values, but take *opposite* truth-values.

803. i.e. in the discussion of the difference between the contraries and the affirmation / negation opposition at 13b12-19.

804. i.e. subsequently at 13b27-35.

805. But the objection is that it is not possible here!

806. i.e. any more than puppies, who are agreed not to have sight when they are born.

807. sc. with oil. Cf. Soranus in *Gynaeciorum Libri IV* ed. J. Ilberg, Leipzig 1927, 2.13.2 (p. 60,15-17), Oribasius in *Oribasii Collectionum Medicarum Reliquiae* vol. 4 ed. J. Raeder, Leipzig 1933, 29.3 (p. 120,26). (I am grateful to Michael Chase for his help with this note and with n. 809 below.)

808. Reading <*ek*>*pesein*, as suggested by Kalbfleisch, who compares Galen 4.247,19-248,4.

809. According to Empedocles, at birth the infant's internal moisture (*hugrasia*) retreats and the outside air rushes in to fill the vessels (*angeioi*) thereby left open (DK A.74). Also of relevance here are Stoic sources according to which at birth contact with the cold air causes the infant's vital spirit (*pneuma*) to change from a vegetative to an animal one, and the infant's cry is both the consequence of the impact of the cold air and the sign that the transformation to an animal has occurred: see *SVF* 2. §§804-8.

810. sc. because any given thing *x* will be contrary, *ex hypothesi*, to *not-x*, and under *not-x* falls everything other than *x*.

811. The so-called 'indifferent' things of Stoic ethical theory: see *SVF* 3. §§491-9.

812. Intermediates between the morally excellent and the wicked cannot fall under vice and so must fall under non-vice. These intermediates will then be contrary to the wicked, which falls under vice, since *ex hypothesi* vice and non-vice are contraries. Equally, assuming not only that the contrary of vice is non-vice but also that the contrary of virtue is non-virtue (this premiss is suppressed by Simplicius and has to be mentally supplied), intermediates between the morally excellent and the wicked cannot fall under virtue and so must fall under non-virtue. These intermediates will then be contrary to the morally excellent, which falls under virtue, since *ex hypothesi* virtue and non-virtue are contraries. Hence intermediates – i.e. all of them, and hence the same things (a point which Simplicius finds additionally absurd: see next sentence) – will be contrary to both the morally excellent and the wicked.

813. It is an implication of the hypothesis that negation introduces contrariety that the same things (i.e. all intermediates) will indeed be contrary to both the morally excellent and the wicked: see previous note. Why is that absurd? Perhaps Simplicius is reasoning on the Stoics' behalf that it will follow that the same things are *both* morally excellent *and* wicked. Here it is important to note that, though it is standard practice to translate *enantios* as 'contrary', this rendering is not quite accurate, as for example Aristotle's talk of contraries with or without something in between indicates. Rather, in both Plato and Aristotle an *enantion* is a 'contrary extreme' sc. in some suitable range of related properties: see here D. Keyt, 'Plato on Falsity: *Sophist* 263B' in E. Lee, A. Mourelatos and R. Rorty eds, *Exegesis and Argument* (*Phronesis* Supp. vol. 1, 1973), 285-305, at p. 300 n. 33, where he suggests 'polar incompatible' as conveying the right sense. On this understanding of the term, only black and white in the colour spectrum count as contraries, not, say, black and green: for even though black and green are no less incompatible than black and white, they are not *polar* incompatibles. The thought behind Simplicius' claim here of absurdity might then be that if an intermediate were contrary to both the morally excellent and the wicked it would itself be located, absurdly, at both those extremes.

814. Nicostratus here relies on Porphyry's characterisation of the *idion* in the strict sense, as that which (always) belongs to all and only members of some class: *Isagoge* 12,13-22.

815. sc. in the sense explained: see n. 789 above.

816. cf. Ammonius *in Int.* 2,9-3,6, where Ammonius lists various divisions of the *logos*, including Stoic ones, and agrees with Nicostratus here, against the Stoics (cf. 406,22-5 below), that oaths are susceptible of truth and falsity, claiming that the only difference between a declarative sentence and an oath is the addition to the latter of an invocation of a deity.

817. Reading *<hoion> hôs*; cf. Kalbfleisch ad loc.

818. Reading '*hôs kalos ge ho Peiraieus*', *<'ou kalos ge ho Peiraieus'>*, as Kalbfleisch tentatively suggests (p. 574), and, in the next line, reading *hoion* '*<hôs> phaulos estin*'. With the text printed by Kalbfleisch there are two apparent problems: (1) the expression of wonderment has no negative limb, and (2) the words 'he is not worthless' are not expressive of blame. The addition of a negative limb after the expression of wonderment, in line with Kalbfleisch's suggestion, deals with the first problem but exacerbates the second, for the words 'the Piraeus is not beautiful' are not expressive of wonderment any more than 'he is not worthless' are of blame. K. Praechter proposed ('Nikostratos der Platoniker', *Hermes* 57, 1922, 481-517 at p. 488 n. 4) deleting these latter words (i.e. *ou phaulos estin*) from 406,12, remarking: 'Beim *thaumastikos logos* ('*hôs kalos ge ho Peiraieus*') fehlt ganz mit Recht das *antikeimenon* ('*ou kalos ge ho Peiraieus*'), denn das wäre eben kein *thaumastikos logos*. Der *thaumastikos* und der *psektikos logos* sind wohl untereinander als *antikeimena* gedacht, wiewohl die Beispiele einander nicht entsprechen ...'. Praechter's suggestion that the expression of wonderment might be opposed to that of blame is, however, ruled out not only by the lack of correspondence between the examples, but also by Simplicius' construction (*kai tois thaumastikois ... to auto huparkhei, ... kai tois psektikois* sc. *to auto huparkhei*), which clearly implies that expressions of wonderment on their own divide the true and the false, and that expressions of blame do so too. Hence Kalbfleisch's suggestion that a negative limb should be added to the expression of wonderment seems to me correct. That leaves problem (2), now apparently exacerbated by the solution to problem (1). But here I think that there is no obligation to suppose that *both* positive *and* negative limbs of the oppositions under consideration need express wonderment or blame: it suffices for Nicostratus' point if just one limb in each opposition does so. For then we will, so he can claim, in each case have an *opposition* which divides the true and the false, but not, strictly speaking, an *antiphasis* (contradictory pair of statements: see n. 746 above), since in each case at least one of the members of the opposition is not a statement. One further change is necessary. At 406,32-4 it is clearly implied that there is a *word* expressive of blame, as there is of wonderment (*hôs*): the suggestion of M. Frede, *Die Stoische Logik*, Göttingen 1974, at p. 43, with reference to D.L. 7.67, that the *pathos* with which an expression of blame is uttered might, as it were, do duty for the missing extra word, is not satisfactory. The most economical solution is to restore a *hôs* at 406,12, rendering the constructions in lines 11 and 12 entirely parallel. (Note that *hôs* at line 11 is not clearly present in all MSS. I conjecture that it has fallen out of line 12, as also *hoion* from line 11, on the basis of an erroneous supposition that *hoion hôs* is pleonastic, whereas in fact the *hoion* is part of Simplicius' construction and the *hôs* belongs to the example.)

819. Reading *hoion* '*<hôs> phaulos estin*': see previous note.

820. The allusion is to Aristotle's famous discussion of future contingency in *Int.* 9.

821. i.e. the Stoics: their identity as the referent of 'they' is secured by the definition of the proposition at 406,22 and Simplicius' statement at 406,27.

822. i.e. dividing the true and the false.

823. Hence Nicostratus' initial point – that there are other types of sentence which divide truth and falsity – is irrelevant, because we are dealing only with the contrast between contradictory opposites and the other kinds of opposition (contraries, relatives, possession / privation). But even if the point of distinction is so circumscribed, acceptance of the claim that not *all* contradictory oppositions divide the true and the false (Nicostratus' second point) will undermine the contrast with statements predicating contraries. For it has already been accepted that, in some cases, statements predicating contraries do divide the true and the false. The point of distinction between contradictory opposites and such statements was not that the former always, and the latter never, divide the true and the false, but rather that the former always, and the latter only sometimes, divide the true and the false: this distinction appears now to be precarious.

824. i.e. the Stoic definition: cf. D.L. 7.65; Sextus *AM* 8.12; Cicero *Acad.* 2.95.

825. i.e. even if the propositional content of an oath is (or turns out to be) true or false. The Stoic position, as here reported, fits with the evidence of Ammonius (n. 816 above), who attacks the Stoics on the ground that sentences expressing oaths are propositional, and so do admit of truth and falsity as such. Simplicius below (406,28ff.) argues that sentences expressing oaths are not as such true or false, but that whether one swears truly or forswears oneself is a function of the truth-value of the embedded proposition. This is a position which was explicitly rejected by the Stoics, who argued that the issue of swearing truly / forswearing oneself is not settled by the truth-value of the embedded proposition, but that other factors – in particular the intentions and conduct of the oath-taker – are decisive. Chrysippus (*SVF* 2.§197) distinguished between swearing an oath whose propositional content is true or false (*alêthorkein / pseudorkein*) on the one hand, and swearing truly / forswearing oneself (*euorkein / epiorkein*) on the other. As against Cleanthes, who identified the oath-taker's *intentions* at the time of taking the oath as settling whether he has sworn truly or not (*SVF* 1.§581), Chrysippus insisted that the oath-taker's *conduct* up to the time of fulfilment of the oath is also relevant, since an oath is like a contract.

Simplicius at 406,28ff. presumably has in mind the sort of past-oriented example mentioned by Nicostratus, but even in these cases it is plausible to suppose that what is relevant to the issue of swearing truly / forswearing oneself is not the sheer truth-value of the embedded proposition but also one's state of mind (whether one believes that the proposition is true). And as far as future-oriented, promissory oaths go, it is even more compelling to suppose that the issue of swearing truly / forswearing oneself is not settled by the sheer truth-value of the embedded proposition, but that whether the agent intends to carry out the oath (Cleanthes) and whether he makes proper efforts to do so (Chrysippus) are also relevant: for someone who swears a future-oriented oath which he intends to carry out, and which he makes every effort to execute, but who is frustrated through purely external circumstances (so that the propositional content of the oath turns out to be false) cannot fairly be said to have forsworn himself. The correct position may lie between Simplicius' and the Stoic positions: perhaps the truth of the embedded proposition is sufficient but not necessary for 'swearing truly', and its falsehood necessary but not sufficient for 'forswearing oneself'.

826. i.e. the phrase expressing the adjuration, not the whole sentence of which that forms part.

827. i.e. 'How!' (*hôs*): see n. 818 above.

828. i.e. the ones relating to the present or the past.

829. i.e. it is (now) determinate which part of the contradictory pair having regard to the future is true and which part false. For the Stoic adherence to an unrestricted Principle of Bivalence, see Cicero *de Fato* 20-1, where Chrysippus argues on the basis of Bivalence to universal causal determinism, and [Plutarch] *de Fato* 574D.

830. i.e. the members divide the true and the false between them in the sense explained in n. 789 above.

831. Is the claim meant to be that the *contradictory pair* (as a whole) is either true or false, or that its *members* are true or false? The former seems unlikely because, even if we take 'contradictory pair' (*antiphasis*) as referring to the disjunction composed of the members of the contradictory pair (as Simplicius does at 407,9), the point would still be (a) irrelevant to what is strictly in dispute between the Stoics and the Peripatetics, since both parties agreed (against the Epicureans) that such disjunctions are true, and (b) misleading in its form, for given that the Peripatetics agree that a disjunction of contradictories is (necessarily) *true* (as Simplicius in effect notes at 407,9-10) it is odd to ascribe to them the weaker position that it is true or false. It seems better to take the Peripatetics to be agreeing with the Stoics not merely that a contradictory *disjunction* relating to the future is true or false (the point confirmed by Simplicius at lines 9-10), but also that its *disjuncts* are in some sense true or false (i.e. in some sense one disjunct is true and the other false). In what sense? The qualification they make to their agreement with the Stoics is given immediately (407,7-8).

832. Reading *autês* instead of *autôn*; cf. Kalbfleisch, ad loc.

833. The Stoics argue that although it is metaphysically determinate whether or not there will be a sea battle tomorrow it is also modally contingent (see here Alexander *de Fato* 10), so that they reject the fatalist's inference from truth to (real) necessity, even though they accept an inference from Bivalence to causal determinism (see n. 829 above): the resulting combination of universal causal determinism with metaphysical contingency occasions much ridicule from Alexander (ibid.) and Cicero (*de Fato* 12-15). Simplicius' report is an important witness that the fatalist's *inference* (truth entails real necessity) was accepted in the Peripatetic tradition: in order to avoid the fatalist's *conclusion* (necessitarianism), and so preserve the contingency of the future, the Peripatetics saw themselves forced to reject the fatalist's *premiss*, namely the metaphysical determinacy of the future. 'Unstable' (*astatos*) should not be taken to imply that statements about future contingencies *change* their truth-values over time, but rather that their truth-values are not (yet) determinate: see my *The Sea Battle and the Master Argument*, Berlin/New York 1995, §12, on similar usages in Boethius.

834. In line with note 831 above, I take the point here to be not a mere repetition of what is said in 6-7, but the distinct claim that, in effect, even though the *members* of a future-oriented contradictory pair are merely 'ungraspably' and 'unstably' either true or false – and, as noted, in line with Aristotle's and Simplicius' usage we can take 'either true or false' here to be shorthand for 'one member is true and the other false' – the *disjunction* consisting of that pair can still be *true*, and hence assertible. (In modern parlance, the disjunction can be supervaluated as true even though the disjuncts lack a determinate truth-value: see n. 836 below.)

835. i.e. in the cases of statements of the form 'There is a sea battle today', 'There was a sea battle yesterday'.

836. If Nicostratus is to be answered, the Peripatetic position must be that the members of an antiphasis having regard to the future must *in some sense* be either true or false, and Simplicius has indeed stated that this is their position at 407,6-7, on the interpretation of those lines which I offered in n. 831 above. But for their position to be distinct from the Stoics', there must also be a *sense* in which the members are *not* either true or false. The way to capture this slippery middle ground is to say that the *disjunction* that there will either be a sea battle tomorrow or not is true, but that neither *disjunct* is true (so the disjunction is, as a whole, non-truth-functional). I argue in my *The Sea Battle and the Master Argument* that this indeed represents Aristotle's and the general Peripatetic position. So if this interpretation of Simplicius is correct, he will be in accord with that position. The interpretation depends not only on interpreting 407,6-7 in the way I have indicated, but also on understanding an implicit 'determinately' (*aphôrismenôs*) in 407,12-13 (transferred from 10-11): '... those [parts of contradictory pairs] which are specified as being about the future are not yet [sc. *determinately*] either true nor false'. But it is arguable that exactly the same licence is required to make sense of Aristotle's solution to the problem of future contingency in *Int.* 9: at *Int.* 19a39-b2 we need similarly to understand an implicit 'determinately', as Boethius rightly remarks. The claim there is that it is not necessary that of every affirmation and opposed negation one be [sc. *determinately*] true and the other [sc. *determinately*] false (see my op. cit., p. 163).

837. Simplicius reiterates for the *Postpraedicamenta* the claim he made for the *Categories* as a whole, that Aristotle has derived his account from Archytas: 2,24-5.

838. On 'divine' as an epithet in Simplicius for Iamblichus see L. Siorvanes's note to Simplicius *in Phys.* 611,8, in J. Urmson, *Simplicius: Corollaries on Place and Time*, p. 31 n. 23.

839. i.e. Pseudo-Archytas' book *On Opposites*.

840. = Thesleff 15,14-20.

841. Pseudo-Archytas replaces the simple Aristotelian *pros ti* with the Stoic category *pros to pôs ekhonta* (see n. 138 above). Szlezák, pp. 113-14, suggests that the reason may be the influence of Boethus' writing on these terms (cf. Simplicius *in Cat.* 163,6-7).

842. = Thesleff 15,23-16,31.

843. Deleting *genesios* with Kalbfleisch.

844. Reading *toutôn* instead of *toutôi*, as suggested by Kalbfleisch. (William of Moerbeke has *ab his*.)

845. Following Kalbfleisch's suggestions I read *<logou> eidea* and omit the third *kai* of 408,10. William of Moerbeke has *Affirmatio autem et negatio orationis species magis sunt et veri et falsi magis sunt significativa*. (Thesleff also omits the second *kai* and the *mallon* of 408,10: but these changes seem to me mistaken.)

846. Here it looks as if the 'signified object' must be a *complexe significabile*, i.e., something like a proposition (in the modern sense) or Meinongian objective, or possible state of affairs, if negative existential statements are to be accommodated. For in the case of the statement *that a man does not exist* the signified object obviously cannot be a man.

847. Reading *kataphasios <kai apophasios>* with Kalbfleisch.

848. Reading *sunuparkhen* (= *sunuparkhein*), as Kalbfleisch conjectures, instead of *sunuparkhon*.

849. i.e., inheres in man.

850. Reading *sunuparkhen* (= *sunuparkhein*), as Kalbfleisch conjectures, instead of *sunuparkhon*. (William of Moerbeke has *coexistere* here, though he had *coexistens* at the previous occurrence.)

851. Deleting *hupo* with Kalbfleisch.

852. i.e. common-places, argumentational strategies designed to promote one's own position in a dialectical debate and reveal weaknesses in the opponent's case. The name 'topic' derives from the technique of memorising arguments by assigning them places (*topoi*) in the mind's eye: cf. Simplicius *in Phys* 642,4-5 with L. Siorvanes's note ad loc (in J. Urmson, *Simplicius: Corollaries on Place and Time*, p. 76 n. 113).

853. Proof (*pistis*) is arrived at either by syllogistic reasoning or by induction: *Top.* 103b2-7; *An. Pr.* 68b9-14.

854. On induction (reasoning from the particular to the general) see *Top.* 105a13-14, *EN* 1039b26-31, *An. Post.* 71a5-9.

855. cf. *EN* 1108b11-35.

856. cf. Simplicius *in Phys.* 1080,15-20.

857. sc. whereas Aristotle only mentions one bad thing contrary to each of his examples of a good: 13b36-14a1.

858. With this discussion cf. Philoponus *in Cat.* 187,27-188,17; Ammonius *in Cat.* 101,14-22; Eustratius *in EN* 44,25-8; Alexander *in Top.* 106,6-8.

859. There are three components in the model which construes virtue as the mean between an excess and a deficiency, but for the purposes of the good-bad contrariety the two excessive extremes should be taken together, so that just one bad thing (what is extreme) is the contrary of the mean *qua good*. Simplicius will make this point more clearly below at 410,22-4. Again, although the contrary of any given extreme *qua bad* is the mean, *qua extreme* the contrary of an extreme is only the opposed extreme. This response to the first point also deals, in outline, with the second one. See further next note.

860. The point, to be made more clearly below, is that deficiency and excess are contraries in the category of quantity and good and bad (balance and imbalance) contraries in the category of quality. In the category of quantity the two extremes (excess and deficiency) are separated the most (cf. *EN* 1108b26-30), whereas in the category of quality good and bad are separated the most. (The virtues fall under the category of quality: *Cat.* 8b29.) On the definition of contraries as those things which differ most from one another (in the same genus) cf. above 387,17ff. So these contrarieties arise in virtue of distinct categorial allegiances, and the relativisation accordingly removes any appearance of absurdity.

861. The point we want is that affections (i.e. affective states) can be modelled in a quantitative way, as admitting of degrees corresponding to excess, mean and deficiency, and hence that they occur in the category of quantity as well as that of quality, thereby allowing for the two sorts of opposition Simplicius is discussing. But the point which this clause actually contains is a different one. It is derived from *Metaph.* 1020a26-30, where Aristotle says that affections are quantities by virtue of the quantitative divisibility of the things to which they attach. Both the original Aristotelian point and the version of it which Simplicius here purveys appear to be irrelevant to the argument, and it is possible that we have to do here with a marginal gloss which has intruded into the text.

862. A Stoic term of art: see 386,26 above and below 410,30.

863. Used here and in the ensuing discussion not in the Aristotelian sense of a mean between excessive and deficient extremes, but in the Stoic sense of a morally indifferent property: see n. 865 below.

864. Normally *methuein* and *oinousthai* (here we have the verb in the form *oinôsthai*, just as in Aristotle we find the participle in the form *oinômenos*) both mean 'to be drunk', but in this passage the former is used in two senses: (1) being drunk and (2) merely taking wine, while the latter is used in the sense of merely taking wine. My rendering is an attempt to preserve the ambiguity. We find the same contrast as at 410,33-4, between *oinôsthai* in the weaker sense of 'drinking wine' and *methuein* in the sense of 'being drunk', at D.L. 7.118; Plutarch *de Garrulitate* 503F-504B (= Ross, *Aristotelis Fragmenta* p. 11), *Quaestiones Convivales* 644E-645A; and Philo *de Plantatione* 34.141ff. (= Ross, *Aristotelis Fragmenta* p. 10), where it is also remarked that *methuein* has the two senses we find here in Simplicius.

865. On Stoic theory children are 'intermediate' agents, i.e. agents who are neither *spoudaioi* (morally excellent) nor *phauloi* (wicked): see here Philo *Legum Allegoriarum* 1.93.1-95.3 Cohn = *SVF* 3.§519.

866. The objection was that being sober (as an intermediate) is opposed to drinking (as a bad), and that imbibing (as an intermediate) is opposed to being sober (as a good). The reply is that in the being sober/imbibing opposition being sober functions, like imbibing, as an intermediate, and that in the being sober/drinking opposition (1) if being sober is taken as a good, then drinking is opposed to it as a bad, whereas (2) if being sober is taken as an intermediate, then the drinking which is opposed to it is also an intermediate.

867. On prudent walking cf. 224,22-30; Stobaeus *Ecl.* 2.7.5c (Wachsmuth p. 68,24-69,4) = *SVF* 3.§103, *Ecl.* 2.7.5g (Wachsmuth p. 71,15-72,6) = *SVF* 3.§106, *Ecl.* 2.7.11e (Wachsmuth p. 96,18-97,5) = *SVF* 3.§501.

868. A Platonic term: cf. *Rep.* 396D1, 517C5.

869. i.e. whereas Stoic intermediates are contrary to one another by virtue of the different particular qualities which, case by case, they have, bad things are contrary to one another and to Aristotelian means not by virtue of the different particular ways in which they are bad, case by case, but by virtue of the unified properties (which all bad things share) of being either excessive or deficient. And, as we saw (410,3ff.), there are two sub-cases here: bad is contrary to bad, in the category of quantity, as excess to deficiency; and bad is contrary to mean, in the category of quality, as imbalanced to balanced. In each sub-case, the only relevant properties of bad are excess and deficiency, either regarded as contraries of one another (in the former sub-case) or regarded, taken together, as contrary to the mean good (in the latter sub-case).

870. Contingencies, as opposed to necessities and impossibilities, sometimes fall out one way and sometimes the other: cf. Ammonius *in Int.* 88,12-28; 91,22-92,2.

871. It is possible both to husband resources and to be generous, and the good man will find the point of intersection.

872. Deleting *tade* with Kalbfleisch.

873. = Thesleff 17,20-3.

874. Reading *auto*, conjectured by Kalbfleisch, instead of *auta*.

875. Kalbfleisch's comma after *elleipsei* should be a period.

876. i.e. as well as the opposition of bad to good. (For on this hypothesis the opposition of bad to bad will arise in the very same cases as that of bad to good.)

877. cf. *Cat.*13a37ff. with Simplicius' comments ad loc.

878. The word *suneilêmmenôn* is to be taken as elliptical for *suneilêmmenôn meta tês hulês*. See here *Metaph.* 1025b32-3, 1035a17-30, 1036a26-7, 1037a33-1037b7; 1058b1-3.

879. Contraries 'taken together [with matter]' coincide with contraries said 'in combination': the linguistic characterisation mirrors the ontological and *vice versa*. Contraries said 'in combination' are contrary *predications*; contraries said 'without combination' are isolated *words* like 'black'/'white' (or their referents: *Cat.* 1a16-19,

13a37ff. Contraries taken together with matter, such as 'the sick Socrates'/'the well Socrates' are, in the first instance, complex *names* of composite *individuals*; but these complex names have propositional import, for if there is such a composite individual as the sick Socrates, it follows *that Socrates is sick*, and *vice versa*. Hence in 412,18 Simplicius can move easily from ontology (the composite individual) to language (the proposition expressing that individual's composition). Simplicius' first point is that contraries without combination do not, in general, require each other's existence; the second point is that individualised such contraries even require each other's *non*-existence. These two points follow Aristotle's exposition.

880. *Iliad* 18,107.

881. DK A.22.

882. *Gorgias* 496Cff.

883. cf. above 332,25-6; 386,13-15.

884. sc. which is more light than black and less light than white.

885. Presumably the genus will either be soul *simpliciter*, or the incorporeal: cf. Philoponus *in Cat.* 189,25.

886. i.e. quite generally, without mediation by any individuals instantiating these qualities. Cf. 388,21ff. above.

887. This verb appears to occur only here.

888. sc. as in specifically or generically the same thing.

889. Omitting the first *to* with Kalbfleisch.

890. With Simplicius' answer to the question why Aristotle fails to mention individuals in this passage cf. Philoponus *in Cat.* 189,29-190,5.

891. With the following passage (414,27-416,7) cf. Aquinas, *de Malo* q.1, a.1, ad 11. There are some puzzling incongruities between Aquinas' account of Simplicius and the text we have. In particular, Aquinas' version of what he calls Simplicius' second solution, that all contrarieties can in a certain sense all be reduced to that of good and bad, seems not to be present in our text of Simplicius.

892. cf. here Bonitz *Index Aristotelicus* 514b3ff.

893. cf. Philoponus *in Cat.* 190,20-8.

894. cf. here 388,10-13, where Simplicius raises the possibility that good and bad are qualities, but states that Aristotle's view in many places is that 'good' and 'bad' are homonymous words.

895. I interpret *oude* at 415,17 as an emphatic 'not'; but it may be that it has – or at least that Simplicius interprets it as having – its frequent sense of 'not ... either': see below 415,28-9 with n. 902.

896. I take *legomena* to be understood.

897. i.e. along the lines envisaged by Porphyry and Philoponus, as detailed above: a given contrary pair (such as good and bad) will occur in more than one genus.

898. i.e. the ones referred to by Theophrastus at 415,17.

899. i.e. under these principles (themselves contraries). The point is that the contrary principles are the *ultimate* contraries: there are no further contraries for them to fall under, so that the different genera which they fall under cannot be different by virtue of contrariety.

900. i.e. the principles of contraries, such as excess and deficiency, form and privation. Some fragments of Aristotle's *de Bono* may be relevant here: see Ross, *Aristotelis Fragmenta* p. 111ff., esp. fr. 2 (on excess and deficiency) and fr. 5 (on the many / the one, the like / the unlike, the same / the different, the equal / the unequal).

901. sc. as well as the non-primary ones.

902. The claim that the primary contraries *are not in a single genus* and the claim that they *are not genera* seem to be logically quite distinct. (After all, the categories themselves are not in a single genus, but are for all that genera.)

Perhaps, then, we should regard Simplicius as interpreting Theophrastus' *oude* at 415,17 (see n. 895 above) as containing, as a suppressed further claim, the needed point: '[sc. not only are these primary contraries not genera], they are not in a single genus *either*'. Given also that the non-primary contraries are not genera, it follows that no contraries are genera, and we would then have some (however tenuous) basis for Simplicius' otherwise mysterious assertion at 415,22-8 that Theophrastus claims, in the passage cited, not merely that contraries are not in a *single* genus, but that they are not in *contrary* genera either. Simplicius is of course right to argue (cf. n. 899 above) that if the principles of contraries are to be genuine (first) principles, they cannot fall under contrary genera, but it is hard to see that this point is made by Theophrastus in the passage quoted.

903. i.e. the examples (for which see n. 900) which the Peripatetics use to illustrate the primary contraries.

904. In fr. 5 Ross of Aristotle's *de Bono* Pseudo-Alexander says that Aristotle divided the one into the same, the like and the equal, and divided the many into the different, the unlike and the unequal: so in the sense in which the one and the many are here genera, and hence prior, the same, the like and the equal, and the different, the unlike and the unequal are all species, and hence posterior.

905. cf. *Metaph.* 986a22ff., *de Pythagoreis* fr. 10 Ross (*Aristotelis Fragmenta*, p. 137).

906. These Pythagorean principles are the ten good things arranged in one series along with the ten corresponding bad things in the co-ordinate series: cf. Philoponus *in Phys.* 360,22-4. ('Series' is singular in its occurrence here, though it should more properly be plural, as it is at 418,7.)

907. Reading *proskeisthai* instead of *prokeisthai*, as suggested by Kalbfleisch (p. 574).

908. i.e. by way of reporting a common opinion, rather than asserted as a piece of science. On this distinction cf. *Top.* 162b31-3, *GC* 318b27-8.

909. Kalbfleisch closes the quotation here: but I think that Simplicius' response is better taken as beginning at 416,3, and the intervening comments ascribed to Iamblichus, for Simplicius does not 'pass over' the point raised at 415,34-416,2, as the 'I' of 416,2 says he is doing, but vigorously defends its inclusion (416,3-7, a passage which begins with *ê*, the standard formula for introducing the author's response to an aporia): see further n. 911 below.

910. cf. 148,33-4; 387,25-6.

911. i.e. contraries which are themselves genera. But the immediate target of the objection (415,34-416,2) was not the third but the second point (things falling under contrary genera); furthermore, Simplicius' response (416,3-7) also concentrates just on the first and second points, leaving the third to be dealt with by implication. The question therefore arises whether *to triton* here is sound. What one would expect is *kai to deuteron*: if this is what originally stood, but at some stage *deuteron* was 'corrected' to *triton* on the basis of a mistaken assimilation to the point at 415,33-4, *kai* could have dropped out as making no sense in the new context. With *kai to deuteron* instead of *to triton*, the clause as a whole would mean: '... so that I pass over the second point as having been put forward by way of opinion, as well', a much more satisfactory sense.

912. Hence the point that contraries are what differ most under a single genus can stand: if we analyse sufficiently far we will find a single genus under which any given pair of contraries fall. Virtue and vice, though in the first instance falling under contrary genera, ultimately both fall under the genus (category) of quality. 'State' and 'condition' are two species of the category of quality. Cf. Philoponus *in Cat.* 191,5-14.

913. = Thesleff 17,23-9 (cf. 391,21ff.). 'more securely' i.e. than does Aristotle.

914. Moraux rightly notes (*Aristotelismus* vol. 2, p. 626 n. 125) that Simplicius here appears to go beyond what Archytas himself says.

915. Elsewhere in Simplicius' reports of Archytas this phrase is used to refer to the categories (2,15-17, 347,6ff.), but here it plainly refers to the genera of genera in Archytas' categorisation, since Simplicius cannot be saying that according to Archytas the categories are also species.

916. But if Kalbfleisch's supplementations of Archytas' text at 392,5ff. were along the right lines, Simplicius has misunderstood the purport of this remark, which refers to items like triangle and virtue, i.e. items which are both genera and species, and not to items like good and bad, which Archytas (according to those supplementations) expressly says are *not* species of higher genera.

917. See e.g. *Cat.* 6b15-16 (cf. 10b7-8), 10b12-13, 11b21, 35-6, 12a4-6. Cf. too *Int.* 23a38-24b7.

918. See the passage quoted above at 391,2ff., which contains all the cases mentioned here by Simplicius except the true / false contrariety.

919. A rare term taken from the Platonic tradition: see the pseudo-Platonic *Definitiones* 412E7.

920. *Cat.* 11b22 etc.; Archytas mentions the sight / blindness opposition as being one of possession and privation at Thesleff 18,14, quoted by Simplicius above at 395,34 and below at 417,19.

921. This passage contains a number of technical terms which figure in similar claims made elsewhere in Simplicius' writings: cf. especially the long discussion of the nature and origin of evil in his commentary on the Manual of Epictetus, *in Enchiridion Epicteti*, at Hadot, *Simplicius: Commentaire sur le Manuel d'Épictète*, pp. 322-44.

922. Reading *bouletai* <*einai*> with Kalbfleisch.

923. cf. 142,4-5, 195,25-6.

924. cf. Simplicius *in de Caelo* 430,6-8.

925. cf. Simplicius *in de Caelo* 429,34; *in Phys.* 774,6-10; 1262,7-9. In these passages *ektropê* is used in the sense in which *paratropê* is here used.

926. sc. of each pair in the above list.

927. Reading *apotukhiai* instead of *apotukhia*, as suggested by Kalbfleisch.

928. cf. Simplicius *in Phys.* 774,6-10; *in EE* 230,36-41 Hadot.

929. i.e. good and bad, health and sickness etc.

930. Reading <*hê*> *antithesis*, as suggested by Kalbfleisch.

931. i.e. both members of any given pair of contraries.

932. sc. in each pair, i.e. being sick and having ophthalmia.

933. sc. in each pair, i.e. having died and having been blinded.

934. 'These men' are Aristotle and Archytas: cf. 416,23-7 and 418,3-8 (remember that Simplicius identifies Archytas with the Pythagorean of that name: see n. 10 above). Aristotle and Archytas use exclusively the *perfect* form of the passive infinitive of *sterein* (= to deprive), *to esterêsthai* (Aristotle at *Cat.* 12a29, 35, 39 and 12b2; Archytas in the passage Simplicius is about to quote and which he has already quoted at 395,32ff.), never a present form such as *to steriskesthai*, here employed (as well the perfect form) by Simplicius, and rendered in my translation by 'to be currently deprived'. Now in fact both Aristotle and Archytas use *to esterêsthai* in the neutral sense of 'to be deprived', without any particular emphasis on its perfective aspect (hence my translation at 395,33 and at 417,18 and 23 below), but here Simplicius feels entitled to take their use of the perfect form of the verb absolutely literally, given that they list what Simplicius regards as cases of being currently deprived under the contraries (see nn. 917 and 918 above), and confine their attention in their discussions of privation to (what Simplicius ranks as) cases of having been deprived. Accordingly Simplicius accuses them of ignoring the privative dimension of cases of current deprivation.

935. In setting out Aristotle's and Archytas' position here Simplicius appears to be influenced by formulations deriving from Proclus: see *de Malorum Subsistentia* ch. 52.

936. sc. of privation, i.e. being currently deprived.

937. = Thesleff 18,12-17 (cf. 395,32ff.).

938. The division here is not specifically of *having been deprived*, but of privation in general, of which *having been deprived* (*to esterêsthai* in the narrow sense) is one differentia. See n. 934 above and n. 940 below.

939. Reading *to ptilôssein* instead of *to ptilôsson*, as suggested by Kalbfleisch (p. 574).

940. Presumably Archytas' first division corresponds to Simplicius' *having been deprived* (*to esterêsthai* in the narrow sense), his second to Simplicius' *being currently deprived*, his third being the new differentia mentioned by Simplicius before the quotation. Simplicius' point here is the following: Archytas officially lists sickness as a *contrary* (see n. 918 above), but in his division of *being deprived*, quoted here by Simplicius, he also recognises having sore eyes (which he would presumably have regarded as a sickness) as a case of *privation*; and in fact (so Simplicius) having sore eyes (hence sickness in general) is properly to be regarded as a case of *being currently deprived*, something implicitly (if not officially) recognised by Archytas in the way he makes his threefold division, since the second differentia corresponds exactly (on Simplicius' view) to *being currently deprived*.

941. cf. above 401,14.

942. That bees were generated from the rotting carcasses of cattle was a widespread belief throughout antiquity. The process is most familiar from the description of it in Virgil's Fourth *Georgic*.

943. i.e. until it is digested.

944. i.e. the Manicheans, who posited two equally fundamental principles of good and evil. If evil is a mere privation of the good, subsisting as a mere appendage to it, then it cannot have the kind of metaphysical prime status the Manicheans attributed to it. On Simplicius' polemic against the Manicheans in his commentary on Epictetus' Manual, see Hadot, *Simplicius Commentaire sur le Manuel d' Épictète*, pp. 114-44.

945. i.e. for Aristotle's and Archytas' treatment of the bad as a contrary, rather than as a privation, of the good.

946. sc. of parallel pairs: cf. 415,32 above with nn. 905 and 906.

947. i.e. as well as making use of the oppositions examined in chs. 10-11: cf. 379,21ff.

948. cf. Philoponus *in Cat.* 191,17-19.

949. Principally at *Metaph.* 5.11, 1018b9ff.

950. cf. D. L. 5.60. But at 423,1ff. Simplicius argues that the other varieties of the prior mentioned by Strato can be reduced to the five specified by Aristotle here.

951. cf. Philoponus *in Cat.* 191,26-192,2; Ammonius *in Cat.* 103,7-8. This point goes back to Porphyry: Boethius *in Cat.* 284A Migne.

952. Reading *poieisthai* instead of *hêgeisthai*, as Kalbfleisch suggests.

953. 32,22-33,21. This view was reported as Porphyry's. Simplicius goes on to reject it.

954. Reading <*ê*> *hê* with Kalbfleisch. This word introduces Simplicius' response to the Porphyrian objection.

955. Primary and secondary substances are homonymous substances, primary substance being substance in the strictest sense since secondary substance is said of it but not *vice versa*.

956. *Iliad* 19,219; 21,440.

957. Probably the Stoics are meant, though I have not located any specifically Stoic source for this characterisation of the prior. Cf. Iamblichus, *in Nicomachi Arithmeticam Introductionem* 10,2-6 Pistelli; *Theologoumena Arithmeticae* 14,4-5 and 21,14-17 De Falco; *de Communi Mathematica Scientia* 14,25-6 Festa; Dexippus *in Cat.* 62,7-9; Simplicius *in Phys.* 1160,28.

958. i.e. is not *thereby* cancelled.

959. Philoponus (*in Cat.* 192,17) and Ammonius (*in Cat.* 103,17-18) call the second sense of priority natural priority, as does Simplicius below (421,12; 422,24-7). (The corresponding variety of the simultaneous is labelled 'natural' by Aristotle at *Cat.* 14b27 and 15a8, and the relatives are said to be simultaneous 'by nature' at 7b15, a usage followed by Simplicius below in his discussion of the simultaneous.) But the label is not very exact, for Simplicius wishes to say that the third and fourth varieties of the prior are also 'by nature' (421,16; 420,24); and Aristotle indeed calls both the fourth and the fifth variety of the prior, and the third variety of the simultaneous, as well as the second one, 'by nature' (*Cat.* 14b5, 14b13, 14b27, 14b33ff.).

960. Reading *akolouthêsin* with v instead of *akolouthian*, adopted by Kalbfleisch.

961. i.e. why did Aristotle not give these particular examples? In fact he does give the example of the genus's being prior to species in the chapter on the simultaneous: 15a4-7.

962. Not all causes: cf. *Cat.* 14b9-23, where Aristotle deals with a purported fifth variety of the prior, the cause of a true sentence (where the cause does *not* precede the effect).

963. cf. Philoponus *in Cat.* 193,13-27 for further criticisms of the appropriateness of Aristotle's examples in this division of priority.

964. i.e. the priority of cause to caused.

965. i.e. as prior and posterior.

966. i.e. being by nature simultaneous, since they reciprocate in respect of the entailment of existence.

967. The implication (absent from Aristotle's text) of the insertion of this word is that this fifth variety of priority is not confined to things which reciprocate in respect of the entailment of existence. And Simplicius will indeed range the material cause under this head (421,8-10, 25-7), in the case of which, as he recognises, there is no such reciprocal entailment.

968. In Aristotle's example, the sentence is *estin anthrôpos*, i.e. 'There is a man' or 'A man exists' or 'Man exists'. What is the object (*pragma*) which is the cause of the truth of this sentence? Is it (a) the (or a) man (an individual), or is it (b) the existence of the (or a) man, or of Man (a state of affairs)? It is perhaps not entirely clear from Aristotle's text which he has in mind, but an earlier passage in the *Categories* (12b5-16) would suggest (b). That was how Gregory of Rimini, one of the principal proponents of the theory of the *complexe significabile* in the fourteenth century, understood our passage, explicitly assimilating it to the earlier passage: *Lectura Super Primum et Secundum Sententiarum* ed. W. Eckermann et al., Berlin / New York 1981, p. 5,17-31; 8,25-9,7. Against Gregory's interpretation, see Paul of Venice, *de Significato Propositionis* in ed. F. del Punta and M. Adams, *Paul of Venice: Logica Magna Part II Fascicule 6*, British Academy 1978, p. 104,10-18 (note that 'noluit' at line 13 needs to be corrected to 'voluit'). See further my 'Simplicius on the Meaning of Sentences'. I translate *pragma* here by the ontologically neutral 'object' so as not to beg this important question, though if (as is probable) Gregory is right, 'state of affairs' would be a suitable translation, as it is indeed in many Aristotelian contexts (see my art. cit., n. 7). (Note that *peri autou* at *Cat* 14b15 might mean 'about him (i.e. a man, or Man)', as I have taken it in my translation of the lemma, or 'about it (i.e. the state of affairs consisting of a man's or Man's existence)', as Ackrill takes it. I take my translation to be neutral as between (a) and (b) above: the sentence 'There is a man' can naturally be said to be 'about' a man without prejudice to the question what the *pragma* which causes its truth, if it is true, is.)

969. Kalbfleisch has *hôs ek gês kai pêlou* ('since it is [made] out of earth and mud'). But clay (*keramos*) is not made of earth and mud (*pêlos*), but is just mud (*pêlos*, which I translate as 'mud', can mean either clay or mire), which is earth mixed with water (Plato *Theaetetus* 147C5-6). Kalbfleisch comments on the contents of these lines (421,8-10) that they are 'neglegentius dicta' (p. 575), but does not specify exactly what he has in mind: he may have in mind the words *hôs ek gês kai pêlou*; he may also (or instead) have in mind the inclusion of the material cause under the fifth variety of the prior (see n. 967 above and next note). As far as the wording of 421,8-9 goes I believe that the mistake, rather than being Simplicius', is his editor's. Some MSS have *hôs gê kai pêlos*, which, when taken together with William of Moerbeke's *ex terra et aqua lutum* and the continuation of the sentence at 421,9, points to what I take to be the right reading, namely *hôs ek gês kai hudatos pêlos*.

970. Note that the matter of the clay and the constituted clay do not reciprocate in respect of the entailment of existence: the material constituents of the clay can exist on their own, without the clay, but not *vice versa*. Cf. n. 967 above and 421,27 below.

971. sc. depending on the perspective one takes up.

972. Reading *ei de <e>ti*: William of Moerbeke has *si autem adhuc*.

973. i.e. the prior in being.

974. *Metaph.* 1035b4ff, cf. 1018b34-7.

975. cf. *EN* 1112b15ff.

976. *Metaph.* 1018b10-1019a3.

977. Simplicius omits 1018b34-7, having already dealt with the point at 421,24-7.

978. Not in his extant writings, but Aristotle reports a Platonist view of ideal numbers as having before and after: *Metaph.* 1080b11. And cf. 1019a1-4 with G. Reale, *Aristotele Metafisica* vol. 3, Milan 1993, p. 246 n. 12.

979. i.e. the first, third and fourth senses of prior.

980. i.e. 421,31-422,13.

981. i.e. the second and fifth senses of prior.

982. i.e. 422,18-20.

983. i.e. the prior in time and the prior in order.

984. Reading *hupo <to> têi* with Kalbfleisch.

985. i.e. the fourth and second varieties of prior respectively.

986. i.e. the dyad entails but is not entailed by the unit, even and odd each entail but are not each entailed by plurality.

987. For the connection between the good and something's function (*ergon*), see *EN* 1097b22ff.

988. cf. *Cat.* 1a20ff.

989. sc. in each case the latter is prior in worth to the former.

990. Hence perception, which is not separable from [sc. human] soul, is prior to desire, which is so separable.

991. sc. and so the eternal is prior to the transient, because good is prior to bad.

992. sc. and so the even is prior to the odd, because the dyad is prior to the triad.

993. Reading *hupo de <to en> tois* with Kalbfleisch.

994. But Simplicius has already noted (421,27), in effect against Strato here, that the material cause of something (and presumably the same applies to a thing's elements) does *not* reciprocate with that thing in respect of the entailment of existence.

995. Reading *<to> auto* with Kalbfleisch.

996. cf. Philoponus *in Cat.* 195,8-10.

997. cf. *Cat.* 14b25-6.

998. i.e. the varieties of the prior and posterior.

999. i.e. the discussion of the prior and posterior.

1000. cf. Philoponus *in Cat.* 195,27-196,17; Ammonius *in Cat.* 104,19-105,6.

1001. Reading *<tôi> hôs aitiôi* with Kalbfleisch.

1002. i.e. further divisions of the same thing. A is first divided into B and C, and then additionally into D and E, leaving in principle four possibilities of combination: B/D, B/E, C/D and C/E. See above 135,32-136,11, and Ammonius *in Porphyrii Isagogen* 9,25-10,8. Simplicius' language here is a little loose. Strictly speaking, only the second of two divisions of the same thing (in this case, the division of body into animate and inanimate) is an *additional* division; the first one (in this case, that of body into hot and cold) is a *division* (*diairesis*). But what determines which of two co-ordinate divisions counts as the basic division and which as the additional division is just (as Ammonius points out at 10,4, and cf. Elias *in Porphyrii Isagogen* 25,33-26,2) the order of their presentation, which is arbitrary: either may be regarded as the additional division if it is placed second in the list, hence both may be – relative to different orders of presentation – considered as 'additional' divisions. (We might restore the appearance of precision by rendering *epidiairesis* 'cross-division', but Simplicius' usage elsewhere, especially at 136,6, indicates that the prefix *epi-* does indeed carry the force of 'additional' in this word.) *Epidiairesis* may, like *hupodiairesis* (see next note), be a Stoic term, though I have not found a Stoic source for it, and it is also possible that the distinction conveyed by the commentators between *diairesis*, *epidiairesis* and *hupodiairesis* goes back to an earlier Peripatetic source.

1003. A Stoic term: D.L. 7.61; cf. Ammonius *in Porphyrii Isagogen* 9,25-10,8.

1004. i.e. contradistinguished species are, like the relatives, simultaneous 'by nature'. Their manner of simultaneity differs from that of the relatives, however, since they are not mutually entailing and cancelling. Simplicius is clear about this point: he will shortly claim that Aristotle has not specified any opposing variety of the prior and posterior to this variety of the simultaneous – so implying that simultaneous things in this sense are *not* mutually entailing and cancelling (425,11-12) – and though Iamblichus is reported as having opposed this variety of the simultaneous to the second variety of the prior and posterior (425,12-18), he too is quoted as expressly rejecting the view that contradistinguished species are simultaneous in the same way as the relatives (425,28-31).

1005. i.e. the species or subspecies produced by one and the same division.

1006. We have to do here with an initial division of a genus followed by subdivisions of the resulting species.

1007. i.e. the species resulting from the first division.

1008. i.e. contradistinguished species of a genus.

1009. i.e. any more than do the one and the two, Aristotle's previous example of priority and posteriority in the second sense, though here, as noted, he adds the genus and species: 15a3-7). Simplicius has already noted that genus is prior to species in the second sense of priority: 419,33-420,5. Cf. Philoponus *in Cat.* 197,5-8.

1010. i.e. as well as the second one.

1011. But in what sense is the third variety of the simultaneous opposed to the second variety of the prior and posterior? The simultaneous in the *second* sense is opposed to the prior and posterior in the second sense by virtue of the fact that whereas the latter do not 'reciprocate in respect of the entailment of existence', the former do; but it seems that the simultaneous in the *third* sense can intelligibly be said to be opposed to the prior and posterior in the second sense only in the opposite respect that while, in the latter case, there is at least an entailment of existence in *one* direction (the species entails the genus, etc.), in the former case there is an entailment of existence in *neither* direction (it does not follow, if there is a terrestrial animal, that there is an aquatic animal, or *vice versa*). But if things which are simultaneous in the third sense do *not* reciprocate in respect of the entailment of existence, it is at least highly misleading to claim, as Iamblichus does here, that they are opposed in this respect to the prior and posterior in the second sense, albeit the *ways* in which the reciprocation fails in each case are different. Ammonius arguably shows confusion on this issue at *in Cat.* 105,1-4. Philoponus avoids it at *in Cat.* 196,20-197,2 by opposing the simultaneous in the third sense to the prior and posterior in the third sense (i.e. in respect of order), a disposition which is also considered by Iamblichus at 425,26-31 and subsequently tentatively endorsed by Simplicius at 426,7-9. Iamblichus goes on to reject the suggestion that this third variety of the simultaneous involves simultaneity in respect of order, continuing to maintain that it is one in respect of nature (426,9-13), but he recognises that this simultaneity in respect of nature is very different from the relatives' simultaneity in respect of nature (425,30-1). Presumably, then, in opposing the third variety of the simultaneous to the second variety of the prior and posterior, Iamblichus intends no more than the superficial point that the third variety of the simultaneous is, like the second variety, dubbed by Aristotle – for whatever reason – 'simultaneity by nature', despite the fact that their logical properties are quite different.

1012. The rational is simultaneous with the non-rational, which is prior to winged. Hence it can be regarded as prior to winged.

1013. sc. and this is the right way to proceed. Stoic divisions are in question: see D.L. 7.68ff., where the division proceeds correctly.

1014. Reading *tou tôi haplôi*, as Kalbfleisch suggests (p. 575), instead of *toutou kai haplou*.

1015. Hence the latter division is wrong because the resulting species are not genuinely co-ordinate: the simple is prior to the conditional and the disjunctive, since these latter are species of the non-simple, with which the simple is simultaneous.

1016. But these cases of simultaneity should properly be opposed to the *fourth* variety of the prior and posterior, as Simplicius points out below at 425,31-426,5.

1017. i.e. which *necessarily* coexist with each other (which reciprocate in respect of the entailment of existence).

1018. Possibly we should emend *sunanairoumena* to *sunanairounta*: William of Moerbeke has *et cointerimunt*. But the overall point would not be affected by the change.

1019. The sense is: several exordia (sc. in several different works) are simultaneous by virtue of their each being in the same position (namely prior) in relation to their respective expositions.

1020. i.e. the simultaneous species produced from a single division of the genus.

1021. Presumably 426,9-13 follows immediately upon the previous citation from Iamblichus, so that the sense is: not only will the third variety of simultaneity not count as simultaneity in respect of nature, where this is construed as involving reciprocation in respect of the entailment of existence (an important proviso: see next note); it will not count as simultaneity in respect of order either, and indeed no kind of simultaneity will, strictly speaking, be simultaneity in respect of order, for order consists in distinction.

1022. We may eke out Iamblichus' point as follows: it would be wrong to react to the difficulties of finding a suitable way of characterising the third variety of the simultaneous by rejecting it; on the contrary, it is widespread, and it is indeed (so Aristotle tells us) a kind of simultaneity *by nature*, even though it is, as we have noted, quite different from the simultaneity by nature exemplified by the second variety of the simultaneous.

1023. cf. above 421,31-422,1.

1024. Achilles' words to Agamemnon at *Iliad* 1.61. At 426,18 the Simplicius MSS are split between *hama* ('simultaneously') and *homou* ('together'). In favour of *homou* there are the following three considerations: (1) Homer has *homou*, (2) *hama* does not scan, and (3) William of Moerbeke has *si itaque 'omu' (id es simul) bellum <domat> et pestilentia Achaicos*. On balance, however, I favour *hama*, with Kalbfleisch, because *homou* does not fit the context (i.e. 426,16-17). Simplicius has either misremembered or else adapted the Homeric line for his purpose, without noticing, or perhaps simply disregarding, the resulting failure of scansion. (We could, following Kalbfleisch's suggestion, emend *polemos* to *ptolemos*, which would save the scansion and Simplicius' literary credentials; but this is hardly necessary.)

1025. In question is whether two people who are at the same place perform an action (e.g. lift an object) together or separately. But since Iamblichus denies that this kind of simultaneity is a case of simultaneity in respect of place, it is rather confusing that the corresponding lack of such simultaneity is placed under the rubric of the separate in respect of place.

1026. *Metaph.* 1018b9-14.

1027. *hosas* is a misprint, and should be corrected to *hosa* (Kalbfleisch, p. 575).

1028. 'The foregoing' refers to the *Categories* proper (chs 1-9), 'the introduction' to the text as a whole, including the *Postpraedicamenta*.

1029. These contentions of Simplicius' can hardly be said to be convincing.

1030. But there is no mention there of the point about causation.

1031. I retain 'movement' as my translation of *kinêsis*, reserving 'change' for *metabolê*. It should be understood that in this context 'movement' does not necessarily entail *spatial* movement. That is a point Simplicius will come to consider below in connection with Democritus' views (431,6ff.). When he wants an unambiguous term for spatial movement, Simplicius uses *phora*, which I translate as 'motion'. At *Cat.* 15a16 I accept Ackrill's suggestion of *auxêsis <ê> meiôsis*.

1032. Most prominently Plotinus, whose views Simplicius has examined thoroughly in his commentary on ch. 9.

1033. With the following cf. Philoponus *in Cat.* 198,1-15.

1034. cf. Philoponus *in Cat.* 198,28-199,9.

1035. Reading *autas* with JP instead of *autos* with the other MSS and Kalbfleisch. (William of Moerbeke has *ipsas*.)

1036. With the following cf. Philoponus *in Cat.* 199,9-24.

1037. Deleting *tauto* with Kalbfleisch.

1038. i.e. movement is of things which subsist throughout the change, generation and destruction of things which change in respect of coming to be and passing away.

1039. i.e. both things which come to be and are destroyed, and subsistent things.

1040. Reading *dokein* instead of *dokei*, as suggested by Brandis.

1041. *Theaetetus* 181C-D.

1042. Simplicius' text is corrupt at this point: on the basis of the Platonic text and Simplicius' citation of this text at *in Phys.* 1267,26 I read here *kai mên kai sunkrinomena men auxanetai*.

1043. If it is not preserved, the object is destroyed, as Plato (who has *hexis*, i.e. state, rather than *taxis*, order) goes on to say.

1044. cf. Philoponus *in Cat.* 201,3-202,9.

1045. The majority of MSS have *posotêtos* ('quantity'), and this reading is accepted by Kalbfleisch. But mathematical figures are precisely not 'beyond' quantity. I adopt the reading of v, *poiotêtos* ('quality'), which gives the right sense and enables the 'since' clause to provide a proper justification (in chiastic arrangement) for the two preceding claims: mathematical figures are unmoveable because they are beyond matter, and unalterable because they are beyond quality.

1046. sc. by the Stoics. Cf. 'Simplicius' *in de Anima* 217,36-218,2.

1047. See T. Heath, *Mathematics in Aristotle* (Bristol: Thoemmes, 1996), pp. 20-1.

1048. These rectangles are named by stating the endpoints of one of their diagonals: so, for example, by AI is meant the figure AEGI.

1049. Reading <*ta men bk kg*> *tetragôna esti* with Kalbfleisch.

1050. i.e. because the defined figure ABCD is a square, GICF and EBIH are primary and AEGI and IHFD complements rather than *vice versa*.

1051. i.e. with either GICF or EBIH.

1052. Simplicius reopens the question broached at 428,14ff. Cf. Philoponus *in Cat.* 201,3ff.

1053. i.e. generation, destruction, increase and diminution of size.

1054. *oudamou*, used here for *oudamoi*.

1055. sc. on the shapes and composition of the atoms.

1056. i.e. the qualities of gross objects.

1057. Reading *kat' autas* as suggested by Kalbfleisch, instead of *kat' auta*.

1058. cf. *Metaph.* 985b4-22.

1059. sc. let alone being the same thing as it.

1060. Reading *kai* <*hai*> *kata* with Kalbfleisch.

1061. *stasis* is the condition of the heavens, a condition not incompatible with motion, but rather constituted by regular, uniform motion. *êremia* is a sublunary phenomenon, achieved temporally by phenomena whose motions are irregular and non-uniform. See here Plotinus *Enn.* 6.3.27, part of which is quoted by Simplicius below (433,20-7).

1062. i.e. staying the same in respect of any quality is opposed to changing from that quality to another.

1063. Kalbfleisch registers a lacuna, and suggests *kai tên en tôi leukôi êremian: hê gar en tôi melani êremia antikeitai têi leukansei*, which I translate.

1064. I read Kalbfleisch's conjecture *tôi pro tou einai* instead of the text's *tôi prôteuein*, which yields no acceptable sense.

1065. *Enn.* 6.3.27.

1066. Reading *dio* with JA instead of *dioti* adopted by Kalbfleisch. William of Moerbeke has *propter quod*.

1067. i.e. as well as not being in the genus of movement.

1068. Reading *hêkei* from Plotinus instead of *hê ekei*, and deleting *esti* in 433,22.

1069. These words (*kai hoti hê kinêsis ergon*) are not in Plotinus.

1070. sc. as Plotinus by implication claimed.

1071. Reading *megethos <megethos> oude tên kat' ousian <ousian>* with Kalbfleisch.

1072. i.e. quality, size and substance. I read *kata tauta* instead of Kalbfleisch's *kat' autas*.

1073. Deleting *touto* (which is not translated by William of Moerbeke), and accepting instead Kalbfleisch's suggestion of *topon*. The point is that time is changing anyway, whether a thing is at rest or in motion: so what makes movement *similarly* related to both time and place is that in this case (contrast: rest) place is changing as well.

1074. i.e. when size is changing as well as time.

1075. i.e. the time in which the thing exists is changing, while its size is staying the same.

1076. Things at rest are contrarily related to time on the one hand and place, size, quality or substance on the other, whereas things which are moved are related in the same way to time on the one hand and place, size, quality or substance on the other, and this difference between things at rest and things which are moved is itself a contrariety.

1077. *Phys.* 219b1-2.

1078. *Parm.* 129E1, *Soph.* 254D5. In translations of these texts *kinêsis* and *stasis* are often rendered by 'change' and 'rest'.

1079. Deleting *kathaper* with Kalbfleisch.

1080. i.e. Aristotle and his followers.

1081. i.e. the person lying on the bed undergoes changes of position, without changing his place (the bed).

1082. i.e. when, relative, acting, undergoing, being-in-a-position, having.

1083. i.e. substance, quantity, quality, where.

1084. cf. n. 1080 above.

1085. i.e. a second-order time, in which the rate of changes in first-order time can be measured. The difficulties inherent in this notion do indeed constitute a very powerful objection to traditional conceptions of 'flowing' time.

1086. *in Phys.* 408,15ff.; 859,16ff.

1087. *Olympian Ode* 2,87.

1088. I read Kalbfleisch's conjecture: *mêpote de tou hebdomou touto esti sêmainomenou tou hôs ktêma.*

1089. cf. Philoponus *in Cat.* 205,18-19.

1090. *Iliad* 2,581-603.

1091. i.e. his treatment in the *Metaphysics*.

1092. i.e. before the *Postpraedicamenta*.

1093. i.e. the first two examples of having in Aristotle's list here are drawn from the categories of quality and quantity respectively, not from the category of having, strictly taken.

1094. i.e. containing inanimate things, whereas having in the sense of the genus requires the contained thing – the haver – to be animate.

1095. Kalbfleisch prints *hothen oukh hôs ho medimnos kai ho keramos periekhei* ('hence it does *not* contain like the [corn] measure and the [wine] jar') and records that JP omitted *oukh hôs*. In the William of Moerbeke MS tradition *non* is absent from all MSS except A. I can only make sense of this clause here by deleting *oukh*, but even so the clause sits awkwardly, and it is possible that the entire phrase, including *oukh*, was originally a marginal gloss on *alla to kuriôs ekhein aneu sumplokês* ('but having in the strict sense is without combination') in the next line (437,21), which then found its way into the text at 437,20 (the deletion of *oukh* being then explicable as an attempt to render the clause intelligible in that context). To make the clause fit in its current location, I also delete *hothen*.

1096. Each of these phrases is expressed in Greek by just one word.

1097. sc. but insofar as they animate or inanimate etc.

1098. i.e. acting, undergoing, being-in-a-position, having.

1099. So, on this view, these two kinds of having (the first two items in Aristotle's list, here taken as representative of all the items) are not simply to be reduced to the categories of quality and quantity respectively, as Simplicius had suggested (437,16ff.), but rather we have here, yet again, a case of things which fall under more than one category.

1100. Hence, contrary to initial appearances, having is indeed *not* simple.

1101. sc. whereas things had in the sense of the genus ought to be separate substances.

1102. The son or field (for the collocation see 366,25) is under the parental or legal control of the owner, but that is not the sense of 'control' meant here, which applies to physical control over small objects. The text is corrupt at this point. Kalbfleisch prints *all' oute ho huios ê ho agros pros tôi apsukhôi perikeimenon krateitai*, and obelises the words *pros tôi apsukhôi*. In his apparatus he suggests *all' oute ho huios ê ho agros tôi empsukhôi perikeimenos krateitai* ('but neither the son nor the field are placed on the animate being and controlled by him'). A comparison with 437,26ff., however, suggests that *tôi apsukhôi perikeimenon* is unobjectionable; but *pros* has to go. The reference to something placed on an inanimate object has nothing to do with the son/field example, but is a further example of an apparent, but not genuine, case of having in the sense of the genus. So we need a suitable conjunction to introduce it: in the context that can only be *oute*. We also need a definite article for *perikeimenon*. Instead of *ê* JA offer the better *oute*, which I adopt (but it would be possible to keep *ê*). My reading is then: *all' oute ho huios oute ho agros oute to tôi apsukhôi perikeimenon krateitai*.

1103. This final prayer contains an allusion to the fundamental place of Aristotle's *Categories* in the Neoplatonic curriculum: this text is an essential viaticum for the student of the higher mysteries (cf. Hadot, *Simplicius: Commentaire sur le Manuel d'Epictète*, pp. 15-16).

English-Greek Glossary

absence: *apousia*
absolute: *apolutos*
accident: *sumbama, (kata) sumbebêkos, sumptôma*; accident, be an: *sumbainein*
accompany: *epakolouthein, sumparêkein*; accompaniment: *epakolouthêsis*
accomplish: *epitelein, sumperainein*
account: *logos*
accretive: *palin kai palin*
accrue: *paragignesthai, prosgignesthai, prospiptein*
acquired: *epiktêtos*
act: *dran, energein, poiein, prattein*; acting: *poiein, poiêma*; action: *poiêsis, pragma*; active: *drastêrios, drastikos, orthos, poiêtikos*; active principle: *drastêrion*
actuality: *entelekheia*
admit (of): *epidekhesthai*
adventitious: *epeisaktos*; be/enter adventitious(ly): *epeisienai*
affection: *pathos, peisis*; affective: *pathêtos, pathêtikos*; affective quality: *pathêtikê, poiotês*
affirmation: *kataphasis*; affirmative: *kataphatikos*
alter: *alloioun*; alteration: *alloiôsis, heteroiôsis*
analogy: *analogia, anaphora*
analyse: *diarthroun*; analysis, *diarthrôsis*
animate: *empsukhos*
apodeictic: *apodeiktikos*
appellative: *prosêgorikon*
apply: *sunaptein, tattein*
apprehension: *antilêpsis*
argument: *epikheirêsis*
arrange (under): *(dia)tattein, katatattein*; arrange properly: *euthetizein*; proper arrangement: *euthetismos*; arrange before:

protattein; arrange together: *suntattein*
artificial: *tekhnêtos*
ask: *zêtein*
assign: *apodidonai*; assignment: *suntaxis*
atom: *atomos*
attributes: *parakolouthounta*
axiom: *axiôma*

balance: *summetria*; balanced: *summetros*
beginning: *arkhê*
being: *ousia*
behave passionately: *pathainesthai*
belong: *epiballein, huparkhein*; belong together with: *sunuparkhein*
bring about: *poiein*
body: *sôma*; bodily: *sômatikos*; of bodily form: *sômatoeidês*
boundary: *perigraphê*

cancel: *(sun)anairein*; cancellation: *anairesis*
capable of receiving: *(epi)dektikos, hupodektikos*
capacity: *dunamis*
category: *kategoria*
cause, causality: *aitia, aition, aitios*; caused: *aitiatos*; causal: *aitiôdês*; causeless: *anaitios*; able to cause: *parektikos*; being a co-cause: *sunaitios*
change: *metabolê, tropê*; change, to: *ameibein, metabainein, metaballein, methistasthai, trepein*
character, *kharaktêr*; characterise: *kharaktêrizein*; way of characterising: *kharaktêristikos, kharaktêr*
choice: *proairesis*
circumscribe: *perigraphein*
circumstance: *peristasis*

idiomatic: *sunêthês*
imagination: *phantasia*
imbalance: *asummetria*; imbalanced: *asummetros*
immaterial: *aülos*
immediate: *amesos*
imperceptible: *anepaisthêtos*
imperfect: *atelês, atelestos*; imperfection: *ateleia*
imply: *sunemphainein, sunepipherein*
impulse: *aphormê*
inactive: *argos*
inanimate: *apsukhos*
incapacity: *adunamia*; incapable: *adunamos*
incessant: *akatapaustos*
include: *periekhein*; inclusive: *periektikos, perilêptikos*
incompatible: *asunaktos*
incomplete: *atelês*
incomprehensible: *akatalêptos*
incongruous: *akatallêlos*
inconsistency: *anomologia*
incorporeal: *asômatos*
increase: *auxêsis, epitasis*
indefinite: *aoristos*
indifference: *adiaphora*; be indifferent: *adiaphorein*; indifferent: *adiaphoros*
individual: *atomos*; individualise: *idiotropein*
indivisible: *ameristos, atomos*
inert: *adranês*
infinite: *apeiros, aperioristos*
inflection: *ptôsis*; inflected: *ptôtikos*
inhere: *enuparkhein*; inherent: *autophuês*
inquiry: *skepsis, zêtêsis*
inseparable: *akhôristos*
instant: *nun*
instrument: *organon*
insubstantial: *anupostatos*
intellective: *noêtikos*
intellectual: *noeros*
intelligible: *noêtos*
intercourse: *sumplokê*
intermediate: *mesos*; having an intermediate: *emmesos*; without an intermediate: *amesos*
intimate: *paremphainein*; intimation: *paremphasis*
intuition: *epibolê*

investigate: *zêtein*; investigation: *theôrêma*

juxtapose: *paratithenai*; juxtaposition: *parathesis*

kin: *sungenês*; kinship: *sungeneia, oikeiotês*
knowledge: *epistêmê, gnôsis, gnôrisis*; knowledgeable: *epistêmôn*; knowable: *epistêtos*; object of knowledge: *epistêton*

laid about, be: *perikeisthai*
last: *teleutaios*
lie: *keisthai*
limit: *peras*; delimit: *sumperainein*
linguistic: *lektikos*
likeness: *homoiotês*
location: *hedra*
logical: *logikos*
loss: *apobolê, apoleia*

magnitude: *megethos*
manifest: *emphainein*; manifest along with / co-manifest: *sunemphainein*
manner: *tropos*
matter: *hulê*; enmattered: *enulos*; material: *hulikos*
mean: *mesotês*
meaning: *sêmasia*; real meaning: *huponoia*; with many meanings: *polusêmos*
metaphor: *metaphora*
mind: *nous*
mix: *(sum)mignunai*; admix: *paramignunai*; mixed: *(sum)miktos*; mixture: *mixis*; commingled: *summigês*; commixture: *summixis*
moment: *khronos*
move: *kinein*; movement: *kinêsis*; motion: *kinêma, phora*; moving: *kinêtikos, kinêtos*; moveable, moved: *kinêtos*
multifarious: *polueidês*
mutually cancelling: *anairêtika allêlôn*

name: *onoma*; naming: *onomasia*
nature: *phusis*; of the same nature: *homophuês*; be naturally united / naturally unite: *sumphuein*;

naturally united: *sumphuês*;
natural: *phusikos*; naturally
inhering: *sumphutos*; natural
attributes: *sumphuta*; be a natural
offshoot: *paraphuein*
negation: *apophasis*; negative:
apophatikos
notion: *epinoia*

object: *pragma*
obliterate: *(sun)anairein*
observe: *noiein, theôrein*
obtain: *huparkhein*; obtaining:
huparxis
operation: *energeia, energêma*;
operate: *energein*; operative:
energêtikos; operationally: *energeiai*
opinion: *doxa*; opinion-forming:
doxastikos
oppose: *antitithenai*; opposed:
antithetos; be opposed, opposite:
antikeisthai; range in opposition:
anti(dia)tattein
opposition: *antithesis*
order: *taxis*; order, to: *diatattein*;
ordering: *diakosmêsis*; in order:
tetagmenôs
origin: *arkhê*; originate: *arkhein*;
originating, originator: *arkhêgos*

part: *meros, morion*; partition:
merizein; partless: *amerês*;
partlessness: *amereia*; particle:
morion
partake: *ephaptesthai, metekhein*
participate: *metalambanein,
metekhein*; participation: *methexis,
metokhê, metousia*
particular: *kath' hekaston, merikos*
passive: *huptios*; passively undergo:
peponthenai; passivity: *peponthêsis*
peculiar: *idios*; peculiar marks:
idiotês; of a peculiar kind:
idiotropos
perception: *aisthêsis*; perceivable:
aisthêtos
perfect: *suntelikos, teleios, teleos*;
perfect, to: *teleioun*; perfecting:
telesiourgos; perfective: *teleiôtikos*;
perfection: *teleiôsis, teleiotês*;
perfect in itself, *autotelês*
period: *khronos*

permanence: *stasis*
per se: kath' hauto
perversion: *paratropê*
physical: *phusikos*
place: *taxis, thesis, topos*; place, to:
tattein; place foremost / before:
protattein; place on: *perikeisthai*;
placing around: *perithesis*; placed
around: *perithetos*
plurality: *plêthos*
point: *sêmeion*
portion: *moira*
posit: *(hupo)tithenai*
position: *thesis*; being-in-a-position:
keisthai; positioned, be: *keisthai*;
position side by side: *sumparistêsis*;
transposition: *antimetastasis,
metathesis*
possession: *hexis, skhesis*; possessive
condition: *kathexis*; non-possession:
aekheia
posterior: *husteros*
postulate: *aitêma*
potential(ity): *dunamis*
power: *dunamis*
practice: *sunêtheia*; practical:
praktikos; practical affair: *pragma*
precede: *proêgeisthai, proüparkhein*
preconception: *prolêpsis*
predicate: *katêgorêma*; predicate, to:
katêgorein; predication: *kategoria*
preposition: *prothesis*
present, be: *huparkhein*; come to be
present: *paragignesthai*; presence:
parousia
primary: *arkhêgikos, proêgoumenos,
prôtourgos*
principal: *arkhêgikôtatos, genikôtatos*
principle: *aitia, aition, arkhê, logos*;
principle of constitution: *logos*
prior: *proteros*; be prior: *protereuein*;
treat as prior: *protattein*; have
prior existence: *proüparkhein*
privation: *sterêsis*; deprive:
(apo)sterein; currently deprive:
steriskein; privative: *sterêtikos*
produce: *poieisthai, (ap)ergazesthai,
apotelein*; productive: *poiêtikos*;
production: *poiêma*
project: *proballein*; projection: *probolê*
proposition: *axiôma*
proof: *pistis*; prove: *pistousthai*

theôrêtikos; theorem: *theôrêma*;
theory: *theôria*
think (of): *(epi)noein*
thought: *(dia)noêma, dianoia, noêsis*;
discursive thought: *dianoia,
dianoêsis*; thought of: *noêtos*
time: *khronos*; in time: *enkhronos*;
timeless: *akhronos*; temporal:
khronikos
topic: *topos*
transfer: *anapherein, metagein*
transform: *alloioun*; capable of
transforming: *alloiôtikos*
transition: *metabasis*
transposition: *antimetastasis,
metathesis*

unchangeable: *ametablêtos*
uncompounded: *asunthetos*
unconnected: *adiataktos*
undefined: *adioristos*
undergo: *paskhein*; undergoing:
paskhein, pathêma
underlie: *hupokeisthai*
unexamined: *anexetastos*
ungenerated: *agenêtos*
unhindered: *akôlutos*
uninterrupted: *adiastatos*

unite: *sunagein*; uniting: *sunagôgos*;
union: *henôsis*; unifying: *henôtikos*
universe: *pan*; universal: *katholou*
unlikeness: *anomoiotês*
unmixed: *amigês*
unmoved: *akinêtos*; be unmoved:
akinêtein; be unmoving:
akinêtizein; unmoveable,
unmoving: *atreptos*
unqualified: *apoios*
unreasonable: *alogos*
usage: *khrêsis, sunêtheia*
use: *khreia, khrêsis*

variety: *tropos*
verb: *rhêma*
virtue: *aretê*

way: *tropos*; being a certain way: *pôs
ekhon*
when: *pote*
where: *pou*
wish: *boulê*
word: *logos, phônê*
world: *kosmos*
worth: *axia*

Greek-English Index

*= not attested elsewhere

adiairetos, indivisible, 346,27ff.
adiaphorein, be indifferent, 365,23
adiaphoria, indifference, 341,2
adiaphoros, indifferent, 386,26;
403,14.15; 410,26ff.; not different,
396,14
adiaphorôs, identically, 384,1.5
adiastatos, dimensionless, 303,2;
304,23; 362,3
adiataktos, in a disordered manner,
379,26
adioristos, undefined, 438,26
adranês, inert, 361,16
adunamia, incapacity, 418,16
adunamos, incapable, 417,13
aeikinêtos, ever-moving, 318,2
aekheia, (state of) non-possession,
395,6ff.
agenêtos, ungenerated, 364,9
agôgê, drawing on, 307,12
aidios, eternal, 318,2; 327,35; 336,23;
338,24; 423,23
aiôn, eternity, 304,23; 343,18ff.;
357,11; 364,11
aiônos, eternal, 304,24
aisthêsis, perception, 305,21;
308,21.24; 318,3.6; 319,31; 330,4ff.;
344,25; 380,2; 383,25ff.; 395,25;
422,15.16; 423,21; 435,30
aisthêtos, perceivable, 300,25; 305,2;
318,2.19.25; 339,18; 344,6; 378,3;
380,2; 383,16ff.; 428,17.19
aitêma, postulate, 420,12
aitia, causality, 329,28; cause, 303,8;
310,15; 312,20; 313,22; 314,17ff.;
315,33; 316,4; 319,21; 320,17ff.;
322,11ff.; 325,13; 328,16; 328,21ff.;
331,4ff.; 337,17ff.; 374,19; 376,20;
420,34; 421,3; principle, 322,33;
reason, 296,5; 311,8; 312,22;
313,12; 320,23; 340,27.28; 341,14;

357,31; 367,33; 379,21; 383,20;
435,21; 437,13
aitiasthai, censure, 302,26; 406,6;
410,25; 411,6
aitiatos, caused, 420,6.8; 424,17.20
aitiôdês, causal, 423,28
aition, cause, 303,15; 312,12; 317,21;
322,2ff.; 327,10ff.; 331,8ff.; 332,11;
333,33; 336,29ff.; 342,11; 362,30ff.;
401,14; 420,6ff.; 422,22.28;
424,17ff.; principle, 364,2; reason,
341,1; 351,5; 383,27; 385,9; 418,3
aitios, cause, 322,20; 364,4;
responsible, 315,16
akataleptos, incomprehensible,
345,10; 346,29
akatallêlos, incongruous, 410,34
akatapaustos, incessant, 327,34
akhôristos, inseparable, 327,21;
346,14ff.; not separate, 305,23.24;
364,5
akhronos, outside time, 308,30.34;
309,10; timeless, 309,11ff.
akinêtein, be unmoved, 436,2.11
akinêtizein, be unmoving, 434,31;
436,4.11
akinêtos, motionless, 308,20; 309,19;
311,24; 317,29; 345,36ff.; 354,22;
378,14; unmoved, 302,12; 304,25;
305,2; 306,18; 309,22; 312,12;
324,33; 350,28; 351,12
akolouthêsis, entailment, 419,22ff.;
424,16ff.
akôlutos, unhindered, 303,2
akousis, hearing, 324,7
akousma, sound, 334,29
alêptos, ungraspable, 407,8
alloiôsis, alteration, 319,15;
321,10.18; 325,11ff.; 330,27; 331,30;
346,24; 427,22ff.; 433,3ff.
alloiôtikos, capable of altering,
366,2ff.

dêmiourgikos, creative, 323,2.6;
  331,16
dêmiourgos, creator, 321,34; 322,32;
  323,7
dexiotês, being on the right, 310,3
diadokhos, subsequent, 320,32;
  succeeding, 328,31
diairein, distinguish, 303,16;
  314,4ff.; 318,27; 319,13.16;
  322,12.13; 331,27; 332,31; 351,26;
  354,1; 394,16; 427,16; divide (up),
  297,10; 300,11.12; 306,27; 310,10;
  320,2; 329,15; 330,14; 331,22;
  346,27ff.; 353,6; 359,10; 367,19ff.;
  386,10; 387,16; 391,2; 395,32;
  399,20; 404,4ff.; 405,22; 406,7;
  415,1; 421,30; 427,19ff.; 437,15ff.
diarêma, divided thing, 425,1
diairesis, division, 297,9ff.;
  298,17.19; 300,34; 306,4; 317,13;
  328,12; 330,28; 331,25; 336,14ff.;
  359,7; 373,33; 378,17; 381,16;
  382,3ff.; 409,10; 410,26; 414,26.33;
  417,23; 418,24; 424,26ff.; 427,25;
  437,12ff.; school, 317,28
diairetos, divisible, 304,11; 345,25ff.;
  410,16
diakeisthai, be disposed, 366,27;
  389,7
diakosmêsis, ordering, 329,13
diakrinein, differentiate, 303,17;
  304,27; 312,21; 316,11; 317,20;
  356,28; 359,31; 365,18; 366,9;
  402,18; 434,18; separate, 306,30;
  429,9
diakrisis, distinction, 330,1; 426,10;
  division, 385,23.24; separation,
  429,11
diakritikos, separative, 327,30
dialektikê, dialectic, 380,13
dialexis, discourse, 361,5
dialogismos, discursive reasoning,
  318,16
diamorphoun, give form to, 306,24
dianoêma, thought, 397,7
dianoêsis, discursive thought,
  317,30; 397,23
dianoia, thought, 317,17; 318,31;
  335,16; discursive thought, 318,1
diaphora, difference, 298,16.18;
  302,25; 306,19; 313,15; 327,29;
  335,36; 340,10.33ff.; 358,19ff.;

367,25ff.; 384,26; 386,3; 387,28ff.;
  397,32ff.; 399,13ff.; 402,13ff.;
  403,33; 407,16ff; 411,29; 412,14;
  418,10; 428,31; 429,26; 431,22;
  differentia, 297,32ff.; 300,11.12;
  301,17; 314,6.12; 317,14; 324,18;
  336,15ff.; 359,7.11; 367,3ff.; 380,29;
  382,6; 386,33ff.; 389,34ff.; 399,22;
  411,31; 415,14.33; 417,16; 427,32;
  438,5ff.; differentiation, 298,21;
  308,17; 320,5.6; 367,27ff.; 386,7;
  391,1; 416,3; 438,25
diaphoros, different, 301,15; 318,33;
  336,12; 348,26; 350,4; 363,12;
  372,8ff.; 389,12; 390,28; 393,21ff.;
  429,13; 432,8; differentiated,
  370,16; 434,8
diaphorotês, differentiation, 354,25
diaphtheirein, destroy, 316,36;
  321,18ff.; 331,13; 352,31ff.; 382,21;
  407,29ff.; 423,11; 428,10ff.
diarithmein, denumerate, 309,25;
  enumerate, 368,13
diarithmêsis, denumeration, 335,9
diarthroun, analyse, 301,2; 379,16ff.;
  427,1
diarthrôsis, analysis, 379,17.20
diastasis, dimension(ality), 308,15;
  309,26; 338,9ff.; 341,24.32; 356,19;
  357,11; 362,4; separation, 303,1;
  320,34; 359,20; 361,18; 387,29;
  399,33
diastatos, having dimension, 304,23;
  339,35; 361,33; 362,29
diastêma, extension, 337,27ff.;
  350,12ff.; 361,16ff.
diatattein, arrange, 306,4.34; 329,35;
  376,27; 379,26; 380,12; 387,24;
  438,12
diataxis, disposition, 337,11; 405,14;
  415,31; 418,4
diatelein, bring to an end, 417,6
diatetagmenôs, in due order, 379,26
diathesis, condition, 298,25;
  323,19.20; 333,34.37; 368,19ff.;
  401,18; 414,30; 416,7; 436,20
diathrôsis, close examination,
  379,17.20
diathroun, describe in detail, 301,2;
  379,16ff.
diatithenai, dispose, 322,6; 365,30

hairesis, philosophical system, 306,14; 352,2
hama, simultaneous, 296,2; 300,33; 359,21.25; 364,10; 371,17; 379,5; 380,1.3; 424,1ff.
haphê, touching, 303,8; sense of touch, 400,2; 405,18.19; 413,4
hapsis, contact, 302,31.32
haptein/ haptesthai, concern, 361,5; 368,28; touch, 303,6
hedra, location, 335,20ff.
hektikos, in a (habitual) state, 369,1ff.; 394,23
hektos, haveable, 369,19.22
henoeidês, of one form, 363,34
henôsis, union, 374,23
henôtikos, unifying, 327,30
heteroiôsis, alteration, 311,30
heterotês, diversity, 308,16; 354,24; 355,22; 384,20ff.; 387,33; 417,30
hexis, state, 298,19.ff; 310,1; 324,24; 346,17; 366,23ff.; 388,8ff.; 402,24.25; 414,30; 416,7; 436,20; (state of) possession, 334,15; 370,24ff.; 381,11; 382,13; 385,34; 390,33; 392,13ff.; 394,14ff.; 396,22ff.; 396,31ff.; 397,29ff.; 399,10ff.; 400,35ff.; 402,15ff.; 404,6.36; 405,12; 407,23ff.; 416,28ff.; 423,16
homalês, regular, 345,28
homoeidês, uniform, 333,2; 389,26
homogenês, homogeneous, 304,25
homoiotês, likeness, 310,3; 369,36; 393,23; 419,15
homônumia, homonymy, 301,5; 365,18; 371,20; 379,6; 380,8ff.
homônumos, homonymous, 301,4; 311,14; 317,24; 318,7; 350,25; 363,10; 365,18ff.; 379,16; 380,31ff.; 388,13; 395,22; 414,34ff.; 419,8ff.; 436,19ff.
homophuês, of the same nature, 374,28.30
homou, together, 426,16ff.
horasis, seeing, 312,25
horismos, definition, 346,10ff.; 389,34; 398,23; 421,25
(ap)hôrismenos, defined, 317,31; 379,1; definite, 297,34; 337,21; 358,35; determinate, 345,28;

349,23; 361,18; 379,1; 400,16ff.; 407,10; 413,28; 414,3; 431,24
horistikos, definitional, 364,33.35; 389,33
horizein / horizesthai, bound, 344,25; define, 307,16; 343,28; 345,21; 361,20; 364,20; 369,19; 382,17.24; 417,6; 421,31ff.; 426,32; 430,22; make determinate, 407,3
hormê, impetus, 306,25.26; impulse, 318,26; 323,9; 371,30
horos, bound, 344,27; 362,12.13; definition, 306,31; 350,17; 361,11.17; 381,3.18; 387,27ff.; 406,21; 408,21; 420,11; 427,18
hulê, matter, 306,24; 316,24ff.; 327,13; 331,3; 332,9ff.; 334,24ff.; 372,2.5; 401,15.17; 417,31; 421,26; 429,19; subject-matter, 411,24
hulikos, material, 304,9; 329,5.8; 330,36; 421,8ff.
hupagein, subsume, 319,10; 343,24; 380,30
huparkhein, belong, 295,24; 296,30; 298,14; 305,14; 308,15; 319,23.24; 334,28ff.; 349,31; 379,33; 393,5; 399,24ff.; 401,24; 402,18; 406,8ff.; 431,13; be (present), 327,21; 341,28; 345,29; 365,26; 401,23; exist, 298,10; 303,29; 304,23; 319,6; 329,32; 341,30; 356,35; 371,12; 378,13; 386,8ff.; 390,9.13; hold, 381,7; 383,2.6; 385,19; 406,11; obtain, 301,28; 305,34; 311,31; 334,32; 349,24; 362,32; 405,17; 408,12.14; 412,20.28; 421,3
huparxis, existence, 361,2; 421,20; substance, 301,26; 365,24; underlying reality, 295,23; 333,3ff.
hupeinai, subsist, 296,7; 340,32; 357,24; 361,22
huperbolê, excess, 409,26ff.; 411,18ff.; hyperbole, 336,6
huperekhein, excel, 308,10
huperokhê, excess, 415,19.25; 425,33; superiority, 342,1; 420,21
hupheimenos, inferior, 303,37; 304,1
huphistanai / huphistasthai, consist 299,5; 318,8; 343,31; 397,11; set up, 357,31; subsist, 307,26; 310,4.31; 311,27; 336,24; 341,15ff.; 347,7ff.; 349,23ff.; 364,4;

Subject Index

Academy, 369,19
acting, 295,1ff.; 299,1ff.
affirmation, 403,26ff.
alteration, 427,22ff.
Andronicus, 332,15; 342,23; 347,6.19; 357,28; 358,10; 359,16; 379,9
Archytas, 296,4; 300,13; 314,15ff.; 317,12ff.; 330,1; 331,25; 332,7; 334,8ff.; 337,32; 338,9.25; 340,28; 342,13.22; 347,6.14; 348,25; 350,11ff.; 357,21ff.; 361,14ff.; 365,3ff.; 367,7; 373,3; 376,35; 378,1; 382,8ff.; 391,1; 395,32; 407,16ff.; 411,29; 416,8ff.; 436,18; 438,31
Boethus, 302,16; 339,19; 348,2; 373,8ff.; 433,28
change, 308,11ff.; 427,9ff.
Chrysippus, 350,16; 389,22; 394,31; 395,10; 396,20; 401,7; 403,6
contraries, 296,20ff.; 385,30ff.; 432,24ff.
Cornutus, 351,23; 359,1
Democritus, 428,14ff.
Empedokles, 337,2
Epicurus, 431,24
gnomon, 430,5ff.
having, 297,18ff., 298,10ff.; 299,36ff.; 365,1ff.; 436,13ff.
Heraclitus, 412,23.25
Iamblichus, 297,24; 298,21; 299,29; 302,16.26; 303,36; 307,2; 308,1; 314,10ff.; 318,35; 321,11.23; 322,32; 325,17ff.; 327,7; 330,9; 331,5; 332,28; 333,8; 336,25; 339,8.34; 341,12; 342,1; 345,8; 349,10; 350,10; 351,4; 353,19ff.; 357,17; 361,7ff.; 367,13ff.; 369,14ff.; 374,8ff.; 379,22; 380,17ff.; 394,12; 403,7; 407,18; 413,7; 414,1.15; 415,20ff.; 421,22; 425,12ff.; 433,14; 436,23ff.
Melissus, 308,25
more and less, 297,1ff.

movement, 302,5ff.; 427,9ff.
negation, 403,26ff.
Nicostratus, 368,12ff.; 381,23; 385,10; 388,4; 390,15; 402,12.32; 406,6; 407,14; 410,25; 414,27; 428,3; 429,13
operation, 302,5ff.
opposites, 380,16ff.
owning, 366,6ff.
Peripatetics, 308,11; 351,5; 380,24; 381,3; 407,6
place, 334,6ff.; 340,14ff.; 357,7ff.
Plato, 308,16; 327,9; 350,28; 351,11; 356,8; 366,8; 370,10; 413,5; 428,21; 429,7; 434,21
Plotinus, 302,11; 303,32; 304,28; 306,13; 307,30; 308,12.33; 309,9.32; 314,10; 315,31; 317,11; 319,16; 320,1ff.; 321,8ff.; 324,9; 325,3ff.; 338,21ff.; 342,29ff.; 347,15.19; 349,5; 358,8; 359,33; 368,2; 370,12; 433,20
Porphyry, 297,24; 298,21; 302,18; 303,30; 379,13; 381,24; 414,34
possession, 392,15ff.
position, 297,12ff.; 334,6ff.
posterior, 418,19ff.
prior, 418,19ff.
privation, 392,15ff.
Pythagoreans, 317,28; 321,22; 351,4ff.; 415,31; 418,6
quantity, 342,21ff.
relatives, 382,1ff.
rest, 432,25ff.
simultaneous, 424,1ff.
Stoics, 302,30; 306,14ff.; 310,14.26; 313,23; 350,13ff.; 361,10; 373,7; 386,26; 387,19ff.; 401,34; 402,22; 403,32; 405,25ff.; 410,30; 436,3
Strato, 346,14; 418,26; 423,1ff.
Theophrastus, 304,32; 346,16; 402,20; 415,15; 435,26
time, 340,14ff.

Index of Passages Cited by Simplicius

Numbers in **bold** type refer to the passages of the works cited; numbers in ordinary type refer to the pages and lines of Kalbfleisch's *CAG* edition. References to *Cat* 1-8, and to Simplicius' commentary on it, are indexed, but not those to *Cat* 9-15, or to Simplicius' commentary on it.

Lightning Source UK Ltd.
Milton Keynes UK
UKOW06f0833070815

256546UK00001B/87/P